T3-BUW-185

Minnesota Symposia on Child Psychology

Meeting the Challenge of Translational Research in Child Psychology

Volume 35

Edited By

Dante Cicchetti

Megan R. Gunnar

John Wiley & Sons, Inc.

This book is printed on acid-free paper. ♾

Published by John Wiley & Sons, Inc., Hoboken, New Jersey.
Published simultaneously in Canada.

For general information on our other products and services please contact our Customer Care Department within the United States at (800) 762-2974, outside the United States at (317) 572-3993 or fax (317) 572-4002.

Wiley also publishes its books in a variety of electronic formats. Some content that appears in print may not be available in electronic books. For more information about Wiley products, visit our website at www.wiley.com.

Library of Congress Cataloging-in-Publication Data:

Minnesota Symposia on Child Psychology (35th : 2007: University of Minnesota) Meeting the challenge of translational research in child psychology/edited by Dante Cicchetti, Megan R. Gunnar.

p.; cm.—(Minnesota symposia on child psychology; v. 35)

Includes bibliographical references and index.

ISBN 978-0-470-34513-9 (cloth: alk. paper)

1. Child psychology—Congresses. I. Cicchetti, Dante. II. Gunnar, Megan R. III. University of Minnesota. Institute of Child Development. IV. Title. V. Series: Minnesota symposia on child psychology (Series); v. 35.

[DNLM: 1. Child Development—Congresses. 2. Child Psychology—Congresses. 3. Child Development Disorders, Pervasive—Congresses. 4. Child. W3 MI607 v. 35 2009/ WS 105 M6643m 2009]

BF721.M544 2009
155.4—dc22

2008042937

Printed in the United States of America

10 9 8 7 6 5 4 3 2 1

Contents

Contributors

Dante Cicchetti, PhD
McKnight Presidential Chair and Professor
Institute of Child Development and Department of Psychiatry
University of Minnesota

Elena L. Grigorenko, PhD
Associate Professor
Yale University

Megan R. Gunnar, PhD
Regents Professor
Institute of Child Development
University of Minnesota

Andrew N. Meltzoff, PhD
Job and Gertrud Tamaki Endowed Chair
Institute for Learning and Brain Sciences
University of Washington

Peter Mundy, PhD
Lisa Capps Chair in Neurodevelopmental Disorders and Education
School of Education and the M.I.N.D. Institute
University of California, Davis

Seth D. Pollak, PhD
Letters and Science Distinguished Professor
University of Wisconsin at Madison

Michael I. Posner, PhD
Professor Emeritus
Department of Psychology
University of Oregon

Mary K. Rothbart, PhD
Professor Emerita
Department of Psychology
University of Oregon

M. R. Rueda, PhD
Assistant Professor of Psychology
University of Grenada, Spain

Jenny R. Saffran, PhD
Associate Professor
Department of Psychology & Waisman Center
University of Wisconsin, Madison

Daniel S. Shaw, PhD
Professor
Department of Psychology
University of Pittsburgh

Brad E. Sheese, PhD
Assistant Professor of Psychology
Illinois Wesleyan University

Yiyuan Tang, MD, PhD
Informatics Institute
Dalian, Bejing Technical University

CHAPTER

1

Meeting the Challenge of Translational Research in Child Development

Opportunities and Roadblocks

Megan R. Gunnar
Dante Cicchetti

In this 35th volume of the Minnesota Symposia series we focus on the rewards and challenges of conducting translational research in developmental science. The Institute of Child Development at the University of Minnesota was founded in 1925 along with other child welfare stations on the belief that the scientific study of the child was essential to the promotion of child welfare (Hartup, Johnson, & Weinberg, 2001; Sears, 1975; Senn, 1975). The translation of basic research into practice was at the heart of this "child development movement" in the United States (Senn, 1975). Stokes (1997) labeled this *use-inspired basic research* and asserted the criticality of grounding research in practice in order to meet the needs of society. Further, he believed that the relationship between research and practice should be bidirectional, with each contributing to the knowledge base of the other.

As the six editions of the *Handbook of Child Psychology* (see Carmichael, 1946, 1954; Damon, 1998, 2006; and Mussen, 1970, 1983) and the growing number of journals in the field of developmental psychology attest, during the past century child development researchers have produced tremendous amounts of basic scientific information on the typical progression of perceptual, cognitive, linguistic, social, and emotional development and on the patterns of family and extrafamilial experiences associated with variations in developmental outcomes (Bornstein, 2006; Lamb & Ahnert, 2006). The burgeoning knowledge about developmental processes contributed to the adoption of social policies such as Head Start that were implemented to improve the development and eventual circumstances of children residing in disadvantaged poverty environments (McLoyd, Aikens, & Burton, 2006; for a history of Head Start, see Zigler & Valentine, 1997). Likewise, increased attention was devoted to children who were developing with handicapping conditions, such as those who were suffering from organic or cultural-familial forms of Mental Retardation (Zigler & Balla, 1982) and children whose parents were afflicted with mental disorders (Garmezy & Streitman, 1974). The discovery that even adults with the most serious forms of psychopathology (e.g., Bipolar Disorder, Schizophrenia) (Zigler & Glick, 1986), as well as their offspring, could escape the most dire predictions of the extant developmental theories not only led to reformulations of the existing models (e.g., from *main effect* and *interactional* to *ecological transactional*), but it also led to important research aimed at discovering the processes contributing to resilience (Cicchetti & Garmezy, 1993; Luthar, Cicchetti, & Becker, 2000; Masten, 2001).

Each of the expansions in focus of the field of developmental psychology has conspired to help forge the disciplines of developmental psychopathology and prevention science (Cicchetti, 1984, 1990; Ialongo et al., 2006), whose missions were even more explicitly to develop the scientific basis for improving children's mental health and their academic and social success. In addition, the knowledge gains in child psychology made it possible for developmentalists to embark upon large-scale collaborative studies—such as the National Institute of Child Health and Human Development Early Child Care Research Network—to address a variety of issues of social significance.

In the past several decades, technological advances in genomics and neuroimaging have ushered in opportunities for developmental geneticists, neuroscientists, psychologists, and psychopathologists to contribute to clinical research and to reduce the burden of mental illness (Gottesman & Hanson, 2005). Specifically, the International Hap Map Project, an organization whose goal is to develop a haplotype map of the human genome, has provided the tools for mapping the common patterns of human genetic variation (Crawford & Nickerson, 2005; Insel & Quirion, 2005). We now have an unprecedented opportunity to investigate how genomic variation, in interaction with well-defined environmental pathogens, confers risk for, or resilience to, the development of mental disorders (Moffitt, Caspi, & Rutter, 2006; Rutter, 2006). Likewise, brain imaging research and studies of brain event-related potentials (ERPs) and the resultant increases in spatial and temporal resolution in brain research are making possible functional studies of the neural circuits underlying psychopathology and resilience (Charney, 2004; Cicchetti & Curtis, 2007; Thomas & Cicchetti, 2008).

Although the field of developmental psychology has made a number of important contributions to improving the lives of children and families, we now are immersed in a new era in which heightened emphasis is being paid to the translation of basic research into practical application and treatments. The translational *push* is designed to speed up the translation of basic scientific findings into practical applications. Indeed, over 4 decades ago Martin and Lois Hoffman (1964) advocated greater communication between researchers and social service providers toward the goal of having behavioral science contribute to the social good.

Consistent with the prevailing viewpoint that it is essential to apply findings from basic research to the context of practice, the past two editions of the *Handbook of Child Psychology* have included volumes devoted to "Child Psychology in Practice" (Sigel & Renninger, 1998; Sigel, 2006). Unlike chapters in prior editions that "served as a standard of dispassionate, scientific rigor," contributors were asked to write reviews that bridged research and practice (Sigel & Renninger, 1998, p. xxii).

In the closing paragraphs to the "Child Psychology in Practice" volume of the *Handbook of Child Psychology*, Sigel (2006) posed the following question: "Should not developmental research offer useful and meaningful explanations for the course of development and where needed provide approaches for the prevention and amelioration of conditions that may hinder the optimization of the developmental trajectory?" (p. 1022). We echo this question and strongly agree with Sigel that the application of research to practice "requires stretching and/or adapting the root metaphors in which we have been trained so that collaborations between researchers and practitioners are the basis of research and of any application of research to practice" (Sigel, 2006 p. 1022).

The new era of translational research is not only exerting impacts on developmental psychology, it is also affecting all fields of research in the medical, physical, social, and clinical sciences. Furthermore, the push for translational research is closely tied to funding priorities at the major federal agencies that provide financial support for university research. The impetus to conduct translational research in the behavioral sciences has emanated largely from the National Institute of Mental Health (Insel, 2005; Insel & Scolnick, 2006) and was spurred by the recognition of the tremendous individual, social, and economic burden associated with mental illness (National Advisory Mental Health Council, 2000). Hence, the emphasis on translational research at the funding agencies is quickly translating itself into priorities within the academy.

There is an old saying, "If I open the window, then it is a breeze; if someone else opens it, then it's a draft." Some basic researchers who have conducted their work for years with the expectation that someone else would take their findings and translate them into practical applications are experiencing this new era as an unwelcome, and even threatening, *draft*. And there are potential pitfalls and threats to basic research. However, the increased emphasis on translating basic research into application also carries tremendous opportunities for advancing not only the welfare of children and families, but also the health of our field and the next generation of child development researchers. If we meet these challenges well, then advances in our understanding of the basic processes of development should not suffer. Indeed, as many of the chapters in this volume attest, our knowledge of basic processes should thrive in this translational era.

In the following chapter, we will discuss some of what is needed to support a healthy climate for translational research in developmental science. This discussion will include what we can expect to be roadblocks in the process of enhancing a translational climate for developmental research. One of the critical issues that face us is how to organize graduate and postgraduate training to permit students to develop enhanced capacities for participating in multidisciplinary, translational research, without at the same time delivering such diluted training that our students become dilettantes and not experts. Other issues involve questions of when our basic science is solid enough to attempt translational work; the types of partnerships that we need and how these can be encouraged; the role of curiosity-driven basic research in an era of translational effort; and so on. We are aided in this discussion by the authors of the chapters in this volume. Each was asked not only to discuss their research, but also to lift the curtain to reveal some of the underlying issues and quandaries facing the researcher who moves his or her research into a more translational realm.

WHAT IS TRANSLATIONAL RESEARCH?

Despite the current emphasis on translational research, there is little consensus on what constitutes a translational research program. National meetings organized around discussion of the importance of translational research (National Institute of Mental Health, 2005) have involved long discussions of the definition without reaching a clear consensus. Program announcements from various funding agencies tend to emphasize the translation of basic ideas, insights, and discoveries into the treatment or prevention of human disease (National Institute of Neurological Disorders and Stroke, 2005). Likewise, statements from the National Institute of Mental Health emphasize the translation of basic research into improvements in diagnosis, prevention, treatment, and delivery of services for mental illness (Pellmar & Eisenberg, 2000). This would seem to limit translational research to a small subset of the research conducted by developmental researchers. However, we argue that these definitions actually describe the goals of translational research rather than define the universe of what constitutes translational research.

Clearly, the goal of translational research is to move basic findings more rapidly through the pipeline into novel treatments and preventive efforts to reduce or alleviate physical, emotional, and behavioral health problems. It is widely recognized that information must flow in both directions through the pipeline. That is, it is not enough for the basic researchers to hand their findings off to the clinicians and prevention scientists who then develop novel treatments and approaches. The information gleaned from testing those treatments and intervention programs needs to feed back to inform basic research. When basic and applied scientists attend different meetings, read different journals, and use different metrics for evaluating findings, the pipeline remains clogged and information flows poorly, if at all. Information exchange requires integration across different disciplines and subdisciplines so that clinicians, prevention scientists, and basic researchers are all at the actual or metaphorical table (Cicchetti & Toth, 1998, 2006a, b; Shonkoff, 2000; Sigel, 2006; Toth, Manly, & Nilsen, 2008). This, in turn, requires a melding and integration of concepts, metrics, and goals. Developing a common language is often discussed as one of the critical components of successful translational efforts; however, the need for a common language is based on the need to establish multidisciplinary approaches to identifying and solving inherently translational problems. Hence, the concept of multidisciplinary work is often conflated with that of translational research. The true relationship between translational and multidisciplinary research is better described as a Venn diagram. Not all translational efforts require multidisciplinary teams of researchers and not all multidisciplinary research has translational goals. But the two are closely linked. This is especially true for developmental research where effective intervention and treatment often require an understanding of multiple facets of development and the multiple contexts in which children develop. This is why in this volume we have included chapters from researchers who have adopted multidisciplinary programs of research that allow them to move comfortably between basic information to application and back again with greater fluidity.

To foster the translation of basic findings to application along the metaphorical pipeline often requires creating links among multiple points of discovery. Moving from one point to the other can be inherently translational, even if the work does not involve a novel treatment or intervention or improvement in diagnostic tools. That is, it can be translational if the *end goal* is to get the findings into a form in which their applicability to a human developmental problem can be more readily discerned, and the motivation to achieve that end goal is not simply to satisfy the need to write a few lines in the *Significance* section of a grant. For example, researchers studying the neural basis of fear and anxiety have identified a distributed neural network of which the amygdala often plays a critical role (Davis, Walker, & Lee, 1997). This work has often been conducted first on rats. Identifying a behavior common to humans and rats and dependent, in rats, on an intact neural fear system (Davis, Falls, Campeau, & Kim, 1993); then testing the behavior for its relevance in human fear disorders (Davis et al., 1997), establishing its neural basis in primate models whose development and neural functioning is more similar to our own (Antoniadis, Winslow, Davis, & Amaral, 2007); and then documenting that theoretically identified aspects of experimentally induced early experience may alter the behavior (Sanchez et al., 2005) are all components of translational research, even though they do not involve testing a novel treatment or examining the efficacy of a novel preventive intervention—or even the study of children. Nonetheless, movement through the pipeline is not complete until this basic research makes contact with studies of, in our case, human development and human developmental treatment and intervention research. Once technological advances permit the conduct of such research with humans and if similar results are obtained, then the inclusion of neurobiological and behavioral measures in the design and evaluation of randomized preventive interventions aimed at reducing fearful and anxious symptoms will provide an important opportunity for developmental psychologists and psychopathologists to enhance their understanding of the processes underlying neural and behavioral plasticity (Cicchetti & Gunnar, 2008).

As this example demonstrates, critical aspects of the research needed to enhance our understanding of the development of children's mental and physical health and disorders may often lie in the work of individuals who use animal models. Moving that work into the human domain and closer to treatments and preventive intervention demands that researchers are not only able to talk across disciplines, but also to talk across species. As there is no animal that evolved to serve as a model for human development, talking effectively across species requires training ourselves and our students to effectively and appropriately apply animal data to problems of human development. The chapter by Pollak (Chapter 6) demonstrates effective use of animal neuroscience data to address critical questions in human development by using those data as a guide to potential neural systems of interest, while not ignoring species differences in the ecology of development.

Likewise, translational research can involve assessing similar behaviors and, as critically, developmental processes in both typically and atypically developing children. The belief that the study of normative developmental processes informs our understanding of pathological development and, conversely, that the study of pathological development informs our understanding of normative development is one of the central tenets of *developmental psychopathology*—an interdisciplinary science that strives to reduce the schisms that so often separate scientific research from the application of knowledge to clinical populations (Cicchetti, 1993; Cicchetti & Toth, 1998). As one of us has previously stated, " . . . all pathology is, strictly speaking, a process. As a process, it is extended through time, and so must be understood in its temporal aspect. Since all pathology may also be conceived of as a disturbance, distortion, or degeneration of normal functioning, it thus follows that, if one would better understand pathology, then one must better understand normal functioning against which pathology is defined" (Cicchetti, 1984, p. 2). Moreover, " . . . the deviations from and distortions of normal development that are seen in pathological processes indicate . . . how normal development may be better studied and understood" (Cicchetti, 1984, p. 4).

Developmental psychopathology has emerged as a discipline through the integration of multiple single disciplines from embryology to genetics, neurophysiology, psychiatry, psychoanalysis, clinical psychology, sociology, and developmental psychology (Cicchetti, 1990). As such, developmental psychopathology provides an example of the synergistic contributions of previously disparate fields that result in the emergence of a new discipline (Cicchetti, 1984). Despite the fact that the bidirectional flow of information provided by integrating the study of typical and atypical developmental processes is widely acknowledged among developmental psychopathologists, to date the majority of research on the normal–abnormal equation has emphasized the contributions that information on basic normative processes can make in the service of understanding pathology.

One of the chapters in this volume (Saffran, Chapter 5) provides evidence that the joint study of typically and atypically developing children can enhance our understanding of normative processes. In applying principles of statistical learning to understanding processes in language development, Saffran describes elegant studies with typically developing children. More recently, however, she and her colleagues have begun to probe processes of atypical language development using concepts and methods from her basic research. The results reveal processes that, because they are more evident among children with specific language impairments, make more salient issues that apply to typical language learners. Hence, our understanding of atypical development is not only informed by studying typically and atypically developing children in concert, but it also results from atypical learners informing our understanding of normative processes in language learning. Although likely, it remains to be determined whether this knowledge can be used to develop or evaluate novel treatments or to improve diagnosis. Saffran's work, consistent with all work that examines processes using both typically and atypically developing children, makes the point that research that attempts to *translate* our understanding of developmental *processes* between children developing along typical and atypical trajectories is inherently translational.

Such research also underscores the fact that basic research on typically developing children is essential if we are to sustain a healthy translational research climate in our field. This point is also made very clearly in the chapter by Mundy (Chapter 3). Mundy's chapter describes research that is much further along the translational pipeline, as it now includes evidence for novel treatments and approaches. However, as Mundy makes clear, the translational research program he describes would not have been possible were it not for the years of very basic research on the development of social interaction processes in infancy that preceded it. The basic infant work involved seemingly esoteric questions such as when do infants first follow a point and when and why do they spontaneously attempt to share their emotional experiences with others? This work gave rise to efforts first to apply the methods and findings to the study of children with autism. The findings from this translational work changed the field of autism research and our understanding of core deficits in this disorder. This in turn has led to the development of novel preventive interventions focused on training joint attention behavior and evidence that focusing on joint attention skills improves other aspects of the social behavior of children with autism in ways that focusing on other social deficits (e.g., social play) does not. Mundy's chapter provides a road map for how translational research can proceed, beginning with very basic developmental studies, through translating those findings to atypically developing children, and finally though translating insights from that work into the development and testing of novel treatments.

In sum, it is easier to describe the goals than the precise definition of *translational research* because the process of moving basic information along the path from discovery to the testing of novel treatments and interventions is a bit like the game of telephone. There are multiple points of information exchange, translation is involved at each point so that the information remains accurate, and movement from any point to the next can be *translational research.* But, if the information stops at any point, then we have a problem. Thus, a critical issue for the field to address is how to keep the information flowing. These issues or roadblocks come in two forms: scientific and structural. The former involves issues of conceptualization and how fields go about organizing their modes of information exchange. The latter involves problems inherent within the academy that have to do with disciplinary boundaries, financial constraints, and the rules of judging individuals for promotion, tenure, and compensation. As the latter issues go beyond the bounds of the work addressed in this volume, we will constrain our remarks to the scientific roadblocks that slow translational research.

SCIENTIFIC ROADBLOCKS

The need to develop a common language is frequently discussed as a roadblock to multidisciplinary research. As translational research in developmental science often requires working across disciplines or subdisciplines, this roadblock also frequently applies to translational research in our science. Terms and concepts develop rich webs of meaning as they emerge and become established within single disciplines or schools of thought. Weaving teams together that include individuals from two or more disciplines in order to approach common translational problems requires educating one another sufficiently so communication and joint problem solving is possible. Depending on the number of disciplines at the table and the number of critical constructs required to address the translational question, this process of mutual education can take considerable time.

However, if the problem of *language* were merely one of explaining constructs, then this roadblock would be relatively easy to surmount. The more intransigent problem that also falls under this heading occurs when modes of judging the validity of theories and hypotheses also must be melded in order for the research team to make progress. The following three differences in philosophies represent common roadblocks in many multidisciplinary translational endeavors: correlation versus experimentation, clinical insight versus objective measures, and elegance versus complexity. Much child development and developmental psychopathology research involves causal interpretations of inherently correlational data. If the translational problem requires bringing researchers trained to disparage findings based *merely* on correlations together with researchers trained to wrest causality from correlational designs, then the viability of the translational effort will require coming to some degree of consensus on judging scientific validity and designing valid research.

A similar chasm exists between those whose research data are weighted toward clinical insights and qualitative data and those who were trained to be skeptical of conclusions based upon such insights and data. This chasm can make it difficult to bring practicing clinicians and researchers together. Clinicians place high value on the richness of clinical insights derived from years of treating patients, while researchers are often trained to discredit conclusions that are not based on quantifiable data. Failure to recognize and overcome these biases can seriously impede translational research efforts. Despite these challenges, we feel confident that successful community clinical, funder, and research partnerships can occur. For example, two theory-driven randomized clinical trials for maltreated infants and preschoolers indicate that it is possible to create successful evidence-based interventions, even within the complex world of the child welfare system (Cicchetti, Rogosch, & Toth, 2006; Toth et al., 2008).

Finally, different disciplines place varied emphases on conducting elegant, simple studies versus studies that embrace more complexity. There is little doubt now that the fields of genetics and neuroscience are advancing so rapidly that our ability to translate basic developmental research into improvements in diagnosis, treatment, and prevention of mental disorders will require that we work and integrate information across levels of analysis from genes to social context. Researchers conducting investigations at the cellular and molecular level of analysis and those working in the neurosciences, however, have been trained to think in terms of reducing complex problems to their simplest levels in order to design and implement elegant, clean experiments. In contrast, researchers studying social and emotional development have been trained to recognize that reducing problems of human socioemotional functioning into more simple elements often risks developing knowledge that when translated back into the reality of human life may have reduced external validity. When placed on the same research team, those trained to work from the bottom up tend to work to simplify designs and to focus measures, whereas those trained at more molar levels tend to develop research paradigms that add measures and concomitant complexity. Although it is possible to achieve designs that reflect acceptable compromises, it is also possible that these biases will defeat the research endeavor and two designs will emerge that do not have sufficient bridging points to permit a coherent translational outcome.

Overcoming the biases we have outlined, and others that we have not addressed, is more difficult for some researchers than for others. To some extent, whether a researcher is able to look past his or her biases in order to work effectively across disciplinary boundaries is a matter of differences in temperament and personality. However, to a larger extent it is also a matter of training and experience. Researchers who have previous experience successfully working across disciplinary boundaries come to new integrative endeavors with insights that allow them to more rapidly develop the common language and perspectives needed to achieve results. To the extent that experience and training matter, questions of when this training should begin arise. In the section on training, we will take up the question of whether we need to build teaching the skills and attitudes needed to work across disciplinary boundaries into our graduate curricula.

Another significant roadblock or clog in the translational pipeline arises from highly valued facets of our scientific training (Shonkoff, 2000). Scientists are trained to be cautious. We are trained to identify errors in theory, hypotheses, experimental designs, data analyses, and conclusions. In sum, we are trained to focus on what we do not know as much as or more so than what we do know. We take it as evidence of our scientific merit to recognize the mantra that "more research is needed" is precisely the correct inference to draw from the results of any research endeavor. Furthermore, the more we burrow into any research domain, the more we recognize the fragility of our knowledge. It does not help that in developmental science we have become increasingly aware that patterns of development and our known correlates of these patterns have a nasty habit of changing when we broaden our focus to include both boys and girls, for example, or individuals from different cultural or subcultural groups, or individuals growing up in different settings, urban or rural, or in different economic strata of our society. Cautious scientists are quite aware that in many ways they do not yet know enough to pass what they know down the pipeline with surety, let alone to use that information to develop novel treatments or intervention programs.

Scientific caution is necessary for good science, but it slows the translation of basic research into practical applications. None of us want to burden children and families who already may be struggling with the child's physical, emotional, or behavioral disorder with the demands of a research program based on questionable basic research or theory. Nor do we want to subject these children and families to unwarranted treatments or intervention programs. Discussions of the ethics of both attempting translational research and failing to do so should become a more common part of our discourse. Establishing forums to conduct such discussions that include both basic researchers and those who are involved in providing treatment and interventions may prove valuable in helping basic researchers overcome their hesitancy to take the next translational steps with their work. The more the basic researcher understands about the treatments and interventions that are in use and their evidence base, the more the basic researcher may be able to discern when what he or she knows is of sufficient certainty to attempt to move it into translation. Fortunately, there are indeed settings, such as centers on developmental psychopathology (Cicchetti, Toth, Nilsen, & Manly, in press) and academic departments in clinical psychology and psychiatry, where research and practice coexist and mutual respect is accorded to members of each discipline. An examination of the structure and philosophy of such settings should prove to be instructive in facilitating similar successful research and practice collaborations.

In his chapter, Shaw (Chapter 8) provides an excellent discussion of the process he and his colleagues went through in deciding that they knew enough about the antecedents of conduct problems to risk translating that knowledge into a preventive intervention. Although Shaw notes that he is a clinician, and thus might seem to be in an excellent position to straddle the translational divide, he found that he needed to form close professional relations with individuals who had extensive histories of working in the prevention field. Their discussions led first to a limited intervention focused on children (primarily African American boys) on whom he had conducted his basic longitudinal research and then later to the melding of research sites and a reasonably cautious *leap of faith* in applying their intervention to both boys and girls and to multiple ethnic groups.

The need for basic researchers and clinicians to share ideas and insights points to a second critical clog or roadblock in the translational pipeline. Although the field of developmental psychopathology emphasizes the need for integration of research on typically and atypically developing children, it is often the case that those who conduct research have little contact with those who treat children with physical, emotional, or behavioral disorders. Nor do researchers investigating basic normative processes typically have training in clinical child psychology, psychiatry, pediatrics, neurology, or hearing, speech, and language disorders. Thus, basic researchers may have only a vague idea that they are studying a phenomenon that has clinical applicability. Even when they do, they may have little ready access to the patient populations who might benefit from their research. Conversely, pediatricians, child neurologists, child psychiatrists, and other clinicians often lack training in basic research in developmental science and, once in practice, even those that have had this training often have little further contact with basic developmental science researchers. Funding agencies are well aware that this is one of the roadblocks to translational research. Prominent in announcements (RFAs) for translational research networks is the requirement that researchers bring clinicians onto their research teams. The hope of this requirement is that in listening to one another discuss research and cases, the divide between clinical practice and basic research will be overcome. It is unlikely, however, that such minimal efforts will achieve their translational goal.

Instead, as a field it would seem prudent to create more opportunities for researchers studying basic normative processes to learn about clinical problems and issues. We should enhance opportunities for basic normative researchers to discuss their work with colleagues in clinical fields as well. In part to achieve this goal, we need to break down barriers between developmental and clinical programs and establish more programs in developmental psychopathology. But we also need to lower barriers between developmental psychology and programs in speech, hearing, and language disorders, neuroscience, molecular genetics, pediatrics and neonatology, child neurology, and the many other disciplines where basic research on human development may find application. As Saffran (Chapter 5) notes, this is increasingly happening for researchers studying typical and atypical language development. These domains are integrating, common meetings are being held, and researchers are increasingly aware of each other's work. In our own department, barriers between pediatrics and developmental psychology have been lowered through the cross-appointment of a neonatologist who studies the impact of micronutrients on brain and behavioral development. Similarly, the formation of centers that bring together researchers from multiple departments, including those where patients are treated, facilitates the lowering of these barriers.

This last problem points to another roadblock to translational research. Clinical disorders are described as syndromes of symptoms, while basic research typically focuses on more circumscribed phenomena. *Caseness* is an issue in clinical research; variations along the normal distribution are the focus of basic normative research. Developmental psychopathologists are interested in both categorical and dimensional approaches to disorder. Disorders share common features, such as problems with attention, emotion regulation, and so on. Basic normative researchers and developmental psychopathologists tend to study processes that contribute to these common features. It is often difficult to meld these very different approaches and perspectives. As Grigorenko (Chapter 7) has articulated, it seems possible, however, that the rising interest in endophenotypes as targets of behavior genetics and molecular genetics research on disorders will have a broader, facilitative effect in building bridges between basic developmental research and research on disorders of development.

Endophenotypes and intermediate *phenotypes* are discrete, measurable traits associated with clinical disorders that may be linked to specific genes. These traits or characteristics are typically closer to the behavioral processes studied by basic child development researchers. The chapter by Rothbart and Posner (Chapter 4) provides a prime example. Their work reflects the merging of research on infant temperament with basic research on adult cognition. The point of contact arose when Rothbart began to note stable individual differences in orienting and attentional control in her infant studies and approached Posner with the question, "What is attention?" Their joint research has examined various aspects of attention, including orienting, inhibition of return, and facets of executive attention. These components of attention and attention regulation, in turn, are known to be disturbed in various mental disorders and are increasingly intermediate phenotypes and endophenotypes of genetic studies (Rothbart & Posner, 2006). This has permitted Rothbart and Posner to bring the study of molecular genetics into their research and to develop focused intervention strategies for improving aspects of attentional control in young children (Posner, Rothbart, & Sheese, 2007). While their collaborative work has not yet progressed to the study of individuals with specific disorders, the solid framework they have constructed provides numerous opportunities for such translational efforts. Furthermore, their work has immediate implications for education—another translational domain for the developmental sciences.

A final roadblock to translational research involves a shift in thinking about the role of research participants that may be difficult for some of us. Scientific objectivity distances researchers from the objects of their study. Researchers design, implement, interpret, and disseminate research, while research participants do what researchers request. Both the distance and the sharp differentiation of the roles of *researcher* and *researched* were not only true of our field over most of its history, they were true of all medical and behavioral sciences. However, beginning with the advocacy organization of the AIDS community, demands that the public participate more actively in setting priorities for research and sit at the table when studies are conceived and fielded have grown stronger. Indeed, to a very real extent, the increased push for more rapid translation of basic findings into practice is an outgrowth of patient organization and advocacy. While most basic developmental researchers are unlikely to experience this sea change as more than simply the need to talk about research *participants* rather than *subjects*, for those conducting translational research at points in the pipeline that involve working with target populations this shift in thinking is necessary and large.

In his chapter, Shaw (Chapter 8) provides an excellent discussion of the need to bring participants into the research process not only so that the work makes sense to their implicit theories of child development, but also so that it is tailored to fit their particular concerns. He notes that researchers can gain a good deal from following procedures that therapists have learned in order to motivate individuals to seek and use available therapies. These procedures involve establishing collaborative relationships in which the targets of intervention efforts become partners in the process. Based on these insights and work in the area of motivating alcoholics to seek treatment (e.g., Miller & Rollnick, 2002), Dishion and Kavanagh (2003) designed a motivational interview procedure for parenting intervention work called the Family CheckUp, which invites parents to choose which areas of their family life or child's behavior they would like help in changing. Shaw and his colleagues adapted the Family CheckUp for their preventive intervention work and he describes how it facilitated parents' motivation to take part in their work.

However, bringing participants into the research process can mean more than using techniques to motivate their participation. It can also mean working closely with representatives of target groups to tailor research questions, dissemination of results, and follow-up work so that the research more directly addresses their needs. For example, the National Institutes of Health has an initiative called Community-Based Participatory Research that partners scientists with agencies and requires research participants (e.g., women who have been incarcerated) to be included. While the Family CheckUp allows parents to choose from a menu of researcher-determined problems, when representatives of target groups sit at the research table, the researchers need to be open to adding or omitting research questions to their work. Conducting translational research does not require that the researcher move to such an extreme participatory-research model; nonetheless, those who have implemented procedures to bring greater representation of their target populations to the research table have found that doing so can improve rather than impede good research.

One of us (Gunnar) has been operating with a board of parent advisors for almost a decade in her work on internationally adopted children and she has hired individuals from the community's adoption agencies in order to establish community links on the front end of her research. While the primary goals of Gunnar's research address basic science questions (e.g., the neurobiological consequences of early deprivation and the capacity of impacted neural and behavioral systems to recover following adoption), working closely with a board of parent advisors and adoption professionals has helped to ensure that the way she addresses her basic science questions contributes to core questions of concern to the families and children and establishes the professional relationships that support dissemination of findings back to adoption professionals.

Translational research conducted at Mt. Hope Family Center highlights the potential for developmental and clinical scientists to export theory and research to the broader community, especially those families involved with child welfare (Cicchetti et al., in press; Toth et al., 2008). This work demonstrates that rigorous science and intervention research can take place within the community, if the time and effort are made in developing mutually supportive partnerships between researchers and community agencies. Mutuality is perhaps the most important ingredient in giving away our developmental knowledge, in that the implementation and conduct of randomized clinical trials and data collection in the child welfare community cannot occur without a process that benefits all parties. By developing relationships between policy makers and researchers, social policy initiatives also can build upon empirical evidence. Furthermore, because the basic research conducted with maltreating families at Mt. Hope Family Center was designed with policy questions at the forefront, rather than as a post hoc afterthought, a true research-informed policy agenda could be achieved that could benefit the welfare of maltreated children and their families (Cicchetti et al., in press; Toth et al., 2008).

We have undoubtedly not covered all of the conceptual roadblocks in our field that slow the translation of basic research into improvements in diagnostic tools, treatments, or preventive interventions. What we hope we have done, however, is to show how the roadblocks are not only surmountable, but also ways in which surmounting these obstacles may create opportunities to enhance our science. While removing these roadblocks requires that we think differently and go about doing our work differently, the changes needed do not threaten the viability of our basic research endeavors. Rather, making these changes can energize and enrich both our questions about basic processes in human development and our ability to address these basic questions. We hope that future generations of researchers will find this discussion of roadblocks somewhat quaint instead of a discussion of problems with which they are still grappling. Whether or not they do, however, will depend on how we train and equip our current students to meet the translational challenges of their generation.

TRAINING RESEARCHERS IN THE TRANSLATIONAL ERA

The goal of graduate and postdoctoral training is both to develop the next generation of scientists in aggregate and, individually, to protect and enhance each student's ability to find employment and launch his or her own research career. Graduate programs grapple with the twin problems of ensuring that students gain a sufficient working knowledge of the broad domain of the field, while protecting sufficient time for them to be trained to conduct research and become experts in a particular research area. Every general requirement added that demands coursework or reading outside of their specific area of expertise takes away time they can devote to becoming expert researchers in their own domain. As knowledge in a field accrues, tension between adding requirements to ensure breadth while protecting time to become experts grows. Ultimately, we know that students will not secure the best postdoctoral positions or tenure-track jobs based on their general knowledge of the field. Instead, they will obtain those positions based on their demonstrated expertise and research acumen in a focused set of research questions. This is why generalist training is concentrated in the first year or two of graduate work, with the latter years focusing increasingly on the development of a particular, narrow domain of expertise. Postdoctoral training may be used to broaden students' area of expertise, although it often is used to permit the students to add technical skills that were not available or that they had no time to learn during their graduate training. The net result, often lamented in discussions of how we are going to *push* translational efforts, is that we gear our graduate and postgraduate training precisely to create the narrow expertise that results in clogs in the translational pipeline.

From the student's perspective, the explosion of knowledge in the developmental sciences over the last decades, the increasing integration of genetic and neuroscience research in domains previously dominated by more purely psychological and behavioral approaches, and the rapid advance of complex technologies means that students are torn by decisions about whether to spread themselves broadly and thinly across the many areas they need to know something about, or to meet only the generalist requirements of their program and otherwise burrow deeply into a narrow area of expertise. And even when they choose to narrow their range in areas critical to translational research such as developmental behavioral neuroscience, the sheer number of techniques they feel they need to master is daunting.

Questions about how to imbue graduate and postdoctoral training to increase the number and quality of researchers who can contribute to the flow of information through the translational pipeline needs to be considered in the context of the tensions in graduate training previously outlined. However, it also may be helpful to consider that funding agencies and universities are encouraging graduate faculty to develop training programs that are implicitly more interdisciplinary, multidisciplinary, and/or translational. Two decades ago, Cicchetti and Toth (1991) urged clinical psychology programs to adopt a developmental psychopathology framework and called for the importance of interdisciplinary training within graduate curricula in developmental and clinical psychology. Recently, the University of Minnesota has established a series of initiatives designed to both foster more interdisciplinary research and enhance interdisciplinary training of graduate and postdoctoral students. The National Institute of Health as part of its Roadmap initiative first offered in 2003 and renewed in 2005 training grant funds under its program, "Training for a New Interdisciplinary Research Workforce." Plans to explicitly train graduate and postdoctoral students in interdisciplinary research and skills are required in these training programs, including the development of interdisciplinary courses and research experiences.

This leads to the question of what skills are needed, how best to encourage the development of those skills, and when in a student's training is it the right time to do so? Is it sufficient, or even a good idea, to require that the student train in the research laboratories of individuals in two related but different disciplines? Will completing coursework for a minor degree in a related discipline be sufficient or wise in all cases? If we want to encourage students to recognize the clinical relevance of their basic research, then should we be encouraging more of them to obtain clinical degrees? Or will the rigors of clinical training detract from the time they need to develop expertise in the multiple disciplines and research skills necessary to contribute to the research required to improve the flow of information in the translational pipeline? If not clinical degrees, would it simply be sufficient to expose them to some clinical coursework or have them participate in clinical rounds, follow-up clinics, and case discussions? If we increase our emphasis on developing facility in multiple domains, then do we risk producing a generation of researchers who have a little knowledge in a lot of areas, but who are not fully experts in any? And is there a way to train students in the attitudes and flexible approaches to problem solving they will need to work effectively with researchers from different research traditions?

There are no ready answers to these questions. However, it seems likely that some of the answers may lie in the attitudes and research activities of the faculty who are involved in students' training. As faculty become more involved in work that moves information along the translational pipeline, students will become involved in this work. Attitudes about the value of basic research and translational efforts will shift. Lectures and reading groups will become imbued with more integrated approaches to the issues and problems in the field. As faculty become involved in integrated research groups organized in centers that reflect multiple disciplines, training opportunities will arise out of these centers. Students will have the opportunity to experience how their disciplinary training narrows their ability to understand the perspectives of researchers trained in other disciplines, and this will provide a platform for establishing attitudes that permit crossdisciplinary discourse before their disciplinary attitudes solidify. Observing their mentors shift between disciplinary-speak and patterns of communication that rise above narrow disciplinary boundaries will provide templates for becoming scientific multilinguists. Thus, while we should worry about how to equip our students to be successful in this translational era, it may be that if we focus our attention on how we as faculty approach this era some of our concerns about training may abate.

CHAPTERS IN THIS VOLUME

We hope that the chapters in this volume will encourage faculty and their students to evaluate how their work can enhance the flow of information in the translational pipeline. For this symposium volume, we chose researchers whose work represented different points in the translational process and we asked them to provide a bit of history of how their research program evolved. Several of the contributors began their careers addressing very basic questions in developmental behavioral science (see Meltzoff, Chapter 2; Rothbart and Posner, Chapter 4; and Saffran, Chapter 5). However, in each case the work has become increasingly translational over time. These authors provide evidence that moving basic research onto a more translational path can enhance not only our ability to use basic science to address issues of diagnosis, treatment, and prevention of disorders, but it can also enhance our understanding of basic developmental processes. Several authors began their work focused on providing improved understanding of children with clinical disorders (see Mundy, Chapter 3) or at-risk children (see Shaw, Chapter 8); their work has progressed to the point of being used in interventions. Two of our authors (Pollak, Chapter 6, and Grigorenko, Chapter 7) focus their work on integrating across levels of organization including genetic and neurobiology data to address behavioral issues. Their work reveals not only the challenges of understanding development through integrating biological and behavioral information, but it also points to the value of these approaches for understanding the basis of behavioral disorders and potential targets for diagnosis and intervention. Together, the chapters in this volume provide a glimpse of the field of developmental science in transition from one in which research traditions contribute to clogging the translational pipeline to one in which research traditions increasingly encourage a reciprocal flow of information from discovery to improvements in patient care and preventive interventions.

REFERENCES

Antoniadis, E. A., Winslow, J. T., Davis, M., & Amaral, D. G. (2007). Role of the primate amygdala in fear-potentiated startle: Effects of chronic lesions in the rhesus monkey. *Journal of Neuroscience, 27*, 7386–7396.

Bornstein, M. H. (2006). Parenting science and practice. In A. Renninger and I. Sigel (Eds.), *Handbook of child psychology: Vol. 4. Child psychology in practice* (6th ed., pp. 893–949). New York: Wiley.

Carmichael, L. (Ed.). (1946). *Manual of child psychology*. New York: Wiley.

Carmichael, L. (Ed.). (1954). *Manual of child psychology*. New York: Wiley.

Charney, D. (2004). Psychobiological mechanisms of resilience and vulnerability: Implications for successful adaptation to extreme stress. *American Journal of Psychiatry, 161*, 195–216.

Cicchetti, D. (1984). The emergence of developmental psychopathology. *Child Development, 55*, 1–7.

Cicchetti, D. (1990). A historical perspective on the discipline of developmental psychopathology. In J. Rolf, A. Masten, D. Cicchetti, K. Nuechterlein, & S. Weintraub (Eds.), *Risk and protective factors in the development of psychopathology* (pp. 2–28). New York: Cambridge University Press.

Cicchetti, D. (1993). Developmental psychopathology: Reactions, reflections, projections. *Developmental Review, 13*, 471–502.

Cicchetti, D., & Curtis, W. J. (Eds.). (2007). A multi-level approach to resilience [Special Issue]. *Development and Psychopathology, 19*(3), 627–955.

Cicchetti, D., & Garmezy, N. (1993). Prospects and promises in the study of resilience. *Development and Psychopathology, 5*, 497–502.

Cicchetti, D., & Gunnar, M. R. (2008). Editorial: Integrating biological processes into the design and evaluation of preventive interventions. *Development and Psychopathology, 20*, 737–743.

Cicchetti, D., Rogosch, F. A., & Toth, S. L. (2006). Fostering secure attachment in infants in maltreating families through preventive interventions. *Development and Psychopathology, 18*, 623–650.

Cicchetti, D., & Toth, S. L. (1991). The making of a developmental psychopathologist. In J. Cantor, C. Spiker, & L. Lipsitt (Eds.), *Child behavior and development: Training for diversity* (pp. 34–72). Norwood, NJ: Ablex.

Cicchetti, D., & Toth, S. L. (1998). Perspectives on research and practice in developmental psychopathology. In W. Damon (Ed.), *Handbook of child psychology: Vol. 4. Child psychology in practice* (5th ed., pp. 479–583). New York: Wiley.

Cicchetti, D., & Toth, S.L. (2006a). A developmental psychopathology perspective on preventive interventions with high risk children and families. In A. Renninger and I. Sigel (Eds.), *Handbook of child psychology: Vol. 4. Child psychology in practice* (6th ed., pp. 497–547). New York: Wiley.

Cicchetti, D., & Toth, S. L. (Eds.). (2006b). Translational Research in Developmental Psychopathology [Special Issue]. *Development and Psychopathology, 18*(3), 619–933.

Cicchetti, D., Toth, S. L., Nilsen, W. J., & Manly, J. T. (in press). What do we know and why does it matter? The dissemination of evidence-based interventions for child maltreatment. In H. R. Schaffer & K. Durkin (Eds.), *Blackwell handbook of developmental Psychology in action*. Oxford: Blackwell.

Crawford, D. C., & Nickerson, D. A. (2005). Definition and clinical importance of haplotypes. *Annual Review of Medicine*, 56, 303–320.

Damon, W. (Series Ed.). (1998). *Handbook of child psychology* (5th ed., Vols. 1–4). New York: Wiley.

Damon, W. (Series Ed.). (2006). *Handbook of child psychology* (6th ed., Vols. 1–4). New York: Wiley.

Davis, M., Falls, W. A., Campeau, S., & Kim, M. (1993). Fear-potentiated startle: A neural and pharmacological analysis. *Behavioral & Brain Research*, 58, 175–198.

Davis, M., Walker, D. L., & Lee, Y. (1997). Roles of the amygdala and bed nucleus of the stria terminalis in fear and anxiety measured with the acoustic startle reflex. *Annals of the New York Academy of Sciences, 821*, 305–331.

Dishion, T., & Kavanagh, K. (2003). *Intervening in adolescent problem behavior: A family-centered approach.* New York: Guilford.

Garmezy, N., & Streitman, S. (1974). Children at risk: Conceptual models and research methods. *Schizophrenia Bulletin*, 9, 55–125.

Gottesman, I. I., & Hanson, D. R. (2005). Human development: Biological and genetic processes. *Annual Review of Psychology*, 56, 263–286.

Hartup, W. W., Johnson, A., & Weinberg, R. A. (2001). *The Institute of Child Development: Pioneering in science and application* 1925–2000. Minneapolis: University of Minnesota.

Hoffman, M. L., & Hoffman, L. W. (Eds.). (1964). *Review of child development research.* Chicago: University of Chicago.

Ialongo, N., Rogosch, F. A., Cicchetti, D., Toth, S. L., Buckley, J., Petras, H., et al. (2006). A developmental psychopathology approach to the prevention of mental health disorders. In D. Cicchetti & D. Cohen (Eds.), *Developmental psychopathology: Vol. 1. Theory and method* (2nd ed., pp. 968–1018). New York: Wiley.

Insel, T. R. (2005). Developmental psychobiology for public health: A bridge for translational research. *Developmental Psychobiology, 47*, 209–216.

Insel, T. R., & Quirion, R. (2005). Psychiatry as a clinical neuroscience discipline. *Journal of the American Medical Association, 294*, 2221–2224.

Insel, T. R., & Scolnick, E. M. (2006). Cure therapeutics and strategic prevention: Raising the bar for mental health research. *Molecular Psychiatry, 11*, 11–17.

Lamb, M. E., & Ahnert, L. (2006). Nonparental child care: Context, concepts, correlates, and consequences. In K. A. Renninger and I. E. Sigel (Eds.), *Handbook of child psychology: Vol. 4. Child psychology in practice* (6th ed., pp. 950–1016). New York: Wiley.

Luthar, S. S., Cicchetti, D., & Becker, B. (2000). The construct of resilience: A critical evaluation and guidelines for future work. *Child Development, 71*, 543–562.

Masten, A. S. (2001). Ordinary magic: Resilience processes in development. *American Psychologist*, 56, 227–238.

McLoyd, V. C., Aikens, N., & Burton, L. (2006). Childhood poverty, policy, and practice. In W. Damon, R. Lerner, A. Renninger, & I. Sigel (Eds.), *Handbook of child psychology: Vol. 4. Child psychology in practice* (6th ed., pp. 700–775). New York: Wiley.

Miller, W. R., & Rollnick, S. (2002). *Motivational interviewing: Preparing people for change* (2nd ed.). New York: Guilford.

Moffitt, T. E., Caspi, A., & Rutter, M. (2006). Measured gene–environment interactions in psychopathology: Concepts, research strategies, and implications for research, intervention, and public understanding of genetics. *Perspectives on Psychological Science, 1*, 5–27.

Mussen, P. (Ed.). (1970). *Carmichael's manual of child psychology* (3rd ed.). New York: Wiley.

Mussen, P. (Ed.). (1983). *Handbook of child psychology* (4th ed.). New York: Wiley.

National Advisory Mental Health Council. (2000). *Translating behavioral science into action: Report of the National Advisory Mental Health Counsel's behavioral science workgroup* (No. 00–4699). Bethesda, MD: National Institutes of Mental Health.

National Institute of Mental Health. (2005). *Proceedings of the National Meeting on Enhancing the Discipline of Clinical and Translational Sciences.* Arlington, VA. (Author).

National Institute of Neurological Disorders and Stroke. (2005). *NINDS Cooperative Program in Translational Research* (PAR-05–158). Bethesda, MD: National Institutes of Health.

Pellmar, T. C., & Eisenberg, L. (Eds.). (2000). *Bridging disciplines in the brain, behavioral, and clinical sciences.* Washington, DC: National Academy Press.

Posner, M. I., Rothbart, M. K., & Sheese, B. E. (2007). Attention genes. *Developmental Science, 10*, 24–29.

Rothbart, M. K., & Posner, M. I. (2006). Temperament, attention, and developmental psychopathology. In D. Cicchetti & D. Cohen (Eds.), *Developmental psychopathology: Vol. 2. Developmental neuroscience* (2nd ed., pp. 465–501). New York: Wiley.

Rutter, M. (2006). *Genes and behavior: Nature-nurture interplay explained.* London: Blackwell Publishing.

Sanchez, M. M., Noble, P. M., Lyon, C. K., Plotsky, P. M., Davis, M., Nemeroff, C. B., et al. (2005). Alterations in diurnal cortisol rhythm and acoustic startle response in nonhuman primates with adverse rearing. *Biological Psychiatry, 57*, 373–381.

Sears, R. R. (1975). Your ancients revisited. In E. M. Hetherington (Ed.), *Review of child development research: Vol. 5* (pp. 1–73). Chicago: University of Chicago Press.

Senn, M. J. E. (1975). Insights on the child development movement in the United States. *Monographs of the Society for Research in Child Development, 40* (3–4, Serial No. 161).

Shonkoff, J. P. (2000). Science, policy, and practice. Three cultures in search of a shared mission. *Child Development, 71*, 181–187.

Sigel, I. E. (2006). Research to practice redefined. In K. A. Renninger & I. E. Sigel (Eds.), *Handbook of child psychology: Vol. 4. Child psychology in practice* (6th ed., pp. 1017–1023). New York: Wiley.

Sigel, I. E., & Renninger, K. A. (Eds.). (1998). Preface. In *Handbook of child psychology: Vol. 4. Child psychology in practice* (5th ed., pp. xxi–xxiii). New York: Wiley.

Stokes, D. E. (1997). *Pasteur's quadrant: Basic science and technological innovation.* Washington, DC: Brookings Institution.

Thomas, K., & Cicchetti, D. (Eds.). (2008). Imaging brain systems in normality and psychopathology [Special Issue]. *Development and Psychopathology, 20*, 1023–1349.

Toth, S. L., Manly, J. T., & Nilsen, W. J. (2008). From research to practice: Lessons learned. *Journal of Applied Developmental Psychology, 29*, 317–325.

Zigler, E., & Balla, D. (Eds.). (1982). *Mental retardation: The developmental-difference controversy*. Hillsdale, NJ: Lawrence Erlbaum Associates.

Zigler, E., & Glick, M. (1986). *A developmental approach to adult psychopathology.* New York: Wiley.

Zigler, E., & Valentine, J. (Eds.). (1997). *Project head start: A legacy of the war on poverty*. New York: Macmillan.

CHAPTER

2

Roots of Social Cognition: The *Like-Me* Framework

Andrew N. Meltzoff

ROOTS OF SOCIAL COGNITION: THE *LIKE-ME* FRAMEWORK

There are three chief reasons why people pursue child development. They want to: (a) help their own child, (b) help other people's children, or (c) understand the causes and mechanisms of child development. The first reason is grounded in a concern for an individual. The second is motivated by a class of people. The third is driven by the pursuit of abstract knowledge. The first two are based on practical concerns and the third on a quest for knowledge.

The parents I see in my laboratory are typically motivated by the first reason. Dr. Benjamin Spock devoted his professional life to the second. Piaget was impelled by the third. Of course, these motives are not mutually exclusive. A practitioner may start off wanting to help children and

This research was supported by NICHD (HD-22514), the National Science Foundation (SBE-0354453), and the Tamaki Foundation. The thoughts expressed in the paper are those of the author and do not necessarily reflect the views of these agencies. I thank R. Brooks, P. Kuhl, C. Harris, and C. Fisher for help on this chapter and A. Gopnik and K. Moore for useful conversations on the matters discussed here.

become captured by the purely abstract issues. A researcher may begin by pursuing abstract knowledge and then be touched by real-world concerns. Over the course of their careers some people such as Piaget (1970) and Bruner (1960), both of whom became interested in improving education, successfully span both theory and practice.

Can we weigh these motives or rank them in relation to each other? Leonardo da Vinci, no stranger to combining theory and practice, asserted:

> Those who are in love with practice without knowledge are like the sailor who gets into a ship without rudder or compass and who never can be certain whither he is going. Practice must always be founded on sound theory. (*Notebooks*, entry 19)

Or even more bluntly, "Science is the captain and practice the soldiers" (*Notebooks*, entry 1160). This fits with C. P. Snow's (1964) influential two-culture thesis that emerged from his experiences at Cambridge University:

> We prided ourselves that the science that we were doing could not, in any conceivable circumstances, have any practical use. The more firmly one could make the claim, the more superior one felt. (p. 32)

The modern view differs from this (Stokes, 1997). Funding agencies, universities, and philanthropists are pushing to close the gap between theory and practice. The goal is to inspire research that does not fit easily in the old basic/applied or captain/soldier dichotomies. The concept of *translational research* has emerged (Gunnar & Cicchetti, this volume). Translational research in child development is motivated by the dual desires to advance fundamental understanding of mind and to help children reach their full potential. Translational research addresses a fundamental intellectual puzzle and has a why-society-should-care component. Neither is the captain; both jointly steer the research.

All science occurs in a context (Kuhn, 1962), and the context for today's child development research is different from the one Piaget found himself in when he observed his own children in the 1920s. Piaget did not write for parents, and his discoveries were not streamed into headlines. There were no Swiss newspapers proclaiming: "Babies loose track of objects hidden under Piaget's beret!" Or "Baby memory: Jacqueline has tantrum one day after seeing neighbor boy throw a fit." Or "Are your baby's secondary circular reactions developing on time?"

Today is different. Parents are being assaulted with information about their role in child-rearing. Some headlines claim "parents don't matter." Others lead parents to feel guilty because they matter too much—early experience is destiny. Society is asking questions about the origins of thought, emotion, language, and personality. How should developmental scientists respond?

First, we should realize that the spotlight is on us. From the White House to the state house, there is interest in research on early learning. Discoveries reported in *Science, Developmental Psychology, or Child Development* are rapidly picked up by the media. Discoveries about the mental life of children no longer creep quietly into the professional literature.

Second, basic researchers do not have to give up their day jobs to respond to society's call (Shonkoff & Phillips, 2000). Our studies of child development need not promise to a cure teenage violence. There is plenty of room for those who want to stay close to the laboratory to uncover the basic mechanisms of learning and psychological development. Today's knowledge-driven research turns into tomorrow's applications, and conversely society's most pressing concerns often inspire careful science (e.g., NICHD Early Child Care Research Network, 2001, 2005). We need not insulate ourselves from the real world on the one hand or overpromise on the other.

Third, scientists can play a role in communicating the empirical discoveries to parents, health-care professionals, business leaders, and policy makers. Between pure discovery and the dissemination of programs there is a missing link. The missing link is the *translation* of the research findings. University scientists make discoveries; non-university groups disseminate the information to those who can use it. But there is a translation gap—the science often inadvertently misrepresented by nonprofessionals who are summarizing it. By ensuring that scientists are involved in the translation process, we can close this gap.

The sharing of scientific discoveries can assist parents in two ways. Learning that babies and young children think, want, intend, and even perform their own mini-experiments helps people see and enjoy babies in new ways. After all, if such discoveries keep scientists going late at night, why should it not do the same for parents? Also, communicating research and the scientific process can inoculate parents against pseudoscience. We may not be able to stop organizations from claiming to make better babies, but we can intrigue parents and policy makers with the value of genuine science. If academic astronomers can intelligently debate the origins of the universe in newspapers carrying astrological predictions, we can discuss the origins of the mind amidst the pseudoscience claiming to create super-babies with expanded IQs and pumped-up ethical sensitivities. In our own efforts to close the translation gap (Gopnik, Meltzoff, & Kuhl, 2001), we treat parents and other stakeholders as intelligent consumers of information who are interested in the philosophy, neuroscience, and the behavioral aspects of child development.

Many discoveries from the modern science of early child development have captured the attention of the public, policy makers, and practitioners. This chapter is focused on discoveries concerning early *social cognition*—what infants know about people. Parents care about IQ, but parents and professionals alike now realize that children's understanding of other people has more impact on school readiness and success and happiness in life than previously thought (e.g., Collins & Laursen, 1999; Ladd, Birch, & Buhs, 1999). Policy makers and parents want to know when children become attuned to other people and come to identify with them. Are children born social, or are they born in a state of "normal autism," as claimed by psychiatrists Mahler, Pine, and Bergman (1975, p. 41), unable to differentiate people from things? Moreover, both parents and policy makers want to know whether children's social environment, beyond the extremes of neglect and abuse, makes a difference to their eventual outcome.

In this chapter I will discuss new research on imitation, joint visual attention, and emotion. I will show that infants are carefully watching our actions and imitating what they see. Parents matter because babies are learning from us. Young children, even infants, look to us for guidance.

I have found that this information makes a special difference to fathers and the male policy makers. While the fathers and grandfathers might have thought that their little ones were not learning before they were old enough to go fishing or hold up their end of a conversation, it alters the paternal worldview to learn that preverbal children are already watching and learning. It is not just that adults are role models for teenagers. The new research shows that we are role models for our young children, even our babies. It is basic science that matters to people in the real world.

Overturning the Myth of the Asocial Infant

Within our professional lifetimes, we have witnessed the overturning of one of the most pervasive myths in social science—the myth of the asocial infant. On classical views of human development offered by Freud, Piaget, and Skinner, the newborn is cut off from others. Freud and his followers made a distinction between a physical and psychological birth (Freud, 1911; Mahler et al., 1975). When the baby is born, there is a physical birth but not yet a psychological one. The baby is like an unhatched chick, incapable of interacting as a social being because a "stimulus barrier" or "protective shield" cuts the newborn off from external reality (Freud, 1920, pp. 25–30). Freud provided the following metaphor to describe the human newborn: "A neat example of a psychical system shut off from the stimuli of the external world . . . is afforded by a bird's egg with its food supply enclosed in its shell; for it, the care provided by its mother is limited to the provision of warmth" (Freud, 1911, p. 220). These and other related claims influenced generations of psychiatrists and their practices (Beebe, Rustin, Sorter, & Knoblauch, 2003; Beebe, Sorter, Rustin, & Knoblauch, 2003).

Piaget used a philosophical rather than biological metaphor to endorse a similar point about the asocial infant. He believed that the baby is "radically egocentric" or even "solipsistic" (Piaget, pp. 352–357). The neonate has only a few reflexes at his or her disposal (e.g., sucking, grasping), and people are registered only to the extent that they can be assimilated to these action schemes. The infant breaks free of the initial solipsism by 18 months. It is a long journey from solipsism to understanding of others' minds, emotions, and the rest of social cognition.

One cannot readily quote Skinner's view about how children crack the puzzle of social cognition, because in a sense he does not think they ever do. Even adults are conceptualized as reacting to behaviors but not knowing the minds of their interactive partners. Human beings have finely tuned contingency detectors, and that is all there is. To use Skinner's phrase, social cognition is largely a "matter of consequences" (Skinner, 1983), by which he means that people are not role models who are observed and internalized, but merely reinforcement agents who sculpt the child's behavior through administering rewards and punishments.

The *Like-Me* Theory

If the human infant is born neither a social isolate nor with an adult-like grasp of other people's thoughts, feelings, intentions, and desires, from whence comes such understanding? What gets social cognition off the ground? Skinnerian blank slates, Freudian isolated eggs, and Piagetian solipsism will not get us from the newborn to the adult because there is not enough innate structure to interpret and make good use of the experience received in social interaction. Based on modern empirical work in developmental science, Meltzoff (2007a, 2007b) proposed the *Like-Me* theory to describe the infant's initial state and early phases of social cognition.

The *Like-Me* theory has three developmental steps, depicted in Figure 2.1. It describes the infant's innate state (Step 1) and also provides a mechanism for developmental change (Steps 2 and 3). The older child and adult are not locked into the same understanding as the newborn. Their interpretation of others as intentional agents is modified by their own experiences.

Step 1: Innate equipment

Newborns detect and use equivalences between observed and executed acts. When newborns see adult biological motion, including hand and face movements, these acts are mapped onto the infant's body movements. This mapping is manifest by newborn imitation. Self and other are intrinsically bound through an innate coding of human acts that is abstract enough to unite the perception and production of behavior. My own felt acts and the acts I watch you make are registered by the

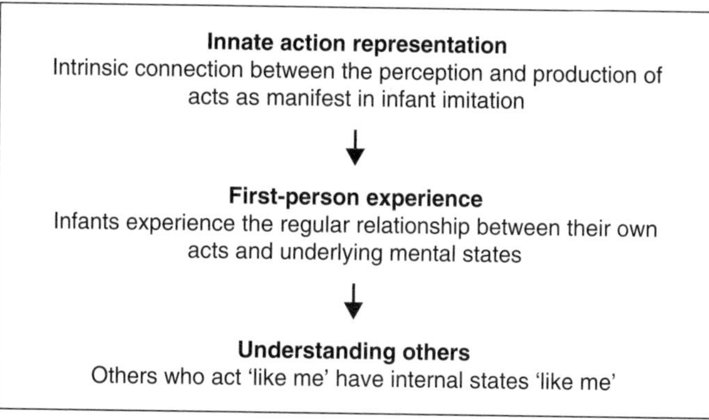

Figure 2.1 'Like Me' developmental theory. (Adapted from: Meltzoff, 2007b).

same abstract code. Meltzoff and Moore (1977, 1997) called this a *supramodal representation* because it cuts across particular modalities. It is because of the infant's action represention—the supramodal code—that the movements of people are special to young babies. The child, even the newborn, can watch the movements of other people and immediately recognize that "those acts are like these acts" or "that looks the way this feels." The supramodal representation of human action provides the lingua franca for connecting self and other.

Step 2: First-person experience

Through everyday experience infants map the relation between their own bodily states and mental experiences. For example, there is an intimate relation between striving to achieve a goal and the concomitant facial expression of concentration and effortful bodily acts. Infants experience their own unfulfilled desires and their own matching facial/postural/vocal reactions. They experience their own inner feelings and behavioral facial expressions and construct a detailed bidirectional map linking mental experiences and behavior (Kuhl & Meltzoff, 1982; Meltzoff & Brooks, 2008; Meltzoff & Moore, 1997).

Step 3: Attributions to others

When infants see others acting in a way that is similar to how they have acted in the past—acting *like me*—they make an attribution. They ascribe the internal feelings that regularly go with those behaviors, based on their self-experience. This gives infants leverage for grasping other minds before language can be used. Infants integrate the ability to relate self–other at the level of action (Step 1) with their own self-experience (Step 2) to yield a deeper understanding of what lays behind the behavior of others. As children's own experiences expand they have an enriched understanding of what another might be feeling, desiring, and perceiving when he or she acts in certain tell-tale ways.

This is not Fodorian nativism (Fodor, 1983). Newborns do not possess the adult theory. Nor is the adult conception of others simply triggered by particular cues or due to the maturation of modules. Rather, infants' initial grasp that the actions of others are *like me*, coupled with their own experiences and observations, provides them with a developmental mechanism for coming to understand the mind others in a new way (Meltzoff & Brooks, 2008).

Action Representation and Imitation

Preverbal infants imbue the acts of others with felt meaning not through a formal process of analytic reasoning, but because the other is processed as *like me*. This is underwritten by the way infants represent action. There is now evidence that young infants parse human action into a common code that links acts they see others perform and ones they themselves produce. Perhaps the best evidence comes from infant imitation. Imitation demonstrates that, at some level of processing, infants use the seen behavior of others as a basis for forming a corresponding action plan. Through imitation, infants make manifest the connection between self and other at the level of shared actions.

When in development does imitation and this coding of action begin? Meltzoff and Moore (1977) reported that 12- to 21-day-old infants imitate facial expressions. Because early imitation ran afoul of the myth of the asocial infant, the report at first engendered surprise; but the finding has now been replicated in more than 24 studies from around the world (for a review see Meltzoff & Moore, 1997). The neonatal imitative response is quite specific; it is not a global or a general arousal reaction. Infants respond differentially to two types of lip movements (mouth opening versus lip protrusion) and two types of protrusion actions (lip protrusion versus tongue protrusion). Infants also differentiate two different types of tongue movements from one another (Meltzoff & Moore, 1994). Early imitation cannot be reduced to simple mimicry or instant resonance. The response can be displaced in time and space from the demonstration. In one study, a pacifier was put in infants' mouths as they watched the display. After the pacifier was removed, the infants imitated the earlier displays (Meltzoff & Moore, 1977). In another study, an adult showed 6-week-old infants a gesture, and then the infants were taken home for a 24-hour memory delay. The next day they were presented with the same adult sitting with a neutral facial expression. If the adult had shown mouth opening the day before, the infants initiated that gesture from memory; if the adult had shown tongue protrusion, infants responded with that gesture (Meltzoff & Moore, 1994). The imitative response is not rigidly fixed in the form of a fixed-action pattern. Infants *correct* their imitative attempts so that they more and more closely converge on the model demonstrated (Meltzoff & Moore, 1997). They are actively matching the target.

Meltzoff and Moore (1983, 1989) tested newborns in a hospital setting. The youngest infant was only 42-minutes old. The results showed that the newborns imitate adult gestures. Nativist claims are commonplace in the philosophical and psychological literatures, but few tests have been conducted on newborns. *Homo sapiens* have an innate capacity to imitate.

Meltzoff and Moore (1997) proposed that facial imitation is based on *active intermodal mapping*—the AIM account. On this view infants can, at some primitive level, recognize equivalence between the acts they see others do and the acts they do themselves. This is not a complex mechanism that requires cognitive machinations by the infant. Rather, there appears to be a very primitive and foundational body scheme that allows infants to unify the seen acts of others and their own felt acts into one common framework. The infants' own facial gestures are invisible to them, but they are not unperceived. They are monitored by proprioception. Conversely, the adult's acts are not felt by proprioception, but they can be seen. Infants can link perception and production through what AIM terms a common *supramodal* coding of human acts. This is why they can correct their imitative movements. And it is why they can imitate from memory: Infants store a representation of the adult's act and it is the target against which they compare their own acts. A more detailed description of the metric of equivalence between self and other is provided elsewhere (Meltzoff & Moore, 1997).

The idea of a supramodal representation of action that we used to explain early imitation 30 years ago fits well with neuroscience discoveries about the mirror neuron system (MNS) and shared neural circuits (Iacoboni et al., 1999; Rizzolatti, Fogassi, & Gallese, 2001). An important task for the future is to analyze the commonalities and differences in these mechanisms, which are proposed at different levels, the neural/sub-personal and the psychological/personal. For example, the MNS is better suited to explain fast, automatic, non-effortful resonance than to explain deferred imitation, response correction, and the imitation of novel acts. Careful analyses are beginning to emerge (e.g., Jackson, Meltzoff, & Decety, 2006; Meltzoff & Decety, 2003; Rizzolatti, Fadiga, Fogassi & Gallese, 2002).

The unique contribution from the human developmental literature is that newborn imitation demonstrates that self–other connectedness is functional at birth.[1] Importantly, I do not argue that the human imitative capacity has reached adult-like levels at birth and have described several interesting developments in imitation in later infancy and early childhood (e.g., Gleissner, Meltzoff, & Bekkering, 2000; Meltzoff, 1995; Repacholi & Meltzoff, 2007; Williamson, Meltzoff, & Markman, 2008). However, the behavioral discoveries do establish that human infants are born learning from their social environment. The idea of a solipsistic newborn—a social isolate—is a myth.

People As Perceivers: Infant Gaze Following

Interpersonal imitation does not exhaust infant social cognition. Another important aspect of social cognition is the realization that people are sources of information about external objects. For adults, particular body movements have special meanings—they are *about* something. If a person looks up into the sky, bystanders follow his or her gaze. This is not

[1]Here it is worth noting that MNS data are lacking using neural measures; the crucial newborn studies remain to be done with monkeys or humans using neuroscience measures. Single cell recordings with newborn monkeys would be useful to evaluate the functionality of mirror neurons at birth in the monkey brain; mu rhythm studies with human newborns may soon become possible.

imitation; the adult is not trying to copy the movement but rather trying to see what the person is looking at. Adults realize that people acquire information from afar, despite the spatial gap between viewer and object. Visual perception is a kind of psychological contact at a distance.

When do infants begin to ascribe visual perception to others? Is there a stage when head turns are interpreted as purely physical motions with no notion that they are *directed toward* the external object, no notion of a perceiver? In fact, children with autism may regard adults' looking behavior in this way. Children with autism have gaze-following deficits, and it can be speculated that they process adults' looking behavior more as a physical movement in space than as a psychological act that connects the perceiver and world (Hobson & Meyer, 2005; Mundy, this volume; Mundy & Sigman, 2006; Mundy, Sigman, & Kasari, 1990; Toth, Munson, Meltzoff, & Dawson, 2006).

The onset of gaze following in typically developing children has profound implications both for language and for emotions. It is relevant for understanding the meaning of an emotional display because people's emotions are often engendered by what they see in the external world (e.g., *that* object is dangerous, appealing, or disgusting). By following a person's gaze you can grasp the cause of his or her emotional display (Moses, Baldwin, Rosicky, & Tidball, 2001; Repacholi & Meltzoff, 2007).

Language acquisition is similarly facilitated by understanding another's line of regard (Baldwin, 1995; Brooks & Meltzoff, 2008; Mundy, Fox, & Card, 2003; Carpenter, Nagell, & Tomasello, 1998). Bruner's (1983) account of early language acquisition gives pride of place to joint visual attention in initial word learning. In the prototypical case, if you want to know what mom is verbally labeling, follow her eyes. She is probably not labeling what is behind her back or on the next page of the book. Infants learn language best from live, socially engaged tutors who engage in joint attention as they are labeling objects (e.g., Conboy, Brooks, Taylor, Meltzoff, & Kuhl, 2008; Kuhl & Rivera-Gaxiola, 2008; Kuhl, Tsao, & Liu, 2003).

There is a debate about the mechanisms underlying infant gaze following and whether it shows that infants have a primitive grasp of *seeing* and *visual contact* in others (Flom, Lee, & Muir, 2007; Mundy & Newell, 2007; Moore & Dunham, 1995). One view is that young infants initially treat others' looking behaviors as mere movements. In the leanest version, young infants visually track the adult's head movement in space and are pulled into the correct hemifield where they catch sight of the salient target object by happenstance (Butterworth & Jarrett, 1991). Over time, infants then learn that the adult's head turn is a reliable cue indicating where an object can be seen (Moore, 1999, 2006). Conversely, others have offered a nativist view suggesting that infants have a built-in module that takes eye gaze as input and automatically makes attributions about seeing and visual experience in others (Baron-Cohen, 1995). A third, developmental view is that infants' understanding of others' vision emerges from more primitive beginnings. Meltzoff & Brooks (2008) propose that a mechanism of change is infants' experience with *their own vision*: Infants develop an understanding of the vision of others, in part through their own acts of turning-in-order-to-see and opening/shutting of their eyes to cut off and reinstate visual experience.

The first issue is to determine whether infants are, as the lean view suggests, simply processing the salient physical movements in space caused by the head. Brooks and Meltzoff (2002, 2005) developed a protocol that zeroed in on the importance of eyes in infant gaze following. In this procedure, an adult turned to look at one of two targets. The manipulation was that the adult turned to the target with eyes open for one group and with eyes closed for the other group. If infants relied simply on head motions, they should turn in both cases. If, infants appreciate that the eyes are relevant for connecting a perceiver and object, they should differentiate the two conditions and turn to look at the target in one case and not the other. The reason such a manipulation is crucial is that we do, in fact, see with our eyes and not with our head. It is an important step forward in social cognition for infants to put special emphasis on eyes (something children with autism may not do; see Mundy, this volume). It is, after all, the eyes that are the *window to the soul*—the head is not such a portal.

Brooks and Meltzoff (2002) used the Gaze Following: Eyes Open/Closed test to assess 12-, 14-, and 18-month-old infants. Each infant at each age was randomly assigned to a condition in which the adult turned to the target with either open or closed eyes. Infants at all three ages followed the adult significantly more often when the adult turned with

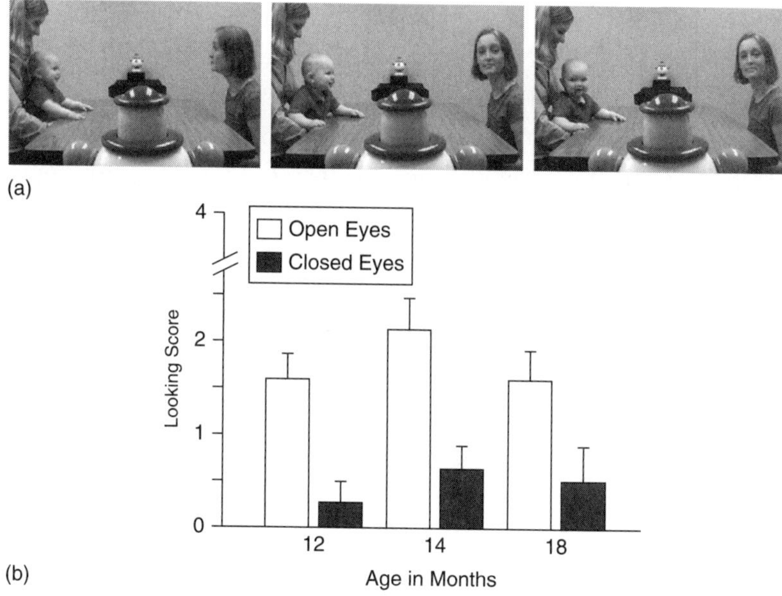

Figure 2.2 (a) Three-panel sequence showing a 12-month-old infant successfully gaze-following. The adult turns in silence and does not point to the target. (b) Infants selectively gaze follow (mean +*SE*) when the adult's eyes are open rather than closed. There were four gaze-following trials, and thus the maximum score if an infant correctly followed the adult's gaze on all trials is 4. (Adapted from: Brooks & Meltzoff, 2002).

open versus closed eyes (Fig. 2.2). At the ages tested, our current findings disprove the leanest interpretation, because head movement was controlled, and infants were more likely to look at the correct target when the social partner could see it.

Eye closure is only one way to block a person's line of sight. Another way is to use an inanimate object. For an adult, an opaque physical barrier has the same function as closed eyes—both prevent visual access. Importantly, this is not the case for 12-month-olds. As shown in the next study, these infants understand that vision is cut off by the biological motion of eye closure in advance of understanding that an inanimate barrier does so.

In the study of inanimate occluders, the person turned toward a target wearing either a headband or a blindfold (Brooks & Meltzoff, 2002).

In both instances, the same cloth covered part of the experimenter's face, but in one situation the adult could see and in the other she could not. We found that 14- and 18-month-old infants looked at the adult's target significantly more often in the headband than in the blindfold condition. In contrast, the 12-month-old infants did not distinguish between the two conditions. They systematically looked at the indicated target whether the adult turned wearing the blindfold or the headband. This is not just a matter of blindfolds causing a general suppression of activity. Rather, 12-month-old infants make the mistake of following the "gaze" of the adult wearing the blindfold. Evidently, they recognize that the human act of eye closure blocks contact with external objects, but they do not yet understand the same about inanimate occluders.

An Intervention Study: Self-Experience Changes Infants' Understanding of Other Minds

Infants understand eye closure in advance of view-blockage by inanimate barriers, but the adult's line of sight is blocked in both cases. Why is there a developmental difference? Eye closure is a biological motion with which infants have extensive first-person experience: Infants can control their own vision by closing their eyes when they do not want to look at something. The experience of turning off and on visual access to the world by eye closing/opening might serve as a framework for understanding such behavior in others. Perhaps if infants are given systematic, novel experience that blindfolds block their *own* view, they might make different attributions to others. To test this we designed an experimental intervention that provided blindfold experience to infants (Meltzoff & Brooks, 2008).

In one study, infants were randomly assigned to one of three groups. Infants in the treatment group were provided with various interesting objects to play with on the table; when they looked down to visually inspect an object, the experimenter held an opaque blindfold in between the object and the child's eyes. Thus, the infants experienced that their own view was blocked when the opaque blindfold was held in front of their eyes and was restored again when the blindfold was removed. This experience had nothing to do with the experimenter's viewpoint; it was a first-person experience. Two control groups were used. One involved a specially constructed windowed-cloth, which was made from the same material as the blindfold but had a window cut out of the center. Infants in the window group received the same protocol as just described, thus controlling for the experience of an adult inserting a cloth between them and the objects; however, they could peer through the windowed cloth. Infants in the baseline control group were simply familiarized with the opaque cloth while it was laying flat on the table, so they could see and touch it, but did not receive a tutorial on its view-blocking properties.

At the end of training all three groups were given a standard gaze-following test: Infants were presented with the blindfolded adult who turned toward the distal objects. The results showed that infants who had received first-person training on the opaque blindfold now interpreted the adult's blindfolded turning correctly. They did not turn when the adult wore the blindfold. Importantly, infants who had the windowed-cloth experience and the baseline infants mistakenly followed the blindfolded adult's "gaze" to the distal object when she wore the blindfold (replicating Brooks & Meltzoff, 2002).

In the natural course of development, infants change their understanding of visual perception. By 18 months of age, infants do not act as though adults can see through opaque barriers (Brooks & Meltzoff, 2002; Butler, Caron, & Brooks, 2000; Dunphy-Lelii & Wellman, 2004). Meltzoff and Brooks (2008, Experiment 2) capitalized on this by providing 18-month-olds with a completely *novel* self-experience—one they would not have encountered outside of the laboratory. We constructed a trick blindfold that looked opaque from the outside but was made of special material that could be seen through when held close to the eyes. Infants were randomly assigned to one of three groups: (a) experience with the trick blindfold, (b) experience with the opaque blindfold, and (c) baseline experience in which they simply played with the trick blindfold as an object while it lay flat on the table. As in the previous study, for infants in the first two groups the blindfold was interposed between their eyes and the toys during the training period. The opaque blindfold blocked their view, and the trick blindfold provided infants the experience that the (apparently opaque) blindfold could be seen through.

After training, infants in all three groups saw the adult wear the blindfold in our standard test. As expected, infants in the baseline group and the opaque-blindfold groups refrained from following the adult's head turns when the adult wore the blindfold. The new finding is that infants who had first-person experience with the trick see-through blindfold *followed* the adult's head turns significantly more often than did infants in the two other groups.

This underscores the power of infant self-experience. Infants were given a particular novel experience under experimental control. They immediately used the novel self-experience to change their construal of the behavior of others. They assume the other can see through the blindfold, despite the fact that the adult's eyes were covered and it looked, from the outside, like she could not.

This is the first study showing that infants use first-person experience about a psychological state such as *seeing* to make interpretations about another person. We think these training effects are a case of *like-me* projection with implications for how infants' self-experience transforms their understanding of mind of others who act *like me*, as will be elaborated on later in this chapter.

Integrating Emotion, Gaze, and imitation

Social cognition can be learned by observing third-party interactions not involving the self. Children learn by watching how siblings interact and observe their parental relationship. There has been surprisingly little laboratory research on infants' learning from watching two people interact. Repacholi and I investigated this in what we call *emotional eavesdropping* (Repacholi & Meltzoff, 2007; Repacholi, Meltzoff, & Olsen, 2008). This work examined whether toddlers regulate their imitation as a function of the emotional responses that they witness *others* receive for performing the same action. If others respond negatively, do they refrain from imitating the act?

Toddlers sat at the table much like a dinner table and watched two adults interact. When one adult performed a seemingly innocent act, the second adult became angry (saying, "*that* is so irritating!"). We manipulated the emotional response of the adult and whether or not that adult was looking when the child subsequently played with the objects. Our hypothesis was that children would be loathe to imitate the act that caused the adult's anger (perhaps recognizing it was a *forbidden act*) if the previously angry adult was currently watching the child. If the angry adult had left the room or could no longer see the child's response, the child would imitate.

In more detail, the experimental set up was as follows. Eighteen-month-olds were randomly assigned to three groups. In all three groups an adult demonstrator performed a specific action on a novel object. What varied was the emotional reaction that another adult expressed. For one control, the Emoter became angry at the adult demonstrator as she performed the target action. The Emoter then assumed a neutral face and looked in the child's direction while the child was handed the object to see if he or she would imitate. For a second control, the Emoter also became angry but then left the room while the child was handed the toy for imitation, so she could not monitor the child's imitation. In the third group, the Emoter did not become angry and simply commented neutrally on the adult's demonstration (saying, "*that* is so entertaining") and watched as the child was handed the object. The results showed that toddlers in the latter two groups had significantly higher imitation scores than those in the first group (Repacholi & Meltzoff, 2007). infants

Repacholi et al. (2008) next zeroed in on the role of the adult watching the child. This work followed the same general procedure, but the previously angry Emoter assumed a neutral face and either: (a) stayed facing the child, (b) stayed facing the child but picked up a magazine to read (so not looking at the infant), or (c) stayed facing the child but closed her eyes (so not looking at the child). Children were significantly more likely to imitate the demonstrator's act in these latter two non-looking conditions than when the previously angry Emoter monitored the child's response.

This research shows that toddlers use *emotional eavesdropping*. Toddlers are not restricted to gleaning information from interactions that directly involve them but are also capable of learning from emotional exchanges between others. Interestingly, children regulated their behavior based on whether or not the previously angry person had *visual access* to their own actions. Children inhibited their imitative performances when the previously angry adult was looking at them; but when she was not, they reproduced the forbidden actions. The work is significant because it shows that children do not blindly and automatically imitate (see also Williamson et al., 2008). Children self-regulated: They chose whether or not to duplicate the acts they saw.

The work is relevant to the child clinical literature on family emotional climate. Children from families in which there are high levels of interparental anger are at risk for behavior problems (Hudson, 2005). It is sobering to contemplate that children's eavesdropping on a brief anger display in the laboratory inhibits their imitation. If infants eavesdrop on repeated events of interparental anger, it might more generally reduce their imitative learning. Repacholi and I are interested in the individual differences we observed in our studies. A small number of children not only did not imitate but refrained from even touching the test object in one or more trials; conversely, there were some who imitated on every trial, whether or not the previously angry Emoter was watching. One wonders whether these observations have predictive value—do they predict aspects of later executive functioning? Are these differences themselves the outcome of identifiable biological factors or family variables (e.g., interparental anger)? We are currently pursuing such questions.

Scope and Implications of the *Like-Me* Theory

The fundamental puzzle of social cognition stems from the fact that persons are more than physical objects. Enumerating a person's height, weight, and eye color does not exhaust our description of that person. We have skipped over their psychological makeup. If a self-mobile, human-looking body was devoid of psychological characteristics it would not be a person at all, but a robot or, to use the philosopher's favorite, a zombie. A fundamental issue is how we come to know others as persons like ourselves. Each of us has the phenomenological experience that we are not alone in the world, not the unique bearer of psychological properties. We know that we perceive, feel, and intend, and we believe others have psychological states just like ours.

Philosophers seek to justify the inference that the dynamic sacks of skin we see are animated by psychological states. They contemplate whether this is a fiction and assemble criteria for knowing whether it is or is not (Russell, 1948; Ryle, 1949; Strawson, 1959). Developmental psychologists ask different questions. We inquire how such a view takes hold regardless of whether it is logically justified. Is it innately specified? Does it differ in children with autism?

Fodor (1987) thinks that infants innately assign adult commonsense psychology to people:

> Here is what I would have done if I had been faced with this problem in designing *Homo sapiens*. I would have made a knowledge of commonsense *Homo sapiens* psychology innate; that way no one would have to spend time learning it. . . . The empirical evidence that God did it the way I would have isn't, in fact, unimpressive. (p. 132)

The opposing school is that newborns lack any inkling that other humans have psychological properties. It is claimed, for example, that the child is born a solipsist (Piaget, 1954) or is in a state of so-called normal autism (Mahler et al., 1975), treating people the same as things. It is a long way—I would say an impossible path—to get from there to commonsense psychology.

Modern developmental scientists, including myself, have been trying to develop a third way. It grants far more to the newborn than the second view, while stopping short of the first. In my view, infant imitation and the neural representations that underlie it provide an innate foundation for building the adult understanding of people, but infants do not possess the adult framework. Infants imitate at birth, but they do not infer intentions or fully understand visual perception as a mental state in others (Brooks & Meltzoff, 2005; Meltzoff, 1999). This is hardly grounds for Fodorian nativism. It is equally true that young infants outstrip Piagetian theory. What we need is a new theory of social development that includes a rich initial understanding and a mechanism of change that can transform this into the adult state based on structured interpersonal experience.

Infants' action representation and imitation demonstrate that they map other people's behavior onto their own bodies. Because human acts are seen in others and performed by the self, the infant can grasp the social connection: You can act *like me* and I can act *like you*—this interpersonal bridge based on shared action provides the initial state of social cognition.

This construal of certain movements in the environment as *me relevant* then has cascading developmental effects. First, the world of material objects can be divided into those entities that perform these acts (people) and those that do not (things). Second, the lingua franca of human acts provides access to other people that are not afforded by things. The ability of young infants to interpret the bodily acts of others in terms of their own acts and experiences provides an engine for social development.

The *Like-Me* theory depicted in Figure 2.1 can helps explain several findings in the developmental literature. Consider infants' growing understanding of the meaning of other peoples' reaching behavior (Sommerville, Woodward, & Needham, 2005). The infant wants something he or she reaches out and grasps it. The infant experiences his or her own internal desires and the concomitant bodily movements. According to *Like-Me* theory the experience of grasping to satisfy desires gives infants leverage for *feeling with* the other who grasps for things. When the child sees another person reaching for an object, these movements are imbued with meaning, in part because of the child's own experience. This may be the avenue by which the infants' reaching experience modifies their understanding of the reaching of others (e.g., Sommerville et al., 2005): The infants' own goal-directed acts help them interpret the similar acts of others—*like me* in action.

A similar argument applies to the studies on intention reading. The Meltzoff (1995) study showed 18-month-old infants an unsuccessful act that did not fulfill the actor's intentions. Infants who saw the unsuccessful attempts completed the target acts at a significantly higher rate than controls. This and other research (e.g., Tomasello, Carpenter, Call, Behne, & Moll, 2005) suggests that toddlers can understand our goals even if we fail to fulfill them. *Like-Me* theory holds that one key element is the infant's own self-experiences. Infants have subjective desires and act intentionally. They have experienced their own thwarted desires, failed plans, and unfulfilled intentions. Indeed in the second half-year of life infants are obsessed with the success and failure of their plans. They mark such self-failures with special labels (e.g., "uh-oh," Gopnik, 1982; Gopnik & Meltzoff, 1986); and they actively experiment with their own failed efforts (Gopnik & Meltzoff, 1997; Moore & Meltzoff, 2004), varying their strategies and try-and-try-again behavior. According to the *Like-Me* view, this *intra*subjective exploration deepens their *inter*subjective grasp about the motivation and meaning of others' behaviors. When an infant sees another act in this way, the infant's self-experience suggests that there is a purpose, desire, or intention beyond the surface behavior. Thus, infants now interpret the behavioral envelope of adults' failed attempts as a pattern of strivings rather than ends in themselves. (For brain-imaging work on neural correlates of goal attribution, see Blakemore et al., 2003; Chaminade, Meltzoff, & Decety, 2002).

Gaze following admits to a similar theoretical analysis. The understanding of another's looking behavior is modified by intrasubjective experience—in this case, experience of oneself as a perceiver. One-year-olds are well-versed with voluntary looking away and eye closing to cut off unwanted stimuli. This bodily act is well–mastered, and they seem to understand that others with their eyes closed cannot see either. They have more difficulty understanding blindfolds. The Meltzoff and Brooks (2008) intervention experiment provided infants first-person experience with blindfolds, and infants were immediately able to use this to understand the blindfold-wearing other in a new way. This shows the power of using first-person experience and provides evidence for Steps 2 and 3 in Figure 2.1.

Finally, Repacholi and I found *Like-Me* theory useful in explaining the imitation and emotion studies. In this case infants are simultaneously coordinating three converging *like-me* comparisons: (a) they and the other person can both perform the same actions, (b) if they perform the act, that the Emoter is likely to become as angry at them just as she did at the other person, and (c) when the Emoter has her back turned or eyes closed, the Emoter cannot see what action is being performed—just as the child's own perceptual access is blocked in a similar case. It is interesting to speculate what would happen if an age-matched peer is scolded for performing the action. We expect that as the target of the anger becomes increasingly *like me*, the infants will be increasingly reluctant to imitate the act. Our previous work has already established infants' sensitivity to age-matched peers in an imitation setting (Hanna & Meltzoff, 1993).

The Like-Me framework has shown itself to be useful for understanding the development of social cognition and the role that self-experience plays in enriching children's understanding of other minds. It accounts not only for existing findings in the literature, but has been the source of novel empirical work, for example the blind-fold training study (Meltzoff & Brooks, 2008).

WHAT IS NEW AND WHAT IS NEXT?

It has long been thought that the commonality between self and other is integral to our understanding of other minds (e.g., Hume, 1739/1969; Smith, 1759/1976). The place that the philosophers went wrong is that the self–other equivalence was postulated to be late developing—emerging from language or complex cognitive analyses. The last quarter century of research stands this proposition on its head. The recognition of self–other equivalences is the starting point for social cognition—a precondition for infant social development, not the outcome of it. Contemporary philosophers of the mind are being influenced by these developmental findings (Goldman, 2005; Gordon, 2005).

Like-Me theory is proving to be useful for generating interdisciplinary predictions and tests in autism, robotics, and neuroscience. For example, deficiencies in the like-me comparison may help illuminate the puzzling pattern of impairments exhibited by children with autism. They have specific deficits in imitation, gaze following, and emotion understanding (e.g., Dapretto et al., 2006; Dawson, Meltzoff, Osterling, & Rinaldi, 1998; Meyer & Hobson, 2005; Mundy, this volume; Mundy & Newell, 2007; Nadel, 2006; Rogers, 1999, 2006)—all of which are underwritten by a like-me understanding.

In computer science, researchers are beginning to design algorithms that enable artificial agents to learn from observing the behavior of others. Instead of laboriously programming a fixed number of skills, the robot can be given imitative skills so that it can learn flexibly from watching humans. Developmental science is translating its theories and findings to computer science and engineering in the quest to construct socially intelligent robots (e.g., Buchsbaum, Blumberg, Breazeal, & Meltzoff, 2005; Demiris & Hayes, 2002; Demiris & Meltzoff, 2008; Rao, Shon, & Meltzoff, 2007; Shon, Storz, Meltzoff, & Rao, 2007).

Work in developmental psychology is also impacting adult social neuroscience. Brain-imaging studies reveal that observing body actions from a first- versus third-person perspective (me versus not-me) leads to different neural processing and speed of imitation (Jackson, Meltzoff, & Decety, 2006). Studies of human empathy shows that adults' neural signatures to injuries vary as a function of the like-me-ness of that entity (Jackson, Brunet, Meltzoff, & Decety, 2006; Lamm, Nusbaum, Meltzoff, & Decety, 2007).

Fodor is correct that solipsism and blank-slate empiricism are too impoverished to characterize the human starting state. However, this does not mean that adult theory of mind is implanted in the mind at birth or matures independent of social experience. I here propose a developmental alternative to Fodor's creation myth. Nature designed a baby with an imitative brain. Culture immerses the child in social play with psychological agents perceived to be *like me*. The adult understanding of mind and empathy for others is the outcome.

Some of the most interesting advances in the next decade will come from developmental social neuroscience. This will allow us to explore the mechanisms and development of imitation, empathy, gaze following, and intersubjectivity in the context of discoveries about the mirror neuron system and shared neural representations. The goal will be to crack one of the most urgent and ancient cries for human meaning: Am I alone? Do others feel what I am feeling? Is there anybody out there like me? The importance of these questions for developmental science, clinical science, and neuroscience will not be lost in translation.

REFERENCES

Baldwin, D. A. (1995). Understanding the link between joint attention and language. In C. Moore & P. J. Dunham (Eds.), *Joint attention: Its origins and role in development* (pp. 131–158). Hillsdale, NJ: Erlbaum.

Baron-Cohen, S. (1995). *Mindblindness: An essay on autism and theory of mind.* Cambridge, MA: MIT Press.

Beebe, B., Rustin, J., Sorter, D., & Knoblauch, S. (2003). An expanded view of intersubjectivity in infancy and its application to psychoanalysis. *Psychoanalytic Dialogues, 13*, 805–841.

Beebe, B., Sorter, D., Rustin, J., & Knoblauch, S. (2003). A comparison of Meltzoff, Trevarthen, and Stern. *Psychoanalytic Dialogues, 13,* 777–804.

Blakemore, S. J., Boyer, P., Pachot-Clouard, M., Meltzoff, A. N., Segebarth, C., & Decety, J. (2003). The detection of contingency and animacy from simple animations in the human brain. *Cerebral Cortex, 13,* 837–844.

Brooks, R., & Meltzoff, A. N. (2002). The importance of eyes: How infants interpret adult looking behavior. *Developmental Psychology,* 38, 958–966.

Brooks, R., & Meltzoff, A. N. (2005). The development of gaze following and its relation to language. *Developmental Science,* 8, 535–543.

Brooks, R., & Meltzoff, A. N. (2008). Infant gaze following and pointing predict accelerated vocabulary growth through two years of age: A longitudinal, growth curve modeling study. *Journal of Child Language,* 35, 207–220.

Bruner, J. (1960). *The process of education.* Cambridge, MA: Harvard University Press.

Bruner, J. S. (1983). *Childs talk: Learning to use language.* New York: Norton.

Buchsbaum, D., Blumberg, B., Breazeal, C., & Meltzoff, A. N. (2005, August). *A simulation-theory inspired social learning system for interactive characters.* Paper presented at the 14th IEEE International Workshop on Robot and Human Interactive Communication (RO-MAN 2005), Nashville, TN.

Butler, S. C., Caron, A. J., & Brooks, R. (2000). Infant understanding of the referential nature of looking. *Journal of Cognition and Development, 1,* 359–377.

Butterworth, G., & Jarrett, N. (1991). What minds have in common is space: Spatial mechanisms serving joint visual attention in infancy. *British Journal of Developmental Psychology,* 9, 55–72.

Carpenter, M., Nagell, K., & Tomasello, M. (1998). Social cognition, joint attention, and communicative competence from 9 to 15 months of age. *Monographs of the Society for Research in Child Development,* 63(4, Serial No. 255).

Chaminade, T., Meltzoff, A. N., & Decety, J. (2002). Does the end justify the means? A PET exploration of the mechanisms involved in human imitation. *NeuroImage, 15,* 318–328.

Collins, W. A., & Laursen, B. (Eds.) (1999). *The Minnesota Symposia on Child Psychology: Vol. 30. Relationships as developmental contexts* Mahwah, NJ: Lawrence Erlbaum Associates.

Conboy, B., Brooks, R., Taylor, M., Meltzoff, A., & Kuhl, P. (2008, March). *Joint engagement with language tutors predicts brain and behavioral responses to second-language phonetic stimuli.* Poster presented at the meeting of the International Conference on Infant Studies, Vancouver, BC.

Dapretto, M., Davies, M. S., Pfeifer, J. H., Scott, A. A., Sigman, M., Bookheimer, S. Y., et al. (2006). Understanding emotions in others: Mirror neuron dysfunction in children with autism spectrum disorders. *Nature Neuroscience, 9,* 28–30.

Dawson, G., Meltzoff, A. N., Osterling, J., & Rinaldi, J. (1998). Neuropsychological correlates of early symptoms of autism. *Child Development, 69,* 1276–1285.

Da Vinci, L. (1935). *Leonardo Da Vinci's notebooks* (E. McCurdy, Trans.). New York: Empire State Book Co. (Original work published 1888).

Demiris, Y., & Hayes, G. (2002). Imitation as a dual-route process featuring predictive and learning components: A biologically plausible computational model. In K. Dautenhahn & C. L. Nehaniv (Eds.), *Imitation in animals and artifacts* (pp. 327–361). Cambridge, MA: MIT Press.

Demiris, Y., & Meltzoff, A. N. (2008). The robot in the crib: A developmental analysis of imitation skills in infants and robots. *Infant and Child Development, 17,* 43–53.

Dunphy-Lelii, S., & Wellman, H. M. (2004). Infants' understanding of occlusion of others' line-of-sight: Implications for an emerging theory of mind. *European Journal of Developmental Psychology, 1,* 49–66.

Flom, R., Lee, K., & Muir, D. (Eds.). (2007). *Gaze following: Its development and significance.* Mahwah, NJ: Erlbaum Associates.

Fodor, J. A. (1983). *The modularity of mind: An essay on faculty psychology.* Cambridge, MA: MIT Press.

Fodor, J. A. (1987). *Psychosemantics: The problem of meaning in the philosophy of mind.* Cambridge, MA: MIT Press.

Freud, S. (1911). Formulation on the two principles of mental functioning. In J. Strachey (Ed.), *The standard edition of the complete psychological works of Sigmund Freud: Vol. 12* (pp. 215–226). London: Hogarth Press.

Freud, S. (1920). *Beyond the pleasure principle.* In *The standard edition of the complete works of Sigmund Freud: Vol. 18* (J. Strachey, Trans.) (pp. 4–67). London: Hogarth Press.

Gleissner, B., Meltzoff, A. N., Bekkering, H. (2000). Children's coding of human action: Cognitive factors influencing imitation in 3-year-olds. *Developmental Science, 3,* 405–414.

Goldman, A. I. (2005). Imitation, mind reading, and simulation. In S. Hurley & N. Chater (Eds.), *Perspectives on imitation: From neuroscience to social science: Vol. 2. Imitation, human development, and culture* (pp. 79–93). Cambridge, MA: MIT Press.

Gopnik, A. (1982). Words and plans: Early language and the development of intelligent action. *Journal of Child Language*, 9, 303–318.

Gopnik, A., & Meltzoff, A. N. (1986). Relations between semantic and cognitive development in the one-word stage: The specificity hypothesis. *Child Development*, 57, 1040–1053.

Gopnik, A., & Meltzoff, A. N. (1997). *Words, thoughts, and theories*. Cambridge, MA: MIT Press.

Gopnik, A., Meltzoff, A. N., & Kuhl, P. K. (2001). *The scientist in the crib: What early learning tells us about the mind*. New York: Harper Paperbacks.

Gordon, R. M. (2005). Intentional agents like myself. In S. Hurley & N. Chater (Eds.), *Perspectives on imitation: From neuroscience to social science: Vol. 2. Imitation, human development, and culture* (pp. 95–106). Cambridge, MA: MIT Press.

Hanna, E., & Meltzoff, A. N. (1993). Peer imitation by toddlers in laboratory, home, and day-care contexts: Implications for social learning and memory. *Developmental Psychology*, 29, 701–710.

Hobson, R. P., & Meyer, J. A. (2005). Foundations for self and other: A study in autism. *Developmental Science*, 8, 481–491.

Hudson, J. L. (2005). Interparental conflict, violence and psychopathology. In J. L. Hudson & R. M. Rapee (Eds.), *Psychopathology and the family* (pp. 53–69). New York: Elsevier.

Hume, D. (1969). *A treatise of human nature*. London: Penguin Books (Original work published 1739).

Iacoboni, M., Woods, R. P., Brass, M., Bekkering, H., Mazziotta, J. C., & Rizzolatti, G. (1999). Cortical mechanisms of human imitation. *Science*, 286, 2526–2528.

Jackson, P. L., Brunet, E., Meltzoff, A. N., & Decety, J. (2006). Empathy examined through the neural mechanisms involved in imagining how I feel versus how you feel pain. *Neuropsychologia*, 44, 752–761.

Jackson, P. L., Meltzoff, A. N., & Decety, J. (2006). Neural circuits involved in imitation and perspective-taking. *NeuroImage*, 31, 429–439.

Kuhl, P. K., & Meltzoff, A. N. (1982). The bimodal perception of speech in infancy. *Science*, 218, 1138–1141.

Kuhl, P. K., & Meltzoff, A. N. (1984). The intermodal representation of speech in infants. *Infant Behavior and Development*, 7, 361–381.

Kuhl, P. K., & Rivera-Gaxiola, M. (2008). Neural substrates of language acquisition. *Annual Review of Neuroscience*, 31, 511–534.

Kuhl, P. K., Tsao, F. M., & Liu, H. M. (2003). Foreign-language experience in infancy: Effects of short-term exposure and social interaction on phonetic learning. *Proceedings of the National Academy of Sciences*, 100, 9096–9101.

Kuhn, T. S. (1962). *The structure of scientific revolutions*. Chicago: University of Chicago Press.

Ladd, G. W., Birch, S. H., & Buhs, E. S. (1999). Children's social and scholastic lives in kindergarten: Related spheres of influence? *Child Development, 70*, 1373–1400.

Lamm, C., Nusbaum, H., Meltzoff, A. N., & Decety, J. (2007). What are you feeling? Using functional magnetic resonance imaging to assess the modulation of sensory and affective responses during empathy for pain. *PLoS One, 2(12): e1292*, doi:10.1371/journal.pone.0001292.

Mahler, M. S., Pine, F., & Bergman, A. (1975). *The psychological birth of the human infant*. New York: Basic Books.

Meltzoff, A. N. (1995). Understanding the intentions of others: Re-enactment of intended acts by 18-month-old children. *Developmental Psychology, 31*, 838–850.

Meltzoff, A. N. (1999). Origins of theory of mind, cognition and communication. *Journal of Communication Disorders, 32*, 251–269.

Meltzoff, A. N. (2007a). 'Like Me': a foundation for social cognition. *Developmental Science, 10*, 126–134.

Meltzoff, A. N. (2007b). The 'like me' framework for recognizing and becoming an intentional agent. *Acta Psychologica, 124*, 26–43.

Meltzoff, A. N., & Brooks, R. (2008). Self-experience as a mechanism for learning about others: A training study in social cognition. *Developmental Psychology, 44*, 1257–1265.

Meltzoff, A. N., & Decety, J. (2003). What imitation tells us about social cognition: A rapprochement between developmental psychology and cognitive neuroscience. *Philosophical Transactions of the Royal Society of London. Series B, Biological Sciences, 358*, 491–500.

Meltzoff, A. N., & Moore, M. K. (1977). Imitation of facial and manual gestures by human neonates. *Science, 198*, 75–78.

Meltzoff, A. N., & Moore, M. K. (1983). Newborn infants imitate adult facial gestures. *Child Development, 54*, 702–709.

Meltzoff, A. N., & Moore, M. K. (1989). Imitation in newborn infants: Exploring the range of gestures imitated and the underlying mechanisms. *Developmental Psychology, 25*, 954–962.

Meltzoff, A. N., & Moore, M. K. (1994). Imitation, memory, and the representation of persons. *Infant Behavior & Development, 17*, 83–99.

Meltzoff, A. N., & Moore, M. K. (1997). Explaining facial imitation: A theoretical model. *Early Development and Parenting*, 6, 179–192.

Meyer, J. A., & Hobson, R. P. (2005). Orientation in relation to self and other: The case of autism. *Interaction Studies*, 5, 221–244.

Moore, C. (1999). Gaze following and the control of attention. In P. Rochat (Ed.), *Early social cognition: Understanding others in the first months of life* (pp. 241–256). Mahwah, NJ: Erlbaum Associates.

Moore, C. (2006). *The development of commonsense psychology*. Mahwah, NJ: Erlbaum.

Moore, C., & Dunham, P. J. (Eds.). (1995). *Joint attention: Its origins and role in development*. Hillsdale, NJ: Erlbaum Associates.

Moore, M. K., & Meltzoff, A. N. (2004). Object permanence after a 24-hr delay and leaving the locale of disappearance: The role of memory, space, and identity. *Developmental Psychology*, 40, 606–620.

Moses, L. J., Baldwin, D. A., Rosicky, J. G., & Tidball, G. (2001). Evidence for referential understanding in the emotions domain at twelve and eighteen months. *Child Development*, 72, 718–735.

Mundy, P., Fox, N., & Card, J. (2003). EEG coherence, joint attention and language development in the second year. *Developmental Science*, 6, 48–54.

Mundy, P., & Newell, L. (2007). Attention, joint attention and social cognition. *Current Directions in Psychological Science*, 16, 269–274.

Mundy, P., & Sigman, M. (2006). Joint attention, social competence and developmental psychopathology. In D. Cicchetti and D. Cohen (Eds.), *Developmental psychopathology: Volume 1. Theory and Methods* (2nd ed., pp. 293–332). Hoboken, N.J.: Wiley.

Mundy, P., Sigman, M., & Kasari, C. (1990). A longitudinal study of joint attention and language development in autistic children. *Journal of Autism and Developmental Disorders*, 20, 115–128.

Nadel, J. (2006). Does imitation matter to children with autism? In S. J. Rogers & J. H. G. Williams (Eds.), *Imitation and the social mind* (pp. 118–137). New York: Guilford Press.

NICHD Early Child Care Research Network. (2001). Nonmaternal care and family factors in early development: An overview of the NICHD Study of Early Child Care. *Journal of Applied Developmental Psychology*, 22, 457–492.

NICHD Early Child Care Research Network. (2005). Early child care and children's development in the primary grades: Follow-up results from the NICHD study of early child care. *American Educational Research Journal*, 43, 537–570.

Piaget, J. (1952). *The origins of intelligence in children* (M. Cook, Trans.). New York: International Universities Press.

Piaget, J. (1954). *The construction of reality in the child* (M. Cook, Trans.). New York: Basic Books.

Piaget, J. (1970). *Science of education and the psychology of the child* (D. Coltman, Trans.). New York: Orion Press.

Rao, R. P. N., Shon, A. P., & Meltzoff, A. N. (2007). A Bayesian model of imitation in infants and robots. In C. L. Nehaniv & K. Dautenhahn (Eds.), *Imitation and social learning in robots, humans, and animals: Behavioural, social and communicative dimensions* (pp. 217–247). Cambridge, UK: Cambridge University Press.

Repacholi, B. M., & Meltzoff, A. N. (2007). Emotional eavesdropping: Infants selectively respond to indirect emotional signals. *Child Development, 78,* 503–521.

Repacholi, B. M., Meltzoff, A. N., & Olsen, B. (2008). Infants' understanding of the link between visual perception and emotion: "If she can't see me doing it, she won't get angry." *Developmental Psychology, 44,* 561–574.

Rizzolatti, G., Fadiga, L., Fogassi, L., & Gallese, V. (2002). From mirror neurons to imitation, facts, and speculations. In A. N. Meltzoff & W. Prinz (Eds.), *The imitative mind: Development, evolution, and brain bases* (pp. 247–266). Cambridge, UK: Cambridge University Press.

Rizzolatti, G., Fogassi, L., & Gallese, V. (2001). Neurophysiological mechanisms underlying the understanding and imitation of action. *Nature Reviews Neuroscience, 2,* 661–670.

Rogers, S. J. (1999). An examination of the imitation deficit in autism. In J. Nadel & G. Butterworth (Eds.), *Imitation in infancy* (pp. 254–283). Cambridge, UK: Cambridge University Press.

Rogers, S. J. (2006). Studies of imitation in early infancy: Findings and theories. In S. J. Rogers & J. H. G. Williams (Eds.), *Imitation and the social mind: Autism and typical development (pp. 3–26).* New York: Guilford Press.

Russell, B. (1948). *Human knowledge: Its scope and limits.* New York: Simon & Schuster.

Ryle, G. (1949). *The concept of mind.* London: Hutchinson.

Shon, A. P., Storz, J. J., Meltzoff, A. N., & Rao, R. P. N. (2007). A cognitive model of imitative development in humans and machines. *International Journal of Humanoid Robotics, 4,* 387–406.

Shonkoff, J. P., & Phillips, D. A. (Eds.) (2000). *From neurons to neighborhoods: The science of early childhood development.* Washington, DC: National Academy Press.

Skinner, B. F. (1983). *A matter of consequences.* New York: Alfred A. Knopf.

Smith, A. (1976). *The theory of moral sentiments*. New York: Oxford University Press. (Original work published in 1759).

Snow, C. P. (1964). *The two cultures and a second look: An expanded version of the two cultures and the scientific revolution*. Cambridge, UK: Cambridge University Press.

Sommerville, J. A., Woodward, A. L., & Needham, A. (2005). Action experience alters 3-month-old infants' perception of others' actions. *Cognition, 96*, B1–B11.

Stokes, D. E. (1997). *Pasteurs quadrant: Basic science and technological innovation*. Washington, DC: Brookings Institution Press.

Strawson, P. F. (1959). *Individuals: An essay in descriptive metaphysics*. London: Methuen & Co.

Tomasello, M., Carpenter, M., Call, J., Behne, T., & Moll, H. (2005). Understanding and sharing intentions: The origins of cultural cognition. *Behavioral and Brain Sciences, 28*, 675–691.

Toth, K., Munson, J., Meltzoff, A. N., & Dawson, G. (2006). Early predictors of communication development in young children with autism spectrum disorder: Joint attention, imitation, and toy play. *Journal of Autism and Developmental Disorders*, 36, 993–1005.

Williamson, R. A., Meltzoff, A. N., & Markman, E. M. (2008). Prior experiences and perceived efficacy influence 3-year-olds' imitation. *Developmental Psychology*, 44, 275–285.

CHAPTER

3

Lessons Learned From Autism: An Information-Processing Model of Joint Attention and Social-Cognition

PETER MUNDY

This chapter describes one way in which translational science has transformed the way we think about the diagnosis and treatment of autism. It is a story of how the study of the cognitive capacity to share knowledge between people helped to define the social deficits of autism. This chapter also describes how the translation of basic cognitive science to autism has begun to encourage new ways of thinking about the phylogeny and ontogeny of the development of human social-cognition. In particular, human social-cognition may be viewed as the outgrowth of a special form of human information processing that we call *joint attention* (Mundy & Newell, 2007). The development of this form of human information processing is impaired in specific ways in autism. Recognizing

The research and theory development reported in this paper were supported by NIH Grants HD 38052, MH 071273, as well as the Lisa Capps Chair Endowment Fund to the UC Davis MIND Institute and School of Education. The support of the University of Miami/Vanderbilt University Marino Autism Research Institute (MARI) is also gratefully acknowledged.

and understanding the specific pattern of joint-attention impairment in autism has contributed to new perspectives about the development of social-cognition in all people (Mundy, 2003). The reciprocal interplay between cognitive science, developmental science, and the science of psychopathology in the study of autism provides a seminal illustration of a school of translational research that began to be codified more than 2 decades ago when a farsighted group outlined the new discipline of *developmental psychopathology* (Cicchetti, 1984; Sroufe & Rutter, 1984).

The chapter begins with a brief description of the history of thought and research on autism. One message of this first section is that, for the want of applied research on social development, the accuracy of the diagnosis of autism was rough and inexact until the early 1990s, or 50 years after it was initially described (Asperger, 1944; Kanner, 1943). Advancing the precision of the diagnosis of autism required the translation of basic research paradigms for the study of social and cognitive development in infants. In particular, research paradigms for the study of the preverbal development of the ability to coordinate attention and share experience with others have helped to define autism (Mundy & Crowson, 1997). The final section of the chapter illustrates how translational research on autism has much to teach us about basic facets of human nature. Insights from research on the social attention and neurodevelopmenal deficits of autism have begun to to provide the framework for a new model of human social-cognition development. According to this model, infants become capable of the joint or parallel processing of information about self attention and the attention of others during the first 24 months of life. The joint processing of social attention information involves the gradual development of integrated processing of information across distributed elements of the anterior and posterior attention systems. This distributed process requires efficient neural interconnectivity between frontal, temporal, and parietal neural networks. With practice in infancy, the integrated processing of this distributed cortical system becomes a social executive substrate that contributes to the human capacity to appreciate shared meaning in symbols and to understand intentionality in self and others. It also supports our competence in the rapid activation and inhibition of behaviors in adaptive social interactions (Mundy & Sigman, 2006).

The basic tenets of this model as applied to autism are as follows: *Autism*, in some fundamental way, is a disorder of attention and information processing. This, however, is true for many other forms of psychopathology. Therefore, a primary task of developmental psychopathology is to understand attention development and related aspects of information processing well enough to allow us to better perceive essential differences between pathologies. Before social-cognition there is the joint processing of information about the *overt* attention of self and the overt attention of other people. This *joint attention* processing requires the integrated activation of two distributed cortical networks involving elements of the anterior (intentional) and posterior (responsive) attention-allocation systems. Self-initiated practice in infancy leads the integrated activation of this distributed attention network for the processing of one's own deployment of overt attention and the deployment of overt attention of other people to become internalized. Internalized joint attention involves the capacity to monitor one's own attention to mental representations and monitor representations of the other people's attention to objects and events. As such, internalization of joint-attention processes is a major supportive substrate for the development of symbolic activity and social-cognition and *remains an executive substrate for both types of cognition throughout the lifespan*. Varying degrees of impairment in the early stages of overt joint attention lead to developmental vulnerability of the capacity for covert joint attention, socially shared symbolic activity, and social-cognition. Such impairments contribute to mental, emotional, and behavioral pathology in many, if not all people with autism (Mundy, 1995, 2003; Mundy & Newell, 2007).

A BRIEF HISTORY OF RESEARCH ON AUTISM

Autism is a biologically based disorder that is characterized by impaired social development, impaired language and/or pragmatic communication skill acquisition, and the presence of repetitive behaviors and thoughts (Asperger, 1944; Bailey, Philips, & Rutter, 1996; Dawson, Osterling, Rinaldi, Carver, & McPartland, 2001; Kanner, 1943). Recent research suggests that symptoms of autism are often observable by 24 months of age (Stone, Coonrod, & Ousley, 1997), with children expressing one of two different courses of symptom onset. Some children may display clear symptoms by the end of the first year or early part of the second year of life. Other children may display more typical development through the early part of the second year but lose competencies during a period of developmental regression, with symptoms apparent by the beginning of the third year of life (Rogers, 2004).

Leo Kanner (1943) displayed impressive clinical acumen when he was able to discern three fundamental elements of autism amongst a large clinical sample of children. Kanner observed that autism likely was: (a) a biological impairment, (b) of affective relatedness to others, (c) which resulted in a developmental disorder that primarily impaired the capacity for typical social interactions. The recognition of this triumvirate of biological, affective, and social–behavioral foundations for the syndrome was a remarkable achievement that is as valid today as it was in 1944. Unfortunately, Kanner's initial perspective on autism did not fit well with the psychodynamic zeitgeist of the time. The psychodynamic perspective emphasized the primacy of environmental over biological factors in the etiology of all psychopathology. Sufficient challenges were brought to bear in this regard that Kanner (1949) recanted his initial biological view of autism.

In the ensuing 30 years the science of autism drifted from conceptual model to conceptual model. Autism was commonly characterized as a disorder caused by an aloof parenting style in which the children grew up to be emotionless (Bettleheim, 1959). Convincing evidence against the parenting style hypothesis was quickly marshaled (Rimland, 1964). However, the prototype of all people with autism as emotionless and aloof remained for a long time. Little data were available to critically appraise this prototypic view because the social-emotional development of children with autism was not a focus of empirical inquiry through the 1970s. Rather, theory at that time suggested that sensory, perceptual, or language impairments were primary in the etiology of autism (Mundy & Sigman, 1989a). Research on these topics advanced our understanding of autism in many ways. However, a downside was that they implicitly relegated the social-emotional impairments of autism to the status of epiphenomenon of what were considered to be primary sensory or language problems.

The relegation of social-emotional symptoms to secondary status constrained the theory and methods used to establish the diagnostic criteria for autism. So, in the first organized attempts to establish a rigorous symptom definitions for autism (e.g., American Psychiatric Association [APA], 1980), only five criteria were proposed: (a) onset before 30 months of age; (b) a pervasive lack of responsiveness to other people; (c) gross deficits in language development; (d) if speech is present, peculiar speech patterns, such as immediate and delayed echolalia, metaphorical language, pronominal reversal; (e) bizarre responses to various aspects of the environment, (e.g., resistance to change, peculiar interest in or attachments to animate or inanimate objects) and (f) absence of delusions, hallucinations, loosening of associations, and incoherence as in Schizophrenia.

Notice that only one criterion was specific to describing the social deficits of autism and this was the rather broad and vague item of a *pervasive lack of responsiveness to other people*. There had been so little research on defining the nature of the social-emotional deficits of autism through 1980 that we simply had no idea what was involved in the social disturbances of autism, even though Kanner had argued that social deficits were central to the syndrome. Pat Howlin (1978) made this limit to our knowledge clear in an early review of research on the social deficits of autism. Pat was able to exhaustively summarize the field of social developmental research on autism in seven pages with 39 citations. Of those 39 citations, only a handful involved peer-reviewed empirical research publications. Fortunately, in the intervening decade there was a virtual explosion of research on the social deficits of autism. Pat Howlin's work again provides an illustration of this growth in our knowledge base. She published a second review of research on the social development of autism 8 years later (Howlin, 1986). By that time, her review required 24 pages and 116 citations to adequately cover the field. Seventy-nine citations involved empirical peer reviewed publications on early social development and autism. Several other empirical papers presented at scientific conferences were also cited.

This welcome increase in the understanding of the social nature of autism occurred because of translational research. Several research groups in the United States, the United Kingdom, and throughout the world began to recognize that theory and methods from the study of early human and primate social development could provide useful tools to examine and define the social deficits of autism (e.g., Dawson & McKissick, 1984; Langdell, 1978; Sigman & Ungerer, 1984). This new wave of research involved the translation of basic science on infant imitation, social learning, preverbal gestural communication, attachment, face processing and other domains. One fairly immediate and vital impact of this surge of translational social developmental research was the dawning awareness that the description of the social impairments of autism singularly as a *pervasive lack of responsiveness to others* was at best limiting, and at worst misguided. It established a categorical prototype that many individuals with autism did not resemble (Mundy & Sigman, 1989a; Wing & Gould, 1979).

Studies began to show that children with autism displayed a range of social styles and social behaviors that corresponded with their intellectual abilities. Many of the children with Severe or Moderate Mental Retardation appeared to be aloof and came closest to expressing pervasive impairments in responsiveness to others. However, those children with Mild Mental Retardation, or normal to high IQs, were either passive but socially responsive or proactive in initiating interactions, but atypical and maladaptive in conducting these interactions (Wing & Gould, 1979; Volkmar, Cohen, Bregman, Hooks, & Stevenson, 1989). By the end of the 1980s, research had also shown that many children with autism, even those with Moderate Mental Retardation, had social strengths as well as weaknesses, rather than a *pervasive lack of responsiveness to others*. They responded when others imitated them, some could learn from modeling, many increased their social output in structured situations, and they varied greatly in their use of gestures and eye contact to communicate (Curcio, 1978; Mundy & Sigman, 1989a). Perhaps most remarkably, observations by Marian Sigman and others indicated that children with autism displayed levels of attachment behaviors that were commensurate with their mental development and *not atypical* relative to other groups with developmental disorders (Shapiro, Sherman, Calamari, & Koch, 1987; Sigman & Ungerer, 1984; Sigman & Mundy, 1989).

Consequently, by the late 1980s translational developmental research indicated that key elements of the nosology of autism were incorrect.

All children with autism did not display what could be described as a *pervasive* lack of responsiveness to others. This inaccurate view promoted a narrow view of autism that excluded many children with the syndrome who frequently made eye contact or displayed caregiver attachment, or any of a number of other social abilities. The development and perseverance of this inaccurate taxonomic prototype likely contributed to a historic underestimation of the prevalence of autism (Wing & Potter, 2002). Indeed, only with the publication of the most recent nosology (e.g., American Psychiatric Association [APA], 1994) have we had sufficiently well-defined guidelines to begin to capture something of the full range of expression of autism. Therefore, it is likely that some significant part of the increasing prevalence of autism observed in North America, Europe, Scandinavia, and Japan since about 1987 has been due to a vast improvement in social diagnostic description of this syndrome (Wing & Potter, 2002). We simply could not identify all the children with autism in the 1970s, 1980s, and early 1990s if we limited ourselves to those who met the restrictive criteria of *a pervasive lack of responsiveness to others*.

The empirically based revisions of social diagnostic criteria of autism culminated in common criteria used in the APA Diagnostic and Statistical Manual (DSM IV (1994; 2000) and the World Health Organization's International Classification of Disease (ICD 10, 1991). In both the DSM and ICD systems the qualitative impairment in social interaction in autism became defined as the expression of at least two of the following: (a) a marked impairment in the use of multiple nonverbal behaviors such as eye-to-eye gaze, facial expression, body postures, and gestures to regulate social interaction; (b) a failure to develop peer relationships appropriate to developmental level; (c) a lack of spontaneous seeking to share experience, enjoyment, interests, or achievements with other people (e.g., by a lack of showing, bringing, or pointing out objects of interest); and (d) lack of social or emotional reciprocity.

The criterion of a lack of appropriate peer skills is extremely useful, but not until 3 or 4 years of age. Earlier identification and diagnosis is largely based on the the other three social symptoms. In particular, the notion that the early development of autism could be described and measured in terms of a *lack of spontaneous seeking to share experience, enjoyment, interests, or achievements with other people* began to be central to our understanding of the nature of the disorder (Mundy & Crowson, 1997; Mundy & Sigman, 1989b). The recognition of the centrality of this social deficit in autism followed from the translation of basic cognitive research on how infants develop the ability to share knowledge and experience with each other (Bruner, 1975). This diagnostic criteria emphasizes that a disturbance in the tendency to *spontaneously seek* or *initiate* social behaviors is as much a part of autism as is an impairment in ability to process or *respond* to the social behaviors of others.

HOW INFANTS SHARE EXPERIENCES WITH OTHER PEOPLE

Well before infants learn to use symbols and language, they begin to be able to share information with other people. They do so by coordinating their attention with another person and by using eye contact and gestures to show objects to others or request aid obtaining and manipulating objects.

In 1975, Scaife and Bruner reported in *Nature* that between 6 to 18 months of age infants increasingly displayed the ability to follow the direction of gaze of a social partner. That is, when testers turned their heads to the left or right many infants displayed the ability to track and follow the visual attention of the testers with their own line of regard. This observation was groundbreaking. It was inconsistent with the prevailing notion of egocentrism in early cognitive development (Piaget, 1952). According to Piaget, infants could not adopt dual perspectives, such as the perspective of self and another person, until late in the second year. However, Scaife and Bruner's (1975) observations suggested that infants begin to discriminate and adapt their own visual perspective relative to another person's perspective much earlier in life than previously believed.

Bruner (1975) adopted the general term *joint attention* for this newfound infant ability domain. He recognized that this ability allowed infants and caregivers to adopt coreference to the same object or event. This, in turn, enabled caregivers to more readily scaffold their infants' development of the human faculty for sharing knowledge with other people. At its heart, Bruner's work was translational. One of his goals was to understand how we best learn in order to improve educational curriculums. However, instead of studying only how we acquire knowledge (learning), he studied how we develop the ability to share knowledge (social learning) because he saw social learning as essential to all forms of pedagogy. His work through the 1970s suggested that the development of the ability to participate in joint attention marked a critical turning point in some unknown set of early cognitive processes that were foundational to human learning and education. More specifically, Bruner perceived that the capacity for coreference was elementary to our human ability to perceive shared meanings, and this type of perception was necessary for the development of symbolic thinking and language development.

In the early days of empirical research it became apparent that infants did not just develop skill with joint attention. Rather, they developed skill with multiple forms of joint-attention behaviors. One type of behavior already noted is displayed when infants follow the direction of another person's gaze (Scaife & Bruner, 1975). This ability can easily be tested. Infants sit facing an adult social partner who shifts his or her gaze to objects to the left, right, behind, or below the observing child. Infants can demonstrate *responding to joint attention* (RJA) behavior (Seibert, Hogan, & Mundy, 1982; see Fig. 3.1) by correctly turning head and eyes to follow the visual line of regard of the adult. Another dimension of joint attention that arises in the first year involves the infant's use of eye contact and/or gestures (i.e., pointing or showing) to spontaneously direct and coordinate attention to share an experience with a social partner. This type of behavior functions like a nonverbal declarative act (Bates, Benigni, Bretherton, Camaioni, & Volterrra, 1979) and may be referred to as *initiating joint attention* (IJA) behavior (Seibert et al., 1982; Fig. 3.1).

The primary social information–sharing functions of IJA and RJA can be juxtaposed with other early nonverbal behaviors that involve attention coordination for more instrumental and imperative purposes. Young infants also learn to prelinguistically direct the attention of other people to request aid in obtaining objects or actions (Bates et al.,

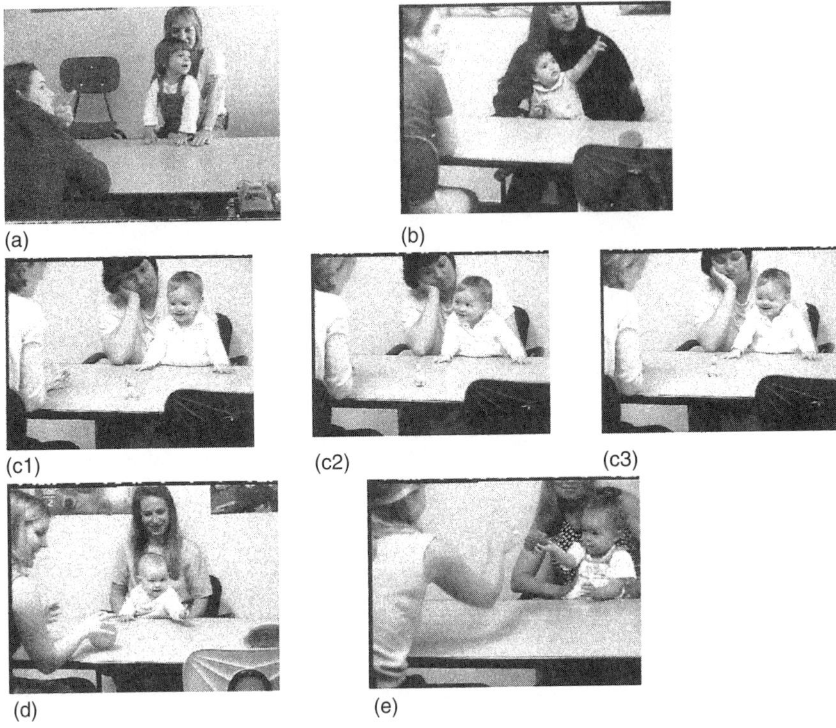

Figure 3.1 Illustrations of different types of infant social attention coordination behaviors.

1979). In addition, they learn to respond to the attention-directing bids that adults use to request objects or actions from infants. These may be referred to as *initiating behavioral requests* (IBR) and *responding to behavioral requests* (RBR; Fig. 3.1).

As the theory and measurement concerning infant joint attention was developing in the 1970s, an important practical issue came to the fore in clinical and developmental psychological science. Researchers wanted to identify valid *infant* markers of cognitive impairments because this would enable the potentially powerful application of early interventions to children at risk for developmental disorders. However, the types of sensorimotor measures that were being used in the 1960s and 1970s to assess infant *intelligence* and cognitive *risk* were no more valid than sensorimotor measures had been when they were used as the first measures of adult and childhood *intelligence* at the turn of the 20th century (Lewis &

McGurk, 1978). Without valid measures of early cognitive development, it was challenging to determine with any precision which infants were at risk for developmental disorders. Without valid early markers of atypical cognitive development, it was also difficult to know what constituted valid targets for early intervention or how to adequately evaluate outcomes of early intervention. This impasse in the 1970s and early 1980s began to clear as applications of basic research indicated that measures of infant visual attention could be used as valid indicators of early cognitive development that were related to individual differences in childhood intellectual outcomes (Bornstein & Sigman, 1986).

One laboratory for the translation of research on infant attention to clinical applications was created by Jeff Seibert and Anne Hogan at the Debbie School of the Mailman Center at the University of Miami. The Debbie School served 1- to 5-year-olds who had moderate to severe motor problems, as well as developmental impairments. Their motor impairments ruled out the use of sensorimotor-based cognitive assessment and intervention strategies. Jeff and Anne, however, were attuned to the work of Bruner, Bates, and others. So they began to develop an early assessment and intervention curriculum that focused on joint attention and preverbal communication skill development. One of the lasting contributions of their program of research was the development of the Early Social Communication Scales (ESCS). The ESCS organized precise observations of joint attention and social attention coordination into stages of development that could be used for assessment as well as to guide intervention along a sequence of prescribed developmental milestones (Seibert et al., 1982).

Another lasting contribution of the ESCS, along with related measures such as the Communication and Symbolic Behavior Scales (Wetherby, Allen, Cleary, Kublin, & Goldstein, 2002) and the Screening Tool for Autism in Two-year-olds (Stone et al., 1997), was that it turned out to be a powerful instrument for the study of the nature of the social deficits of autism. The recognition of this utility of the ESCS was bolstered by the type of serendipitous scientific communication that nourishes translational research. By the time the first version of the ESCS was being tested (1978–1982), Marian Sigman at UCLA had begun studying autism by applying theory and measures gleaned from the literature on infant object-oriented cognitive development (e.g., Ungerer & Sigman, 1981). Relatively quickly, Marian concluded that research on autism needed to go beyond research on object-oriented problem solving to included models and measures of infant social development. She gave a talk to that effect in the late autumn of 1980 at the University of Miami Mailman Center for Child Development. That talk kindled a long collaboration in translational research on autism that involved applications of joint-attention theory, and ESCS methods, to defining the nature of early social competence and the social deficits of autism (Mundy & Sigman, 1989b, 2006).

JOINT ATTENTION AND DEFINING THE SOCIAL DEFICITS OF AUTISM

To my knowledge, it was Frank Curcio at the University of Boston who first noted that many children with autism capably initiated nonverbal requests in social interactions (Curcio, 1978). Indeed, 50% of the elementary school–aged children with autism he observed in classrooms systematically used eye contact and conventional gestures to express their requests. However, Curcio reported that the children with autism displayed very little evidence of the use of eye contact or gestures to initiate nonverbal joint attention bids in social interactions. Curcio concluded that impairments in the capacity to initiate declarative joint attention communicative functions may be central to the nature of the social impairments of autism.

Curcio's observations were intriguing but did not provide information about whether joint-attention deficits were specific to autism or to a more general phenomenon associated with developmental delays and Mental Retardation. However, subsequent studies indicated that a developmental disturbance of joint attention did appear to be specific to the syndrome of autism (Loveland & Landry, 1986; Mundy, Sigman, Ungerer, & Sherman, 1986; Wetherby & Prutting, 1984).

In our own work, we compared mental age, chronological age, and IQ-matched samples of 4- to 7-year-old children with autism or Mental Retardation (MR) as well as a mental age–matched sample of typically

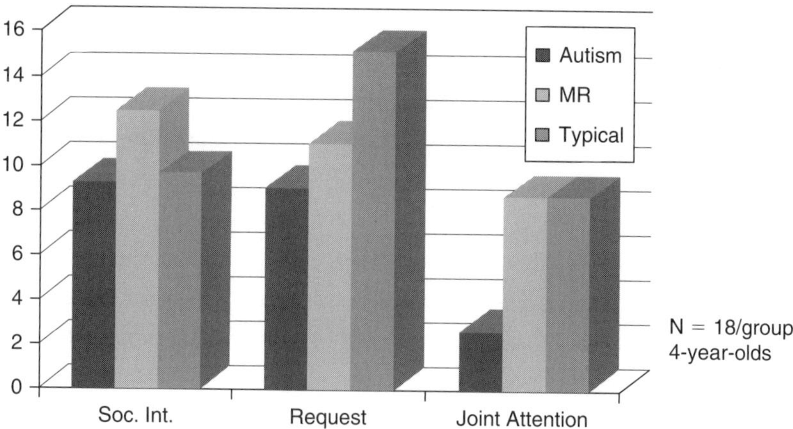

Figure 3.2 Illustration of the group differences on the ESCS joint-attention, requesting, and social interaction measures observed for children with autism, Mental Retardation, and typical development reported in Mundy et al., 1986.

developing children (Mundy et al., 1986; Sigman, Mundy, Sherman, & Ungerer, 1986). We found the children with autism displayed deficits in joint attention in interactions with unfamiliar testers or their familiar parents relative to both comparison groups. However, although they displayed less requesting than the typical group, they were not different from the MR sample on requesting. These studies also lead to several new and surprising observations. One of these was that children with autism often did well in social interactions measured with social turn-taking games in which they systematically exchanged objects in play with an adult-tester (Mundy et al., 1986; see Fig. 3.2).

The other surprise was that young children with autism did display abiding differences in eye contact compared to children with Mental Retardation on the ESCS. They displayed comparable levels of eye contact in requesting and turn-taking social interactions. However, an eye contact–disturbance specific to autism was clearly manifested in the attenuation of the use of alternating eye contact to spontaneously initiate sharing of their experience of a mechanical toy with the tester (IJA–Alternates Eye Contact, see Fig. 3.1, $c_{1,2,3}$). This one type of eye-contact behavior discriminated the autism sample from the comparison samples with a combined sensitivity and specificity of 96% (Mundy et al., 1986). This aspect of our 1986 data is especially useful to note today because many believe that the IJA disturbance is manifest most clearly in impairments of conventional gestures such as pointing and showing. Impairments in pointing and showing do occur in autism. Showing, in particular, provides the prototypic illustration of the social function of IJA bids. However, these impairments emerge in the second year of life and are not displayed by all young children with a sufficiently high frequency to be optimal for the early discrimination of young children with developmental delays. Alternatively, since 1986 our data have consistently suggested that the IJA disturbance of autism was apparent in reliable rating of a specific sharing function of eye contact that emerged before the second year of life.

We cannot definitively know a young child's intent in alternating eye contact. Nevertheless, during administration of the ESCS the adult tester often subjectively arrives at the impression that alternating eye contact serves to acknowledge others' common experience of an event or garner attention to the child's own experience of the event (Fig. 3.1; see Mundy & Sigman, 2006, for discussion). Hence, observing alternating eye contact in a young child affects the perception of the child's relatedness to the tester. Thus, it may well be that that diminished IJA alternating eye contact was the crucial element of the behavior pattern that Leo Kanner observed that led him to speculate in 1943 that autism was characterized by impairments in relatedness and affective contact with others (Mundy & Sigman, 1989a).

The idea that IJA was related to a disturbance in affective contact in autism was subsequently supported by research that showed that about 60% of the IJA bids displayed by typical infants and children with Mental Retardation involved the conveyance of positive affect (Kasari, Sigman, Mundy, & Yirmiya, 1990; Mundy, Kasari, & Sigman, 1992). However, positive affect is much less frequently part of the IJA behaviors of children with autism (Kasari et al., 1990). The onset of the systematic conveyance of positive affect as part of IJA bids begins to develop early in life at about 8 to 10 months of age (Venezia, Messinger, Thorp, & Mundy, 2004). Thus, joint-attention impairments reflect what are likely to be early arising deficits in the tendency of children with autism to socially share positive affect. This in turn may involve a disturbance in their early appreciation of the positive social *value* of shared attention. That is to say, motivation factors or sensitivity to reward value of social gaze may play a role in joint-attention disturbance in autism (Mundy, 1995).

During the time that several research groups were describing the possible centrality of joint-attention impairments in autism (e.g., Loveland & Landry, 1986; Wetherby & Prutting, 1984), another kind of translation research was beginning to emerge in research with children with autism. Premack and Woodruff (1978) began to describe observational methods that enabled them to evaluate whether primates were aware of the thoughts or intention of conspecifics. That is, they began to study if apes had a theory of mind (ToM). In the United Kingdom, Wimmer and Perner (1983) further operationalized the construct of ToM with the development of the false-belief task. With this paradigm they began to study the course of development of ToM, or social-cognition in young preschool and elementary school–age children. Very quickly thereafter other research groups in London began to translate Wimmer and Perner's basic *false-belief* developmental paradigms to the study of autism. This led to another seminal sequence of observations. Children with autism appeared to have more difficulty with the development of social-cognition than other aspects of cognitive development (e.g., Baron-Cohen, Leslie, & Frith, 1985; Leslie & Happe, 1989; Frith, 1989).

At about the same time theory had linked the development of joint attention to the emergence of social-cognition (Bretherton, 1991). However, the parallel observations of deficits in joint-attention development and ToM development in autism during the mid-1980s provided the first empirical, albeit indirect, link between these two domains of development. Susequently, the social cognitive view of autism and typical social development became so compelling in the literature that joint attention disturbance began to be interpreted as a manifestation of social cognitive impairment in autism (Baron-Cohen, 1989; Leslie & Happe, 1989). This was also true for the theory on typical development, in which a prominent view remains that joint attention is not possible without social cognition (Tomasello & Call, 1997).

So some have argued that social-cognition precedes and gives rise to joint attention (Tomasello, Carpenter, Call, Behne, & Moll, 2005), and impairments in social-cognition may explain the cause of joint-attention impairment in autism (Baron-Cohen, 1989). For just as long it has been suggested that it may be inadvisable to take what may be a later-arising and complex epistemological process of cognitive development (e.g., ToM) and use it to explain an earlier arising, information-processing form of cognitive development such as joint attention (Mundy & Newell, 2007; Mundy & Sigman, 1989b; Mundy, Sigman, & Kasari, 1993). Information-processing systems do not necessarily involve the ability to interpret *meaning* for their growth and maturation (Hunt, 1999). Nevertheless, information processing can contribute to the development of the capacity to perceive and share meanings across people, such as is involved in social-cognition. I will have more to say about this in the second half of this chapter.

THE DISSOCIATION OF JOINT-ATTENTION DEFICITS IN AUTISM

One of the observations that began to raise questions about the social cognitive hypothesis of joint-attention impairments was the dissociation in IJA and RJA development observed in children with autism. We initially understood that deficits in joint attention in autism were pervasive in the sense that they were expressed in younger and older children (Baron-Cohen, 1989), in interactions with familiar caregivers (e.g., Sigman et al., 1986), with unfamiliar testers (e.g., Loveland & Landry, 1986; Mundy et al., 1986; Wetherby & Prutting, 1984), and in classroom interactions (e.g., Curcio, 1978). However, we did not know if impairments were expressed equally across initiating and responding forms of joint-attention behavior.

This issue was first examined in a study of 30 3- to 6-year-old children with autism who were compared with developmentally matched samples of children with typical development or Mental Retardation (Mundy, Sigman, & Kasari, 1994). We observed that children with autism who had lower mental ages, estimated between 8 and 22 months (n = 15), displayed syndrome-specific deficits on *both* IJA and RJA measures relative to mental age matched typically developing children,

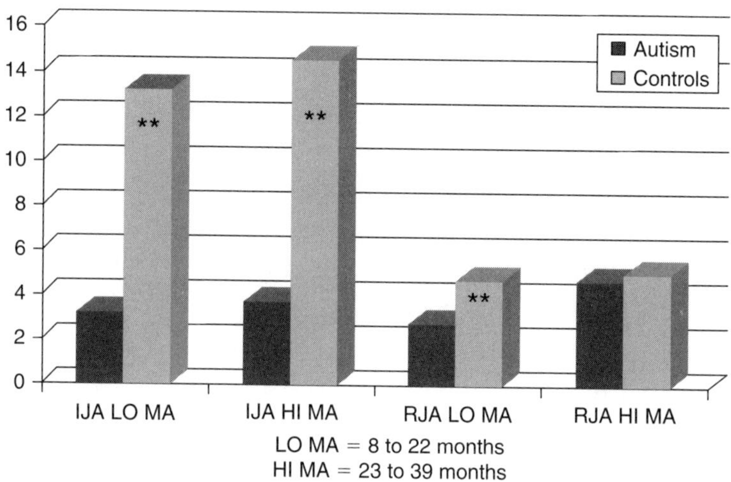

Figure 3.3 Illustration of the moderating affect of mental age on diagnostic group differences on RJA versus IJA reported in Mundy et al., 1994.

as well as chronological and mental age matched children with Mental Retardation. On the other hand, children with autism who had higher mental age, estimated between 23 and 39 months (n = 15), *only* displayed significant deficits on IJA compared to controls. In contrast, autism-related RJA performance deficits were not observed in this higher mental age subgroup compared to controls (see Fig. 3.3). These data raised the strong possibility that an essential *developmental dissociation* characterized joint-attention disturbance in autism. Both IJA and RJA deficits were exhibited during the earliest periods of mental development in this disorder. However, after a mental age of 2 to 3 years, only IJA remained as a robust syndrome-specific focus of joint-attention disturbance (Mundy et al., 1994).

Individual differences data analyses in the 1994 study also provided evidence of important differences between IJA and RJA deficits. Differences in IJA, but not RJA, performance were significantly related to differences in parent report of symptom presentation in the children with autism. Higher IJA scores were associated with parent reports of fewer problems on the Social Relatedness subscale of the Autism Behavior Checklist (ABC). This suggested that there was also a dissociation between

RJA and IJA with respect to their relations with symptom presentation in autism. Moreover, this type of specific IJA but not RJA association with parent reports of social relatedness was also evident in the data for children in the typically developing control sample (Mundy et al., 1994).

These data provided objective evidence for the hypothesis that IJA was associated with what adults perceive as an impairment in social relatedness among children with autism (Karsari et al., 1990; Mundy & Sigman, 1989a). The data also indicated that this association might be specific to initiating rather than responding forms of joint attention. Finally, the data suggested that the association between IJA and social competence was a general developmental phenomenon that was not only apparent in the development of children with autism, but it was also apparent in the development of infants not affected by autism. More recent data from samples with typical development, as well as those at risk for developmental disturbance, provide striking support for the last proposition (Sheinkopf, Mundy, Claussen, & Willoughby, 2004; Vaughan Van Hecke et al., 2007).

Evidence for the dissociation between IJA and RJA development has grown over the years in research on typical development, as well as autism. With regard to the latter many studies have shown that young children readily acquire RJA skills after 2 years of life (Nation & Penny, 2008). For example, Leekam and colleagues (2000) reported that while only 25% of a sample of 16 young children with autism initially displayed gaze-following competence, an additional 8 children (50%) displayed gaze-following after only four brief operant learning trials. Some initial reports had been interpreted to suggest that children with autism did not use RJA or gaze-following skills in language development (e.g., Baron-Cohen, Baldwin, & Crowson, 1997). However, that type of observation may have been an artifact of assessment methods, or sample characteristics, because larger scale longitudinal research has indicated that early differences in RJA (but not IJA) predict responsiveness to early language intervention (Bono, Daley, & Sigman, 2004) as well as developmental difference in language acquisition through late childhood and early adolescence (Sigman & Ruskin, 1999). Indeed a recent comprehensive review reports little evidence of a chronic or consistent syndrome-specific impairment in the ability to respond to joint attention or process the direction of gaze in people with autism (Nation & Penny,

2008). Rather, individual differences in the development of gaze following and RJA abound in autism with a substantial portion of the variance in this domain due to general developmental factors.

Alternatively, IJA-related deficits appear to be a more chronic component of the syndrome of autism (Mundy & Crowson, 1997). Moreover, IJA but not RJA has been observed to predict individual differences in outcomes measured in terms of differences in social initiations and social symptoms reports in childhood and early adolescence (Charman, 2003; Lord, Floody, Anderson, & Pickles, 2003; Sigman & Ruskin, 1999). IJA, but not RJA, responsiveness is also related to longer-term outcome in early intervention for children with autism (Kasari, Freeman, & Paparella, 2007).

Research with at-risk as well as typically developing infants also suggests that RJA and IJA reflect unique constellations of multiple processes in early development. Studies of at-risk and typically developing infants most often report no significant correlations between performance on RJA and IJA measures, suggesting these domains of development are at best modestly associated in early development (e.g., Brooks & Meltzoff, 2008; Mundy et al., 2007; Sheinkopf et al., 2004; Slaughter & McConnell, 2003; but also see Carpenter, Nagell, & Tomasello, 1998). Pertinent research also indicates that IJA and RJA measures are differentially related to measures of childhood IQ (Ulvund & Smith, 1996), frontal brain activity (Caplan et al., 1993; Mundy, Card, & Fox, 2000; Henderson, Yoder, Yale, & McDuffie, 2002), inhibiting and switching behavioral responses (Dawson et al., 2002; Griffith, Pennington, Wehner, & Rogers, 1999; Nichols, Fox, & Mundy, 2005), attention regulation (Morales, Mundy, & Rojas, 2005), self-monitoring (Nichols et al., 2005), the expression of positive affect associated with social motivation (Kasari et al., 1990; Mundy et al., 1992; Vaughan et al., 2003), attachment (Claussen, Mundy, Malik, & Willoughby, 2002), as well as learning and reward sensitivity (Dawson et al., 2002; Corkum & Moore, 1998; Nichols et al., 2005).

JOINT ATTENTION AND AUTISM DIAGNOSIS

By 1994, research had begun to suggest several things about autism. First, autism was associated with a specific pattern of developmental disturbance in joint attention. Both RJA and IJA impairments seemed to be characteristic of the early development of autism, but problems with IJA were more chronic and robust through later periods of development. The chronic nature of the disruption of initiating joint attention reinforced the long-standing notion that autism could be construed as a disturbance of the spontaneous generation of social behaviors, as much as or more than a disturbance of the perception and responses to the social behaviors of others (Koegel, Carter, & Koegel, 2003). Furthermore, the phenomenon of dissociation in the development of IJA and RJA was not specific to autism. Rather, the dissociation in joint-attention impairments in autism seemed to be indicative of a more general dissociation in joint-attention development that was also evident in the course of typical development. Therefore, if the nature and ramifications of this developmental dissociation could be understood, this would contribute to our understanding of the strengths and weaknesses of the social development of children with autism (Mundy et al., 2007).

Second, *neither IJA nor RJA deficits in autism were absolute*. Joint-attention deficits in autism are not absolute because all studies using frequency measures indicate that some children with autism display some level of IJA and RJA behaviors (Mundy et al., 1986). Moreover, correlation analyses have repeatedly informed us that individual differences in joint attention among children with autism are meaningful (e.g., Mundy et al., 1994; Sigman & Ruskin, 1999).

The availability of information on the dissociation between IJA and RJA deficits in autism contributed to the formulation of the diagnostic criteria and methods we use today. We began to describe initiating joint attention and its deficits in autism as related to sharing experience with others (e.g., Mundy et al., 1992; Mundy & Sigman, 1989a, b). Subsequently, the developers of the Pervasive Developmental Disorder (PDD) diagnostic criteria for DSM-IV (APA, 1994) also adopted the notion of impairments in IJA behaviors, such as showing and pointing, as a central symptom indicative of a deficit in the capacity to adaptively share experience in autism. So, "A lack of spontaneous seeking to share enjoyment, interests, or achievements with other people, (e.g., by a lack of showing, bringing, or pointing out objects of interest to other people)" (APA, 2000, pp. 69–70), became one of the four essential social symptoms of autism. The gold-standard diagnostic structured interview, called the Autism Diagnostic Interview (ADI), and an objective observation instrument, called the Autism Diagnostic Observation Schedule (ADOS), incorporated measures in joint attention. These measures even assumed the IJA and RJA nomenclature first used in the ESCS. Moreover, the ADOS recognized the developmental dissociation in symptom presentation of RJA and IJA. ADOS Module 1, used for the youngest groups of children, included both IJA and RJA measures in its diagnostic algorithms. However, Module 2, for older preschool children, includes IJA but not RJA measures in its diagnostic criteria.

JOINT ATTENTION AND THE TREATMENT OF AUTISM

Behavioral learning theory was used to establish the first documented effective treatment for autism (Lovaas, 1987). These methods involved increasing positive and decreasing negative behaviors in children with autism using operant, stimulus-response reinforcement on discrete learning trials. The discrete trials were adult-directed learning opportunities designed to remediate and incrementally rebuild typical development one skill at a time and one step in development at a time. Some but not all children with autism displayed significant cognitive gains in response to this treatment modality (Smith, Groen, & Wynn, 2000). Because the response to behavioral treatment was variable, the field began to realize that discrete trial learning may not be the only modality to consider in attempts to address the social-communication impairments of autism. So researchers turned to *developmental* interventions. The central assumption of this type of intervention is that it may be critical to attempt to build the ability of children with autism to actively learn in social interactions, in addition to teaching them discrete skills. One explicit target of this new developmental approach to early intervention is joint-attention skill development, because joint attention embodies self-organizing characteristics that facilitate early learning. For example, much of early language learning takes place in unstructured or incidental social learning situations. Parents do not intentionally set up training

Figure 3.4 Illustration from Baldwin (1995) depicting the referential mapping problem encountered by infants in incidental social word learning situations.

sessions to teach language to their infants and toddlers one word at time. Rather, language acquisition often occurs by way of unstructured or incidental social learning situations in which parents provide new words that refer to novel objects or events. In these unstructured situations infants need to contribute to their own learning. They often must choose which of an array of possible objects to attend to in order to achieve the correct referential mapping associated with the new word provided by their parent. Joint attention assists infants in optimally organizing social information processing to avoid referential mapping errors in these situations (Baldwin, 1995).

To narrow the field of possible referents, infants utilize their ability to follow the direction of gaze of the parent (RJA skill) to look to the area of the environment that most likely holds the correct referent. This increases the statistical likelihood of correct word mapping and learning (Fig. 3.4). This narrowing of the field of possible referents represents an endogenous mechanism of constraint that is related to learning (Aslin & Fiser, 2005) that allows infants to avoid possible referential mapping errors (Baldwin, 1995). Similarly, parents can follow the gaze of infants or infants may direct the gaze of parents via initiating bids for joint attention. In either case, a responsive caregiver follows the child's line of regard and take advantage of the child's focus of attention and manifest interest to provide a new word in a context that maximizes the opportunity to learn (Tomasello & Farrar, 1986). Thus, parent gaze following and infant initiating joint attention also serve related learning support functions by reducing referential mapping errors and facilitating accurate lexical acquisition in incidental learning opportunities.

Research has also begun to suggest that joint attention increases depth of processing of information. Striano and colleagues (Striano, Chen, Cleveland, & Bradshaw, 2006; Striano, Reid, & Hoel, 2006) observed infants studying pictures in two conditions. One included a social partner who first made eye contact with the infants and then passively looked at pictures with them. In a second condition the social partner looked at the pictures with the infant but did not make eye contact. Infants in the first condition (analogous to IJA-alternating gaze) displayed brain activity indicative of deeper stimulus processing and also displayed better picture recognition memory in a novelty preference paradigm.

Thus, the self-organizing and information-processing characteristics of joint attention that facilitate early learning make it an essential target for early developmental interventions for autism. Theoretically, if joint attention in children with autism can be improved it may be possible to enhance their life-long ability to learn in social interactions (Mundy & Crowson, 1997). The literature on joint attention in typical development also emphasizes that following the child's line of regard and capitalizing on his or her manifest interest, rather than redirecting the child's attention to adult-selected learning tasks, may be especially useful in early intervention. This method also has the potential to give the child more experience with child-directed sharing of attention. This experience may help to increase the child's own tendency to initiate episodes of joint attention with others. Improving the capacity of children to spontaneously initiate adaptive social behaviors, such as initiating joint-attention bids, has long been a central goal of early intervention in autism (Koegel et al., 2003).

Several studies and research groups have reported success in this new developmental approach to intervention with autism. One of the more influential presentations of this approach has been provided by Connie Kasari (e.g., Kasari, Freeman, & Paparella, 2006), who conducted a randomized control trial of three intervention conditions groups of approximately 20 3-year-old children with autism. In one condition children received an experimental mother-child interaction treatment targeting joint attention, especially IJA. Another group received mother-child interaction treatment targeting symbolic play skills. And a third comparison control group received a standard community-based intervention. The results indicated that the symbolic play intervention significantly increased both symbolic play and joint attention in children with autism relative to controls after 12 months. The joint-attention intervention had a more specific impact on that domain rather than symbolic play. However, both joint-attention and symbolic play interventions were associated with comparable expressive language scores 12 months later compared to the control sample (Kasari et al., 2006). Moreover, longer term follow-up has revealed that only improvements in IJA were positively associated with language and cognitive outcomes in the experimental treatment groups 4 years later. Furthermore, improved IJA was also associated with a decrease in symptoms of social impairment as rated on the ADOS at the 4-year outcome assessment (Kasari et al., 2007). These longer-term or ongoing developmental improvements are expected if increasing joint attention enhances learning abilities in children with autism.

In summary, the application of basic research on joint attention and how infants learn to share experience gave impetus to translational studies that helped to define the nature of the social deficits of autism and improve its diagnosis. Recent insights into the self-organizing role of joint attention in early learning have added vital information for the formulation of developmental intervention strategies that hold the promise of improving the quality of life for many children afflicted with this disorder. In addition, particulars gleaned from research on autism have begun to have an impact on basic science theories of attention, joint attention, and social-cognition. This type of feedback from translational research on autism to basic science is described in the next section of this chapter.

THE SOCIAL COGNITIVE AND INFORMATION-PROCESSING MODELS OF JOINT ATTENTION

As noted earlier in the chapter, a prominent current perspective is that the development of *social cognition*, defined as understanding intentionality in others, enables the development of true joint attention. The essential logic of this model was expressed by Tomasello and Call (1997) with the statement: "An organism would only attempt to tune into the attention of others, or get others to tune into their attention, if they understood them as beings able to intentionally direct their attention to specific entities on demand" (p. 405). Consequently, joint attention is often viewed as a facility of mind that begins to emerge at the cusp of the first and second years of life as the consequence of incipient development of understanding intentionality in others (e.g., Tomasello et al., 2005).

As I have said, research on joint attention in autism, though, has raised several questions about the nature of the relations between joint attention and social-cognition. These questions began to arise with the observation of a dissociation between initiating and responding joint-attention development in autism (Mundy et al., 1994) and typical development (e.g., Mundy & Gomes, 1998). Social cognitive theory, to my knowledge, does not speak to a dissociation in the development of initiating and responding forms of joint attention since both are assumed to reflect similar if not identical aspects of social cognitive development (e.g., Baron-Cohen, 1989; Tomasello, 1995).

Other questions have been raised by observations that children with autism and typical development display a range of meaningful individual differences in early joint-attention development (e.g., Morales et al., 1998; Morales, Mundy, Crowson, Neal, & Delgado, 2005; Mundy & Gomes, 1998; Sheinkopf et al., 2004; Ulvund & Smith, 1996; Vaughan Van Hecke et al., 2007). The issue here is not that the social-cognitive model cannot explain individual difference phenomenon. Rather, its current formulations simply do not acknowledge that individual differences exist or are an important phenomenon to explain in a fully informed model or theory (Mundy et al., 2007). It is also the case, though, that IJA and RJA measures display unique developmental patterns of correlations with language, cognitive, and behavioral outcome measures (Claussen et al., 2002; Mundy et al., 2007; Sheinkopf et al., 2004; Smith & Ulvund, 2003; Vaughan Van Hecke et al., 2007). The observations of these divergent patterns of development and orthogonal correlation data on construct validity belie the idea that IJA and RJA reflect one common aspect of early social cognition. Instead, the developmental differences between IJA and RJA suggest that there are multiple paths and processes involved in joint-attention development. According to this view, IJA and RJA reflect different constellations of processes that may be related to social-cognition. This notion is emphasized by the observation that joint-attention development appears to involve the interactive functions of two distributed cortical attention systems.

The Two Cortical Systems of Joint Attention

If autism is a neurodevelopmental disorder, and joint-attention impairment is central to autism, then understanding the neurodevelopment of joint attention is a vital task for research on autism (Mundy, 1995). This logic set in motion a sequence of planned and serendipitous research that examined the neurodevelopmental correlates of different forms of joint attention. The first study was an opportunistic collaboration between researchers at UCLA. Thirteen infants were evaluated with Positron Emission Tomography (PET) to evaluate metabolic activity in dorsal frontal, orbital frontal, temporal, and occipital regions (Caplan et al., 1993). They were then presented with an intervention to minimize activity in the hemisphere afflicted with seizure activity. The ESCS was used to appraise social communication development before and after intervention. The results indicated that preintervention resting-state metabolic activity in the dorsal media frontal lobes was a specific predictor of postintervention IJA development in the 13 infants in this study. RJA and initiating behavior regulation, however, were not associated with frontal, temporal, or occipital PET measures of cortical metabolic activity.

A second set of studies were conducted in the developmental electrophysiological laboratories of Nathan Fox at the University of Maryland. The first of these involved the participation of 32 typically developing infants assessed at 14, 16, and 18 months of age (Mundy et al., 2000). At each age infants were assessed with the ESCS and an EEG assessment to collect bilateral resting-state brain activity data from medial frontal, central, temporal, parietal, and occipital electrode sites. Two primary observations emerged from this study. Fourteen-month EEG measures of parietal activation predicted differences in RJA performance of infants at 18 months. The observation of this posterior cortical association is consistent with several studies indicating that gaze following and RJA skill development is associated with activity in parietal areas specialized for spatial orienting along with temporal systems specialized for processing the gaze direction of others (Atsushi, Johnson, & Csibra, 2006; Cavanna & Trimble, 2006; Frieschen, Bayliss, & Tipper, 2007; Mundy & Vaughan Van Hecke, 2008).

In contrast to the pattern of predictors of RJA, a more complex pattern of EEG coherence between medial-frontal and central activity at 14 months was a predictor of differences in IJA performance among 18-month-old infants (Mundy et al., 2000). Although the source location of the frontal EEG data could not be definitively determined, the frontal correlates of IJA involved activity from electrode F3 of the 10/20 placement system. This electrode was positioned above a point of confluence of Brodmann's areas 8 and 9 of the medial-frontal cortex of the left hemisphere (Martin, 1996). This area includes aspects of the frontal eye fields and supplementary motor cortex commonly observed to be involved in an anterior system of attention control (Posner & Petersen, 1990). This study (Mundy et al., 2000) was the first to suggest a dual-process model of joint-attention development that involved a distributed system of frontal and posterior cortical functions.

Subsequent research from the Fox laboratory indicated that frontal EEG coherence was not only associated with IJA at 18 months but also predicted language development at 24 months (Mundy, Card, & Fox, 2003). However, above and beyond variance that was associated with the EEG measure, IJA also displayed evidence of an association with 24-month language development. This suggested that the connection between IJA and language could not be entirely explained in terms of the common neurological processes measured in this study. This observation was consistent with the idea that, beyond its neurodevelopmental substrate, joint-attention *behaviors* affect self-organizing of learning and subsequent development. Nichols, Fox, and Mundy (2005) have also reported that performance on a delayed nonmatch to sample (DNMS) task was significantly associated with performance on a measure of IJA, but not RJA. This type of DNMS task has previously been associated with functions of a temporal-ventromedial-frontal circuit involved in reward-based discriminant learning. This was consistent with the theory on the potential role of reward sensitivity in the development of self-initiated joint-attention bids (Mundy, 1995). Nichols and colleagues (2005) also observed that IJA but not RJA was associated with a self-recognition measure used to assess self-monitoring. Alternatively, other studies that examined the neuropsychological correlates of joint attention in children with autism and controls reported that both IJA and RJA are correlated with performance on a spatial reversal task that presumably taps into dorsolateral frontal response inhibition, memory, and planning processes (e.g., Griffith et al., 1999). Thus, IJA and RJA may share some frontal functions, such as inhibition, but not others involved in self-monitoring and aspects of reward based learning. Furthermore, although IJA may involve temporal and even parietal functioning, parietal cortical functional associations appear to be a more robust correlate of gaze following/RJA behaviors.

The specificity of a frontal functional association with IJA has also been emphasized by the observation of Henderson and colleagues (2002). This research group examined the neural correlates of pointing for declarative (IJA) and imperative (IBR) functions in infants. Henderson and colleagues observed no significant correlations between any of their 14-month resting state EEG data and IBR pointing at 18 months. However, IJA pointing at 18 months was predicted by 14-month EEG data indicative of greater brain activity recorded from dorsal-frontal sites. In this study IJA pointing at 18 months was also predicted by activity recorded from electrodes over the orbito-frontal, temporal, and dorsolateral frontal cortical regions. Thus, Henderson et al. (2002) observed that IJA development was associated with the distributed activation in dorsal cortical, ventral *social brain* and dorso-lateral frontal networks. Data consistent with the observations from resting state EEG studies have also recently been provided using evoke response (ERP) methods. Torkildsen, Thormodsen, Syvensen, Smith, and Lindgren (2008) presented 20- to 24-month-old infants with sets of video vignettes of two people interacting. In one condition (IJA), each vignette showed one person pointing to an object to show it to their social partner while making eye contact. In the second condition (IBR), each vignette showed one person pointing or reaching to request an object from their social partner while making eye contact. EEG-ERP data were collected anchored to the occurrence of eye contact in both conditions. The results indicated that infants displayed more evidence of frontal activation in the IJA than IBR condition.

Using fMRI, Astafiev and colleagues (2003) compared cortical activation associated with attention, looking, and pointing to peripheral targets in adults. They found that activation of the frontal eye fields and intraparietal sulcus was common to all activities. However, pointing also recruited activation of the supplementary motor cortex as well as the precuneus, parietal lobes, and posterior superior temporal sulcus. In another study, Williams and colleagues (2005) examined cortical activation in adults in two conditions. In the congruent *joint-attention* condition, the participants visually tracked a moving dot on a monitor and the full face image of another person on the screen also appeared to visually track the dot. In a second incongruent condition, the participant tried to track the dot while the image of the other person on the screen appeared to make errors in visually tracking the dot. Experience of the former *joint-attention* simulation condition uniquely elicited activation not only in the dorsal and medial frontal cortex, but also in the dorso-lateral frontal cortex, orbital frontal cortex, and parietal cortex compared to the incongruent social gaze condition.

Research of this kind has provided part of the foundation for the new hypothesis that fully realized joint-attention skill in the second year of life is an outcome of the interaction of distributed neural systems associated with the anterior and posterior attention systems (see Fig. 3.5; Mundy & Newell, 2007). The posterior orienting and perceptual attention system plays a primary role in responding to joint-attention (RJA) development in infancy. This relatively involuntary system begins to develop in the first months of life and prioritizes the capacity to orient in the direction of biologically meaningful stimuli (Posner & Rothbart,

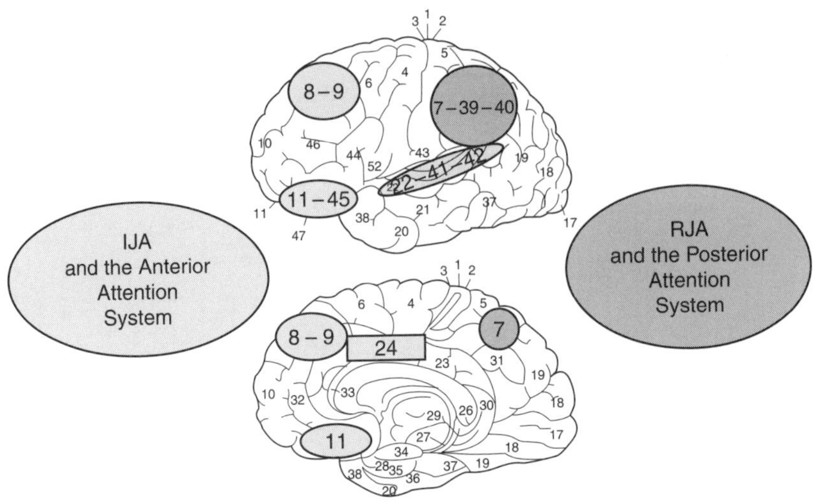

Figure 3.5 Illustration from Mundy & Newell, 2007.

2007). It is supported by the parietal and superior temporal cortices, which serve aspects of representational development, imitation, and the perception of the eye and head orientations of others, as well as the perception of spatial relations between self, other, and the environment. The neural substrates and functions of this system are common to many primates. Shorthand for one of the goal-related cognitive output from this system is the understanding that "where others' eyes go, behavior follows" (Jellema, Baker, Wicker, & Perrett, D, 2000).

Alternatively, initiating joint attention is supported by the later-developing anterior attention system. This system controls volitional, goal-directed attention allocation that is constrained and corrected by reward-related self-appraisal of behavior. It involves a neural network that includes the frontal eye fields, prefrontal association cortex, orbital frontal cortex, and anterior cingulate (Fig. 3.5). Elements of this system (e.g., anterior cingulate) also regulate integrated activity across the anterior and posterior attention systems. This integration yields the distinct form of human attention we call *joint attention*. EEG and imaging data attest to the integrated activation of the anterior and posterior systems in human joint attention (Henderson et al., 2002; Williams et al., 2005).

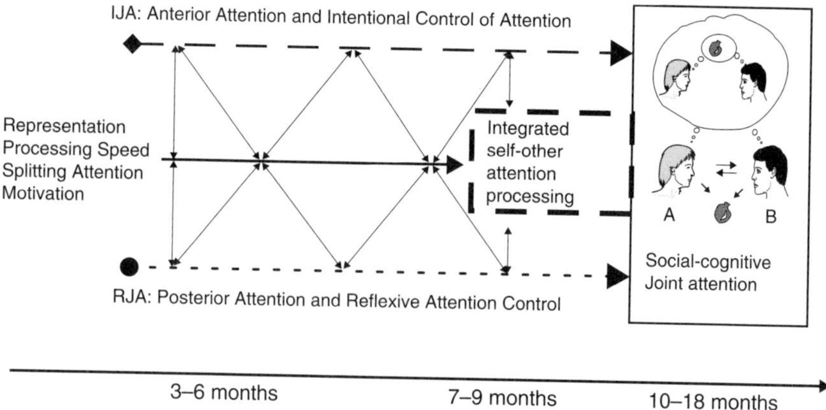

Figure 3.6 An illustration of the information processing systems model of joint attention and social-cognition, from Mundy & Newell, 2007.

This attention network also has much in common with the neural substrates of social-cognition (Mundy, 2003).

Shorthand for an initial cognitive output from the anterior system is a *self-awareness* of intentional attention control and the understanding that "where *my* eyes go, my *successful* behavior follows." Mundy and Newell (2007) suggested that an executive function of the anterior attention system integrates internal information about self-initiated goal-related attention deployment (my eyes → my behavior) with external information from posterior system processing of the attention and behavior in others (others' eyes → others' behavior). As this integrative processing matures with experience and practice in social interactions, a fully functional adaptive human social-cognitive system emerges (Fig. 3.6). Information about self-initiated goal-related attention leads to the development of the self concept (where my eyes intentionally go → my goal-directed behavior follows). Subsequently, the conditional association of (*if* my eye direction precedes my intentional goal directed action *then* other people's eye direction signals *their* intentions) may be realized and the seeds of social-cognition begin to grow. Thus, the social coordination of *overt* aspects of visual attention early in infancy provide information and experiences that nourish the development of the human capacity for social coordination of *covert* aspects of attention (i.e., social-cognition), such as when social partners share attention to psychological phenomena including ideas, intentions, and emotions (Mundy, 2003).

Elements of this perspective are consistent with current social cognitive models. However, an explicit tenet here is that the rapid, real-time processing of information about one's own attention and the attention of others, in conjunction with the integrated development of a distributed cortical attention network, makes a fundamental contribution to the human development of social-cognition. A corollary of this hypothesis is that processes that affect the organization, accuracy, and speed of integrated processing, within or across the anterior and posterior attention systems, may contribute to phylogenetic and ontological differences in joint attention and social-cognition. This observation brings us back to autism.

A recent advance in our thinking about autism has been the emergence of connectivity theory, which suggests that problems in communication between brain regions, especially anterior and posterior cortical connections, may be primary to the cognitive impairments of autism (e.g., Cherkassky, Kana, Keller, & Just, 2006). Our multiple-process perspective of joint attention is consonant with elements of this theory and suggests that the primacy of the joint-attention deficit in autism may occur because it is a form of early behavior development that is especially sensitive to neurodevelopment processes associated with abnormalities of distal neural connectivity (Mundy & Newell, 2007). This combination of ideas about information processing and distributed cortical systems does not only have relevance for how we think about joint attention in children with autism. It also has relevance for how we think about joint attention in human development more generally, especially with respect to how we envision the relations between joint attention and social cognition.

A Social Cognitive Model of Joint Attention

One of the more articulate and elegant social cognitive models of joint attention has been provided by Tomasello and his colleagues (2005). It incorporates three important hypotheses. The Phylogentic Hypothesis suggests that aspects of joint attention (i.e., IJA) and social cognition

Figure 3.7 An illustration of the stage model of early social attention.

distinguish human cognitive capacities from those in evidence in other primates (Tomasello & Carpenter, 2005; Tomasello et al., 2005). The Cultural Learning Hypothesis suggests that social cognition, and to a lesser extent joint attention, provides the foundation for the development of human cultures and the intergenerational transmission of knowledge. The Ontogenetic Hypothesis states that the early development of joint attention and social cognition can be understood in terms of three stages, which are characterized by changes in what infants *know about other people* early in development (see Fig. 3.7). In sequence, these stages are Understanding Animate Action, Understanding the Pursuit of Goals, and Understanding Choice of Plans. It is only in this last stage that Tomasello and colleagues believe that *proper* joint attention and social cognition are manifest in infancy. This model emphasizes the role of what we perceive and understand about others, rather than ourselves in the development of joint attention and social-cognition.

In the Understanding Animate Action stage, 3- to 8-month-old infants can understand other persons as animate agents. They experience contingencies between our own animate actions and emotions and their animate actions and behaviorally expressed emotions. However, infants at this age do not represent the internal mental goals of others that may be associated with these actions. Tomasello et al., (2005) note that mutual gaze is a prototypic element of early dyadic activity where "the *infant is not monitoring the adult's looking* at her or any object: it is direct engagement" (p. 682); but there is "nothing inside the heads" of infants in terms of *awareness of intentionality in others*" (p. 681, italics added). Without understanding intentionality, infants engage in extended bouts of social interactions with others because of an undefined human biomotivational system that promotes the tendency to share experiences, such as our emotions, with others from early in life.

Things begin to change at about 9 months with the next Understanding of Pursuit of Goals stage of development. At this point, infants' motivations to share experience with others provides the impetus for infants and their social partners to begin to share goal-directed actions on objects (e.g., building a block tower together). Infants begin to understand others as capable of goals and of themselves as capable of pursuing shared goals, or of doing things together with other people. Tomasello and colleagues (2005) suggest that, at this stage, infants become capable of perceiving the association of their actions with those of others in acts of *joint perception*. Others have referred to this type of joint activity as *infant joint attention* (Bruner, 1975). However, Tomasello and colleagues (2005) argue that the types of social cognition necessary for joint attention are not available to children at this age. They suggest that 9- to 12-month-old infants may represent others as capable of behavioral goals (e.g., actions on the world) and perceptions such as seeing. However, they are not yet capable of representing others as capable of internal mental actions, plans, or intentions.

The capacity for representation of others as capable of mental intentions characterizes the next Understanding Choice of Plans stage of development and demarks the transition from joint *perception* to true joint *attention*. This is a qualitative change that occurs between 12- to 15-months of age (Tomasello et al., 2005). By 12 to 15 months, most infants become much more active in initiating episodes of joint engagement by alternating their eye contact between interesting sights and caregivers (Fig. 3.1, $c_{1,2,3}$) or by pointing to and showing objects (Bakeman & Adamson, 1984). For Tomasello and colleagues (2005), this shift to an active stance in joint engagement is critical and is explained by infants' development of an appreciation that others can make internal mental choices about alternative actions that affect their attention deployment. This increase in depth of knowledge about cognition and behavior in other people motivates infants to become increasingly active in attempts to guide, elicit, and share attention with others. Infants can now know themselves as agents that initiate collaborative activity based on their own goals, and they also know that they can follow the goals and motivations of others in collaborative interaction (Carpenter, Call, & Tomasello, 2005). Thus, according to this model the development of true joint attention at this stage is based on the capacity to adopt two perspectives (e.g., speaker-listener) and is based on a social cognitive ability that emerges at this stage of development.

The capacity to adopt two perspectives, such as that of the speaker and the listener, is also assumed to be an inherent and essential functional characteristic of symbols. Tomasello and colleagues (2005) convincingly argue that linguistic symbols not only demand self–other perspective taking but that they also serve to orient or socially coordinate attention so that the intentions of the listener align with those of the speaker. *Thus, a primary function of linguistic symbols is the efficient social coordination of covert mental attention to a common abstract representation among people.*

This is a significant insight that is at once intuitive and grand in its implications. However, Tomasello and colleagues suggest that facility with this function of symbols, as well as facility with true joint attention, develops in the second year because of the emergence of social cognitive knowledge about self and others. However, an information-processing perspective on joint attention encourages us to look at this equation from a slightly different angle. Accordingly, if a primary function of symbols is the social coordination of *covert (mental) attention* to common representations, then the development of the capacity for symbolic thought, including language, may first require extensive practice with the executive demands of joint attention and the social coordination of *overt (visual) attention* to external objects or events.

Perhaps we should not think of joint attention as replaced in stages of development marked by the emergence of social cognition or symbolic thinking. Rather, it may be important to understand that *joint-attention processes continue to provide a fundamental foundation for the functions of symbols, language, and social cognition throughout our lives* (Werner & Kaplan, 1963).

Indeed, a basic assumption of the information-processing model of joint attention is that extended practice with the coordination of *overt* aspects of attention (e.g., coordination of gaze) in the first 15 months of life allows for a cognitive shift to internal mental management of the social coordination of covert attention of self and others. This cognitive shift allows the distributed cortical management of joint attention to act as an executive substrate to support the development of the ability to socially coordinate *covert* attention (e.g., attention to mental representations) so that the intentions of the listener align with those of the speaker (Mundy, 2003; Mundy & Newell, 2007). This social executive attention-management function provides a needed foundation for symbolic thought and shared consciousness (i.e., intersubjectivity) in human development.

An Introduction to the Information-Processing Model of Joint Attention

The information-processing view of joint attention has emerged largely from research on autism (Mundy, 2003). It involves the following set of assumptions. Joint attention is an executive form of information processing. The phylogenetic and ontogenetic emergence of joint attention and social-cognition is generated by: (a) elaborations of the capacity to self-monitor and control goal-related attention; (b) elaborations of neural networks that integrate *inside-out* processing of self-generated attention behavior with *outside-in* processing of the attention behavior of other people; (c) elaborations of representation mental processes and causal thinking about animate and inanimate objects, and (d) motivation associated with the positive value of social attention.

This model adopts a continuous view of joint-attention development. It emphasizes how the early development of the joint processing of information about attention in self and others in the first 9 months of life contributes to social and cognitive developments. Research affiliated with this model often involves longitudinal and quasiexperimental paradigms designed to examine the correlations of varied psychological processes (e.g., executive, affective, social cognitive) with joint-attention skills across ages in development. Theory related to this model is characterized by the explicit assumption that differences in the frequencies of joint-attention bids are important to measure because of joint attention's self-organizing role in social learning. It is also assumed that *different measures of joint attention may reflect different constellations of multiple basic mental processes* in development. Hence, understanding the nature and meaning of individual differences is considered to be a phenomenon of principle theoretical consequence in understanding human joint attention and social cognitive development (Mundy et al., 2007).

This model adopts an *inside-out* processing perspective. First, from the earliest points in development we receive more information about self-intended actions (e.g., active looking) through proprioception than we receive about other's intended actions through exteroception. We learn as much *or more* about intentionality from observing our own actions compared to observing the actions of others. Hence, this is a self-organizing and constructivist model that emphasizes the role of self–other perception as a foundation for the attribution of meaning to the perception of others behaviors. Thus, when we model the phylogenetic or ontogentic changes that give rise to advances in joint attention and social-cognition we need to consider the possibility that improvement in the fidelity and complexity of proprioceptive self-monitoring may be fundamental to human development and evolution.

This model is not competing or incompatible with current social cognitive models (see Mundy, in preparation). Rather, information processing and knowledge based social cognitive models address different issues and questions about the same domain of development. Hence, the models are complimentary and should be synergistic. When they are contrasted or combined they serve to clarify and deepen our view of the multifaceted nature of human joint attention and social cognition. They concur that joint attention and social-cognition are inexorably linked in human development and evolution. They differ, however, in their perspectives on the timing and nature of the developmental links between joint attention and social cognitive development. The social cognitive model focuses on a stage of development when joint attention becomes infused with *social cognition*, defined as an elaborated awareness of intentionality in others. On the other hand, the information-processing model (IPM) focuses on the development of the integrated processing of the attention of self and of other people that precedes, and indeed may provide a foundation for, social-cognitive development. This difference between the models has numerous implications.

One of these differences is semantic. Adherents of the IPM do not ascribe to the view that joint attention may be singularly defined by what infants *know*, such as the presence or absence of knowledge about intentions in others. This epistemological view is not invalid, but it does limit the conceptualizations and study of joint attention. Therefore, the distinction made by Tomasello and colleagues (2005) between *joint perception* at 9 to 12 months and *joint attention* at 12 to 15 months is not central to the IPM. The IPM acknowledges that a significant social cognitive transition takes place in the context of joint attention after about 9 months of age (see Fig. 3.6). However, the information-processing characteristics that are thought to be at the heart of joint attention begin to emerge as a very real domain of human mental activity and development after 3 to 4 months of age (e.g., D'Entremont, Hains, & Muir, 1997; Farroni, Massaccesi, & Francesca, 2002; Hood, Willen, & Driver, 1998; Striano & Stahl, 2005). It is at this point in development that infants' posterior and anterior neural development allows them to not only orient in adaptive responses to biologically meaningful external stimuli, but to also begin to exert intentional control of their own attention (Posner & Rothbart, 2007).

Another explicit assumption of the IPM is that the integrated processing of information about the attention of self and others is a fundamental form of primate and human cortical executive functions. Executive functions are frontal cortical processes that emerge from experience with goal-directed behavior. They typically involve the transmission of bias signals throughout the brain to selectively inhibit comparatively automatic behavioral responses in favor of activation of more volitional, planned, and goal-directed ideation and action in problem-solving contexts. These frontal bias signals act as regulators throughout much of the rest of the brain, affecting visual processes and attention as well as other sensory modalities and systems responsible for task-relevant response execution, memory retrieval, emotional evaluation, and so on. *The aggregate effect of these bias signals is to guide the flow of neural activity along pathways that establish the proper mappings between inputs* (i.e., outside-in processing), *internal states, and outputs* (i.e., inside-out processing) *needed to perform a given task more efficiently* (Miller & Cohen, 2001). Once well-practiced and established, the executive activation and integration aspects of attention deployment and information processing require little effort to engage. At that point in development, they require little mental effort to deploy and serve as a cognitive substrate that makes higher-order problem solving more efficient and effective.

Our human ability to coordinate attention with other people develops gradually in the first year of life. Once codified, though, it becomes a specific social application of executive functions (Mundy, 2003). At this point, joint attention begins to act like an automatic information-processing subroutine that increases higher cognitive efficiency in adaptive social interactions. For example, recall that the capacity to adopt two perspectives, that of the speaker and of the listener, is thought to be an inherent and essential functional characteristic of symbols. Linguistic symbols not only demand self–other perspective taking but they also serve to orient or socially coordinate attention so that the intentions of the listener align with those of the speaker (Tomasello et al., 2005). Thus, a primary function of linguistic symbols is to coordinate attention to a representation of information shared by two or more people. This type of advanced cognition requires at least two elemental processes. One is a reasonably well-established capacity for representational thought. The other is the establishment of a rapid, facile, and relatively low-effort capacity for social attention coordination. Thus, joint attention may be regarded as a social executive attention function that provides a necessary but not sufficient neuropsychological substrate for symbolic thought process.

As previously noted, a core assumption of the IPM is that practice with overt aspects of social attention coordination (e.g., gaze following) in the first 9 months lead to an internalized (representational) capacity for social attention coordination. After approximately 9 months, joint attention begins to act as an executive substrate to support the

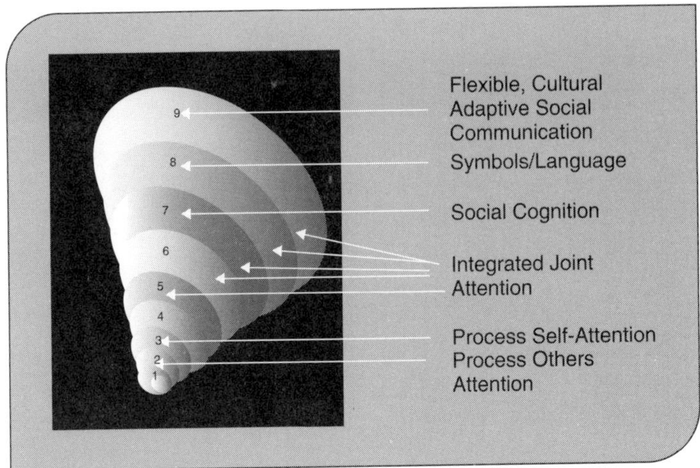

Figure 3.8 An illustration of the continuous information-processing model of social attention, joint attention, and social cognition.

development of the ability to socially coordinate *covert* attention (e.g., attention to mental representations) so that the intentions of the listener align with those of the speaker (Mundy, 2003; Mundy & Newell, 2007; Tomasello et al., 2005). So the IPM considers the development of management and coordination of overt aspects of attention in the 4- to 12-month period to be true joint attention, while Tomasello and colleagues only view the phase of internalization of social attention coordination and awareness of intentionality to involve true joint attention.

Beyond infancy, joint attention continues to be refined and elaborated in conjunction with the extended period of human functional frontal cortical neurodevelopment. Rather than thinking of joint attention as being replaced by new stages of social cognition or language or symbolic development, I prefer to think of joint attention as a primary and enduring stratum of a more *continuous spiral* of human neurocognitive development (see Fig. 3.8).

Some aspects of joint attention, such as RJA, may be relatively well-developed and common to many apes, some primates, other mammals, and even some birds. However, what makes human joint attention different is the balanced and interactive development of *both* initiation and response behavior modalities. The addition of the self-initiation of joint attention in human development is telling. An emphasis on examining the importance of inside-out processing involved in the initiation of joint attention is a hallmark of the IPM and highlights the model's affinity with a constructivist perspective on development.

A quintessential constructivist theory of human development was provided by Piaget (e.g., Piaget, 1952), who argued that infants did not learn about their world through the passive perception of objects in the world. Rather, he proposed that infants take action on objects and learn from these (causal) actions. They then modify their actions to learn new things about their physical world. Piaget viewed self-initiated actions on objects as singularly important in providing infants with the type of information that was necessary to fuel the engines of cognitive development.

The constructivist developmental perspective has always struck a chord with me. Moreover, in recent years scientists have begun to suggest that the constructivist viewpoint fits with basic biological principles of typical and atypical neurocognitive development (e.g., Elman, 2005; Mareschal et al., 2007; Meltzoff, 2007; Mundy & Burnette, 2005). One notion here is that the vast number of functional neural connections that are made in the early years of brain development are too numerous to be specified by our genes alone. Instead, genes specify channels, or narrow but not completely specified paths for potential neural network connections. Within these channels, important specifics about functional neural connections are carved into our developing nervous systems by experience. Since most of us experience a relatively similar range of events, environments, and experiences in early life, the specifics nature of our functional, neural network connections display significant similarities across most people. This transaction between neurodevelopment and experience has been called *experience-expectant* developmental processes. Greenough, Wallace, and Black (1987) coined this term and also suggested that infants generate actions and observe reactions from the social world that make critical contributions to experience-expectant social cognitive neurodevelopment (see Greenough et al., 1987). So, just as Piaget envisioned infants learning about themselves and the physical world from their repeated experiences of the effects of their self-generated actions on objects, we may also expect that infants learn about themselves and the social world from their repeated experiences of the effects of their self-generated actions on people.

Active Vision and the IPM

To the degree the foregoing assumptions are valid it is important to recognize that *it is the actions infants take, as much as their perceptions of others, that aids in constructing social knowledge*. If we only think about outside-in processing and focus singularly on questions about how infants perceive or know about the actions of others, we are at risk of missing much of the picture regarding critical inputs to typical and atypical social cognitive development (Mundy, 2003; Mundy et al., 1993). So what *actions* can we take as infants to construct our social knowledge? A core assumption for me is that one of the first and most vitally informative actions we take involves self-control over our own looking behavior.

We can learn a lot about our own agency and intentional control of the environment through active vision (see Findlay & Gilchrist, 2003). Findlay and Gilchrist (2003) provide a an instructive discussion of how the science of vision has been transformed by moving away from a singular emphasis on the study of *seeing*, or passive visual perception, to the study of *looking*, or volitional visual action and attention deployment. Their account helped crystallize my thinking that early on we learn a lot about our self-agency, and perhaps especially social agency, through our own goal-directed active looking. From an inside-out processing perspective, when we engage in active looking we often engage in coactive analysis of internal (proprioceptive) information about our behavior and corresponding changes in the (social) environment. The latter information is gleaned from external outside-in (i.e., exteroceptive) sensory perception. Our active looking does many things. It selects much of the information we process, and it can elicit contingent behavior responses from other people such as smiles or head turns. It also is one of the first types of volitional actions we develop that can be used to exert control over the stimulus level of the external environment and assist in self-regulation of our arousal and affective states (Posner & Rothbart, 2007). *Volitional control of visual attention is an early self-generated action* that we learn from and use to optimize our arousal states for learning in early development.

Among the sensory systems, looking behavior also has the unique property of signaling the direction of our attention to other people. Even as infants, our eye movements may often be accurately interpreted by others as indicative of the spatial direction of our attention. Comparable information about the spatial direction of our attention, however, is not so clearly available from movement of our nose or our sense of touch, or taste, or even early vocalizations. Eye direction of very young infants is a unique indicator of the spontaneous direction of their interest and attention.

The informative nature of eye movements may be especially true for apes and higher primates, as well as many predatory animals, whose frontal binocular eye positions allow for enhanced spatial processing and depth of perception through parallax perception. The eyes of humans and apes are also affected by intricate musculatures that, in combination with parallax processing, allow for rapid visual focus on objects that are far or near. Finally, of all the primates the *direction of attention* information of the human eyes is highlighted by the contrast between the dark coloration of the pupil and iris versus the light to white coloration of the sclera. This contrasting pattern of coloration allows the direction of the eyes, and even the direction of the pupils, to be the more prominent source of information in the human face than in other primates. The latter observation is relevant to the suggestion that the evolution of the human eye has facilitated our capacity for processing information about others' direction of attention and intentions. Quite reasonably, this observation has led to the ideas about how the clarity of perception of eyes enhances the ability to process the direction of *others'* attention, and how this may affect the phylogentic and ontogenetic development of social-cognition (e.g., Tomasello, Hare, Lehman, & Call, 2006). However, *it is also likely to be true that these characteristics of the human eye allow intentional saccades of infants to be readily observable, eliciting reactions from their social environment*. Indeed, observations of shifts of visual attention are so readily and meaningfully observed that science has long used them to make inferences about the cognitive development of infants in the first months of life (Bornstein & Sigman, 1986).

It makes sense to me, then, that one initial, primary path to understanding ourselves as intentional agents is through our active control of vision. Imagine the type, quantity, and quality of information that self-monitoring of volitional shifts of attention can provide to infants about their own agency early in development. Moreover, consider the possibility that human evolution, as well as human ontology, is marked not only by advances in the capacity for processing external sources of information, but just as significantly the capacity for the rapid processing of proprioceptive (self) information *in relation to* external information. One outcome of this advance is improved early self-monitoring of our own shifts of visual attention and increased processing (awareness) of social reactions to our own eye movements. Because of visual acuity, attention control, and the morphology of our eyes, socially contingent reactions to infant eye movements may be more likely to occur in humans than other primates. In conjunction with this inside-out view of processing information about the social effects of visual attention, the information about the direction of other people's visual attention also enhances infants' capacity to perceive external social attention information that can be integrated into the infants' developing awareness of the causal or goal-related nature of visual attention deployment.

All this really begins to developmentally synergize just as frontal *cognitive control* allows us to become increasingly capable of attending to multiple sources of information during development. When we can attend to multiple sources of information we can begin to relate our self-perception of intentional visual attention control, with the reactions of others to our direction of gaze, and our own reactions to the direction of the looking behavior of other people. With improvements in the capacity to attend to multiple sources of information, *triadic attention* behaviors begin to become more common at about 6 months of age (Scaife & Bruner, 1975; Morales et al., 1998). The context of triadic attention provides us with a richer field of comparative information upon which to begin to impute that others may have intentional control over their looking behavior that is similar to our own.

IPM and Other Models of Precursors of Social-Cognition

The IPM has several points of congruence with the *Like-Me* hypothesis of social cognitive development (e.g., Meltzoff, 2007). Ostensibly, this model describes the contribution of outside-in processing associated with imitation to social-cognition. Nevertheless, Meltzoff is aware of the importance of inside-out processing and the role that self-action plays in developing an interpretive framework for the perception of meaning in others' actions. Indeed, he has recently provided a wonderfully instructive example of *inside-out* joint-attention learning (Meltzoff, 2007).

Brooks and Meltzoff (2002) have observed that 12-month-old infants often follow the *gaze direction* of testers whose eyes are open or closed. After 12 months, though, infants infrequently follow the gaze of testers whose eyes are closed. This suggests that the social cognitive meaning of *eye* gaze may change for infants in this developmental period. Brooks and Meltzoff then conducted an experimental intervention study to explore this developmental shift. Comparable to their eye-open and eyes-closed data, they observed a group of infants who followed the gaze of testers who were blindfolded or not blindfolded. They then provided the infants with the experience of how blindfolds occluded their own looking behavior. After gaining this self-referenced experience with blindfolds, the infants no longer followed the head turn of blindfolded testers, but they did follow the head turn and gaze of nonblindfolded testers (see Meltzoff, 2007, for details). One interpretation here is that the infants demonstrated inside-out learning and constructed a new element of social-cognitive awareness about others from experience with the effects of blindfolds on their own active looking behavior.

SUMMARY

In my opinion, joint attention involves a lot of inside-out constructivist learning. Joint attention may be best viewed as a transactional platform in which integrations of the perceptions about our own looking behavior interact with perceptions about the looking behavior of others. The effects of practice with this integration of perceptions of self attention and other attention that accrue over time and incrementally contribute new social cognitive and interpersonal capabilities. Because of its transactional nature, it may not be plausible to assign primacy to inside-out processing and self-awareness, or outside-in processing and other-awareness in social cognitive development. Indeed, it is likely that we need to have the juxtaposition of information about external others to cast our own internal information in sufficient relief for *self*-awareness to become an articulated and differentiated element of our phenomenology (Piaget, 1952). It is equally likely, though, that we cannot perceive the level of meaning in the actions of others that is necessary for this differentiation to occur without foundational elements of self-awareness of our own intentional actions.

This dialectical or dynamic systems view of joint attention is bolstered by an appreciation of the nature of the two cortical components of attention networks described by Posner and others (e.g., Posner & Rothbart, 2007). One involves the self-control of our own looking behavior regulated by a volitional anterior-cortical attention system. The other involves a more reflexive orienting system involved in gaze following and processing information about the looking behavior of others. The later is regulated by a posterior-cortical attention system. The degree of integrated development and action of the anterior and posterior attention systems may be unique to humans relative to other primates. Indeed, we have suggested that human social cognition and its contributions to language may be viewed as emergent properties of this special human faculty for integrated development of these distal and distributed neural attention systems (Mundy & Newell, 2007).

The development of this perspective on joint attention and social cognition owes much to clinical research on autism. Research on autism has encouraged developmental science to better understand the dissociation of initiating and responding forms of joint-attention development. Attempts to understand autism have also given impetus to the need to understand joint attention from a neurodevelopmental perspective. In return, research and theory on the inside-out processing view of joint attention have begun to emphasize the self-organizing, constructivist nature of joint attention and social cognitive development. This raises the notion that it may be useful to conceive of autism as a form of *social constructivist developmental disorder*. This idea is useful because it emphasizes that teaching children with autism discrete skills in early intervention may not be enough. Instead, we may need to develop methods to help children with autism develop the capacity and motivation for joint attention so that they may become more active (constructivist) participants in their own social learning (Kasari et al., 2006; Koegel et al., 2003; Sherer & Schreibman, 2005).

REFERENCES

American Psychiatric Association. (1980). *Diagnostic and statistical manual of mental disorders* (3rd ed.). Washington, DC: Author.

American Psychiatric Association. (1994). *Diagnostic and statistical manual of mental disorders* (4th ed.). Washington, DC: Author.

American Psychiatric Association. (2000). *Diagnostic and statistical manual of mental disorders* (4th ed., text revision). Washington, DC: Author.

Aslin, R., & Fiser, J. (2005). Methodological challenges for understanding cognitive changes in infants. *Trends in Cognitive Sciences* 9, 92–98.

Asperger, H. (1944). Die "Autistischen Psychopathen" im Kindesalter. *Archiv Für Psychiatrie und Nevenkrankheiten, 117*, 76–136.

Astafiev, S., Shulman, G., Stanley, C., Snyder, A., Essen, D., & Corbetta, M. (2003). Functional organization of human intraparietal and frontal cortex for attending, looking and pointing. *Journal of Neuroscience, 23*, 4689–4699.

Atsushi, S., Johnson, M., & Csibra, G. (2006). The development and neural basis of referential gaze perception. *Social Neuroscience, 13*, 220–234.

Bailey, A., Philips, W., & Rutter, M. (1996). Autism: Towards an integration of clinical, genetic, neuropsychological, and neurobiological perspectives. *Journal of Child Psychology and Psychiatry, 37*, 89–126.

Bakeman, R., & Adamson, L. (1984). Coordinating attention to people and objects in mother-infant and peer-infant interaction. *Child Development, 55*, 1278–1289.

Baldwin, D. (1995). *Understanding the link between joint attention and language*. In C. Moore & P. Dunham (Eds.), *Joint attention: Its origins and role in development* (pp. 131–158). Hillsdale, NJ: Erlbaum.

Baron-Cohen, S. (1989). Joint attention deficits in autism: Towards a cognitive analysis. *Development and Psychopathology, 3*, 185–190.

Baron-Cohen, S., Baldwin, D., & Crowson, M. (1997). Do children with autism use the speaker's direction of gaze strategy to crack the code of language? *Child Development, 68*, 48–57.

Baron-Cohen, S., Leslie, A., & Frith, U. (1985). Does the autistic child have a theory of mind? *Cognition, 21*, 37–46.

Bates, E., Benigni, L., Bretherton, I., Camaioni, L., & Volterrra, V. (1979). *The emergence of symbols: Cognition and communication in infancy*. New York: Academic Press.

Bettleheim, B. (1959). Joey: A "mechanical boy." *Scientific American, 200*, 117–126.

Bono, M., Daley, T., & Sigman, M. (2004). Joint attention moderates the relation between intervention and language development in young children with autism. *Journal of Autism and Related Disorders, 34*, 495–505.

Bornstein, M., & Sigman, M. (1986). Continuity in mental development from infancy. *Child Development, 57*, 251–274.

Bretherton, I. (1991). *Intentional communication and the development of an understanding of mind.* In D. Frye & C. Moore (Eds.), *Children's theories of mind: Mental states and social understanding* (pp. 49–75). Hillsdale, NJ: Erlbaum.

Brooks, R., & Meltzoff, A. (2002). The importance of eyes: How infants interpret adult looking behavior. *Developmental Psychology, 38*, 958–966.

Brooks, R., & Meltzoff, A. (2008). Infant gaze following and pointing predict accelerated vocabulary growth through two years of age. *Journal of Child Language, 35*, 207–220.

Bruner, J. S. (1975). From communication to language: A psychological perspective. *Cognition, 3*, 255–287.

Caplan, R., Chugani, H., Messa, C., Guthrie, D., Sigman, M., Traversay, J., et al. (1993). Hemispherectomy for early onset intractable seizures: Presurgical cerebral glucose metabolism and postsurgical nonverbal communication patterns. *Developmental Medicine and Child Neurology, 35*, 574–581.

Carpenter, M., Call, J., & Tomasello, M. (2005). Twelve and 18 month olds copy actions in terms of goals. *Developmental Science, 8*, 13–20.

Carpenter, M., Nagell, K., & Tomasello, M. (1998). Social-cognition, joint attention, and communicative competence from 9- to 15-months of age. *Monographs of the Society for Research in Child Development, 63* (4, Serial No. 255).

Cavanna, A., & Trimble, M. (2006). The precuneous: A review of its functional anatomy and behavioural correlates. *Brain, 10*, 1–20.

Charman, T. (2003). *Why is joint attention a pivotal skill in autism?* In U. Frith and E. Hill (Eds.). *Autism: Mind and brain* (pp. 67–87). New York: Oxford University Press.

Cherkassky, V., Kana, R., Keller, T., & Just, M. (2006). Functional connectivity in the baseline resting state network in autism. *Neuroreport, 17*, 1687–1690.

Cicchetti, D. (1984). The emergence of developmental psychopathology. *Child Development, 55*, 1–7.

Claussen, A., Mundy, P., Malik, S., & Willoughby, J. (2002). Joint attention and disorganized attachment status in at risk infants. *Development and Psychopathology, 14*, 279–292.

Corkum, V., & Moore, C. (1998). Origins of joint visual attention in infants. *Developmental Psychology, 34*, 28–38.

Curcio, F. (1978). Sensorimotor functioning and communication in mute autistic children. *Journal of Autism and Developmental Disorders, 8*, 281–292.

Dawson, G., & McKissick, F. C. (1984). Self-recognition in autistic children. *Journal of Autism and Developmental Disorders, 14*, 383–394.

Dawson, G., Osterling, J., Rinaldi, J., Carver, L., & McPartland, J. (2001). Brief report: Recognition memory and stimulus-reward associations: Indirect support for the role of ventromedial prefrontal dysfunction in autism. *Journal of Autism and Developmental Disorders, 31*, 337–341.

Dawson, G., Webb, S., Schellenberg, G., Dager, S., Friedman, S., Ayland, E., et al. (2002). Defining the broader phenotype of autism: Genetic, brain, and behavioral perspectives. *Development and Psychopathology, 14*, 581–612.

D'Entremont, B., Hains, S., & Muir, D. (1997). A demonstration of gaze following in 3- to 6- month-olds. *Infant Behavior and Development, 20*, 569–572.

Elman, J. (2005). Connectionist models of cognitive development: Where next. *Trends in Cognitive Science*, 9, 111–117.

Farroni, T., Massaccesi, S., & Francesca, S. (2002). Can the direction of gaze of another person shift the attention of a neonate? *Giornole-Italiano-di-Psicologia, 29*, 857–864.

Findlay, J., & Gilchrist, I. (2003). *Active vision: The psychology of looking and seeing*. New York: Oxford University Press.

Frieschen, A., Bayliss, A., & Tipper S. (2007). Gaze cueing of attention: Visual attention, social-cognition and individual differences. *Psychological Bulletin, 133*, 694–724.

Frith, U. (1989). *Autism: Explaining the enigma*. Oxford, UK: Basil Blackwell.

Greenough, W., Black, J., & Wallace, C. (1987). Experience and brain development. *Child Development, 58*, 539–559.

Griffith, E., Pennington, B., Wehner, E., & Rogers, S. (1999). Executive functions in young children with autism. *Child Development, 70*, 817–832.

Henderson, L., Yoder, P., Yale, M., & McDuffie, A. (2002). Getting the point: Electrophysiological correlates of protodeclarative pointing. *International Journal of Developmental Neuroscience, 20*, 449–458.

Hood, B., Willen, J., & Driver, J. (1998). Adult's eyes trigger shifts of visual attention in human infants. *Psychological Science*, 9, 131–134.

Howlin, P. (1978). *The assessment of social behavior*. In M. Rutter and E. Schopler (Eds.), *Autism: A reappraisal of concepts and treatment* (pp. 63–69). New York: Plenum Press.

Howlin, P. (1986). *An overview of social behavior in autism*. In E. Schopler & G. Mesibov (Eds.), *Social behavior in autism* (pp. 103–131). New York: Plenum Publishing.

Hunt, E. (1999). *Intelligence and human resources: Past, present and future.* In P. Ackerman, P. Kyllonen, & R. Roberts (Eds.), *Learning and individual differences: Process, trait and current determinants* (pp. 3–30). Washington, DC: APA Books.

Jellema, T., Baker, C., Wicker, B., & Perrett, D. (2000). Neural representation for the perception of intentionality of actions. *Brain and Cognition, 44,* 280–302.

Kanner, L. (1943). Autistic disorder of affective contact. *Nervous Child, 2,* 217–250.

Kanner, L. (1949). Problems of nosology and psychodynamics of early infantile autism. *American Journal of Orthopsychiatry, 19,* 416–426.

Kasari, C., Freeman, S., & Paparella, T. (2006). Joint attention and symbolic play in young children with autism: A randomized controlled intervention study. *Journal of Child Psychology and Psychiatry, 47,* 611–620.

Kasari, C., Freeman, S., & Paparella, T. (2007, April). *The UCLA RCT on Play and Joint Attention.* Paper presented at the Biennial Conference of the Society for Research on Child Development, Boston, MA.

Kasari, C., Sigman, M., Mundy, P., & Yirmiya, N. (1990). Affective sharing in the context of joint attention interactions of normal, autistic, and mentally retarded children. *Journal of Autism and Developmental Disorders, 20,* 87–100.

Koegel, L., Carter, C., & Koegel, R. (2003). Teaching children with autism self-initiations as a pivotal response. *Topics in Language Disorders, 23,* 134–145.

Langdell, T. (1978). Recognition of face: An approach to the study of autism. *Journal of the Child Psychology and Psychiatry, 19,* 255–268.

Leekam, S., Lopez, B., & Moore, C. (2000). Attention and joint attention in preschool children with autism. *Developmental Psychology, 36,* 261–273.

Leslie, A., & Happe, F. (1989). Autism and ostensive communication: The relevance of meta-representation. *Development and Psychopathology, 1,* 205–212.

Lewis, M., & McGurk, H. (1978). Evaluation of intelligence in infants. *Science, 178,* 1174–1177.

Lord, C., Floody, H., Anderson, D., & Pickles, A. (2003, April). *Social engagement in very young children with autism: Differences across contexts.* Paper presented at the Society for Research in Child Development, Tampa, FL.

Lovaas, O. I. (1987). Behavioral treatment and normal educational and intellectual functioning in young autistic children. *Journal of Consulting and Clinical Psychology, 55,* 3–9.

Loveland, K., & Landry, S. (1986). Joint attention and language in autism and developmental language delay. *Journal of Autism and Developmental Disorders, 16,* 335–349.

Mareschal, D., Johnson, M., Sirois, S., Spratling, S., Thomas, M., & Wasserman, G. (2007). *Neuroconstructivism: Volume 1. How the brain constructs cognition.* Oxford, UK: Oxford University Press.

Martin, J. (1996). *Neuroanatomy: Text and atlas* (2nd ed.). New York: McGraw-Hill.

Meltzoff, A. (2007). "Like me": a foundation for social-cognition. *Developmental Science, 10*, 126–134.

Miller, E., & Cohen, J. (2001). An integrative theory of prefrontal cortex functioning. *Annual Review of Neurosciences, 24*, 167–202.

Morales, M., Mundy, P., Crowson, M., Neal, R., & Delgado, C. (2005). Individual differences in infant attention skills, joint attention, and emotion regulation behavior. *International Journal of Behavioral Development, 29*, 259–263.

Morales, M., Mundy, P., & Rojas, J. (1998). Following the direction of gaze and language development in 6-month olds. *Infant Behavior and Development, 21*, 373–377.

Mundy, P. (1995). Joint attention and social-emotional approach behavior in children with autism. *Development and Psychopathology, 7*, 63–82.

Mundy, P. (2003). The neural basis of social impairments in autism: The role of the dorsal medial-frontal cortex and anterior cingulate system. *Journal of Child Psychology and Psychiatry and Allied Disciplines, 44*, 793–809.

Mundy, P. (in preparation). *Joint attention and our sharing minds.* New York: Guilford.

Mundy, P., Block, J., Vaughan Van Hecke, A., Delgadoa, C., Venezia Parlade, M., & Pomares, Y. (2007). Individual differences and the development of infant joint attention. *Child Development, 78*, 938–954.

Mundy, P., & Burnette, C. (2005). *Joint attention and neurodevelopment.* In F. Volkmar, A. Klin, & R. Paul (Eds.), *Handbook of autism and pervasive developmental disorders* (3rd ed., pp. 650–681). Hoboken, NJ: Wiley.

Mundy, P., Card, J., & Fox, N. (2000). EEG correlates of the development of infant joint attention skills. *Developmental Psychobiology, 36*, 325–338.

Mundy, P., & Crowson, M. (1997). Joint attention and early social communication: Implications for research on intervention with autism. *Journal of Autism and Developmental Disorders, 27*, 653–676.

Mundy, P., Fox, N., & Card, J. (2003). Joint attention, EEG coherence and early vocabulary development. *Developmental Science, 6*, 48–54.

Mundy, P., & Gomes A. (1998). Individual differences in joint attention skill development in the second year. *Infant Behavior and Development, 21*, 469–482.

Mundy, P., Kasari, C., & Sigman, M. (1992). Nonverbal communication, affective sharing, and intersubjectivity. *Infant Behavior and Development, 15*, 377–381.

Mundy, P., & Newell, L. (2007). Attention, joint attention and social-cognition. *Current Directions in Psychological Science, 16*, 269–274.

Mundy, P., & Sigman, M. (1989a). *Specifying the nature of the social impairment in autism*. In G. Dawson (Ed.), *Autism: New perspectives on diagnosis, nature, and treatment* (pp. 3–21). New York: Guilford.

Mundy, P., & Sigman, M. (1989b). Theoretical implications of joint attention deficits in autism. *Development and Psychopathology, 1*, 173–184.

Mundy, P., & Sigman, M. (2006). *Joint attention, social competence and developmental psychopathology*. In D. Cicchetti and D. Cohen (Eds.), *Developmental Psychopathology: Vol. 1. Theory and Methods* (2nd ed., pp. 293–332). Hoboken, NJ: Wiley.

Mundy, P., Sigman, M., & Kasari, C. (1993). *The autistic person's theory of mind and early nonverbal joint attention deficits*. In S. Baron-Cohen, H. Tager- Flusberg, D. Cohen, & F. Volkmar (Eds.), *Understanding other minds: Perspectives from autism* (pp. 181–201). Oxford, UK: Oxford University Press.

Mundy, P., Sigman, M., & Kasari, C. (1994). Joint attention, developmental level, and symptom presentation in children with autism. *Development and Psychopathology*, 6, 389–401.

Mundy, P., Sigman, M. D., Ungerer, J., & Sherman, T. (1986). Defining the social deficits of autism: The contribution of non-verbal communication measures. *Journal of Child Psychology and Psychiatry, 27*, 657–669.

Mundy, P., & Vaughan Van Hecke, A. (2008). *Neural systems, gaze following and the development of joint attention*. In C. Nelson & M. Luciana (Eds.), *Handbook of developmental cognitive neuroscience* (pp. 819–837). New York: Oxford University Press.

Nation, K., & Penny, S. (2008). Sensitivity to eye gaze in autism: Is it normal? Is it automatic? Is it social? *Development and Psychopathology, 20*, 79–97.

Nichols, K. E., Fox, N., & Mundy, P. (2005). Joint attention, self-recognition and neurocognitive functioning. *Infancy, 7*, 35–51.

Piaget, J. (1952). *The origins of intelligence in children*. New York: Norton.

Posner, M. I., & Petersen, S. (1990). The attention system of the human brain. *Annual Review of Neuroscience, 13*, 25–42.

Posner, M. I., & Rothbart, M. (2007). *Educating the human brain*. Washington, DC: APA.

Premack, D., & Woodruff, G. (1978). Does the chimpanzee have a theory of mind. *Behavioral and Brain Science, 1*, 515–526.

Rimland, B. (1964). *Infantile autism: The syndrome and its implications for a neural theory of behavior*. New York: Appleton-Century-Crofts.

Rogers, S. (2004). Developmental regression in autism spectrum disorders. *Mental Retardation and Developmental Disabilities Research Reviews, 10,* 139–143.

Scaife, M., & Bruner, J. (1975). The capacity for joint visual attention in the infant. *Nature, 253,* 265–266.

Seibert, J. M., Hogan, A. E., & Mundy, P. C. (1982). Assessing interactional competencies: The early social-communication scales. *Infant Mental Health Journal, 3,* 244–258.

Shapiro, T., Sherman, M., Calamari, G., & Koch, D. (1987). Attachment in autism and other developmental disorders. *Journal of the American Academy of Child and Adolescent Psychiatry, 26,* 480–484.

Sheinkopf, S., Mundy, P., Claussen, A., & Willoughby, J. (2004). Infant joint attention skill and preschool behavioral outcomes in at-risk children. *Development and Psychopathology, 16,* 273–293.

Sherer, M., & Schreibman, L. (2005). Individual behavioral profiles and predictors of treatment effectiveness for children with autism. *Journal of Consulting and Clinical Psychology, 73,* 525–538.

Sigman, M. & Mundy, P. (1989). Social attachments in autistic children. *Journal of the American Academy of Child and Adolescent Psychiatry, 28,* 74–81.

Sigman, M., Mundy, P., Sherman, T., & Ungerer, J. (1986). Social interactions of autistic, mentally retarded, and normal children and their caregivers. *Journal of Child Psychology and Psychiatry, 27,* 647–656.

Sigman, M., & Ruskin, E. (1999). Continuity and change in the social competence of children with autism, Down's syndrome, and developmental delays. *Monographs of the Society for Research in Child Development, 64* (1, Serial No. 256).

Sigman, M., & Ungerer, J. (1984). Attachment behaviors in autistic children. *Journal of Autism and Related Disabilities, 14,* 231–244.

Slaughter, V., & McConnell, D. (2003). Emergence of joint attention: Relationships between gaze following, social referencing, imitation, and naming in infancy. *Journal of Genetic Psychology, 164,* 54–71.

Smith, L., & Ulvund, L. (2003). The role of joint attention in later development among preterm children: Linkages between early and middle childhood. *Social Development, 12,* 222–234.

Smith, T., Groen, A., & Wynn, J. (2000). Randomized trial of intensive early intervention for children with pervasive developmental disorder. *American Journal on Mental Retardation, 105,* 269–285.

Sroufe, L. A., & Rutter, M. (1984). The domain of developmental psychopathology. *Child Development, 55*, 17–29.

Stone, W., Coonrod, E., & Ousley, C. (1997). Brief report: Screening tool for autism in two year olds (STAT): Development and preliminary data. *Journal of Autism and Developmental Disorders, 30*, 607–612.

Striano, T., Chen, X., Cleveland, A., & Bradshaw, S. (2006a). Joint attention social cues influence infant learning. *European Journal of Developmental Psychology, 3*, 289–299.

Striano, T., Reid, V., & Hoel, S. (2006b). Neural mechanisms of joint attention in infancy. *European Journal of Neuroscience, 23*, 2819–2823.

Striano, T., & Stahl, D. (2005). Sensitivity to triadic attention in early infancy. *Developmental Science, 8*, 333–343.

Tomasello, M. (1995). *Joint attention as social-cognition.* In C. Moore and P. Dunham (Eds.), *Joint attention: Its origins and role in development* (pp. 103–130). Hillsdale, NJ: Lawrence Erlbaum.

Tomasello, M., & Call, J. (1997). *Primate cognition.* New York: Oxford University Press.

Tomasello, M. & Carpenter, M. (2005). The emergence of social-cognition in three chimpanzees. *Monographs of the Society for Research in Child Development, 70*, No. 279, 1–131.

Tomasello, M., Carpenter, M., Call, J., Behne, T., & Moll, H. (2005). Understanding sharing intentions: The origins of cultural cognition. *Brain and Behavior Sciences, 28*, 675–690.

Tomasello, M., & Farrar, M. J. (1986). Joint attention and early language. *Child Development, 57*, 1454–1463.

Tomasello, M., Hare, B., Lehman, H., & Call, J. (2006). Reliance on head versus eyes in the gaze following of great apes and humans: The cooperative eyes hypothesis. *Journal of Human Evolution, 52*, 314–320.

Torkildsen, J., Thormodsen, R., Syvensen, G., Smith, L., & Lindgren, M. (2008, March). *Brain correlates of nonverbal communicative comprehension in 20–24 month olds*. Paper presented at the International Conference on Infant Studies, Vancouver, BC, Canada.

Ulvund, S., & Smith, L. (1996). The predictive validity of nonverbal communicative skills in infants with perinatal hazards. *Infant Behavior and Development, 19*, 441–449.

Ungerer, J., & Sigman, M. (1981). Symbolic play and language comprehension in autistic children. *Journal of the American Academy of Child Psychiatry, 20*, 318–337.

Vaughan, A., Mundy, P., Block, J., Burnette, C., Delgado, C., Gomez, Y., et al. (2003). Child, caregiver, and temperament contributions to infant joint attention. *Infancy, 4*, 603–616.

Vaughan Van Hecke, A., Mundy, P., Acra, F., Block, J., Delgado, C., & Venezia, M. (2007). Infant joint attention, temperament, and social competence in preschool children. *Child Development, 78*, 938–954.

Venezia, M., Messinger, D., Thorp, D., & Mundy, P. (2004). Timing changes: The development of anticipatory smiling. *Infancy*, 6, 397–406.

Volkmar, F. R., Cohen, D. J., Bregman, J. D., Hooks, M. Y., & Stevenson, J. M. (1989). An examination of social typologies in autism. *Journal of the American Academy of Child and Adolescent Psychiatry, 28*, 82–86.

Werner, H., & Kaplan, B. (1963). *Symbol formation*. Oxford, UK: Wiley.

Wetherby, A., Allen, L., Cleary, J., Kublin, K., & Goldstein, H. (2002). Validity and reliability of the communication and symbolic behavior scales developmental profile with very young children. *Journal of Speech, Language, and Hearing Research*, 45, 1202–1218.

Wetherby, A., & Prutting, C. (1984). Profiles of communicative and cognitive-social abilities in autistic children. *Journal of Speech and Hearing Research, 27*, 367–377.

Williams, J., Waiter, G., Perra, O., A., Perrett, D., Murray, A., & Whitten, A. (2005). An fMRI study of joint attention experience. *NeuroImage, 25*, 133–140.

Wimmer, H., & Perner, J. (1983). Beliefs about beliefs: Representation and constraint functions of wrong beliefs in young children. *Cognition, 13*, 102–128.

Wing, L., & Gould J. (1979). Severe impairments of social interaction and associated abnormalities in children: Epidemiology and classification. *Journal of Autism and Developmental Disorders*, 9, 11–29.

Wing, L., & Potter, D. (2002). The epidemiology of autistic spectrum disorders: Is the prevalence rising? *Mental Retardation and Developmental Disabilities Research*, 8, 151–161.

CHAPTER

4

Enhancing Self-Regulation in School and Clinic

Mary K. Rothbart, Michael I. Posner, M. R. Rueda, Brad E. Sheese, Yiyuan Tang

In this chapter, we describe a program of translational research on temperamental effortful control and executive attention. This program, carried out in Oregon and New York over the past 3 decades, combined two major strands of theory and research. The first strand was research on individual differences in effortful control (Rothbart, 2007). The construct of effortful control has added a new perspective to the study of individual differences in temperament, taking it beyond emotional reactivity to include the development of self-regulation. The second strand was the discovery of a specific set of brain areas (the executive attention network; Posner & Raichle, 1994) that work to regulate the operation of cognitive and emotional networks to which they are connected. Evidence for the executive attention network's involvement in self-regulation led us to combine our research efforts on the development of individual differences in attention. Our research and that of our

This research was supported by NICHD grant HD 38051 and by the James S. Bower and John Templeton Foundations and the Dana Foundation Grant for the Arts.

colleagues has linked behavior to efficiency of brain networks and to the influence of genes and experience on behavior. In addition, we used our basic advances in the study of brain and behavior to devise interventions to improve executive attention in children and adults.

TRANSLATIONAL RESEARCH

Ideas about translational research are not new (Cicchetti & Gunnar, this volume). Indeed, developmental psychologists have long been engaged in the study of evolutionarily conserved systems, especially those involved in self-regulation, with their implications for plasticity and change in development. Because these systems develop and are multiply influenced, their adequate study requires longitudinal and experimental study at multiple levels of analysis (Cicchetti & Blender, 2004). A critical aspect of this analysis is behavioral. Behavioral study is needed not only to establish meaningful links with the neural substrate, but also to permit study of the organism in context, allowing examination of influence from the social and individual levels down as well as from the neural levels up. Finally, interactions across these levels bring us back to the evolutionary issues: Cognition, emotion, and behavior all contribute to survival. In this chapter, we describe the steps in theory and research that have led us to the implementation of interventions to train a self-regulative network—the executive attention network. At the paper's conclusion, we also present a few reflections on our translational research.

Working As a Team

The vision emerging from our collaboration (MIP and MKR) has been to ask questions we would not have asked if working independently. The seeds of our collaboration were sown when Rothbart, in her infant-temperament research, began to note that individual differences in orienting and attentional control were critical aspects of temperament. This led to joint discussion around fundamental questions like, What is attention? (see an important answer by Posner & Petersen, 1990, and Posner & Raichle [1994]). In the course of this discussion, we were inspired to attempt to apply an attentional network, theoretical framework to guide developmental research.

In 1980 at the Nebraska Symposium on Motivation (Rothbart & Posner, 1980), we started to formally put our ideas together. This was followed by grant proposals and eventually by funding from the National Institutes of Health to support an attention and temperament laboratory for the study of the development of self-regulation. We began with studies of orienting and postdoctoral and graduate students soon joined us. At the time we felt like rather hesitant pioneers, because in the early 1990s, crossing the boundaries between cognition and emotion was relatively uncharted territory.

Studying Effortful Control

Our work on the executive attention network and its offshoots was inspired by our temperament research. *Temperament* is defined as constitutionally based individual differences in emotional, motor, and attentional reactivity (measured by latency, intensity, and recovery of response) and self-regulation (processes that modulate reactivity) (Rothbart & Bates, 2006; Rothbart & Derryberry, 1981). Temperamental processes develop over time, and are influenced by both genes and experience.

Examining caregiver reports of children's temperament has revealed three higher-order factors (Ahadi, Rothbart, & Ye, 1993; Rothbart, Ahadi, Hershey, & Fisher, 2001). The first two factors are reactive: Surgency/Extraversion—including activity level, sociability, impulsivity, and enjoyment of high-intensity pleasures—and Negative Affectivity, including fear, anger/frustration, discomfort, and sadness. The third broad factor we labeled Effortful Control (EC), including inhibitory control, the ability to focus and shift attention, and sensitivity to low-intensity stimuli. EC describes children's ability to perform under conditions of conflict and their general ability to control themselves.

EC makes a crucial contribution to socialization. It is possible to measure EC by parent questionnaire when the children are in the second or third years of life and beyond. Over the preschool years, children become increasingly able to voluntarily deploy their attention, allowing them to regulate their more reactive tendencies. Individual differences in EC allow children to suppress their more reactive tendencies, take in additional sources of information, and plan more efficient strategies for coping. Whereas children under 2 1/2 years show considerable difficulty in inhibiting one action in order to perform an instructed action, they become increasingly able to control their behavior and to both inhibit and activate responses under instructions.

EC is related to the development of conscience (Kochanska, Murray, & Harlan, 2000) and to empathy, social competence, and compliance. Lower EC is related to higher aggression, more frequent problem behaviors, and adolescent and adult psychopathology (see reviews by Eisenberg, Smith, Sadovsky, & Spinrad, 2004; Rothbart, 2007; Rothbart & Bates, 2006). Higher EC is also related to lower negative emotionality (Rothbart & Sheese, 2007). EC is critically important in the socialization and adaptation of the child.

Our research identified clues to the specific mechanisms through which EC develops. We proposed that the roots of EC lie in the functioning of the executive attention network (Posner & Rothbart, 1998, 2007; Rothbart, Derryberry, & Posner, 1994). Recent imaging data have supported this idea (Whittle, 2007). In the next sections of this paper, we describe advances in our understanding of executive attention at behavioral and neural levels and links between EC and executive attention.

The Anatomy of Executive Attention

The executive attention network is one of three neural attention networks. These networks serve different functions, have different neural anatomies, and involve different neuromodulators (Posner & Fan, 2004; Rueda, Posner, & Rothbart, 2004). The first two networks, the alerting and orienting networks, involve maintenance of an alert state and orienting to attend to potentially meaningful incoming stimuli. The third, the executive attention network, functions to monitor and resolve conflict between information that is being processed by other brain networks (Botvinick, Braver, Barch, Carter, & Cohen, 2001). This conflict-resolution function, which involves both the promotion and suppression of activation in other networks, may be central to conscious self-regulatory efforts.

We begin with a collaborative effort to understand the functions of a high-level attention network (executive attention) found to be active during tasks related to conflict (Botvinick et. al, 2001; Fan, Flombaum, McCandliss, Thomas, & Posner, 2003; Posner, Rothbart, Sheese, & Tang, 2007). In this chapter, we first summarize findings about this network in a way that will make potential applications clear, discussing the functional anatomy of the executive attention network. A number of studies have confirmed close relationships of executive attention to reports of parents concerning children's abilities to display effortful control of their feelings and behavior. These findings are summarized in the section on Development. The relation of individual differences in the efficiency of this network as measured in cognitive tasks to parental reports of their children's effortful control led us to ask how genes and environment shape this network. In the section on Genes and Environment, we propose that human evolution may be selecting genetic variations that make it possible to achieve cultural influence over behavior. Because studies of psychopathology and education both suggest the importance of executive attention, enhancement of network operations could in principle lead to prevention of deficits and support of student achievement. These connections are discussed in the section on Attention in School and Clinic. Since the culture acting through the parents seemed to be important in shaping network efficiency, we were led to propose training exercises that might enhance the operation of the network. These are described in our section on Enhancing Self-Regulation. Using findings on self-regulation to enhance education and performance would be important translations of these basic science discoveries to clinic and school. In the final Translation section we discuss difficulties that need to be overcome before secure translation can be made of these discoveries.

FUNCTIONAL ANATOMY

Studies of attention have revealed a frontal brain anatomy active in a wide variety of difficult cognitive and emotional tasks. This network of brain areas is thought to deal with situations requiring a nonhabitual response when there is conflict between different brain networks (Botvinick et al., 2001). Although all parts of the network may not be fully known, Figure 4.1 illustrates that the anterior cingulate and lateral frontal areas appear

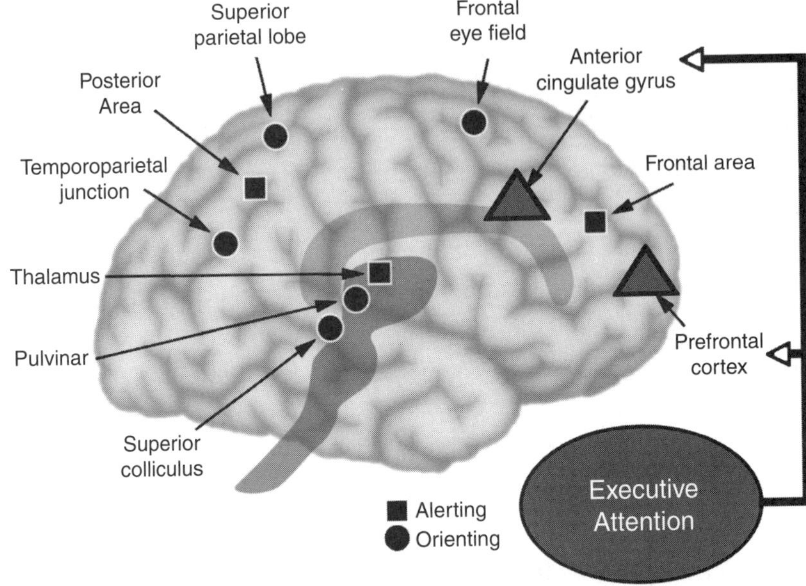

Figure 4.1 The Attention System of the human brain has three networks illustrated in this figure. The executive network in relation to its role in self-regulation is the special focus of this chapter (large triangle). The alerting network (squares) and the orienting network (circles) are also shown.

to be common areas involved in this network (Fan, McCandliss, Fossella, Flombaum, & Posner, 2005). This network is involved in more general cognitive functions. One important study (Duncan et al., 2000) examined a wide range of verbal, spatial, and object tasks selected from intelligence tests that had in common a strong loading on the factor of general intelligence (g). These items were contrasted with perceptually similar control items that did not require the kind of attention thought to be involved in general intelligence. This subtraction led to differential activity in two major areas that are part of this network. One was the anterior cingulate and the second was the lateral prefrontal cortex.

Conflict

Many imaging studies have been conducted using either the Stroop task or variants of it that involved conflict among elements (Bush, Luu, & Posner, 2000). The Stroop task requires the person to respond to the

	Stroop Task (naming the color)	**Number Stroop Task** (counting the items)	**Flanker Task** (indicating the direction of the center arrow)
Congruent condition	**GREEN** (ink color *green*)	3 3 3	→ → → → →
Incongruent condition	**BLUE** (ink color *red*)	6 6 6 6	→ → ← → →

Figure 4.2 Several cognitive tasks shown to activate the executive attention network.

color of ink of a target, which can be a conflicting color word (see Fig. 4.2, top left). Another conflict task, the Attention Network Test (ANT), introduces flanking arrows that either point in the direction of the target or in the opposite direction. In a version of the numerical Stroop task used with trained primates (see Fig. 4.2, bottom panel) it was found that both humans and monkeys took additional time to respond during conflict trials. In fact, the increase in RT was about the same for the two species; but while humans rarely made an error, macaques made almost 25% errors on the conflict trials even after many hundreds of training trials. These findings suggest that their network for resolving conflict is not as efficient as that of human beings (Washburn, 1994).

Using functional magnetic resonance imaging (fMRI) techniques with adult participants, we examined three conflict tasks, two of which were suitable for children, to determine areas of activation for each task (Fan, Fossella, Sommer, & Posner, 2003). We found that all three tasks activated a common focus in the anterior cingulate cortex (ACC) and in addition, all activated similar areas of the lateral prefrontal cortex. In our view, the dorsal area of the anterior cingulate has been shown to be active primarily in cognitive tasks like the Stroop, while tasks that have a more emotional component activate a more ventral part of the cingulate (Bush et al., 2000). Although there are different views about how best to divide the cingulate into functional areas, this view fits with the patterns of connectivity discussed in the following section. We have argued that in humans the role of the anterior cingulate is to regulate the processing of information from other networks, serving as a part of an executive attention network involved in the control of both cognition and emotion. Support for this idea also comes from many studies of the connectivity of the anterior cingulate with other brain areas that are discussed in the next section.

Connectivity

A possible difference between humans and other primates in their control of cognition and emotion may lie in differences in the degree of connectivity that the anterior cingulate has to other parts of the brain. As mentioned previously, the more dorsal part of the ACC has been identified with cognitive control, while the more ventral part with emotional control. One way to examine this issue is to image the structural connections of different parts of the cingulate using diffusion tensor imaging (DTI). *Myelin* is the fatty sheath that forms around the axons of neurons to speed up neuronal transmission. DTI uses the diffusion of water molecules in particular directions due to the presence of myelinated fibers, to provide a way of examining the physical connections present in the brain. A DTI analysis of humans confirms animal studies indicating that the dorsal part of the ACC is connected to cortical areas of the parietal and frontal lobes, while the ventral part of the ACC has strong connections to subcortical limbic areas (Posner, Sheese, Odludas, & Tang, 2006).

It is also possible to use fMRI to examine the functional connectivity between brain areas during the performance of a task (Posner et al., 2006). Two recent studies illustrate the use of fMRI to trace the interaction of the anterior cingulate with other brain areas. In one study, subjects were required to switch between auditory and visual modalities (Crottaz-Herbette & Mennon, 2006). The dorsal anterior cingulate was coupled to visual brain areas when the instruction was to attend to visual events and to auditory brain areas when instructed to attend auditory events. Another study (Etkin, Egner, Peraza, Kandel, & Hirsch, 2006) required subjects to resolve conflict related to negative emotion. The ventral anterior cingulate was shown to be coupled to the amygdala in this form of conflict resolution. Studies requiring people to control their positive (Beauregard, Levesque, & Bourgouin, 2001) or negative emotional reactions (Ochsner et al., 2001) to stimuli have shown strong activation in the anterior cingulate in comparison to viewing the same stimuli without exercising control.

Comparative anatomical studies point to important differences in the evolution of cingulate connectivity between nonhuman primates and humans. While the anterior cingulate is a very ancient structure, it seems to have undergone considerable change in recent evolution. Anatomical studies show a great expansion of white matter, which has increased more in recent evolution than has the neocortex itself (Zilles, 2005). One type of projection cell, the Von Economo neuron, is found only in the anterior cingulate and a related area of the anterior insula (Allman, Watson, Tetreault, & Hakeem, 2005). It is thought that this neuron is important in communication between the cingulate and other brain areas. This neuron is not present at all in macaques and expands greatly in frequency between great apes and humans.

The two brain areas in which von Economo neurons are found (anterior cingulate and anterior insula) are also shown to be in close communication in human studies, even when participants are in the resting state (Dosenbach et al., 2007). There is also some evidence that the frequency of the neuron's activity increases in development between infancy and later childhood (Allman et al., 2005). In our view, this neuron and the rapid and efficient connectivity it provides may be an important reason why self-regulation in adult humans can be so much stronger than in other organisms. Lateral areas of the prefrontal cortex may play a more important role in regulation in macaques, where it has been found that lesions of dorsolateral prefrontal cortex interrupt the resolution of conflict in a task requiring memory, while lesions of the anterior cingulate do not (Mansouri, Buckley, & Tanaka, 2007).

The development of executive attention is also related to achievements in self-regulation that we have documented between infancy and age 7 to 8. In the next section we trace this development.

DEVELOPMENT

Much of the work described in the last section rests upon our ability to image brain activity using methods like fMRI. This method is less available for use with infants and young children because of the difficulty in their keeping still. However, many studies of adults have shown that brain areas involved in attention and other cognitive functions give rise to electrical activity that can be sensed by scalp electrodes (Posner et al., 2006). Our strategy for the study of development has been to use tasks similar to those found to activate attentional networks in adults and to monitor our success by use of large numbers of scalp electrodes that can relate electrical patterns from the scalp to underlying brain areas that are parts of the attentional network.

We (Posner and Rothbart, 2007) have been interested in how the attention system develops in infancy and early childhood. The development of executive attention can be easily observed both by questionnaire and by cognitive tasks after about age 2.5 to 4 years. At this age, parents can identify the ability of their children to regulate their emotions and control their behaviors in accord with social demands. However, in infancy it has been difficult to pose questions that refer to effortful control because most regulation seems automatic or involves the caregiver's intervention. Obviously, infants cannot be instructed to press a key in accord with a particular rule.

Infancy

We have been examining executive attention in infancy to see if we can predict later executive attention and effortful control from infant behavior. Detecting errors has been an important method for activation of the executive attention network (Bush et al., 2000). One study examined the ability of 7-month-old infants to detect errors (Berger, Tzur, & Posner, 2006). In this study, infants observed a scene in which one or two puppets were hidden behind a screen. A hand was seen to reach behind the screen and either add or remove a puppet. The screen was then removed and the infant saw either a correct or incorrect number of puppets. Wynn (1992) found that infants of 7 months looked longer when the number was in error than when it was correct. Whether the increased looking time involved the same executive attention circuitry that is active in adults during error detection was unknown.

Berger and colleges (Berger et al., 2006) replicated the Wynn study but used 128-channel EEG to determine the brain activity that occurred

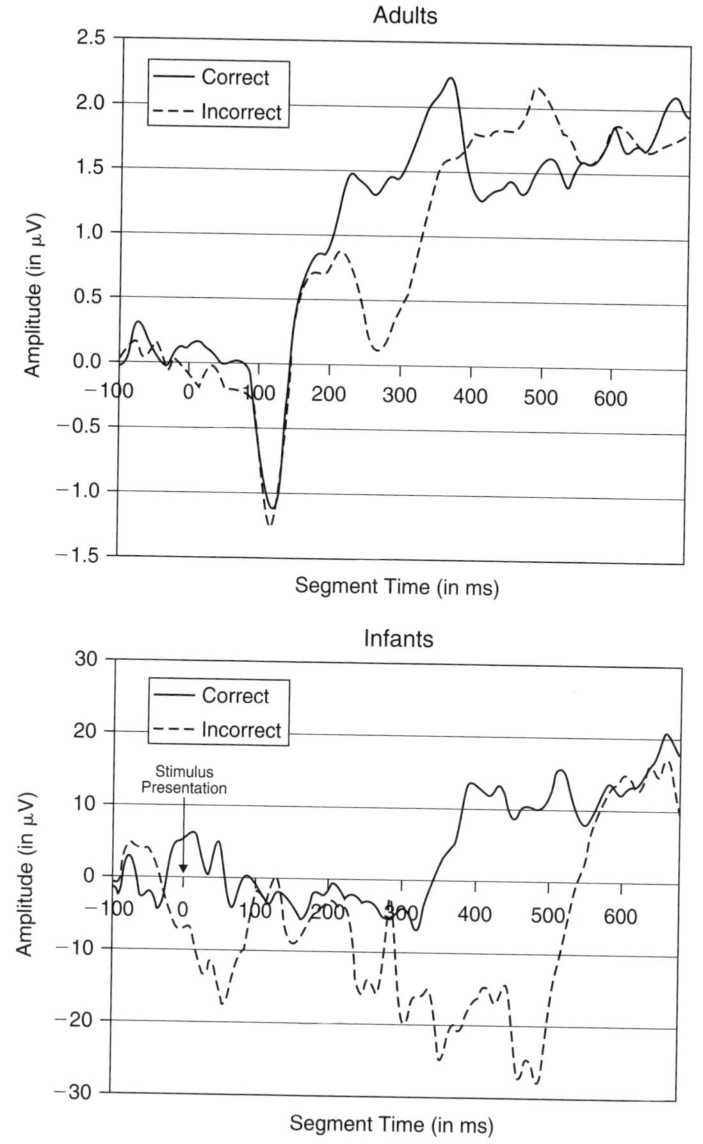

Figure 4.3 Event-related potentials for adults (top) and infants (bottom) for correct and incorrect stimuli (after Berger et al., 2006).

during error trials in comparison with that found when the infant viewed a correct solution. The results, as illustrated in Figure 4.3, indicate that the same EEG component over the same electrode sites differed between conditions for both infants and adults. As you look at the adult data in the top panel you can see that correct and error trials start to differ around 200 millisec in a component of the overall wave form called the frontal N2. This EEG component is thought to come from the anterior cingulate gyrus and/or surrounding mid-frontal areas (Dehaene, Posner, & Tucker, 1994). The infant waveforms in the bottom panel look somewhat different overall, but they show the same departure between error and correct trials at about 300 millisec. It is usual for infant electrical activity to be somewhat slower, but overall it appears that the same brain anatomy is involved as in adult studies. Of course, the result of activating this anatomy for observing an error is not the same as found in adults for self-made errors, where adults actually slow down after an error and adjust their performance. However, it suggests that even very early in life the anatomy of the executive attention system is at least partly in place.

Our most recent longitudinal study also began with infants of 7 months (Sheese, Rothbart, Posner, White, & Fraundorf, in press). We studied eye movements that occurred when attractive stimuli appear in a fixed sequence of locations on a screen in front of the child. On most occasions the children moved their eyes to the stimulus after it appeared, but on some occasions they moved their eyes to the location where the stimulus was about to occur prior to it being presented. We argued that these anticipatory movements represent an early form of executive attention because they rely upon a voluntary response that anticipates the visual event. In support of the idea that the anticipatory movements reflected the executive attention system, we had previously found that 3.5-year-olds showed a correlation between performance in voluntary key press tasks and their correct anticipations when performing in the visual sequence (Rothbart, Ellis, Rueda, & Posner, 2003).

In the first session of our longitudinal study we used the eye-movement task adapted from Clohessy, Posner, and Rothbart (2001). Infants were also given a task in which they were presented with novel objects and one in which they looked at novel, somewhat disturbing masks (Sheese et al., in press). Correct anticipatory looks were related to more hesitant initial approach to the toys, including longer latencies to initial reaching and longer durations of looking without physically touching the toy. Infants rated by their parents as higher in positive affect (often called *surgency*) also showed shorter latencies to physically engage the toys and higher frequencies of engagement. These results suggest that an early form of executive attention may allow for the dampening of positive affect and inhibition of related approach tendencies. Correct anticipatory looks were also positively related to greater use of sucking as a self-soothing mechanism during the mask presentation. These results indicate that anticipatory looking is related both to caution in reaching toward novel toys and to aspects of the regulation of distress in infancy. They also suggest that executive attention is present in infancy and can serve as one basis for the regulation of emotion.

Childhood

Gerardi-Caulton (2000) carried out some of the first research linking effortful control (EC), based on parents' reports of their children's behavior, to underlying brain networks of executive attention measured in conflict situations such as the Stroop task. Because children of preschool age typically do not read, location and identity rather than word meaning and ink color served as the dimensions in the spatial conflict task. Children sat in front of two response keys, one located to the child's left and one to the right. Each key displayed a picture. On every trial, a picture identical to one of the pair appeared on either the left or right side of the screen. Children were rewarded for responding to the identity of the stimulus regardless of its spatial compatibility with the matching response key (Gerardi-Caulton, 2000). Reduced accuracy and slowed reaction times for spatially incompatible trials in comparison with spatially compatible trials reflected the effort required to resolve conflict between identity and location. Performance on this task also produces a clear interference effect in adults and activates the anterior cingulate (Fan, Flombaum, et al., 2003).

Children 24 months of age tended to use one response regardless of what was correct, while 36-month-old children performed at high accuracy levels. Like adults, however, they responded more slowly and with reduced accuracy levels to conflict trials. Greater efficiency in spatial conflict performance was also related to parent reports of effortful control and higher performance on laboratory tests of inhibitory control

		Congruent trials		Incongruent trials		Conflict effect	
AGE	TASK	RT	% correct	RT	% correct	RT	% correct
2	Spatial conflict (touch-screen)	3476	69.1	3378	53.9	−98	−15.2
2½		2489	80.8	3045	57.8	556	−23.0
3		2465	90.1	3072	80.3	607	−9.8
4	Flanker (Child ANT)	1490	89.4	1913	77.1	424	−13.0
6	Flanker (Child ANT)	890	92.0	1005	76.4	115	−15.6
7		828	94.6	891	93.9	63	−0.7
8		791	95.0	862	95.3	71	+0.3
9		724	98.1	791	96.5	67	−1.6
10		624	98.7	693	96.6	69	−2.1
adults		473	99.5	534	97.9	61	−1.6

Figure 4.4 Overall RTs and Conflict scores on child conflict tasks for children age 2 to adults. From age 4 tasks involve Child ANT (after Rueda, Posner, & Rothbart, 2004).

(Gerardi-Caulton, 2000). Similar correspondence between parent reports of temperamental effortful control and performance on laboratory attention tasks have been shown with 24-, 30-, and 36-month-olds (Rothbart et al., 2003); 3- and 5-year-olds (Chang & Burns, 2005); 7-year-olds (Gonzales, Fuentes, Carranza, & Estevez, 2001); and 12-year-olds (Checa, Rodriguez-Bailon, & Rueda, submitted).

The development of executive attention has also been traced into the primary school period (Rueda, Fan, et al., 2004) using a child version of the Attention Networks Test (ANT). The results of several studies using the ANT are shown in Figure 3.4. Reaction times for the children are much longer than for adults, but there is impressive development in the speed of resolving conflict from age 4 to about 7 years of age. Rather surprisingly, the ability to resolve conflict on the flanker task, as measured by the ANT, remained about the same from age 7 to adulthood. Nonetheless, studies in which the difficulty of the conflict task is increased by other demands such as switching rules or holding more information in working memory have shown further development of conflict resolution between late childhood and adulthood (Davidson, Amso, Anderson, & Diamond, 2006).

Adolescence

During adolescence, effortful control has been linked to the brain areas involved in self-regulation by imaging studies (Whittle, 2007). Whittle had 155 adolescents fill out a temperament scale (Ellis and Rothbart, 2001) and also measured the size of different brain structures and their activity. She found that the dorsal anterior cingulate size was positively correlated to effortful control and that the ventral anterior cingulate activity was negatively related to effortful control. These structural and functional findings may relate to the mutual inhibition between the ventral and dorsal cingulate that has been reported in other imaging studies (Drevets and Raichle, 1998).

During adolescence, individual differences in effortful control and executive attention have been related to frequency of antisocial behavior (Ellis & Rothbart, 2001). This may reflect different levels of maturation of prefrontal and subcortical brain areas (Galvan et al., 2006). These findings suggest that while much of the development of executive attention is accomplished in early childhood there remain other aspects of brain networks related to behavior that continue to show changes into adulthood.

GENES AND ENVIRONMENT

The anatomy of executive attention is roughly common to all people and appears to be present even in infancy. This suggests that it has a genetic origin. However, individuals differ in the efficiency of their networks. Studies of effortful control reveal marked individual differences that are stable over relatively long periods. These individual differences could reflect genetic variation. A step toward understanding this genetic variation is to determine if differences in genes are related to individual differences in executive attention and effortful control.

Identifying Genes

Initial studies on genetic influences on attention used adults as participants. The ANT was used to examine the individual efficiency of the executive network (Fan, McCandliss, Sommer, Raz, & Posner, 2002). In a sample of 40 adults, executive network scores were found to be reliable over repeated presentations. The ability to measure differences in attention raised the question of the degree to which executive attention is heritable. To explore this issue, the ANT was used to assess attention in monozygotic and dizygotic same-sex twins (Fan, Wu, Fossella, & Posner, 2001). We found strong evidence for heritability of variations in the efficacy of the executive network.

The executive attention network is modulated by input from dopamine-rich brain areas such as the ventral tegmental area. The association of the executive network with the neuromodulator dopamine led us to examine genes related to dopamine receptors and transporters as a means of searching for candidates that might relate to the efficiency of attentional networks (Fossella et al., 2002). The dopamine 4 receptor was an obvious candidate because of its association with attention-deficit disorders (Swanson et al., 2000).

To carry out these studies, 200 persons performed the ANT and were genotyped to examine frequent polymorphisms in genes related to dopamine. We found significant association of two genes with executive attention: the dopamine D4 receptor (DRD4) gene and the monoamine oxidase A (MAO-A) gene. We then conducted a neuroimaging experiment in which persons with different alleles of these two genes were compared while they performed the ANT (Fan, Fossela, et al., 2003). Groups with different alleles of these genes showed differences in the ability to resolve conflict as measured by the ANT and also produced significantly different activations in the anterior cingulate, a major node of the executive attention network as discussed in the previous section.

Recent studies have extended these observations. In two different studies employing conflict-related tasks other than the ANT, alleles of the catechol-o-methyl transferase (COMT) gene were also found to be related to the ability to resolve conflict (Blasi et al., 2005; Diamond, Briand, Fossella, & Gehlbach, 2004). A study using the child ANT showed a significant relation between the dopamine transporter gene, DAT1, and executive attention (Rueda, Rothbart, McCandliss, Saccamannno, & Posner, 2005). There is also increasing evidence that the serotonin system plays a role in executive attention along with the dopamine system (Canli et al., 2005; Reuter, Ott, Vaidl, & Hennig, 2007).

Gene–Environment Interactions

In our longitudinal study, we used cheek swabs to extract DNA and determine the genetic variation in a dozen of the genes that had been connected to attention in the adult studies. These children had been seen when they were 7 months old, but the genotyping took place when they returned to the laboratory at about 2 years of age. In addition, we added an observation of caregiver–child interaction in which the children played with toys in the presence of one of their caregivers. Raters watched the caregiver–child interaction and rated the parents on five dimensions of parental quality according to a schedule developed by the National Institute of Child Health and Development (NICHD Early Child Care Research Network, 1993). Parent dimensions scored were: support, autonomy, stimulation, lack of hostility, and confidence in the child. Although all of the parents were likely concerned and caring, they did differ in their scores and we divided them at the mean into two groups. One of the groups had been observed to show a higher quality of parenting, and the other a lower quality. We also genotyped the children for several candidate genes, including the DRD4 that had previously been related to executive attention in adults.

The DRD4-gene polymorphism, previously linked to temperamental risk taking is a repeat of 48 base pairs in one part of the gene. Adults and children carrying the 7-repeat allele have been shown to be higher in the temperamental quality of risk taking and to have a high risk for Attention-Deficit Disorder than those with smaller numbers of repeats (Auerbach et al., 1999; Swanson et al., 2001). What we were interested in was whether parent reports of the child's impulsivity and risk taking were related to whether or not the child carried the 7-repeat allele of the DRD4 gene, the parent's scores on parenting quality, or an interaction of gene and parenting. We found a strong interaction effect. For children without the 7-repeat polymorphism, variations in parenting within the range we examined were unrelated to the children's scores on impulsivity and risk taking. For children carrying the 7-repeat gene variant, however, variations in parenting mattered.

Our finding with the DRD4 gene (Sheese, Voelker, Rothbart, & Posner, 2007) seems to have important implications beyond the study of

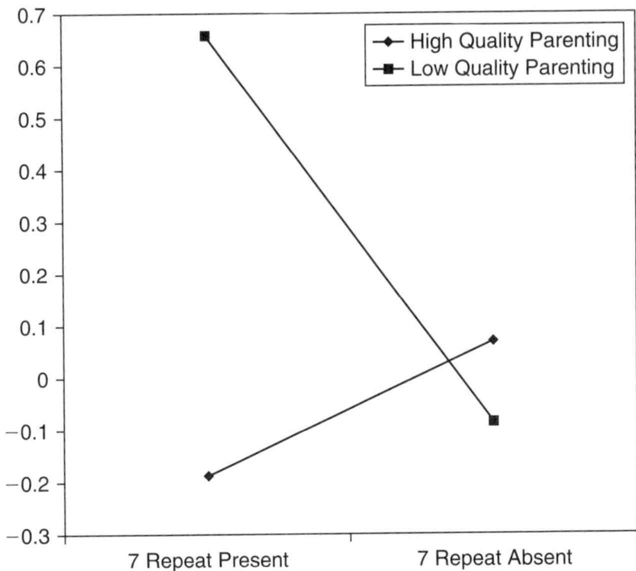

Figure 4.5 A gene–environment interaction. The dependent variable (Y axis) is the scale score for the temperament factor of Impulsivity for 2-year-old children obtained from parent ratings. It is shown as a function of the presence or absence of the 7-repeat allele of the DRD4 gene (X axis) and parental quality (higher quality dark line, lower quality light line) (After Sheese et al., 2007).

one particular gene. We found, as shown in Figure 4.5, that for children with the 7-repeat allele there was a strong influence of parenting quality. Parents who were rated as giving greater support, autonomy, and so on had children who were close to average in the ratings of their impulsivity. Children without the 7-repeat allele showed the same rated impulsivity regardless of parenting, and their impulsivity did not differ from children with the 7-repeat allele who received higher quality parenting. However, children with the 7-repeat allele whose parents had shown lower quality parenting in the laboratory were much higher in impulsivity. Similar results were obtained for activity level and high-intensity stimulation seeking, which we combined into one aggregate measure that we called *risk taking*.

Further evidence that environment can have a stronger influence in the presence of the 7-repeat allele has been reported by others

(Bakermans-Kranenburg & van Ijzendoorn, 2006; van Ijzendoorn & Bakermans-Kranenburg, 2006). Moreover in one study an intervention to increase parental use of positive discipline reduced the externalizing problem behavior in toddlers with the 7-repeat allele of the DRD4 gene significantly more than for those without this allele (Bakermans-Kranenburg, IJzendoorn, Pijlman, Mesman, & Juffer, 2008). This experiment indicated directly the greater influence of environmental events on children with this allele.

The 7-repeat allele of the DRD4 has also been frequently shown to be related to Attention-Deficit/Hyperactivity Disorder (ADHD), with children having this allele being more likely to show the disorder. However, an explicit test of whether children with the 7-repeat were poorer in aspects of attention found no relation between its presence and deficits in attention (Swanson et al., 2000). We believe that the connection between the 7-repeat and ADHD is through the association of this gene polymorphism with temperamental aspects of sensation seeking.

An even more paradoxical finding for an allele associated with developmental psychopathology is that the 7-repeat allele is under positive selective pressure in recent human evolution (Ding et al., 2002). Why should an allele related to ADHD be positively selected? We think that positive selection of the 7-repeat allele could well arise from its sensitivity to environmental influences. Parenting provides training for children in the values favored by the culture in which they live. For example, Rothbart and colleagues (Ahadi et al., 1993) found that in Western culture effortful control appears to regulate negative affect (sadness and anger), while in China (at least in the 1980s) it was found to regulate positive affect (outgoingness and enthusiasm). In recent years, the genetic part of the nature-by-nurture interaction has been given a lot of emphasis, but if genetic variations are selected according to the sensitivity to cultural influences that they produce in children, this could support a greater balance between genes and environment. Theories of positive selection in the DRD4 gene have stressed the role of sensation seeking in human evolution (Harpending & Cochran, 2002; Wang et al., 2004). Our new findings do not contradict this emphasis, but they suggest a form of explanation that could have even wider significance.

It remains to be seen whether the other 300 genes estimated to show positive selection would also increase an individual's sensitivity to variations in rearing environments. We will be examining additional longitudinal data to test these ideas further.

How could variation in genetic alleles lead to enhanced influence of cultural factors like parenting? The anterior cingulate receives input on both reward value and pain or punishment, and this information is clearly important in regulating thoughts and feelings. Dopamine is the most important neuromodulator in these reward and punishment pathways. Thus, changes in the availability of dopamine could enhance the influence of signals from parents related to reward and punishment. Another interaction has been reported between the serotonin transporter gene and parental social support on the temperamental dimension of behavioral inhibition or social fear (Fox et al., 2005). To explain this interaction, Fox, Hane, and Pine (2007) argue that those children with a short form of the serotonin transporter gene who also have lower social support from parents show enhanced attention to threat and greater social fear. However, in our study we did not find that attention was the mechanism by which the genetic variation influenced the child's behavior. In our study there was no influence of the 7-repeat allele on executive attention, rather the gene and environment interacted to influence the child's behavior as observed by his or her caregiver. It is important to consider the multiple mechanisms by which genes may influence behavior. Clearly, one important mechanism lies in the executive attention network we have been discussing in this chapter, but there must be other pathways that influence the same behavior.

In general, our longitudinal study has not found gene–environment interactions in relation to the laboratory tasks we have used like anticipatory looking and infants' approach to novel objects. The gene–environment interaction we found and those reported by others seem to involve more general aspects of behavior as revealed by temperament questionnaires or behavioral checklists. We speculate that the variables defined by neuroimaging or cognitive tasks such as the ANT may show the effects of genetic variation but are less likely to show gene–environment interactions. These interactions may arise mainly because behavior itself is multiply controlled, not only by mechanisms of self-regulation but also by the reactivity of different brain areas to environmental stimulation. Thus, it may be easier for the environment to have its impact on broader behavioral measures than on more narrowly defined endophenotypes. The exact intermediate mechanisms through which gene–environment interactions influence temperamental factors such as fear (HTT) or impulsivity (DRD4) remain to be worked out. We hope that later stages of our longitudinal study will give us the opportunity to contribute to this effort.

ATTENTION IN CLINIC AND SCHOOL

Attentional difficulties are a frequent symptom of different forms of psychopathology and of failure in school (Rothbart & Posner, 2006). However, without a real understanding of the neural substrates of attention, there have not been systematic efforts to remedy attentional problems. This situation has been changed with the application of our understanding of attentional networks to pathological issues. Viewing attention in terms of underlying neural networks provides a means of classifying disorders that differs from the usual internalizing (e.g., depression) versus externalizing (e.g., Conduct Disorder) classifications that have been applied to such disorders. In the following section we consider the relationship between attention networks and some common disorders.

Alerting and Orienting

Studies that have used the ANT or other versions of it have been useful in this effort. For example, there is evidence that ADHD involves a deficit in alerting (Halperin & Schulz, 2006) together with an executive deficit (Johnson et al., submitted). While normal aging influences primarily the alerting network, when aging includes Alzheimers' disease it adds an executive deficit (Fernandez-Duque & Black, 2006). Anxiety disorders appear to involve the orienting network, in particular difficulties in the ability to orient away from a negative target (Derryberry & Reed, 1994; Fox, Russo, Bowles, & Dutton, 2001), whereas autism seems to have a large influence on the orienting network, even for neutral stimuli that do not involve a social aspect (Landry & Bryson, 2004). In this chapter, however, we have stressed research in executive attention and effortful control. For this reason, we discuss in the following disorders that have primarily involved the executive attention network. These include: Borderline Personality Disorder, Schizophrenia, and Chromosome 22Q11 deletion syndrome, all of which seem to have strong links with executive attention.

Executive Attention

Borderline personality

Borderline Personality Disorder is characterized by great lability of affect and difficulties in interpersonal relations. In some cases, patients are suicidal or carry out self-mutilation. Because this diagnosis has been studied largely by psychoanalysts and has a very complex definition, it might at first be thought of as a poor candidate for a specific pathophysiology involving attentional networks. However, we focused on the temperamentally based core symptoms of negative emotionality and difficulty in self-regulation (Posner et al., 2002), including patients who were very high in temperamental negative affect and relatively low in effortful control (Rothbart et al., 2001). We also defined a temperamentally matched control group of normal persons who did not meet the requirements for a personality disorder but were equivalent in scores on these two temperamental dimensions. In the ANT, we found a deficit specific to the executive attention network in borderline patients that was not found in the controls (Posner et al., 2002).

Imaging results suggested overgeneralization of responding to negative words in the amygdala in the borderline patients and reduced responding in the anterior cingulate and related midline frontal areas involved in self-regulation (Silbersweig et al., 2007). Patients with higher effortful control and lower conflict scores on the ANT were also the most likely to show the effects of therapy. This methodology shows the utility of focusing on the core deficits of patients, defining appropriate control groups based on matched temperament, and using specific attentional tests to help determine how to conduct imaging studies.

Schizophrenia

A number of years ago, never-medicated schizophrenic patients were tested with a cued-detection task similar to the orienting part of the

ANT and were studied using positron emission tomography. These patients showed a deficit in orienting similar to what had been found for left parietal patients (Early, Posner, Reiman, & Raichle, 1989). At rest, these subjects also showed a focal decrease in cerebral blood flow in the left globus pallidus (Early et al., 1989), a part of the basal ganglia with close ties to the anterior cingulate. When their visual attention was engaged, they had difficulty in shifting attention to the right visual field and they also showed deficits in conflict tasks, particularly when they had to rely on a language cue. It was concluded that the overall pattern of their behavior was most consistent with a deficit in the anterior cingulate and basal ganglia, parts of a frontally based executive attention system.

The deficit in orienting rightward has been replicated in first-break schizophrenics, but it does not seem to be true later in the disorder (Maruff, Currie, Hay, McArthur-Jackson, & Malone, 1995), nor does the pattern appear to be part of the genetic predisposition for Schizophrenia (Pardo et al., 2000). First-break schizophrenic subjects often have been shown to have hemisphere deficits, and there have been many reports of anterior cingulate and basal ganglia deficits in patients with Schizophrenia (Benes, 1999). The anterior cingulate may be part of a much larger network of frontal and temporal structures that operate abnormally in Schizophrenia (Benes, 1999).

A study using the ANT casts some light on these results (Wang et al., 2005). In this study, the schizophrenic patients were chronic and they were compared to a similarly aged control group. The schizophrenic patients had a much greater difficulty resolving conflict than did the normal controls. The deficit in patients was also much larger than that found for borderline personality patients. There was still a great deal of overlap between the patients and normal subjects, however, indicating that the deficit is not suitable for making a differential diagnosis. The data also showed a much smaller orienting deficit of the type that had been reported previously. These findings suggest that on average there is a strong executive deficit in chronic Schizophrenia, as would be anticipated by the Benes (1999) theory. It remains to be determined whether this deficit exists prior to the initial symptoms, or if it develops with the disorder.

Chromosome 22q11.2 deletion syndrome

This syndrome is a complex one that involves a number of abnormalities, including facial and heart structure, but also mental retardation due to deletion of a number of genes. Children with this syndrome are at a high risk for developing Schizophrenia. Among the genes deleted in this syndrome is the COMT gene, which has been associated with performance in a conflict task (Diamond et al., 2004) and with Schizophrenia (Egan et al., 2003). In light of these findings, it was expected that the disorder would produce a large executive deficit, and findings have corroborated this expectation (Simon et al., 2005; Sobin et al., 2004). Sobin and colleagues also found that the deficit in resolving conflict is associated with the ability to inhibit a blink following a cue that a loud noise would be presented shortly (prepulse inhibition). The authors suggest that the association of high-level attention and prepulse inhibition deficit involves a pathway that includes both the basal ganglia and the anterior cingulate.

Schooling

Effortful control measured in preschool has been shown to be an important predictor of success in kindergarten (Blair & Razza, 2007). In later schooling, effortful control is related to higher grades in a wide range of secondary school subjects and skills important for school success such as rule following, tolerance to frustration, and understanding of the role of the students in the classroom. In addition, effortful control appears to be the key mediator between social adjustment at school and academic achievement (Checa et al., submitted). In the same study, the efficiency of conflict resolution as measured by the ANT, which is indicative of executive attention network function, was more specifically related to performance in secondary school math and regulation of social behavior in the classroom.

Attention is also critical to a wide variety of other subjects that draw upon general intelligence. Anatomically, the network involving resolution of conflict also overlaps with brain areas related to general intelligence (Duncan et al., 2000). In another publication (Posner & Rothbart, 2007), we discussed in detail the training of attention either explicitly or implicitly as part of the preschool curriculum and we will not repeat those arguments here. Rather, in the following section on enhancing attention we explore methods for carrying out this training.

A more specific role for attention in school performance has been based on recent findings of superior performance of multilinguals on executive functions (Bialystok & Martin, 2004) and on executive attention as measured by the ANT (Costa, Hernandez, & Sebastian-Gallés, 2008). The idea is that those using multiple languages might train executive attention because of the need to suppress one language while using the other. Some direct evidence for the role of executive attention in this process comes from a study by Yang and Lust (2006) comparing Korean and Chinese native speakers who were bilingual in English with French and Spanish speakers bilingual in English and with English monolinguals. Both bilingual groups showed better executive attention as measured by the ANT than monolinguals. In addition, the Asian group, whose languages differed the most from English, was superior to the Romance bilinguals. This study demonstrates the close ties between language and attention and also suggests that the need to select among languages may form one important basis for improved executive attention. The effect of second-language learning on executive attention is an intriguing one, but to date the naturalistic nature of these studies has not allowed random assignment of participants to groups. Thus, there is always the possibility that improved executive attention may be due to subtle differences between those who learn second languages and those who do not. The next section deals with this problem in our systematic training studies of attention in children and adults.

ENHANCING ATTENTION

The presence of large individual differences in attention starting early in life and the importance of parenting for behaviors such as activity level and impulsivity suggest that the ability of children to handle the school situation may depend upon the joint interaction of genes and environment. The relation of genetic factors to the functioning of the executive attention system does not mean that the system cannot be influenced by experience. Indeed, the gene–environment interaction discussed previously suggests that sensitivity to the environment might be built into genetic variation. Several training-oriented programs have been successful in improving attention in patients suffering from different pathologies. For example, the use of Attention Process Training (APT) has led to specific improvements in executive attention in patients with specific brain injury (Sohlberg, McLaughlin, Pavese, Heidrich, & Posner, 2000), as well as in children with ADHD (Kerns, Esso, & Thompson, 1999). Work with children with ADHD has also shown that working-memory training can improve attention (Klingberg, Forssberg, & Westerberg, 2002; Olesen, Westerberg, & Klingberg, 2004). In nonclinical samples of adults, training with video games has produced better performance on a range of visual attention tasks (Green & Bavelier, 2003).

Attention Training in Children

To examine the role of experience on the executive attention network, we developed and tested a 5-day training intervention using computerized exercises. We tested the effects of this training during the period of major development of executive attention, between 4 and 7 years of age (Rueda et al., 2005). We hoped to develop methods that could be used to observe improvements in conflict resolution following training, and adapted methods that had been used to train monkeys for work in space (Rumbaugh & Washburn, 2003). The training began with the children learning to use a joystick. First, they moved a cat to the grass so as to avoid mud. Over trials, the grass shrank and the mud increased, requiring more careful control of the cat. These skills were then used to teach prediction, exercise working memory, and finally to practice children in resolving conflict. Children who went through the training were compared with a randomly selected control group who were engaged with interactive videos.

Before and after training the children performed the ANT while their brain waves were recorded. The children who had undergone attention training (see Fig. 4.6) showed clear evidence of improvement in the executive attention network following training in comparison with the control children. As discussed earlier, the N2 component of the scalp recorded average electrical potential has been shown to arise in the anterior

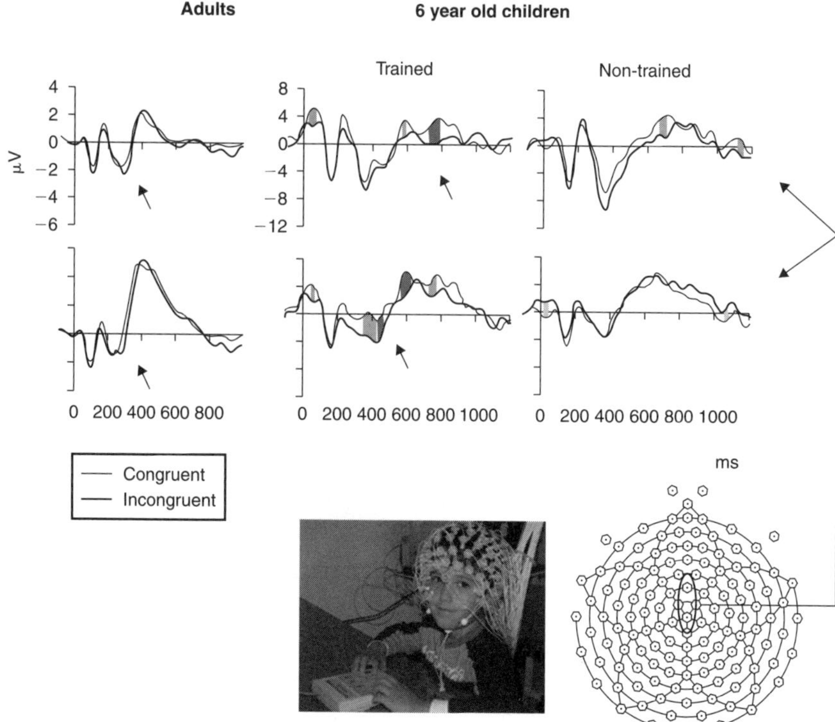

Figure 4.6 ERPs for the child ANT performed by adults (left), trained 6-year-olds, and untrained 6-year-olds. The ERPs come from electrodes over the frontal midline known to arise in the dorsal anterior cingulate. (After Rueda et al., 2005).

cingulate and is related to monitoring or resolution of conflict (van Veen & Carter, 2002; Jonkman, Sniedt, & Kemner, 2007). We found N2 differences between congruent and incongruent trials of the ANT in trained 6-year-olds that resembled differences found in adults. In the 4-year-olds, the training seemed to influence more anterior electrodes that have been related to emotional control areas of the cingulate (Bush et al., 2000). These data suggest that training altered the network for the resolution of conflict in the direction of being more like what is found in adults.

We also found a significantly greater improvement in a measure of intelligence in the trained group compared to the control children. This finding suggested that training effects had generalized to a measure of cognitive processing that is far removed from the training exercises.

The parents did not report changes in temperament over the course of the training, but this was not expected because parents had only the short time elapsing between assessment sessions on which to base their ratings.

Recently, a replication and extension of this study was carried out for 5-year-olds in a Spanish preschool (Rueda, Checa, & Santonja, 2008). Several additional exercises were added and 10 days of training were provided for both experimental and control groups. As in the previous study, the randomly assigned control group viewed child-appropriate videos for the same amount of time as the intervention group was trained. A follow-up session for all children was also given 2 months after the training. Figure 4.7 shows that, unlike the control group, trained children showed improvement in intelligence scores, as measured by the matrices scale of the K-BIT, following training. In addition, the trained group held sustained improvement over the 2 months without further training, while the control group did not. Additionally, the training of attention produced beneficial effects on performance of tasks involving affective regulation, such as the Children's Gambling Task (Hongwanishkul, Happaney, Lee, & Zelazo, 2005).

We hope our training method will be evaluated along with other such methods both as a possible means of improving attention prior to school and for children diagnosed with ADHD and other attention-related disorders. However, we do not have any expectation that our exercises are optimal or even better than other methods. The study of attention training as a whole suggests that networks can be shaped both in informal ways and by formal training. With the availability of imaging and related methods it should be possible to design appropriate methods for children of various ages and with various forms of difficulty (see section on Translation). Our studies, do however, support the importance of educational designs in improving the lives of children.

Adult Attention Training

The exercises we used for young children are too simple for use by adults. However, there is evidence that changes in the attention state induced by meditation or relaxation training (Jha, Klein, Krompinger and Baime,

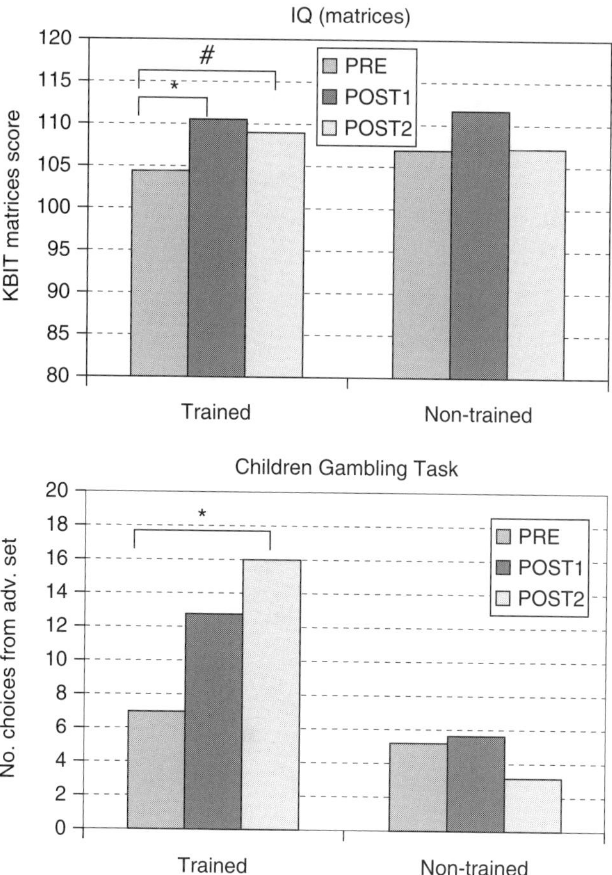

Figure 4.7 IQ (Matrices subscale) and Children's Gambling Task for children that underwent ten 35-minutes sessions of attention training compared to a group of age-matched controls. Scores were taken before training (PRE), immediately after training (POST 1), and 2 months after completion of training (POST 2). (*) $p < .05$; (#) $p < .10$ (Rueda et al., 2008).

2007; Slagter et al., 2007) can also be useful in improving the efficiency of attention. While some of this evidence is impressive, it has not used brief training methods or random assignment to examine changes as we have done for children.

To accomplish this goal, we worked with colleagues in China to evaluate a training method they had developed called Integrative Body–Mind Training (IBMT). This method was adapted from traditional Chinese medicine (Tang et al., 2007). In IBMT, the trainee concentrates on achieving a balanced state of mind through training by a coach and use of a CD that teaches them relaxation, adjustment of breathing, and mental imagery. Because this approach is suitable for novices, it was hypothesized that a short period of training and practice might influence the efficiency of the executive attention network related to self-regulation (Tang et al., 2007). This study used a random assignment of 40 Chinese undergraduates to an experimental group and 40 to a control group for 5 days of training, requiring 20 minutes per day. The experimental group was given a short term of IBMT. Training was presented in a standardized way and guided by a skillful IBMT coach. Each of the coaches in this study had considerable experience with IBMT. The control group was given relaxation training, which is frequently used in the West as a part of some forms of behavioral therapy (Benson, 1975; Bernstein & Borkoved, 1973).

The two groups were given a battery of tests a week before training and immediately following the final training session. The tests included the ANT, the Raven's Standard Progressive Matrices, which is a standard culture fair intelligence test, a measure of mood state, and a mental arithmetic challenge task followed by collection of salivary cortisol as a measure of stress. All of the measures were analyzed by experimenters who were blind to the experimental condition.

The data for the ANT is shown in Figure 4.8. For the conflict network, there was a significant interaction between group and time of testing indicating that the experimental group showed significantly greater improvement in executive attention than the control. Similar results were obtained for self-reports of negative affect and fatigue using the POMS self-report and for the cortisol measure. The experimental group showed less cortisol response to the cognitive challenge following training than did the control, suggesting that training improved the handling of the stressor. Finally, the IBMT training produced an improvement in IQ scores in the Raven's test, although the difference between the trained and control groups on that improvement was marginal.

An additional study used either 5 days or 5 weeks of training. The additional weeks of IBMT training had the expected effect of increased efficiency on the ANT, but with additional training the alerting as well

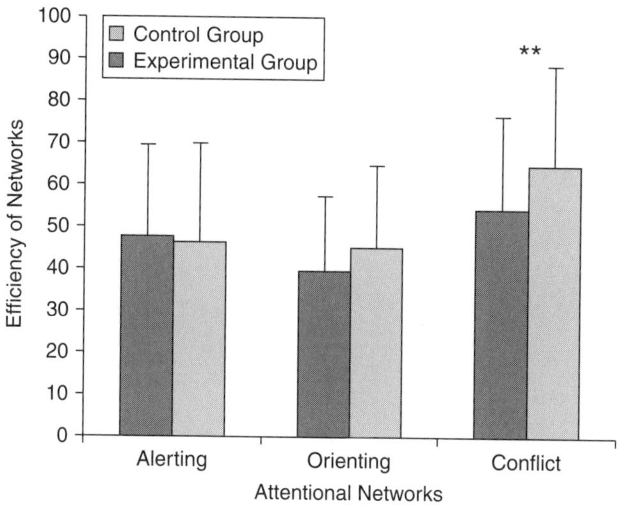

Figure 4.8 ANT scores for alerting, orienting, and conflict for the experimental group after 5 days of IBMT and a relaxation control. The experimental group on the left shows significantly better conflict scores than the control, but only after training (Tang et al., 2007).

as the conflict score showed a significant interaction effect. In addition, the regulation of cortisol secretion was much stronger after the longer period of training (see Fig. 4.9).

Since subjects were randomly assigned to experimental and control groups and objective tests were used, we concluded that the IBMT improved executive attention more than the relaxation control did. The reaction to mental stress was also significantly improved in the experimental group, who had lower levels of cortisol than the control after the additional training. These outcomes after only 5 days of training open a new door for simple and effective investigations of meditation effects. The IBMT provides a convenient method for studying the influence of meditation training using appropriate experimental and control methods similar to those used to test drugs or other interventions. The findings also indicate the potential of IBMT for stress management, body-mind health, and improvement in cognitive performance and self-regulation (Tang, 2005; Tang et al., 2007).

Why does the IBMT work after only a few days practice, while studies with other methods often require months? The following are possible

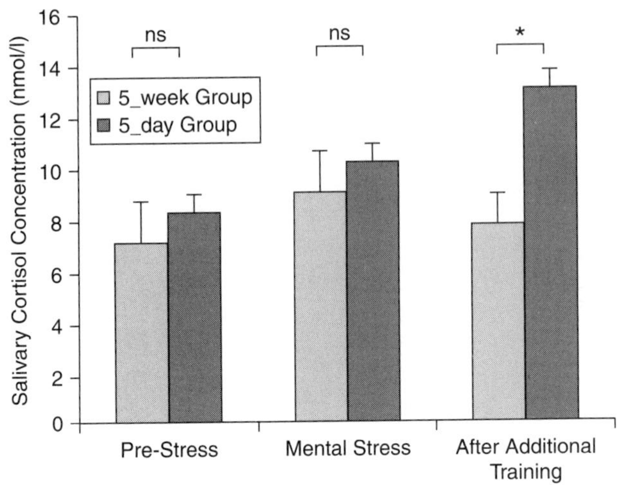

Figure 4.9 Cortisol collected from an IBMT group trained for 5 weeks (left) or 5 days (right) before any training, after stress, and after training and control (right bars). Five-days training produces less improvement in stress regulation than does 5 week training.

reasons. First, the IBMT integrates several key components of body-mind techniques including body relaxation (Benson, 1975), breathing adjustment (Lusk, 2005), mental imagery (Watanabe, Fukuda, & Shirakawa, 2005), and mindfulness training (Shapiro, Arnell, & Raymond, 1997), which have shown broad positive effects in attention, emotion, and social behavior in previous studies. This combination may amplify the training effect over the use of only one of these components. Second, since everyone at times has experienced mindfulness (Hart, 1987), a qualified coach can help each participant increase the amount of this experience and thus guarantee that each practice session achieves a good result (Tang, 2005; Tang et al., 2007). For participants with months to years of meditation, there has been the opportunity to make mistakes, correct them, and gradually find the right way. Recent findings indicate that the amount of time participants spend meditating each day, rather than merely the total number of hours of meditative practice over their lifetime, was the most important influence on attention (Chan & Woollacott, 2007).

In order for mediation practice to improve attention and self-regulation in only 5 days, a very high quality of training is needed.

To ensure this quality, a trainer was used to observe the session. The work of the trainer is critical. The trainer needs to know how to interact with the trainees to obtain the desired state. Although the trainers are not present during the training sessions, they observe the trainees over TV and help them after the session with their problems. The trainers could well be a part of the effective ingredient of IBMT and their role requires additional research.

TRANSLATION

Our work began with basic studies of temperament and of the anatomy and connectivity of a high-level attention system. At the time we had little realization of the potential importance of our findings for psychopathology or for schooling. The relative success of our two training efforts has certainly provided sufficient evidence that attention and self-regulation can be enhanced in children and adults.

One important part of the puzzle that remains is evidence for enhancement of children's performance in school settings. Does attention training improve the prospect for achievement in school over the long run? Would attention training help to prevent or reduce the effect of mental illness involving executive attention? Finding answers to questions like these mean rather complex prospective studies of the influence of training.

Another challenging translational issue relates to the effective ingredient in training. When we started this work, we assumed that it would be difficult to influence the attentional network; but in retrospect that turns out not to be true. If it were true, it is highly unlikely that either of our methods would have worked, or that there would be subsequent reports of similar success of working-memory training and video games, and augmented classroom work and parent training of preschool children (Diamond, Barnett, Thomas, & Munro, 2007; Fanning, Paulsen, Sundbord & Neville, 2007). Our original goal was really a feasibility study. Was attention trainable, and if so, what were its consequences? Now the issue is more how to train well to achieve the desired consequence. Classroom interventions appear to have more practical utility in educational settings, while individualized tutorials may fit clinical applications. In our view, imaging can play an important role in understanding exactly what the consequence of each form of intervention might be in terms of brain function so that it would be possible to develop an optimal method. It would be most unfortunate if the usual sterile debates about what is the *best* way to train attention take place without using the tools to obtain real evidence on the issue.

Even if optimal attention training could be designed and it has very fortunate consequences for the child, there are also serious questions about whether it would be used. For example, we already know that prenatal nutrition is critical but many mothers and infants go without it. If the scientific community could reach a consensus on the utility of enhancing self-regulation, it would certainly help ensure public debate and action. For this reason, in this chapter we have sought to connect interventions with specific brain networks shown to influence children's behaviors in specific ways. This is designed to foster a consensus supporting an effort to train brain networks related to executive function. We hope our papers will receive attention and criticism along with other efforts to train attention and working memory, and that the enhancement of self-regulation will be an important societal goal for our children.

REFERENCES

Ahadi, S. A., Rothbart, M. K., & Ye, R. (1993). Children's temperament in the U.S. and China: Similarities and differences. *European Journal of Personality*, 7, 359–378.

Allman, J. M., Watson, K. K., Tetreault, N. A., & Hakeem, A. Y. (2005). Intuition and autism: A possible role for Von Economo neurons. *Trends in Cognitive Science*, 9, 367–373.

Auerbach, J., Geller, V., Lezer, S., Shinwell, E., Belmaker, R. H., Levine, J., et al. (1999). Dopamine D4 receptor (D4DR) and serotonin transporter promoter (5-HTTLPR) polymorphisms in the determination of temperament in 2-month-old infants. *Molecular Psychiatry*, 4, 369–373.

Bakermans-Kranenburg, M. J., & van Ijzendoorn, M. H. (2006). Gene-environment interaction of the dopamine D4 receptor (DRD4) and observed maternal insensitivity predicting externalizing behavior in preschoolers. *Developmental Psychobiology*, 48, 406–409.

Bakermans-Kranenburg, M. J., van IJzendoorn, M. H., Pijlman, F. T., Mesman, J., & Juffer, F. (2008) Experimental evidence for differential susceptibility: Dopamine D4 Receptor Polymorphism (DRD4 VNTR) moderates effects of toddler's externalizing behavior in a randomized control trial. *Developmental Psychology, 44*, 293–300.

Beauregard, M., Levesque, J., & Bourgouin, P. (2001). Neural correlates of conscious self-regulation of emotion. *Journal of Neuroscience, 21*, RC165.

Benes, F. (1999). Model generation and testing to probe neural circuitry in the cingulate cortex of postmortem schizophrenic brains. *Schizophrenia Bulletin, 24*, 219–229.

Benson, H. (1975). *The relaxation response*. New York: Avon.

Berger, A., Tzur, G., & Posner, M. I. (2006). Infant brains detect arithmetic error. *Proceedings of the National Academy of Sciences of the USA, 103*, 12649–12653.

Bernstein, D. A., & Borkoved, T. D. (1973). *Progressive relaxation training*. Champaign, IL: Research Press.

Bialystok, E., & Martin M. M. (2004). Attention and inhibition in bilingual children: Evidence from the dimensional change card task. *Psychological Sciences, 7*, 325–339.

Blair, C., & Razza, R. P. (2007). Relating effortful control, executive function and false belief understanding to emerging math and literacy ability in kindergarten. *Child Development, 78*, 647–663.

Blasi, G., Mattay, G. S., Bertolino, A., Elvevåg, B., Callicott, J. H., Das, S., et al. (2005). Effect of cCatechol-O-Methyltransferase *val*^{158} *met* genotype on attentional control. *Journal of Neuroscience, 25*, 5038–5045.

Botvinick, M. M., Braver, T. S., Barch, D. M., Carter, C. S., & Cohen, J. D. (2001). Conflict monitoring and cognitive control. *Psychological Review, 108*, 624–652.

Bush, G., Luu, P., & Posner, M. I. (2000). Cognitive and emotional influences in the anterior cingulate cortex. *Trends in Cognitive Science, 4*, 215–222.

Canli, T., Omura, K., Haas, B. W., Fallgatter, A., Todd, R., Constable, R. T., et al. (2005). Beyond affect: A role for genetic variation of the serotonin transporter in neural activation during a cognitive attention task. *Proceedings of the National Academy of Sciences of the USA, 102*, 12224–12229.

Chan, D., & Woollacott, M. (2007). Effects of level of meditation experience on attentional focus: Is the efficiency of executive or orientation networks improved? *Journal of Alternative and Complementary Medicine, 13*, 651–658.

Chang, F., & Burns, B. M. (2005). Attention in preschoolers: Associations with effortful control and motivation. *Child Development, 76*, 247–263.

Checa, P., Rodriguez-Bailon, R., & Rueda, M. R. (submitted). Neurocognitive and temperamental systems of self-regulation and early adolescents' schooling outcomes.

Cicchetti, D., & Blender, J. A. (2004). A multiple-levels-of analysis approach to the study of developmental process in maltreated children. *Proceedings of the National Academy of Sciences of the USA, 101*, 17325–17326.

Clohessy, A. B., Posner, M. I., & Rothbart, M. K. (2001) Development of the functional visual field. *Acta Psychologica, 106*, 51–68.

Costa, A., Hernandez, M., & Sebastian-Gallés, N. (2008). Bilingualism aids conflict resolution: Evidence from the ANT task. *Cognition, 106*, 59–86.

Crottaz-Herbette, S., & Mennon, V. (2006). Where and when the anterior cingulate cortex modulates attentional response: Combined fMRI and ERP evidence. *Journal of Cognitive Neuroscience, 18*, 766–780.

Davidson, M. C., Amso, D., Anderson, L. C., & Diamond, A. (2006). Development of cognitive control and executive functions from 4 to 13 years: Evidence from manipulations of memory, inhibition, and task switching. *Neuropsychologia, 44*, 2037–2078.

Dehaene, S., Posner, M. I., & Tucker, D. M. (1994). Localization of a neural system for error detection and compensation. *Psychological Science, 5*, 303–305.

Derryberry, D., & Reed, M. A. (1994). Temperament and the self-organization of personality. *Development and Psychopathology, 6*, 653–676.

Diamond, A., Barnett, S., Thomas, J., & Munro, S. (2007). Preschool improves cognitive control. *Science, 318*, 1387–1388.

Diamond, A., Briand, L., Fossella, J., & Gehlbach, L. (2004). Genetic and neurochemical modulation of prefrontal cognitive functions in children. *American Journal of Psychiatry, 161*, 125–132.

Ding, Y. C., Chi, H. C., Grady, D. L., Morishima, A., Kidd, J. R., Kidd, K. K., et al. (2002). Evidence of positive selection acting at the human dopamine receptor D4 gene locus. *Proceedings of the National Academy of Sciences of the USA, 99*, 309–314.

Dosenbach, N. U. F., Fair, D. A., Miezin, F. M., Cohen, A. L., Wenger, K. K., Dosenbach, R. A. T., et al. (2007). Distinct brain networks for adaptive and stable task control in humans. *Proceedings of the National Academy of Sciences of the USA, 104*, 11073–11078.

Drevets, W. C., & Raichle, M. E. (1998). Reciprocal suppression of regional blood flow during emotional versus higher cognitive processes: Implications for interactions between emotion and cognition. *Cognition and Emotion, 12*, 285–353.

Duncan, J., Seitz, R. J., Kolodny, J. Bor, D., Herzon, H., Ahmed, A., et al. (2000). A neural basis for general intelligence. *Science, 289*, 457–460.

Early, T. S., Posner, M. I., Reiman, E. M., & Raichle, M. E. (1989). Hyperactivity of the left striato-pallidal projection, Part I: Lower level theory. *Psychiatric Developments, 2*, 85–108.

Egan, M. F., Kojima, M., Callicott, J. H., Goldberg, T. E., Kolachana, B. S., Bertolino, A., et al. (2003). The BDNF val66met polymorphism affects activity-dependent secretion of BDNF and H. *Cell, 112*, 144–145.

Eisenberg, N., Smith, C. L., Sadovsky, A., Spinrad, T. L., (2004). Effortful control: Relations with emotion-regulation, adjustment, and socialization in childhood. In R. F. Baumeister & K. D. Vohs (Eds.), *Handbook of Self-Regulation* (pp. 259-282). New York: Guilford.

Ellis, L., & Rothbart, M. K. (2001, April). *Revision of the early adolescent temperament questionnaire*. Paper presented at the meeting of the Society for Research in Child Development, Minneapolis, MN.

Etkin, A., Egner, T., Peraza, D. M., Kandel, E. R., & Hirsch, J. (2006). Resolving emotional conflict: A role for the rostral anterior cingulate cortex in modulating activity in the amygdala. *Neuron, 51*, 871–882.

Fan, J., Flombaum, J. I., McCandliss, B. D., Thomas, K. M., & Posner, M. I. (2003). Cognitive and brain consequences of conflict. *Neuro Image, 18*, 42–57.

Fan, J., Fossella, J. A., Sommer, T., & Posner, M. I. (2003). Mapping the genetic variation of executive attention onto brain activity. *Proceedings of the National Academy of Sciences of the USA, 100*, 7406–7411.

Fan, J., McCandliss, B. D., Fossella, J., Flombaum, J. I., & Posner, M. I. (2005). The activation of attentional networks. *Neuroimage, 26*, 471–479.

Fan, J., McCandliss, B. D., Sommer, T., Raz, M., & Posner, M. I. (2002). Testing the efficiency and independence of attentional networks. *Journal of Cognitive Neuroscience, 3*, 340–347.

Fan, J., Wu, Y., Fossella, J., & Posner, M. I. (2001). Assessing the heritability of attentional networks. *BioMed Central Neuroscience, 2*, 14.

Fanning, J. L., Paulsen, D., Sunbord, S., & Neville, H. J. (2007, May) *The effects of parent training: Enhancing children's neurocognitive function*. Poster presented at the meeting of the Cognitive Neuroscience Society, San Francisco, CA.

Fernandez-Duque, D., & Black, S. E. (2006). Attentional networks in normal aging and Alzheimeer's disease. *Neuropsychology, 20*, 133–143.

Fossella, J., Sommer, T., Fan, J., Wu, Y., Swanson, J. M., Pfaff, D. W., et al. (2002). Assessing the molecular genetics of attention networks. *BMC Neuroscience, 3*, 14.

Fox, E., Russo, R., Bowles, R. J., & Dutton, K. (2001). Do threatening stimuli draw or hold attention in subclinical anxiety? *Journal of Experimental Psychology–General, 130*, 681–700.

Fox, N. A., Hane, A. A., & Pine, D. S. (2007). Plasticity for affective neurocircuitry. *Current Directions in Psychological Science, 16*, 1–5.

Fox, N. A., Nichols, K. E., Henderson, H. A., Rubin, K., Schmidt, L., Hamer, D., et al. (2005). Evidence for a gene-environment interaction in predicting behavioral inhibition in middle childhood. *Psychological Science, 16*, 921–926.

Galvan, A., Hare, T. A., Parra, C. E., Penn, J., Voss, H., Glover, G., et al. (2006). Earlier development of the accumbens related to orbitofrontal cortex might underlie risk-taking behavior in adolescents. *Journal of Neuroscience, 26*, 6885–6892.

Gerardi-Caulton, G. (2000). Sensitivity to spatial conflict and the development of self-regulation in children 24-36 months of age. *Developmental Science, 3/4*, 397–404.

Gonzalez, C., Fuentes, L. J., Carranza, J. A., & Estevez, A. F. (2001). Temperament and attention in the self-regulation of 7-year-old children. *Personality and Individual Differences, 30*, 931–946.

Green, C. S., & Bavelier, D. (2003). Action video games modifies visual selective attention. *Nature, 423*, 434–437.

Halperin, J. M., & Schulz, K. P. (2006). Revisiting the role of the prefrontal cortex in the pathophysiology of Attention-Deficit/Hyperactivity Disorder. *Psychological Bulletin, 132*, 560–581.

Harpending, H., & Cochran, G. (2002). In our genes. *Proceedings of the National Academy of Sciences of the USA*, 99, 10–12.

Hart, W. (1987). *The art of living: Vipassana meditation: As taught by S.N. Goenka.* New York: Harper and Row.

Hongwanishkul, D., Happaney, K. R., Lee, W. S., & Zelazo, P. D. (2005). Assessment of hot and cool executive function in young children: Age-related changes and individual differences. *Developmental Neuropsychology, 28*, 617–644.

Jha, A., Klein, R., Krompinger, J., & Baime, M. (2007). Mindfulness training modifies subsystems of attention. *Cognitive Affective and Behavioral Neuroscience, 2*, 109–119.

Johnson, K., Robertson, I., Barry, E., Mulligan, A., Daibhis, A., Daly, M., et al. (submitted). Impaired conflict resolution and alerting in children with ADHD: Evidence from the Attention Network Task.

Jonkman, L. M., Sniedt, F. L. F., & Kemner, C. (2007). Source localization of the Nogo-N2: A developmental study. *Clinical Neurophysiology, 118*, 1069–1077.

Kerns, K. A., Esso, K., & Thompson, J. (1999). Investigation of a direct intervention for improving attention in young children with ADHD. *Developmental Neuropsychology, 16*, 273–295.

Klingberg, T., Forssberg, H., & Westerberg, H. (2002). Training of working memory in children with ADHD. *Journal of Clinical and Experimental Neuropsychology, 24*, 781–791.

Kochanska, G., Murray, K. T., & Harlan, E. T. (2000). Effortful control in early childhood: Continuity and change, antecedents, and implications for social development. *Developmental Psychology, 36*, 220–232.

Landry, R., & Bryson, S. E. (2004). Impaired disengagement of attention in young children with autism. *Journal of Child and Adolescent Psychiatry, 45*, 1115–1122.

Lusk, J. T. (2005). *Yoga meditations*. New York: Whole Person Associates.

Mansouri, F. A., Buckley, M. J., & Tanaka, K. (2007). Mnemonic function of the dorsolateral prefrontal cortex in conflict-induced behavioral adjustment. *Science, 318*, 987–990.

Maruff, P., Currie, J., Hay, D., McArthur-Jackson, C., & Malone, V. (1995). Asymmetries in the covert orienting of visual spatial attention in schizophrenia. *Neuropsychologia, 31*, 1205–1223.

NICHD Early Child Care Research Network. (1993). *The NICHD Study of Early Child Care: A comprehensive longitudinal study of young children's lives*. Rockville, MD: National Institute of Child Health and Development. (ERIC Document Reproduction Service No. ED3530870).

Ochsner, K. N., Kossyln, S. M., Cosgrove, G. R., Cassem, E. H., Price, B. H., Nierenberg, A. A., et al. (2001). Deficits in visual cognition and attention following bilateral anterior cingulotomy. *Neuropsychologia, 39*, 219–230.

Olesen, P. J., Westerberg, H., & Klingberg, T. (2004). Increased prefrontal and parietal activity after training of working memory. *Nature Neuroscience, 7*, 75–79.

Pardo, P. J., Knesevich, M. A., Vogler, G. P., Pardo J. V., Towne, B., Cloninger, C. R., et al. (2000). Genetic and state variables of neurocognitive dysfunction in schizophrenia: A twin study. *Schizophrenia Bulletin, 26*, 459–477.

Posner, M. I., & Fan, J. (2008). Attention as an organ system. In J. R. Pomerantz (Ed.), *Topics in integrative neuroscience* (pp. 31–61). New York: Cambridge University Press.

Posner, M. I., & Petersen, S. E. (1990). The attention system of the human brain. *Annual Review of Neuroscience, 13*, 25–42.

Posner, M. I., & Raichle, M. E. (1994). *Images of mind.* New York: Scientific American Books.

Posner, M. I., & Rothbart, M. K. (1980). The development of attentional mechanisms. In J. H. Flowers (Ed.), *Nebraska symposium on motivation* (pp. 1–49). Lincoln: Nebraska University Press.

Posner, M. I., & Rothbart, M. K. (1998). Attention, self regulation and consciousness. *Philosophical Transactions of the Royal Society of London B, 353,* 1915–1927.

Posner, M. I., & Rothbart, M. K. (2007). *Educating the human brain.* Washington, DC: APA.

Posner, M. I., Rothbart, M. K., Sheese, B. E., & Tang, Y. (2007). The anterior cingulate gyrus and the mechanisms of self regulation. *Journal of Cognitive, Affective and Social Neuroscience, 7,* 391–395.

Posner, M. I., Rothbart, M. K., Vizueta, N., Levy, K., Thomas, K. M., & Clarkin, J. (2002). Attentional mechanisms of borderline personality disorder. *Proceedings of the National Academy of Sciences USA,* 99, 16366–16370.

Posner, M. I., Sheese, B. E., Odludas, Y., & Tang, Y. (2006). Analyzing and shaping neural networks. *Neural Networks, 19,* 1422–1429.

Reuter, M., Ott, U., Vaidl, D., & Henning, J. (2007). Impaired executive attention is associated with a variation in the promotor region of the tryptophan hydroxylase-2 gene. *Journal of Cognitive Neuroscience, 19,* 401–408.

Rothbart, M. K. (2007). Temperament, development and personality. *Current Directions in Psychological Science, 16,* 207–212.

Rothbart, M. K., Ahadi, S. A., Hershey, K. L., & Fisher, P. (2001). Investigations of temperament at three to seven years: The Children's Behavior Questionnaire. *Child Development, 72,* 1394–1408.

Rothbart, M. K., & Bates, J. E. (2006). Temperament. In W. Damon, R. Lerner, & N. Eisenberg (Eds.), *Handbook of child psychology: Vol. 3. Social, emotional, and personality development* (6th ed., pp. 99–106). New York: Wiley.

Rothbart, M. K., & Derryberry, D. (1981). Development of individual differences in temperament. In M. E. Lamb & A. L. Brown (Eds.), *Advances in developmental psychology: Vol. 1.* (pp. 37–86). Hillsdale, NJ: Erlbaum.

Rothbart, M. K., Derryberry, D., & Posner, M. I. (1994). A psychobiological approach to the development of temperament. In J. E. Bates & T. D. Wachs (Eds.), *Temperament: Individual differences at the interface of biology and behavior* (pp. 83–116). Washington, DC: APA.

Rothbart, M. K., Ellis, L. K., Rueda, M. R., & Posner, M. I. (2003). Developing mechanisms of temperamental effortful control. *Journal of Personality, 71,* 1113–1143.

Rothbart, M. K., & Posner, M. I. (2006). Temperament, attention, and developmental psychopathology. In D. Cicchetti & D. J. Cohen (Eds.), *Handbook of developmental psychopathology: Vol. 2. Developmental neuroscience* (2nd ed., pp. 465–501). New York: Wiley.

Rothbart, M. K., & Sheese, B. (2007). Temperament and emotion regulation. In J. J. Gross (Ed.), *Handbook of emotion regulation* (pp. 331–350). New York: Guilford.

Rueda, M. R., Checa, P., & Santonja, M. (2008, April). Training executive attention in preschoolers: Lasting effects and transfer to affective self-regulation. Paper presented at the Annual Meeting of the Cognitive Neuroscience Society, San Francisco, CA.

Rueda, M. R., Fan, J., Halparin, J., Gruber, D., Lercari, L. P., McCandliss B. D., et al. (2004). Development of attention during childhood. *Neuropsychologia, 42*, 1029–1040.

Rueda, M. R., Posner, M. I., & Rothbart, M. K. (2004). Attentional control and self-regulation. In R. F. Baumeister & K. D. Vohs (Eds.), *Handbook of self-regulation: Research, theory, and applications* (pp. 283–300). New York: Guilford.

Rueda, M. R., Rothbart, M. K., McCandliss, B. D., Saccamanno, L., & Posner, M. I. (2005). Training, maturation and genetic influences on the development of executive attention. *Proceedings of the National Academy of Sciences of the USA, 102*, 14931–14936.

Rumbaugh, D. M., & Washburn, D. A. (2003). *Intelligence of apes and other rational beings*. New Haven, CN: Yale University Press.

Shapiro, K. L., Arnell, K. A., & Raymond, J. E. (1997). The attentional blink. *Trends in Cognitive Science, 1*, 291–296.

Sheese, B. E., Rothbart, M. K., Posner, M. I., White, L. K., & Fraundorf, S. H. (2008). Executive attention and self-regulation in infancy. *Infant Behavior and Development, 31*, 501–510.

Sheese, B. E., Voelker, P., Rothbart, M. K., & Posner, M. I. (2007). Caregiver quality interacts with genetic variation to influence aspects of toddler temperament. *Development and Psychopathology, 19*, 1039–1046.

Silbersweig, D. A., Clarkin, J. F., Goldstein, M., Kernberg, O. F., Tuescher, O., Levy, K. N., et al. (2007). Failure of fronto-limbic inhibitory function in the context of negative emotion in borderline personality disorder. *American Journal of Psychiatry, 164*, 1832–1841.

Simon, T. J., Bish, J. P., Bearden, C. E., Ding, L., Ferrante, S., Nguyen, V., et al. (2005). A multi-level analysis of cognitive dysfunction and psychopathology associated with chromosome 22q11.2 deletion syndrome in children. *Development and Psychopathology*, *17*, 753–784.

Slagter, H. A., Lutz, A., Greischar, L. L., Francis, A. D., Nieuwenhuis, S., Davis, J. M., et al. (2007). Mental training affects use of limited brain resources. *Public Library of Science*, 5, e138.

Sobin, C., Kiley-Brabeck, K., Daniels, S., Blundell, M., Anyane-Yeboa, K., & Karayiorgou, M. (2004). Networks of attention in children with the 22q11 deletion syndrome. *Developmental Neuropsychology*, *26*, 611–626.

Sohlberg, M. M., McLaughlin, K. A., Pavese, A., Heidrich, A., & Posner, M. I. (2000). Evaluation of attention process therapy training in persons with acquired brain injury. *Journal of Clinical and Experimental Neuropsychology*, *22*, 656–676.

Swanson, J., Deutsch, C., Cantwell, D., Posner, M., Kennedy, J., Barr, C., et al. (2001). Genes and Attention-Deficit/Hyperactivity Disorder. *Clinical Neuroscience Research*, *1*, 207–216.

Swanson, J., Oosterlaan, J., Murias, M., Schuck, S., Flodman, P., Spence, M. A., et al. (2000). Attention deficit/hyperactivity disorder children with a 7-repeat allele of the dopamine receptor D4 gene have extreme behavior but normal performance on critical neuropsychological tests of attention. *Proceedings of National Academy of Sciences*, *97*, 4754–4759.

Tang, Y. (2005). *Health from brain, wisdom from brain.* Dailan, China: Dailan University Press.

Tang, Y. Y., Ma, Y., Wang, J., Fan, Y., Feng, S., Lu, Q., et al. (2007). Short-term meditation training improves attention and self regulation. *Proceedings of the National Academy of Sciences of the USA*, *104*, 17152–17156.

van Ijzendoorn, M. H., & Bakermans-Kranenburg, M. J. (2006). DRD4 7-repeat polymorphism moderates the association between maternal unresolved loss or trauma and infant disorganization. *Attachment and Human Development*, 8, 291–307.

van Veen, V., & Carter, C. S. (2002). The timing of action-monitoring processes in the anterior cingulate cortex. *Journal of Cognitive Neuroscience*, *14*, 593–602.

Wang, E. T., Ding, Y. C., Flodman, P, Kidd, J. R., Kidd, K. K., Grady, D. L., et al. (2004). The genetic architecture of selection at the human dopamine receptor D4 (DRD4) gene locus. *The American Journal of Human Genetics*, *74*, 931–944.

Wang, K., Fan, J., Dong, Y., Wang, C., Lee, T., & Posner, M. I. (2005). Selective impairment of attentional networks of orienting and executive control in schizophrenia. *Schizophrenia Research*, *78*, 235–241.

Washburn, D. A. (1994). Stroop-like effects for monkeys and humans: Processing speed or strength of association? *Journal of Psychological Science, 5*, 375–379.

Watanabe, E., Fukuda, S., & Shirakawa, T. (2005). Effects among healthy subjects of the duration of regularly practicing a guided imagery program. *BMC Complementary and Alternative Medicine, 5*, 21.

Whittle, S. L. (2007). The neurobiological correlates of temperament in early adolescents. Unpublished doctoral dissertation, University of Melbourne, Australia.

Wynn, K. (1992). Addition and subtraction by human infants. *Nature, 358*, 749–750.

Yang, S., & Lust, B. (2006, May). *Cross-linguistic differences in cognitive effects due to bilingualism: Experimental study of lexicon and executive attention in two typologically distinct language groups*. Paper presented at the Boston University Conference on Language Development, Boston, MA.

Zilles, K. (2005). Evolution of the human brain and comparative syto and recepto architecture. In S. Dehaene, J. R. Duhamel, M. D. Hauser, and G. Rizzolatti (Eds.), *From monkey brain to human brain* (pp. 41–56). Cambridge, MA: MIT Press, Bradford Books.

CHAPTER

5

Learning Is Not a Four-Letter Word: Changing Views of Infant Language Acquisition

Jenny R. Saffran

INTRODUCTION

For decades, researchers have endeavored to understand how we develop one of our most central abilities—language use. Fluent language comprehension and production is a hallmark of maturity, and it is all the more fascinating to understand given the typical rapidity of its developmental trajectory. With some notable exceptions (Gleitman & Wanner, 1982; Maratsos & Chalkley, 1980; Slobin, 1973), research in the 1970s and 1980s focused on documenting the incredible linguistic strides made during infancy and early childhood, including the origins of speech perception abilities, the development of the child's early vocabulary, and the

Preparation of this manuscript was supported by a grant from NICHD (R01HD37466), and by a core grant to the Waisman Center from NICHD (P30HD03352). I am grateful to Martha Alibali, Dick Aslin, Julia Evans, Ruth Litovsky, Maryellen MacDonald, Elissa Newport, Seth Pollak, Tim Rogers, Mark Seidenberg, and especially the current and past members of the UW-Madison Infant Learning Lab for many helpful discussions about these issues, to Jessica Rich for her assistance with manuscript preparation, and to the organizers and speakers at the 35th Minnesota Symposium for their contributions to these ideas.

beginnings of productive syntax. At the same time, researchers studying atypical language development were similarly—and largely separately—focused on characterizing the phenotypes of interest.

Armed with compelling descriptions of the timeline of language development, researchers in the 1990s turned their focus away from *when* to begin to ask questions about *how* and *why*. These questions have always informed theoretical approaches to the study of language acquisition, most notably due to their central role in the development of modern linguistics and the ensuing cognitive revolution (e.g., Chomsky, 1959). The development of new computational tools for analyzing corpora of speech to and by children, novel experimental techniques, and other developments in the 1990s combined together to lead to a renewed focus on mechanism. What are the processes underlying language development? How might these processes operate across different learners, including atypically developing as well as typically developing children? The past decade has seen an explosion of research aimed squarely on the question of mechanism in an endeavor to characterize and understand how it is that so much complex knowledge is acquired with such astonishing rapidity over the first few years of postnatal life.

Studying the mechanisms underlying learning provides an invaluable opportunity to bring together research on typical and atypical development. To this end, this chapter will focus on our recent findings in the domain of early language acquisition, through the lens of a developmental psychopathology approach. In particular, we study typical development in order to develop hypotheses concerning the types of learning mechanisms that are critical to successful language learning. This, in turn, provides clues about what could go wrong during language acquisition: If we are correct about the necessary ingredients of learning, we can hypothesize what might occur if one or more of these ingredients is missing. These hypotheses can then be tested in atypically developing children, whose language acquisition follows a different trajectory than typically developing children. At the same time, studies concerning language acquisition and processing in atypically developing children allow us to isolate potentially important mechanisms that are less visible in a high-functioning system. This dual focus—on children who are following a typical language-acquisition trajectory and those who are not—offers a novel perspective on the types of processes that are centrally involved as infants and children negotiate the complexities of their native language(s).

There are many facets of language acquisition that have received attention as researchers have sought to identify potential learning mechanisms. In this chapter, I will focus specifically on statistical learning mechanisms: tracking the patterns and regularities in the input that signal underlying structure. Since the first reports of statistical learning in infancy (e.g., Goodsitt, Morgan, & Kuhl, 1993; Saffran, Aslin, & Newport, 1996), these mechanisms have received a great deal of attention—and scrutiny—from a wide range of researchers (for a recent review, see Saffran & Sahni, in press). Unlike many other types of potential learning abilities, statistical learning mechanisms have the potential to operate at numerous levels of representation and could thus play a potential role in the acquisition of many different types of linguistic knowledge, from sound categories to syntax. Moreover, statistical learning mechanisms are not isolated for use in the language domain; they operate across myriad domains, and even across species (e.g., Baldwin, Andersson, Saffran, & Meyer, 2008; Fiser & Aslin, 2002; Hauser, Newport, & Aslin, 2001; Kirkham, Slemmer, & Johnson, 2002; Saffran, Johnson, Aslin, & Newport, 1999; Toro & Trobalon, 2005). At the same time, very little is known about how these mechanisms operate and, in particular, how they are constrained.

The plan for the chapter is as follows. The first section will consist of a primer on statistical learning and how it is potentially related to language in important and useful ways. Next, critiques of statistical learning approaches will be considered, followed by a discussion of recent research designed to explore the potential utility of statistical learning mechanisms. The final section of the chapter will describe recent work with two populations of children who are atypical language users—school-aged children diagnosed with Specific Language Impairment and deaf toddlers with cochlear implants—and describe preliminary findings focused on underlying differences in how these children learn and process spoken language.

Most broadly, the goal of this chapter is to highlight the importance of studying learning to understand both normative and atypical development. During the latter half of the 20th century, the study of learning was relegated to the back benches of cognitive psychology. The thorough trouncing of behaviorist approaches by proponents of the cognitive revolution broadly impacted research focused on learning. The learning-based approaches in vogue at the time were viewed as overly simplistic and unable to capture how something as abstract and generative as language could be acquired. Fortunately, the study of learning has now been combined with all we have learned from the cognitive revolution about the importance of understanding representations and the abstract nature of thought and behavior. All areas of development, including both typical and atypical development, need to attend to the fact that how we learn determines many aspects of who we are, and that all the genetic structure in the world is of no use unless it interacts with our environments. Learning provides a critical bridge between nature and nurture, regardless of the content area in question. My hope is that readers will be inspired to reconsider their own content areas through the lens of learning, and take on the myriad questions of mechanism that are raised when learning is taken seriously. In turn, understanding how learning operates in a given domain may offer novel insights into how atypical outcomes may unfold over development, either as a function of atypical environments or of atypical learning systems.

WHAT IS STATISTICAL LEARNING?

Statistical learning is one of a class of learning mechanisms that has received attention from researchers across a number of fields over the past few decades (for a recent review, see Saffran, 2008c). The central claim of statistical learning-based accounts is that humans—along with other species including monkeys and rats (e.g., Hauser et al., 2001; Toro & Trobalan, 2005)—learn by detecting probabilistic patterns in the environment that signal underlying structure. This hypothesis may be contrasted with other types of learning mechanisms that invoke explicit strategy use or that entail detection of deterministic (nonprobabilistic) rule-based abstract patterns in the environment. However, it can be difficult to empirically distinguish these types of learning, as in the example of learning by analogy, which may or may not be explicit, and may or may not be probabilistic.

There is currently widespread agreement that learners can exploit statistical patterns to discover at least some types of structure in their environments—the debates concern which patterns and under which circumstances. Of particular interest, given the developmental emphasis of this volume, is that statistical learning mechanisms are available in infancy. Evidence supporting this claim has come from infant research across a number of domains, including the acquisition of visual shape patterns (e.g., Kirkham et al., 2002), visuospatial patterns (e.g., Fiser & Aslin, 2002), visual action patterns (Baldwin et al., 2008), and musical patterns (Saffran et al., 1999; Saffran & Griepentrog, 2001).

The bulk of this research, however, has focused on language learning. Due to decades of research in the area of linguistics and psycholinguistics, a great deal is known about the structure of human languages and the nature of language input to children. This knowledge base contrasts favorably with most other domains; imagine a compendium of nearly complete descriptions of the detailed input to infants in the domain of action, or of emotion, across cultures! Linguistic research provides researchers with extensive knowledge about the nature of the environment in which children are immersed. These descriptions, paired with adult psycholinguistic experiments, provide researchers with clear hypotheses concerning the end state of language development. Similarly, computational models and corpus analyses offer detailed descriptions of the information contained in language input to children. All of these sources provide clues to the potential types of statistics that characterize children's linguistic environments. These clues, in turn, have motivated infancy researchers to perform experiments designed to determine whether, in fact, infants are capable of tracking the types of patterns that would be relevant to language learning.

Initial studies in this domain examined *word segmentation*—the problem of finding word boundaries in continuous speech—which is an important early step in language acquisition (Goodsitt et al., 1993; Saffran et al., 1996). For example, Saffran and colleagues (1996) exposed 8-month-old infants to 2 minutes of a nonsense language, generated via a computer speech synthesizer as continuous speech with no pauses or other acoustic cues to word boundaries. The only information available to signal where one word ended and the next began was statistical information: Sound pairs within words cooccurred with a higher probability than sound pairs spanning word boundaries. Infants successfully distinguished test items based solely on these distributional regularities. Subsequent research expanded these findings, demonstrating that infants are using probabilities, not just frequencies (Aslin, Saffran, & Newport, 1998). These sequential statistical regularities interact with other probabilistic cues to word boundaries. For example, once infants know how syllable stress patterning works in English, they shift from using sequential statistical cues to focusing instead on lexical stress (e.g., Johnson & Jusczyk, 2001; Thiessen & Saffran, 2003, 2007). Infants may use general cues like sequential statistics as a *bootstrapping tool*—discovering cues specific to their native language once they have used general cues to segment some initial candidate words (e.g., Sahni, Seidenberg, & Saffran, 2008).

Studies of statistical language learning have expanded beyond word segmentation to include numerous other aspects of linguistic structure (for recent reviews, see Saffran & Sahni, in press; Saffran, Werker, & Werner, 2006). For example, infants appear to track the distributions of individual sound tokens and can use the presence of bimodal versus unimodal distributions to determine whether a particular sound continuum should be broken up into two categories (as in English /r/ versus /l/) or a single category (as in the Japanese flap that straddles the English /r/ and /l/ categories; Maye, Werker, & Gerken, 2002). Infants can track the patterning of individual words to extract the beginnings of lexical categories (e.g., Gerken, Wilson, & Lewis, 2005; Gómez & LaKusta, 2004). Syntactic patterns also contain statistical information that can be harnessed by infant learners, at least in simple artificial grammars (e.g., Gómez & Gerken, 1999; Saffran & Wilson, 2003). For example, 12-month-old infants can track the statistical dependencies between individual words and word classes to discover simple grammatical phrase structures in artificial language stimuli (Saffran et al., 2008).

All of these findings, taken together, support the claim that infant learners are sensitive to a variety of different types of statistical patterns, including frequencies, modes (bimodal versus unimodal histograms), co-occurrence frequencies, transitional probabilities, and other forms of dependencies. This work has provided the impetus for numerous research programs designed to uncover the types of learning mechanisms underlying language acquisition, including both statistical and nonstatistical approaches. At the same time, this body of research has raised some thorny questions. If rats can do the same types of computations as infants (which they can, at least with respect to transitional probabilities; Toro & Trobalan, 2005), then what is special about language, and why do rats not learn language? If humans are such powerful learners, then why do languages take the particular form that they do, with specific structures recurring ubiquitously across the languages of the world? Are all of these experimental results showing infant statistical learning essentially party tricks done in the lab—could what appear to be impressive infant learning abilities really just be a reflection of the simplicity of these tasks relative to what infants face in the real world?

These are all critically important issues that need to be addressed by theories that take learning seriously as a guiding force in language acquisition. The idea of constraints on learning—a workhorse of studies in the animal learning literature (e.g., Garcia & Koelling, 1966; Marler, 1991)—has been profitably applied to the first two questions (e.g., Saffran, 2003, 2008a, 2008b). In the current chapter, I will take on the third question. What might these studies tell us about *real* learning? Can these results generalize beyond the simple lab tasks that we use to inform us about language learning "in the wild"?

To address these issues, this chapter will describe several recent lines of work that point to the potential of the statistical learning approach. We will begin in the word-segmentation domain with two studies focused on typical language development. In one set of experiments, by Graf Estes and colleagues (2007), we will ask whether the representations that emerge from statistical learning tasks in the lab actually resemble real linguistic structures (words). In the second study, we will ask whether our statistical learning tasks can be scaled up to use real natural language materials, moving away from the artificial language paradigm that has been the sole method to investigate statistical learning to date (Pelucchi, Hay, & Saffran, 2008). The results of these studies suggest that infants use statistics in language-like ways. This is not to say that statistical learning is *for* language—there is ample evidence that statistical learning operates across domains and species (e.g., Saffran & Thiessen, 2007). Instead, we believe that these results support a *constrained statistical learning hypothesis:* Nonlinguistic limitations on learning have shaped the structure of human languages, providing explanations for crosslinguistic universals.

In the last part of the chapter, we will turn to studies of individuals who are atypical language learners. The fields of communicative disorders and typical language development are growing ever closer together, with students training across both fields and developing theoretical and methodological expertise that spans these two disciplines. It is clear that studying atypical development can inform our theories of language acquisition. At the same time, the experimental tasks developed in psychology labs may help us to get a better understanding of various disorders. In particular, methods developed for use with infants and young children who do not yet produce much language may be very helpful for studies of atypical language development, where productive language may be limited. And if we are right about the importance of learning, then our hypotheses have implications for learners who follow different developmental trajectories.

To this end, we have been testing children from a number of different populations who are following atypical paths in their development of spoken language. In this chapter, I will focus on two specific groups of children: grade-school children diagnosed with Specific Language Impairment and deaf toddlers with cochlear implants. These two groups face very different challenges in learning language. While both lines of work are in their earliest stages, the results suggest that investigating the nature of language learning and processing in atypical language learners has potential to be quite illuminating with respect to the underlying mechanisms that may operate differently in these children.

What Is Statistical Learning For?

It is evident, based on the past decade of research, that infants can rapidly learn patterns based solely on statistical information. These lab tasks typically take the following structure. Infants are exposed for several minutes to a sequence of some sort, like a series of co-articulated syllables (*golabupabikututibugolabututibu* . . .) or sine wave tones (AC#FDEGBG#CAC#FBG#C . . .) or grammatically sequenced novel words (*biff rud dupp* . . . *lum dupp tiz vot* . . .). They are then tested, using head-turn preferential listening procedures, habituation/dishabituation methods, or other related techniques, to see whether they can discriminate test items drawn from the exposure corpus (e.g., a sequence consistent with familiarization, such as a word or a novel grammatical sequence) from test items that differ only in their statistical properties (e.g., a sequence that infants heard during exposure but that occurred less regularly, a novel ungrammatical sequence). Positive results consist of a significant discrimination between the two types of test items, suggesting that infants have learned something about whatever makes one item different from the other. Importantly, these studies always include *counterbalancing*, intended to rule out the possibility that what appear to be positive results due to learning actually reflect a preexisting bias for one test item over another.

Much of the experimental design in such studies centers on the choice of these test items. It is the contrast between the relatively familiar items versus the relatively novel items that points to what types of information infants tracked during exposure. In the most rigorous comparison, we can ask whether infants discriminate between test items that were equally frequent in the exposure stream but that contain different internal probabilities (e.g., Aslin et al., 1998; Fiser & Aslin, 2002; Thiessen & Saffran, 2003). Rather remarkably, infants are able to perform this test discrimination, suggesting that they are attuned not just to how often a sound pair occurs, but how probable a syllable pair is—that is, how likely Sound Y is to follow Sound X (or vice versa).

A major question raised by this research is what these successful discrimination patterns actually tell us. It is all fine and good to show that infants discriminate a word like *golabu* from a part-word sequence spanning word boundaries, like *bupabi*. But does that show that infants actually learned *golabu?* More specifically, can such results really be interpreted to suggest that infants segmented *golabu* from the speech stream and are treating it as a candidate word? No, these results do not directly speak to word segmentation. All that can be reasonably concluded is that infants have learned something about the statistics of the speech stream. While that is a very important finding in itself, it does not tell us whether statistical learning plays a role in word segmentation per se—that is, whether or not infants have pulled word-like units out of fluent speech. Moreover, it remains unclear whether any of the myriad infant studies purporting to demonstrate word segmentation actually do so, as they are all based on the same kind of test-discrimination logic as the statistical learning-type studies (though see Hollich, 2006, and Saffran, 2001, for interesting alternative approaches). Showing that infants who have been familiarized with English sentences containing *bike* can now discriminate *bike* from *cup* cannot, itself, demonstrate word segmentation. It is possible that infants are responding to the similarity of these items relative to their familiarization experience, but not actually segmenting them from the fluent speech.

To address this issue more directly, we designed a series of experiments intended to investigate the role of statistical learning in word segmentation and word learning (Graf Estes et al., 2007). Our goal was to ask how infants represent sound sequences like *golabu* following presentation in fluent speech. Are they responding to the test contrast between words and part-words (familiar sequences spanning word boundaries) with respect to the probabilities with which the sounds in each sequence co-occurred? Or are they actually treating *golabu* as a candidate word, available for subsequent mapping to meaning? Perhaps the most important feature of words is that they are sounds that become attached to meanings. However, remarkably little is known about the sound side of this problem (Saffran & Graf Estes, 2006). We thus asked whether the statistical properties of a sound sequence influenced infants' ease of mapping that sound to an object.

To do so, we developed a three-stage task, bringing methods from the word-learning literature (e.g., Stager & Werker, 1997) together with methods from the word-segmentation literature (Graf Estes et al., 2007). Seventeen-month-old infants were first familiarized with a stream of continuous speech, created by concatenating four bisyllabic nonsense words together in a random order, with only statistical cues to word boundaries. At this point, the study diverged from the usual word-segmentation task. Instead of testing infants on their ability to discriminate words and part-words (as measured by preferential looking), infants entered into a label/object association task. During this phase of the experiment, infants were exposed to sounds from the word-segmentation task, presented in isolation as labels for objects. Infants were habituated to the label/object pairs. Following habituation, infants were tested using the Same/Switch procedure, designed for use in word-learning tasks (e.g., Stager & Werker, 1997). Half of the test trials consisted of labels and objects paired correctly, as during the habituation phase (Same trials). In the other half of the trials we flipped the pairings, creating pairs different from the habituation phase (Switch trials). The logic behind this procedure is that if infants have learned the correct mappings, they should dishabituate during Switch trials, as these trials contain incorrect pairings.

The critical manipulation in this task concerned the status of the labels. For some infants, the labels presented during habituation were the *words* from the fluent stream of speech presented at the start of the experiment. For other infants, the labels were *part-words*—sound sequences spanning word boundaries. The materials were designed such that the words and part-words used as labels occurred equally often in the speech stream. We hypothesized that if statistical learning mechanisms were generating representations based on familiarity with a string of sounds, then the words and part-words should be equally good labels for the novel objects presented during habituation. However, if statistical learning was generating new *representational units*—candidate words, available for mapping to meaning—then the word labels should be more readily mapped to meanings (here, objects) than the part-word labels. This is precisely what we found. Only those infants for whom the labels were words showed a Same/Switch effect on the test, showing longer looking times for Switch trials than Same trials, as shown in Figure 5.1. These results suggest that the statistical properties of the speech stream affected subsequent word learning. Sound sequences that were statistically coherent were better labels for objects.

Of course, these results cannot show conclusively that infants use statistical information when learning the sounds of words in their actual native language. These speech streams were extremely stripped down and simplified, and the word-learning task consisted merely of associating a sound with an object. Nevertheless, the results are consistent with the

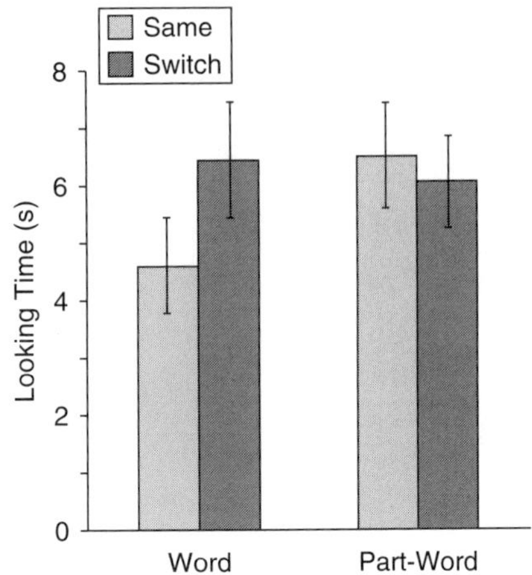

Figure 5.1 Data from Graf Estes et al. (2007), Experiment 2. Permission to reprint granted by Blackwell.

hypothesis that infants can make use of statistical learning mechanisms to generate linguistically relevant representations. In the next study, we further pursued this hypothesis by testing infants' statistical learning abilities given richer, more naturalistic, input to learning.

Statistical Learning in a Natural Language

To date, every infant statistical language-learning study has employed an artificial language paradigm, in which the materials are created using nonsense words. This methodology was adapted from research on adult learning, which has used artificial materials to investigate learning for decades. Two fields in particular have led to the development of artificial language methodologies. Beginning with Reber's (1967, 1969) classic artificial grammar experiments, implicit learning research has long used simple finite-state grammars—usually written over linguistic symbols such as letters or nonsense words—as a tool to investigate the types of information that can be learned without awareness. Researchers interested in language learning have used somewhat more complex artificial systems to investigate the mechanisms underlying adult language learning (e.g., Morgan & Newport, 1981; Morgan, Meier, & Newport, 1987, 1989). As these two fields have developed, they have largely operated independent of one another, though there is beginning to be more interaction given the clear overlap in both method and research questions (Perruchet & Pacton, 2006).

Due to the challenges of infant research, developmental studies using artificial language materials have generally required yet more simplification of the languages in question. For example, the word-segmentation studies in infants have typically used four words, either bisyllabic or trisyllabic (or a mix of the two, as in Thiessen, Hill, & Saffran, 2005), with very high transitional probabilities: usually 1.0 within words, contrasted with .25 to .33 across word boundaries. In contrast, the adult studies that preceded the infant work used six words with a far greater range of probabilities; within-word pairings were not deterministic, as in the infancy work. In general, experiments with infants have employed materials that are stripped down by adult study standards, though there have been some exceptions. For example, Saffran and colleagues (2008) successfully tested 12-month-old infants using a relatively complicated syntactic structure in an artificial grammar that had previously been used with adults—but only after first running infants (and, in this case, cotton-top tamarin monkeys) on a stripped-down, simplified version of the grammar.

Artificial languages afford researchers an unparalleled level of experimental control. In studies focused on statistical learning, for example, it is possible to carefully manipulate the statistics of an artificial language in a way that is nearly impossible given more naturalistic materials. However, the simplicity of these materials leads to concerns about ecological validity—or the lack thereof. What can we learn about actual language acquisition from what infants learn from a monotone, synthesized (or synthesized-sounding), pause-free, intonation-free, isochronous (equal beats, such that there is no rhythmic variability) stream of speech? Natural speech is exquisitely rich and complex. Perhaps the learning abilities we see in the lab cannot be used when learning from actual speech, with all its layers of variability and structure.

Alternatively, it is possible that the richness of speech actually helps infant learners. In particular, infant-directed speech contains attention-drawing prosodic manipulations and phonological cues that are often correlated with statistical information. Three recent studies from our lab support this latter hypothesis. In one study, infants were given a statistical learning task using an artificial language that was produced either with adult-directed intonation contours or with infant-directed intonation contours (Thiessen et al., 2005). The same statistical information was present in both sets of materials, and the intonation contours were uncorrelated with word boundaries. However, the infants showed better performance in the infant-directed condition, suggesting that the intonation contours served to increase their attention and/or motivation. In a second set of studies, we tested infants' memory for word lists that were either spoken or sung (Thiessen & Saffran, 2008). The presence of the melodies enhanced infants' memory recall, even given test items that were themselves spoken. Most recently, we have demonstrated that when infants are exposed to an artificial speech stream containing statistical cues (transitional probabilities) and a novel cue (here, words began with the phoneme /t/), infants were able to use the combination of the two cues to acquire the novel cue (Sahni et al., 2008). Complexity—at least some kinds of complexity—may actually enhance learning.

These studies suggest that statistical learning accounts may have the potential to scale up to include at least some aspects of natural languages. However, to date, no studies have used actual natural language materials to assess statistical learning; it is possible that infants will fail when they are confronted with the variability inherent in natural speech. One hint that infants may be able to harness statistics in natural speech comes from an experiment by Jusczyk, Houston, and Newsome (1999, Exp. 11). This experiment was part of a large set of studies designed to demonstrate the trochaic bias in word segmentation: By 9 months of age, infants treat stressed syllables as word onsets, providing a potent cue to word boundaries. Jusczyk and colleagues (1999, Exp. 11) presented infants with iambic words (weak-strong, like *guiTAR*), followed by the same syllable every time (here, *guiTAR is*). Under these circumstances, infants combined their trochaic bias with information about sequential statistics, (incorrectly) treating *TARis* as a word. These results suggest that statistical information in natural speech is used by infants, at least when paired with stress cues.

In a recent study, we designed a statistical learning task using natural speech materials (Pelucchi et al., 2008). To do so, we created materials from

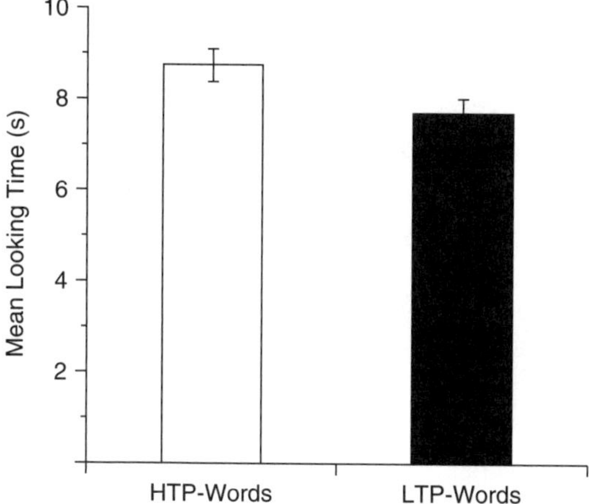

Figure 5.2 Data from Pelucchi et al. (2008), Experiment 3, for the High Transition Probability words versus the Low Transition Probability words.

a natural language that was previously unfamiliar to our Wisconsin infants: Italian. In this set of experiments, we carefully controlled the sequential statistics of the materials and used a native Italian speaker who was asked to produce the sentences naturally, as if she was addressing an infant. The resulting speech stream contained statistical cues to word boundaries as in our previous artificial language experiments, as well as the myriad other features that vary in natural speech. In addition, the target words occurred relatively infrequently, as would be typical of natural speech but quite unlike the artificial speech streams used in previous studies (where four to six words repeat in random order). There were also far more words, syllables, and phonemes represented than in a typical artificial language corpus.

Nevertheless, infants successfully discriminated test items based on exposure to one of two counterbalanced languages. As shown in Figure 5.2, infants were able to discriminate between test words with high transitional probability versus test words with low transitional probability. Both types of words occurred equally often during the familiarization stream and contained the preferred trochaic stress pattern. The results thus suggest that infants are able to track transitional probability information across a corpus of naturally produced speech. This is all the more impressive given that the materials were generated in Italian and thus contained sounds and sound patterns that were entirely unfamiliar to the infants. A situation like this is likely to be even more challenging than learning from native language materials, when infants are already familiar with the sound inventory and perhaps some of the component words.

It thus appears that infants can exploit statistical regularities in contexts rather more complex than those usually presented in lab tasks. On the one hand, this is not surprising, given that there is reason to believe that statistical knowledge subserves aspects of infants' native language knowledge. On the other hand, it is remarkable to see how rapidly infants can harness this knowledge in situations in which it is of no conceivable use. There is no feedback in these experiments and no reward other than learning itself. Infants appear to track statistical regularities quite naturally, even in the face of (or perhaps because of) complicated input containing many layers of potential information.

However, we know that by the time infants are in their second year of postnatal life there are measurable divergences in their language-learning attainments. Recent studies suggest that the roots of these challenges can be measured in infancy. For example, early speech-perception skill is linked to later word-learning outcomes (Tsao, Liu, & Kuhl, 2004). Similarly, infants' lexical-processing skill predicts language outcomes months and even years later (Fernald, Perfors, & Marchman, 2006; Marchman & Fernald, 2008). Even infants' word-segmentation and word-recognition skills have been linked to subsequent language outcomes (Newman, Bernstein Ratner, Jusczyk, Jusczyk, & Dow, 2006). While the particular mechanisms underlying these linkages have yet to be identified, it is clear that individual differences are rampant in early language acquisition, despite textbook claims about the ease of language learning in infancy. In the next section, we turn to studies of atypical development that can help to shed light on potential factors underlying these difficulties.

LANGUAGE LEARNING AND ATYPICAL DEVELOPMENT

There are many reasons to be fascinated by atypical language development. Language acquisition is commonly viewed as effortless and achieved by (almost) all children at roughly the same pace. This textbook view obscures the tremendous range of individual differences that are obvious to parents and practitioners. Some of these individual differences are benign. For example, roughly 15% of toddlers are considered to be *late-talkers* at 24 months—that is, at the bottom end of the distribution for achievement on language-related tasks, with apparently typical functioning in other domains. Of these children, 50 to 70% *catch up* and perform in the normal range on language tasks by school age (for a review, see Leonard, 1998). However, the remaining children show residual language deficits at the outset of school, and they are at risk for lower academic achievement and other negative ramifications of impaired communication abilities.

Roughly 7% of kindergarten-aged children meet diagnostic criteria for Specific Language Impairment, or SLI (Tomblin et al., 1997). These children score in the normal range on nonverbal IQ tests and have no frank perceptual impairments (e.g., their hearing is in the normal range). However, they show challenges in myriad language-related tasks, from vocabulary to grammatical skills to pragmatic abilities. The *specific* aspect of the diagnostic category has been under fire in recent years, as researchers have expanded their investigations beyond IQ and other standardized measurements of nonverbal skill (which appear to be age-typical) to examine more general cognitive abilities such as working memory and processing speed in these children (e.g., Leonard, 1998).

Learning is one aspect of SLI that has received surprisingly little attention. Given that acquiring a native language necessarily entails a great deal of learning, it seems natural to extend investigations of SLI to include these children's ability to learn in both verbal and nonverbal domains. Two recent studies with adolescents and college students revealed provocative findings (Plante, Gomez, & Gerken, 2002; Tomblin, Mainela-Arnold, & Zhang, 2007). When individuals with SLI or related language-learning disorders were tested using implicit learning tasks, including both linguistic and nonlinguistic stimuli, their performance was impaired relative to unaffected individuals. For example, Tomblin and colleagues (2007) tested adolescents with SLI on a serial reaction-time task, in which the dependent measure was reaction time to respond to patterns of visual stimuli (nonlinguistic shapes). Despite the fact that the materials were entirely nonverbal, the adolescents with SLI were markedly slower to acquire the patterns. Moreover, children's language scores from kindergarten were correlated with their performance on this nonlinguistic task, administered in high school. These results suggest that challenges in sequence learning may be related to eventual native language skill.

In a recent study, we tested the hypothesis that statistical learning mechanisms may underlie at least part of the challenge facing children with SLI (Evans, Saffran, & Robe, 2008). Using materials and methods previously developed for testing grade-school children (Saffran, Newport, Aslin, Tunick, & Barrueco, 1997), we tested a group of children diagnosed with SLI on a statistical word-segmentation task, along with a comparison group matched for age and nonverbal IQ. In this task, children listened to a continuous stream of speech generated using an artificial language, with no word boundary cues other than sequential statistics, for 21 minutes. They were then given a forced-choice task in which words from the speech stream were paired with nonwords (consisting of syllables from the stream presented in novel orders) and asked to choose which item was most similar to the speech stream. We used practice trials with English items to ensure that all participants were able to do the task.

The results of this first study were clear. Given 21 minutes of exposure to the sequences, the children with SLI were unable to achieve above-chance performance and performed significantly worse than the comparison group. Both groups showed tremendous individual variation, with some children in the normal language comparison group performing in the range of the SLI group (see Fig. 5.3). Interestingly, we also found that task performance was correlated with measures of English expressive and receptive vocabulary, suggesting that the artificial language task was indeed capturing something in common with these children's native language achievement.

In a second study, we doubled the exposure to 42 minutes in order to ask whether children with SLI were incapable of performing the task, or if they could do so with more time to learn the sequences. Given this additional exposure, the SLI group was able to *catch up* to the normal language comparison group, as shown on the left panel of Figure 5.4. We also tested the same children using *nonspeech stimuli*—tone sequences

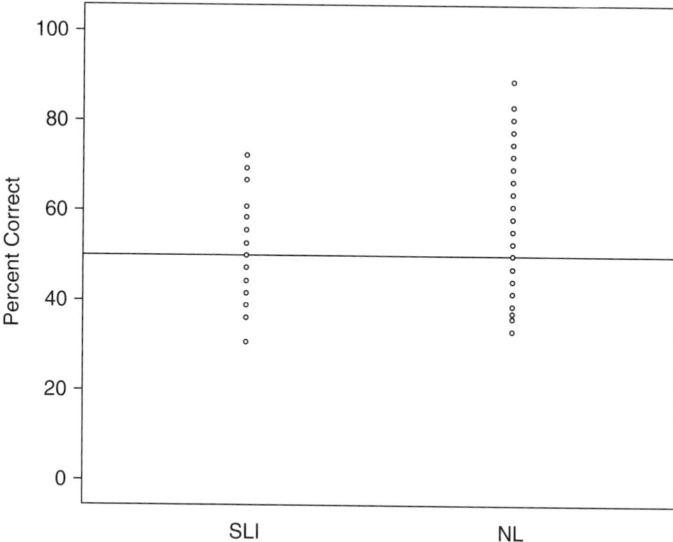

Figure 5.3 Data from Evans et al. (2008), Experiment 1, for the SLI group and the Normal Language (NL) group.

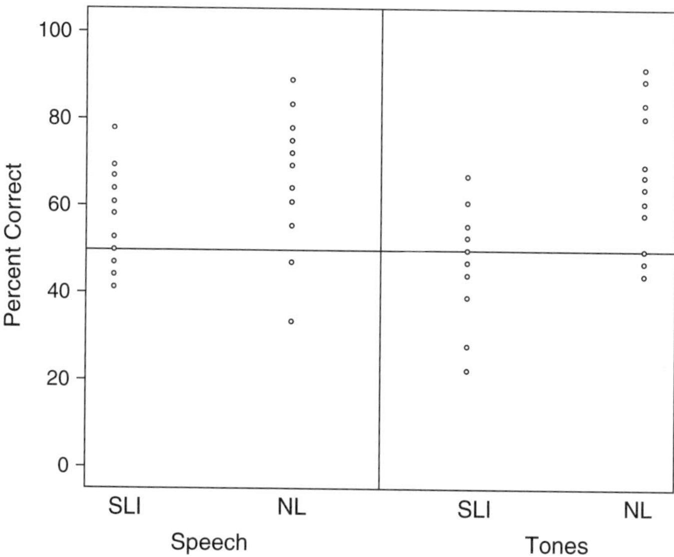

Figure 5.4 Data from Evans et al. (2008), Experiment 2, for the SLI group and the Normal Language (NL) group. The left panel shows performance after 42 min of the speech stimuli; the right panel shows performance after 42 min of the nonlinguistic tone stimuli.

that followed the same statistics as the linguistic stimuli (Saffran et al., 1999). To our surprise, the SLI group was unable to exceed chance performance given the nonlinguistic tone stimuli, as shown on the right panel of Figure 5.4. Despite 42 minutes of exposure, the children with SLI were unable to succeed at the nonlinguistic task, performing worse on the nonlinguistic task than on the linguistic task. Importantly, the typically developing comparison group performed comparably on the linguistic and nonlinguistic tasks, suggesting that the latter task was not inherently more difficult.

These experiments raise more questions than they answer. Why do children with SLI have difficulty at tracking statistical patterns? Is the problem with the statistical computations, or with children's ability to represent the elements over which the statistics are computed (Saffran, 2008b)? Unconfounding these factors is going to be critical in developing new hypotheses about the nature of SLI. Recent studies of the speech-perception abilities of children with SLI suggest that they may have difficulty representing synthesized speech, which contains fewer of the redundant cues present in natural speech (e.g., Coady, Evans, Mainela-Arnold, & Kluender, 2007). It is thus possible that the children with SLI are perfectly capable of tracking the appropriate statistics, but that the units over which the statistics are tracked are not well represented, and that this noise is influencing the results. This would be consistent with the fact that the worst performance was on the tone sequences; these were created from sine wave tones and were extremely unnatural. Additional research manipulating the materials, and the domain from which the materials are drawn, is likely to be extremely helpful in disentangling these possibilities.

Whatever the reason, it is clear that learning—more specifically, challenges in learning—may be part of the difficulty facing children with SLI. Language learning requires a cascade of knowledge. Without fine-grained representations of the sounds of language, it is much more difficult to begin to learn the sound structure of language—which sounds can occur in which positions in syllables and words—and to begin to segment words from speech. Without isolating words from fluent speech, it is much more difficult to begin to map those sounds onto meanings.

And without solid word representations, syntactic structure will remain elusive. Thus, understanding the antecedents of learning, and how they may be challenged in different populations of children, will be critical for developing tailored interventions.

Language Learning and Atypical Perceptual Systems

The previous section focused on learning when perceptual systems are intact, but the machinery underlying language learning (and potentially other learning as well) is operating atypically. What about cases in which the language-learning machinery is presumably intact, but the input to language learning is atypical due to a different set of perceptual systems? Recent technological developments provide aspects of hearing to individuals who are profoundly deaf. Multiple-channel cochlear implants (CIs) are sensory prostheses that provide auditory input to people who are deaf by transforming acoustic information into an electric signal that stimulates the auditory nerve. For children who are born deaf, the electrical stimulation from CIs is a novel sensory input that is introduced following a period of auditory deprivation. When provided at an early age, CIs enable children to learn aspects of spoken language and other auditory skills, with better results associated with earlier implantation, though there are huge individual differences in outcomes across the board (e.g., Svirsky, Robbins, Kirk, Pisoni, & Miyamoto, 2000).

Almost all of the research concerning deaf children with CIs has relied upon standardized measures of language skill. In particular, there are very few studies of infants and young children with CIs that use sensitive measures designed to tap underlying speech and language abilities (e.g., Houston, Pisoni, Kirk, Ying, & Miyamoto, 2003). How infants and young children process and learn from the degraded input provided by CIs remains largely unknown.

We developed a series of experiments designed to assess language processing and acquisition in deaf toddlers with cochlear implants (Grieco-Calub, Saffran, & Litovsky, 2008). In particular, we were interested in how these children process language online, in real time. Do they recognize familiar words in the same way as their peers? These children were all profoundly deaf at birth and received a CI by approximately

13 months of age. What are the effects of months without any auditory stimulation, combined with the impoverished signal provided by the CI?

In these studies, we tested two groups of 2- to 3-year-old children: deaf toddlers with CIs and a hearing comparison group. We used a looking-while-listening task previously developed by Fernald, Swingley, and their collaborators (e.g., Fernald, Pinto, Swingley, Weinberg, & McRoberts, 1998; Fernald, Swingley, & Pinto, 2001; Swingley & Aslin, 2000, 2002). Toddlers were seated in front of a large video monitor. On each trial, two familiar objects were displayed on the monitor, and the toddler heard a prerecorded instruction to attend to one of the two objects: "Look at the ball—can you find it?" We recorded the children's eye movements in order to measure their accuracy (correct looks to the target object) and their latency (the speed with which they looked at the target object). All of the labels were highly frequent and easily depicted objects that children of this age typically name easily, such as ball, dog, and car. As a further manipulation, we ran the same study twice. In one iteration of the task, all of the items were labeled in silence, as is usual in such tasks. In the other iteration, the items were labeled against a noisy background (two-talker babble), which was slightly quieter than the instructions to look at the target object. This manipulation allowed us to assess word recognition in an environment that is more characteristic of language processing, which rarely occurs against a silent background.

The results of this study were intriguing and are shown in Figure 5.5. Despite the use of highly familiar words like *dog* and *ball*, 2- to 3-year-old deaf toddlers with CIs showed decreased accuracy in recognizing these words, as indexed by their eye movements toward the correct target. This is perhaps not surprising, given that these children, on average, will have had one less year of exposure to spoken language than the normal hearing comparison group. The good news is that these children did successfully recognize the words, by and large, when they were presented against a silent background. However, their accuracy lags behind normal hearing infants, tested in prior studies, who are on average a year younger than the children we tested. We also found that the presence of background noise impacted both groups of toddlers, decreasing the accuracy of the normal hearing and the deaf children. In fact, the toddlers with CIs were unable to recognize these common words at above-chance levels in the presence of noise.

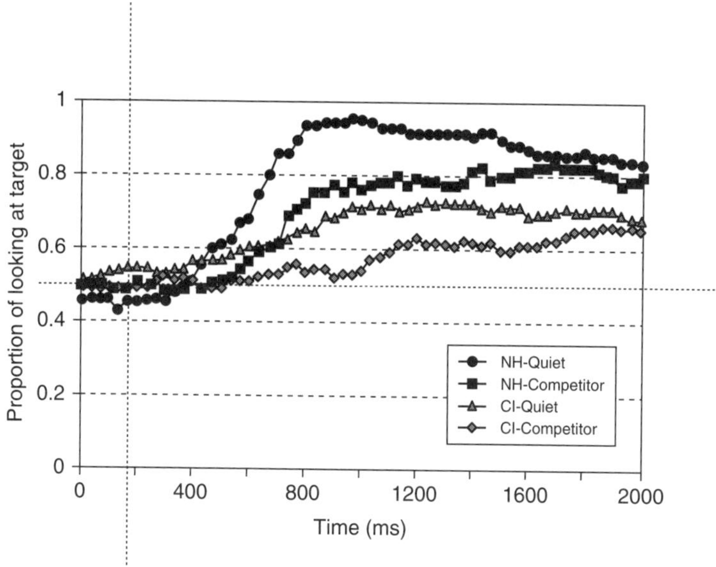

Figure 5.5 Proportion of looks to target as a function of time since target word onset (chance = 50%), for normal hearing toddlers (NH) and toddlers with cochlear implants (CIs). Data are plotted for targets presented in silence and for targets presented with background competitor speech. From Grieco-Calub, Saffran, & Litovsky (2008).

Perhaps the most interesting aspect of these results concerns the time course of word recognition. By coding the toddlers' eye movements, frame by frame, we are able to tell when they first successfully fixate the target object, which provides a time-locked index of lexical access—when do children first look at the right object following the verbal instructions? The normal hearing toddlers are quite quick, with their first looks at the target approximately 600 ms from the onset of the target word to peak accuracy, when the word is presented in silence. However, the deaf toddlers with CIs are markedly slower, with their first looks at the target several hundred milliseconds later than the normally hearing toddlers. This timing difference is immensely important in understanding the challenges facing deaf children with CIs. In normal speech, this time gap could include a syllable, or even two. If deaf children with CIs are processing language more slowly than typical children, there could be huge ramifications for their ability to understand spoken language. Some of the observed individual differences in outcome may be traceable to these timing issues.

In future studies, we will continue to attempt to unpack individual differences in this population. For example, it is possible that early exposure to structured signed input, especially natural languages like American Sign Language, can actually facilitate the acquisition of spoken language, perhaps by providing experience with rapid sequential input (e.g., Mayberry, Lock, & Kazmi, 2002). The most important point is that, without using fine-grained measures that provide temporal information, we would not have observed these differences in processing time across our two groups of toddlers. Experimental methods thus have great promise in going beyond parental report measures to provide insight into differences underlying groups and individuals.

CONCLUSIONS: A ROLE FOR LEARNING IN THE STUDY OF TYPICAL AND ATYPICAL DEVELOPMENT

The goal of this chapter was to provide evidence supporting the central role of learning in language development and to show how statistical learning studies of typically developing children are beginning to inform work with atypical populations and vice versa. The idea that learning is important to language development should not be a controversial one. However, the hypothesis that learning mechanisms play an important causal role in understanding language acquisition—and challenges thereof—has only recently begun to make an impact on the field. In this chapter, we have presented illustrative examples to show how far we have come in our theoretical and empirical work focused on learning mechanisms in language development. It should also be clear just how far we have to go before we have anything resembling a full theory.

It is important to point out that the kind of learning espoused here does not resemble the blank-slate empiricism of the past. These learning mechanisms are complicated and interactive. While we do not believe that the mechanisms themselves are domain-specific, they operate within specific domains in ways that are constrained by our perceptual systems, the material to be learned, and our prior knowledge in the given domain (e.g., Saffran, 2008b, c). There appear to be computational properties of the human mind, including infants' minds, that differ from those of other primates and that may facilitate the acquisition of some critical aspects of language (Saffran et al., 2008). The complexity of the learning machinery underlying language, and its relationship to other aspects of cognition, perception, and social interaction, mirrors the complexity of the system to be learned.

These considerations suggest that understanding the differences between typical and atypical language-development pathways will also require a complex explanation. There will not be a silver bullet, or a *language gene*, that can explain critical individual differences. The studies described in this chapter are just a first step in our attempt to unravel the complex dynamics among perception, learning, processing, and outcomes. The past decade has seen a vast increase in the number of researchers focused on the relationship between typical and atypical language acquisition. Along with this increase in researchers comes an explosion of methods and theories. This is an extremely hopeful sign of progress, and the landscape of this field will likely look very different in another decade—just as the field of typical language development has changed vastly with the introduction of new methods and theories designed to focus on mechanism.

With respect to statistical learning in particular, there is no doubt that infants are remarkable learners. They can track statistics implicitly, across numerous domains. While learning has not been central to studies of atypical language development, it has potential. In particular, learners must be able to perceive and process the input prior to tracking statistics. Without adequate representations of the input, it is not possible to do the right computations. Perception, learning, and their interaction should be taken seriously both within and across developmental domains.

REFERENCES

Aslin, R. N., Saffran, J. R., & Newport, E. L. (1998). Computation of conditional probability statistics by 8-month-old infants. *Psychological Science*, 9, 321–324.

Baldwin, D., Andersson, A., Saffran, J. R., & Meyer, M. (2008). Segmenting dynamic human action via statistical structure. *Cognition*, *106*, 1382–1407.

Chomsky, N. (1959). Review of B. F. Skinner's "Verbal Behavior". *Language, 35*, 26–58.

Coady, J., Evans, J. L., Mainela-Arnold, E., & Kluender, K. (2007). Children with specific language impairments perceive speech most categorically when tokens are natural and meaningful. *Journal of Speech, Language and Hearing Research, 50*, 41–57.

Evans, J., Saffran, J. R., & Robe, K. (2008). Statistical learning in children with Specific Language Impairments. Manuscript in press, *Journal of Speech, Language and Hearing Research.*

Fernald, A., Perfors, A., & Marchman, V. A. (2006). Picking up speed in understanding: Speech processing efficiency and vocabulary growth across the second year. *Developmental Psychology, 42*, 98–116.

Fernald, A., Pinto, J. P., Swingley, D., Weinberg, A., & McRoberts, G. W. (1998). Rapid gains in speed of verbal processing by infants in the second year. *Psychological Science*, 9, 72–75.

Fernald, A., Swingley, D., & Pinto, J. P. (2001). When half a word is enough: infants can recognize spoken words using partial phonetic information. *Child Development, 72*, 1003–1015.

Fiser, J., & Aslin, R. N. (2002). Statistical learning of new visual feature combinations by infants. *Proceedings of the National Academy of Sciences*, 99, 15822–15826.

Garcia, J., & Koelling, R. A. (1966). Relation of cue to consequence in avoidance learning. *Psychonomic Science*, 4, 123–124.

Gerken, L. A., Wilson, R., & Lewis, W. (2005). Seventeen-month-olds can use distributional cues to form syntactic categories. *Journal of Child Language*, 32, 249–268.

Gleitman, L. R., & Wanner, E. (1982). *Language acquisition: The state of the state of the art.* In E. Wanner & L. R. Wanner (Eds.), *Language acquisition: The state of the art* (pp. 3–48). Cambridge, UK: Cambridge University Press.

Gómez, R. L., & Gerken, L. (1999). Artificial grammar learning by 1-year-olds leads to specific and abstract knowledge. *Cognition, 70*, 109–135.

Gómez, R. L., & LaKusta, L. (2004). A first step in form-based category abstraction by 12-month-old infants. *Developmental Science, 7*, 567–580.

Goodsitt, J. V., Morgan, J. L., & Kuhl, P. K. (1993). Perceptual strategies in prelingual speech segmentation. *Journal of Child Language, 20*, 229–252.

Graf Estes, K. M., Evans, J., Alibali, M. W., & Saffran, J. R. (2007). Can infants map meaning to newly segmented words? Statistical segmentation and word learning. *Psychological Science, 18*, 254–260.

Grieco-Calub, T. M., Saffran, J. R., & Litovsky, R. (2008). Spoken word recognition in toddlers who use cochlear implants. Manuscript under editorial review.

Hauser, M. D., Newport, E. L., & Aslin, R. N. (2001). Segmentation of the speech stream in a non-human primate: Statistical learning in cotton-top tamarins. *Cognition, 78*, B53–B64.

Hollich, G. (2006). Combining techniques to reveal emergent effects in infants' segmentation, word learning, and grammar. *Language and Speech, 49*, 3–19.

Houston, D. M., Pisoni, D. B., Kirk, K. I., Ying, E. A., & Miyamoto, R. T. (2003). Speech perception skills of deaf infants following cochlear implantation: A first report. *International Journal of Pediatric Otorhinolaryngology, 67*, 479–495.

Johnson, E. K., & Jusczyk, P. W. (2001). Word segmentation by 8-month-olds: When speech cues count more than statistics. *Journal of Memory and Language, 44*, 548–567.

Jusczyk, P. W., Houston, D. M., & Newsome, M. (1999). The beginnings of word segmentation in English-learning infants. *Cognitive Psychology, 39*, 159–207.

Kirkham, N. Z., Slemmer, J. A., & Johnson, S. P. (2002). Visual statistical learning in infancy: Evidence for a domain general learning mechanism. *Cognition, 83*, B35–B42.

Leonard, L. (1998). *Children with specific language impairment.* Cambridge, MA: MIT Press.

Maratsos, M., & Chalkley, M. (1980). The internal language of children's syntax: The ontogenesis and representation of syntactic categories. In K. Nelson (Ed.), *Children's language: Vol. 2*, pp. 127–214. New York: Gardner Press.

Marchman, V. A., & Fernald, A. (2008). Speed of word recognition and vocabulary knowledge in infancy predict cognitive and language outcomes in later childhood. *Developmental Science, 11*, F9–F16.

Marler, P. (1991). *The instinct to learn.* In S. Carey & R. Gelman (Eds.), *The epigenesis of mind: Essays on biology and cognition*, pp. 37–66. Hillsdale, NJ: Erlbaum.

Mayberry, R. I., Lock, E., & Kazmi, H. (2002). Linguistic ability and early language exposure. *Nature, 417*, 38.

Maye, J., Werker, J. F., & Gerken, L. (2002). Infant sensitivity to distributional information can affect phonetic discrimination. *Cognition, 82*, B101–B111.

Morgan, J., Meier, R., & Newport, E. (1987). Structural packaging in the input to language learning: Contributions of prosodic and morphological marking of phrases to the acquisition of language. *Cognitive Psychology, 19*, 498–550.

Morgan, J., Meier, R., & Newport, E. (1989). Facilitating the acquisition of syntax with cross-sentential cues to phrase structure. *Journal of Memory and Language*, *28*, 360–374.

Morgan, J., & Newport, E. (1981). The role of constituent structure in the induction of an artificial language. *Journal of Verbal Learning & Verbal Behavior*, *20*, 67–85.

Newman, R., Bernstein Ratner, N., Jusczyk, A. M., Jusczyk, P. W., & Dow, K. A. (2006). Infants' early ability to segment the conversational speech signal predicts later language development: A retrospective analysis. *Developmental Psychology*, *42*, 643–655.

Pelucchi, B., Hay, J. F., & Saffran, J. R. (2008). Statistical learning in a natural language by 8-month-old infants. Manuscript under review.

Perruchet, P., & Pacton, S. (2006). Implicit learning and statistical learning: One phenomenon, two approaches. *Trends in Cognitive Science*, *10*, 233–238.

Plante, E. R., Gomez, R., & Gerken, L. (2002). Sensitivity to word order cues by normal and language/learning disables adults. *Journal of Communication Disorders*, *35*, 453–462.

Reber, A. S. (1967). Implicit learning of artificial grammars. *Journal of Verbal Learning & Verbal Behavior*, *6*, 855–863.

Reber, A. S. (1969). Transfer of syntactic structure in synthetic languages. *Journal of Experimental Psychology*, *18*, 115–119.

Saffran, J. R. (2001). Words in a sea of sounds: The output of infant statistical learning. *Cognition*, *81*, 149–169.

Saffran, J. R. (2003). Statistical language learning: Mechanisms and constraints. *Current Directions in Psychological Science*, *12*, 110–114.

Saffran, J. R. (2008a). *Acquiring grammatical patterns: Constraints on learning.* Chapter to appear in J. Columbo, P. McCardle, & L. Freund (Eds.), *Pathways to language from infancy.* Mahwah, NJ: Lawrence Erlbaum. Manuscript in press.

Saffran, J. R. (2008b). What can statistical learning tell us about infant learning? Chapter to appear in A. Needham & A. Woodward (Eds.), *Learning and the infant mind.* Oxford, UK: Oxford University Press. Manuscript in press.

Saffran, J. R. (2008c). What is statistical learning, and what statistical learning is not. Chapter to appear in S. Johnson (Ed.), *Neoconstructivism: The new science of cognitive development*, Oxford, UK: Oxford University Press. Manuscript in press.

Saffran, J. R., Aslin, R. N., & Newport, E. L. (1996). Statistical learning by 8-month-old infants. *Science*, *274*, 1926–1928.

Saffran, J. R., & Graf Estes, K. M. (2006). Mapping sound to meaning: Connections between learning about sounds and learning about words. In R. Kail (Ed.), *Advances in child development and behavior* (pp. 1–38). New York: Elsevier.

Saffran, J. R., & Griepentrog, G. J. (2001). Absolute pitch in infant auditory learning: Evidence for developmental reorganization. *Developmental Psychology, 37*, 74–85.

Saffran, J. R., Hauser, M., Seibel, R., Kapfhamer, J., Tsao, F., & Cushman, F. (2008). Grammatical pattern learning by human infants and cotton-top tamarin monkeys. *Cognition, 107*, 479–500.

Saffran, J. R., Johnson, E. K., Aslin, R. N., & Newport, E. L. (1999). Statistical learning of tone sequences by human infants and adults. *Cognition, 70*, 27–52.

Saffran, J. R., Newport, E. L., Aslin, R. N., Tunick, R. A., & Barrueco, S. (1997). Incidental language learning: Listening (and learning) out of the corner of your ear. *Psychological Science, 8*, 101–105.

Saffran, J. R., & Sahni, S. D. (in press). Learning the sounds of language. Chapter to appear in M. Joanisse, M. Spivey, and K. McCrae (Eds.), *Cambridge handbook of psycholinguistics*. Cambridge, UK: Cambridge University Press.

Saffran, J. R., & Thiessen, E. D. (2007). Domain-general learning capacities. In E. Hoff & M. Shatz (Eds.), *Blackwell handbook of language development* (pp. 68–86). Malden, MA: Blackwell.

Saffran, J. R., Werker, J. F., & Werner, L. A. (2006). The infant's auditory world: Hearing, speech, and the beginnings of language. In D. Kuhn & R. S. Siegler (Eds.), *Handbook of child psychology: Vol 2. Cognition, perception, and language* (6th ed., pp. 58–108). Hoboken, NJ: Wiley

Saffran, J. R., & Wilson, D. P. (2003). From syllables to syntax: Multilevel statistical learning by 12-month-old infants. *Infancy, 4*, 273–284.

Sahni, S. D., Seidenberg, M. S., & Saffran, J. R. (2008). Connecting cues in word segmentation. Manuscript submitted for publication.

Slobin, D. (1973). Cognitive prerequisites for the development of grammar. In C. Ferguson and D. Slobin (Eds.), *Studies of child language development*. New York: Holt, Rinehart, & Winston.

Stager, C. L., & Werker, J. F. (1997). Infants listen for more phonetic detail in speech perception than in word-learning tasks. *Nature, 388*, 381–382.

Svirsky, M. A., Robbins, A. M., Kirk, K. I., Pisoni, D. B., & Miyamoto, R. T. (2000). Language development in profoundly deaf children with cochlear implants. *Psychological Science, 11*, 153–158.

Swingley, D., & Aslin, R. N. (2000). Spoken word recognition and lexical representation in very young children. *Cognition*, *76*, 147–166.

Swingley, D., & Aslin, R. N. (2002). Lexical neighborhoods and the word-form representations of 14-month-olds. *Psychological Science*, *13*, 480–484.

Thiessen, E. D., Hill, E. A., & Saffran, J. R. (2005). Infant-directed speech facilitates word segmentation. *Infancy*, *7*, 53–71.

Thiessen, E. D., & Saffran, J. R. (2003). When cues collide: Use of stress and statistical cues to word boundaries by 7- to 9-month-old infants. *Developmental Psychology*, *39*, 706–716.

Thiessen, E. D., & Saffran, J. R. (2007). Learning to learn: Infants' acquisition of stress-based strategies for word segmentation. *Language Learning and Development*, *3*, 73–100.

Thiessen, E. D., & Saffran, J. R. (2008). How the melody facilitates the message, and vice versa, in infant learning and memory. Manuscript under review.

Tomblin, B., Mainela-Arnold, E., & Zhang, X. (2007). Procedural learning in children with and without specific language impairment. *Journal of Child Language Learning and Development*, *3*, 269–293.

Tomblin, J. B., Records, N. L., Buckwalter, P., Zhang, X., Smith, E., & O'Brien, M. (1997). The prevalence of specific language impairment in kindergarten children. *Journal of Speech Language Hearing Research*, *40*, 1245–1260.

Toro, J. M., & Trobalon, J. B. (2005). Statistical computations over a speech stream in a rodent. *Perception & Psychophysics*, *67*, 867–875.

Tsao, F.-M., Liu, H.-M., & Kuhl, P. K. (2004). Speech perception in infancy predicts language development in the second year of life: A longitudinal study. *Child Development*, *75*, 1067–1084.

CHAPTER

6

The Emergence of Emotion: Experience, Development, and Biology

Seth D. Pollak

> "For I regard human emotions and their properties as on the same footing with other natural phenomena. Assuredly human emotions indicate the power and ingenuity of nature, if not human nature, quite as fully as other things which we admire, and which we delight to contemplate."
>
> (Spinoza, 1677/1957, p. 114)

A central assumption in the study of human emotion is that we are born with certain basic emotions (at least those referred to in Western cultures by words such as *anger*, *sadness*, *fear*, *disgust*, and *happiness*) and that some rudimentary neural circuitry for emotion is preconfigured in the human brain. Indeed, the predominant theories of emotion take as a core tenet that basic emotions are characterized by distinctive signatures of hormonal, muscular, autonomic, and subjective responses that are each coordinated to serve adaptive functions (e.g., Buck, 1999; Cosmides & Tooby,

The writing of this chapter was supported by the National Institute of Mental Health through grant numbers R01-MH61285 and R01-MH68858.

2000; Ekman, 1973, 1992; Izard, 1978, 1993; Ekman, Campos, Davidson, & de Waal, 2003; Johnson-Laird & Oatley, 1992; LeDoux, 2000; Levenson, 2003a,b; Panksepp, 2000; Plutchik, 1982). Often these theories include acknowledgment that influences such as the developing child's learning history may play a role in emotional responding (e.g., Ekman, 1992; Izard, Youngstrom, Fine, Mostow, & Trentacosta, 2006; Keltner & Haidt, 2001; Panksepp, 1998). In general, however, theories of emotional development either emphasize the hard-wired, universal aspect of emotion and devote little attention to learning processes, or they emphasize functional adaptations and underspecify the initial state of emotion in the brain that facilitates learning (Campos, Mumme, Kermoian, & Campos, 1994). In this chapter, I focus on a central question in human development: How do children manage to learn so much about emotion from the examples they see, hear, and experience? Are the emotional signals that children experience too vast and complex a system for children to learn from, or are emotions too inconsistent, unclear, or nuanced to support rapid learning and mastery without some guided predisposition for emotion learning? Whether or not emotional experiences are complex or vague, the reality is that most infants do learn an immense amount about emotions and master a complex social repertoire; yet we understand little about what guides this early learning. Here, I highlight different perspectives on the ontogenesis of emotion. Next, I examine data that are both in favor of and inconsistent with these arguments about the origin of emotion. I conclude by noting the ways in which translational research—both between basic and clinical as well as human and nonhuman studies—may help clarify the developmental mechanisms underlying emotion. Because emotional difficulties are central to all forms of mental health problems, a clear understanding of the origin and development of emotion holds tremendous promise for prevention and remediation of mental illness in children and adults.

WHAT IS THE INITIAL STATE OF THE EMOTIONAL BRAIN?

One view of the origins of emotions maintains that humans are genetically programmed to develop the circuitry that underlies basic emotional behaviors. Darwin (1872/1965), for example, argued that facial expressions are innate. By describing emotions as innate, Darwin meant that the ability to pose, express, and understand the meaning of facial expressions exists in the brain independent of any kind of sensory or learning experience. The most prominent contemporary theories about the ontogenesis of emotion, including those of Silvan Tomkins (1963), Carroll Izard (1991), and Paul Ekman (1994), begin with the basic premise that rudimentary or basic emotions are innate, discrete neurological packages with specific sets of predetermined bodily and facial reactions. These theories about emotion are grounded in a broader rubric called *nativism*, which refers to the view that certain skills or abilities are *native* or hardwired into the brain at birth.

Nativism emerges from a rich intellectual history in psychology, philosophy, and developmental biology. As it is applied to psychological phenomena, nativism stems from the seminal ideas of the philosopher David Hume. Hume (1748/1902) articulated a logical argument: People could not infer notions of causality based upon the perceptual input we receive from the world. Based upon what we actually observe, the most we could hope to infer from our perceptual experiences is that two events happen in succession. We could only reason that A preceded B or that A and B co-occur, but not that B resulted from A. What follows from Hume's argument is the conclusion that concepts such as the ability to understand causality must exist in the mind prior to any sensory or perceptual experience. The extension of this argument is that any psychological construct that organisms acquire, but that could not have been learned based upon sensory input, must be innate. Indeed, the philosopher Immanuel Kant, in his *Critique of Pure Reason* (1902), posited that from birth humans know certain things about objects that they could not have learned based upon their experiences in the world. One example of this type of knowledge is that all objects are successive over time and juxtaposed in space. Schopenhauer (1928) agreed with Kant that humans must have some innate knowledge, but he reduced the number of innate categories back down to the original one—namely, causality, which, he argued, presupposes all other domains of knowledge.

Modern psychology has greatly expanded the domains of knowledge hypothesized to be innate. Arguments in favor of innate knowledge in humans have been advanced for emotion (Ekman, 1999; Izard, 1997), physics (Spelke, 1999), causality (Leslie & Keeble, 1987), animacy (Carey, 1985), grammar (Chomsky, 1959/2003), face processing (Kanwisher, 2000), intentionality (Gergely & Csibra, 2003), numeracy (Dehaene & Cohen, 1997; Xu, Spelke, & Goddard, 2005), theory of mind (Leslie, 1987), attachment (Bowlby, 1988), and most recently social hierarchy (Zink et al., 2008). A related perspective that combines these views is that humans are born with *core knowledge* systems that represent inanimate objects and their mechanics, social agents and their goal-directed actions, numerical relationships, and spatial/geometric relationships (Spelke & Kinzler, 2007).

The contrasting view to nativism is empiricism. *Empiricism* holds that the innate capabilities of the brain do not contain content such as beliefs, knowledge, or specific packages of skills; instead, humans possess inborn capabilities for learning from the environment. This epistemological concept emphasizes the role of sensory experience as the basis of knowledge. The term *empiricism* has a dual etymology. The Latin translation is *experientia*, from which we derive the word *experience*; the word also derives from a more specific classical Greek usage of *empiric*, referring to a physician whose skill derives from practical experience as opposed to instruction in theory. Empiricism was explicitly formulated by John Locke (1709), who argued that the mind is a *tabula rasa* (*clean slate* or *blank tablet*), upon which experiences leave their marks. In this view, the human mind does not possess anything knowable without reference to experience in the sensory world. Any knowledge properly inferred or deduced must be gained from sense-based experience. Empiricism was historically contrasted with a school of thought known as *rationalism*, which, in very broad terms, asserted that knowledge derives from reason independent of the senses. However, this contrast is no longer meaningful. Indeed, the main rationalists (Descartes, Spinoza, and Leibniz) were also advocates of empirical methods.

NATIVISM AND EMOTION

There are many sound reasons to consider some aspects of emotion to be innate. The most frequently cited and compelling evidence is that distinct emotions are observed very early in the infant's life, with relatively little individual variation in form, function, and developmental timing. Although there is considerable debate about how to determine what an infant is feeling, it is clear that young infants demonstrate a surprising facility to acquire and use basic emotions.

Arguments supporting a nativist stance toward emotion typically include some variant of the following claims:

1. Other than in the case of certain neurological conditions, human infants acquire emotions early in life. Typically developing children express and recognize happiness, sadness, anger, fear, disgust, and surprise within the first postnatal year regardless of parental style, culture, or education. There is no evidence that children are explicitly taught to express or recognize emotions. By this, I mean that children are rarely instructed or corrected as to the right way to express an emotion; what children appear to be explicitly taught is when to suppress or mask emotional expressions rather than the pairing of elicitors, subjective feelings, and outward manifestation of emotional expressions.
2. Emotional development is fairly ordered with regularity in developmental timing that varies little across individuals or cultures. This overall stability in emotional development applies to children in vastly different circumstances. There appears to be a high degree of universality in the way humans recognize emotions, and even children born both blind and deaf—who could not have acquired expressions through observation or modeling—produce similar expressions of emotion as typically developing children (Eibl-Eibesfeldt, 1972).
3. Children's errors in emotional expression are rarely noticed by adults and errors in young children's emotion recognition and reasoning appear to be circumscribed and to follow predictable developmental patterns.
4. Basic emotions are universal, with similarities not only across species, but also across human cultures. For example, the signaling intentions of emotions, such as a smiling face as an indication of *welcoming*, are universally understood (Fridlund, 1994).

5. The emotional behaviors evinced by even very young infants may appear simple, yet they represent computationally complex processes linking perceptual information to conceptual and representational knowledge.

Both of the seminal and comprehensive theories of emotional development encompass the basic premises listed. Carroll Izard's (1978) Discrete Emotions Theory is based upon observations that emotional behaviors cohere in infancy, with similar patterns of vocal, facial, and postural reactions across infants to similar elicitors. In this view, discrete emotions are innate and invariant over the life span (Izard, 1984) and the innate qualities include expressions and emotion feelings (Izard & Malatesta, 1987). These basic emotions preempt consciousness and drive narrowly focused sets of responses (Izard, 1977; Tomkins, 1963). Developmental changes in this basic-emotion response system are attributed to learning after the infancy and toddler periods. Here, the innately specified emotion system can be modified or inhibited by cognitive and learned regulatory capacities, which can result in new emotions beyond the basic innate set.

Paul Ekman's (1972) Neocultural Theory posits two factors in emotional development. The first component consists of a small set of fundamental emotions that are innate, biologically based, and universal. By using the term *biological*, Ekman conveys his belief that these emotion processes, if unimpeded, will be expressed naturally as motor programs that include facial expressions such as smiles and frowns. The second component in this theory allows for cultural or social effects on emotional development and includes the display rules that children learn such as when and where each expression should be displayed, suppressed, or masked. The general principle of this theory is that it accommodates both innate and learned components in emotional development in that core emotions are posited to exist prior to sensory or social experience, but they are shaped or socialized according to cultural rules.

Although a comprehensive review of the literature on emotional development is not possible here, a limited sampling of data suggests that there is both merit to, and inconsistency with, nativist perspectives. Nativist theories are supported by observations that neonates preferentially attend to faces. Indeed, infants ranging from 2 to 8 months of age express more interest in a live human face than to a mannequin and more to the mannequin than to a face-shaped object with scrambled facial features (Morton & Johnson, 1991). Extant data suggest that this preference appears to be a general perceptual preference rather than a face- or emotion-specific orientation (for a review, see Turati, 2004).

Although, consistent with nativist theories, early research suggested that young infants responded to emotion-specific categories such as happiness and anger (e.g., Haviland & Lelwica, 1987). It is now understood that infants discriminate facial features such as an open mouth with visible teeth versus a closed mouth. Indeed, what first appeared to be evidence that infants held categories of basic emotional expressions turned out to be evidence that infants are perceptually sensitive to the presence of teeth. At 4, 7, and 9 months of age infants fail to discriminate happy from angry faces if the expressions both involve open mouths (Caron, Caron, & Myers, 1985).

By 3½ months of age, infants can demonstrate that they are aware of when facial expressions of emotion match vocal expressions of the same emotion, looking longer when the facial and vocal cues are mismatched (Kahana-Kalman & Walker-Andrews, 2001). This behavior suggests early appearance of a complex skill. However, it is curious that the 3-month-olds are only able to differentiate nonmatching emotional cues when the expressions are produced by the infant's own mother. Moreover, the ability of infants to accurately pair facial expressions of emotion with affectively concordant or discordant vocal expressions correlates with the amount of parent–infant contact time the infant has had (Montague & Walker-Andrews, 2002), suggesting an effect of learning or experience. By 1 year of age, infants are able to use facial cues produced by their caregivers to evaluate potential threat, as evidenced by *social referencing* behaviors (Sorce, Emde, Campos, & Klinnert, 1985; Klinnert, Emde, Butterfield, & Campos, 1986). Again, this is a computationally complex task that infants appear to be able to master quickly. Yet, as with other studies of emotion recognition, familiarity with the individual expressing an emotion enhances the infant's ability to extract information from that person's emotional expressions.

With regard to emotion production, the experience of both inoculation and goal blockage elicits anger expressions in 4-month-old infants

(Campos, 1996; Izard, Hembree, & Huebner, 1987). Moreover, infant anger and sadness expressions appear to be related to distinct patterns of autonomic nervous system and hypothalamic–pituitary–adrenal system activity (Lewis, Ramsay, & Sullivan, 2006). For example, 10-month-olds showed different patterns of electroencephalograph asymmetry (different right and left frontal activation) during anger and sadness expressions (Fox & Davidson, 1988). It should be acknowledged, though, that when scientists refer to *infant emotional expressions*, it is more precise to describe these behaviors as facial expressions that adult observers interpret as being indicative of underlying emotional states. Such caution highlights the difficulty in validating what a neonate is truly *feeling*. At the same time, it is problematic to require some sort of self-report of subjective feeling states as evidence of an emotion. If a self-report is required to *validate* the presence of an emotional state, then substantive nonhuman animal research on emotion would be excluded from consideration. Nonhuman animal research has been instrumental in furthering understanding of processes such as fear, aspects of depression, stress regulation, and emotional components of neurodevelopmental disorders in humans. Even among adults, self-reports of feeling states provide only one type of information. Reports about subjective feeling states may be informative for addressing how individuals introspect, attend to, or choose to describe their experiences and behaviors. Yet how research subjects say they might feel or respond or think in different situations cannot uncover biological mechanisms because research subjects do not have awareness of the neural processes involved in the processing of their emotional states. Moreover, traditional methods do not lend themselves to the kinds of experimental manipulations necessary to test precise hypotheses about how humans process emotional information (Pollak, Vardi, Bechner, & Curtin, 2005).

Much of the data used to support nativist claims can also be used to highlight a role for learning; however, it is also the case that studies used to support empiricist views can be interpreted from a nativist perspective. A significant role of learning is highlighted by the observation that children do not appear to use distinct categories of emotion until the age of 5 years, with younger children often relying upon labels such as *happy* and *sad* to describe broad categories of *positive* and *negative* emotions (Widen & Russell, 2003). Children slowly learn to differentiate within positive and negative categories until they have acquired concepts for anger, fear, and so on. Such findings raise two significant issues. First, the data on children's development of emotion concepts suggest that children's *errors* in labeling emotion faces and subjective feeling states are systematic rather than random. For example, children initially associate faces and labels largely on the basis of valence—positive versus negative (Bullock & Russell, 1984; Russell & Bullock, 1986). The presence of such systematicity or structure could be taken as evidence of rudimentary, innate emotion knowledge. Second, the overt behavioral performance of young children will necessarily be limited by children's abilities to meet the cognitive and motor demands of particular tasks. Thus, children's competence or conceptual knowledge may not be reflected in overt behavioral performance. Unfortunately, for these reasons, extant data are not sufficient to refute or confirm nativist or empiricist claims; rather, these data highlight the difficulty in supporting one claim over another.

In fact, there are many good reasons to consider that human infants enter the world with something that starts, directs, or facilitates emotional development. What extant data do not adequately address is precisely the nature of those primary building blocks. Darwin (1872/1965) was not studying emotions as we think of them today; rather, he was specifically interested in emotional expression as evidence for evolution. In many respects, Darwin was an exemplar of a translational scientist in that he was attempting to understand emotion expression by contrasting adult, child, and nonhuman animal behavior as well as using both normal and atypical phenomena to inform each other. In his early writings, Darwin described emotional expression as a reflex-like mechanism that was triggered involuntarily. For example, he focused on behaviors such as the raising of the lips that we perceive as a grimace, snarl, or baring of teeth and associate with a response to threat or an expression of hostility. Certain expressions such as eyebrow raising upon greeting, laughter, and crying, and bared teeth paired with wrinkled brows during anger, are seen across cultures (Eibl-Eibesfeldt, 1972; Ortony & Turner, 1990). This type of inborn, reflex-like aspect of emotion noted by Darwin is the type of behavior that Izard and Ekman try to capture as innate, biologically based, and universal. Left uncertain is what the relationship is between a reflex and an underlying representation for an emotion.

EMPIRICISM AND EMOTION

From an empiricist approach, the basis of nativistic arguments consists almost exclusively of assumptions. Indeed, a conceptual problem rarely addressed in the literature on emotion development concerns how the presence of an innate emotion, or innate mechanism of emotional development, could be empirically tested or falsified. At some level, nativistic theories may appear unfalsifiable because there are no fixed criteria for when abilities are innate. Typically, innate is equated with *appearing early in development*, and what appears early in ontogeny is assumed to reflect processes that appear early in phylogeny (e.g., Buck, 1999; Damasio, 1999; Darwin, 1872/1965; Dimberg, Thunberg, & Elmehed, 2000; Ekman, 1994; Izard, 1971; Langer, 1967; Lundqvist & Öhman, 2005; Öhman & Mineka, 2001; Panksepp, 2000; Plutchik, 1982).

This situation reflects what Putnam (1967) called a *what else* argument. By this, Putnam means that there is no positive evidence for any kind of innate mechanism. Rather, we evoke the *infants are born with it* position as the most parsimonious account of behavioral data that lacks an otherwise adequate explanation. This is not unsound reasoning; it merely requires that scientists acknowledge the difference between hypothesized explanations that seem to fit with what we observe about children's emotional behavior as compared with the epistemological status of a developmental claim that has been empirically tested. The predominant theories of emotional development follow the *parsimony* line of reasoning: Given what we observe in human infants, *what else* could account for emotional development other than an innate origin?

In response, the general principles of empiricist accounts are usually some variant of the following argument:

1. It is plausible that there is enough sensory input in the world to learn complex phenomena.

2. Sensory input has an organizing role on brain systems early in development.
3. Nativist theorists may drastically underestimate the power of the human infant's learning abilities.

Empiricist claims raise questions about the soundness of premises used in the formulation of nativist accounts. The first issue is concerned with at what point it could be claimed that a human infant has had absolutely no experience with emotion. Consider that within a few moments of postnatal life a human infant has been exposed to a wide array of emotional experiences such as smiles, laughter, touch, and cries—there is certainly no void of human emotional behavior immediately after childbirth! It is a mistake to consider 3- to 6-month-old babies as proxies for organisms without experience. A strong version of the empiricist view of emotion is that environmental factors play a critical role in the emergence of basic emotions, not just in the refinement, modification, or socialization of emotions. On this view, it is possible that similar forms of early learning in infants could lead observers to the assumption that a feature of emotional development is innate when in fact it was learned quickly and early in development. This is a conceptually complex issue, however, in that equally valid questions can be raised about why sensory input regarding emotion is consistent enough to structure learning similarly across organisms.

Second, although it is true that many forms of complex emotional behaviors appear very early in infancy, the observation that a behavior emerges early in life is not proof that the behavior is innate. Even verification that a behavior or skill is *present at birth* is insufficient to conclude it is innate because some behaviors may be present early in development but are clearly not innate. Neonates show perceptual preferences for their mother's native language (Mehler, Jusczyk, Lambertz, & Halsted, 1988) and for stories that were read aloud during their mother's pregnancy (DeCasper & Spence, 1986). These behaviors are clearly learned. Similarly, pre- and perinatal events can have lasting effects on the mature structure of the immune system by altering the trajectory of immune cells (Hodgson & Coe, 2006). Humans do not have molars in the back of our mouths at birth, yet the process of growing teeth and the eventual location of different types of teeth in our mouths is innately specified. The point here is that many aspects of development may be present at birth but still learned or may not be present at birth yet still reflect innate processes, including the growing of teeth, the emergence of pubic hair during puberty, or genetic diseases for which symptoms do not appear until later in life. These examples highlight that the developmental timing of the emergence of a behavior, regardless of how early or late in life the behavior appears, is inconclusive with regard to determining experience-independence.

Evidence of cross-cultural invariance in emotional development is often used to bolster nativist theories. However, cross-cultural similarities in emotional behavior are not inconsistent with an empiricist perspective. For example, there is some debate about whether scientists have generally underestimated the variance in emotional behavior both within and between cultures (Barrett, 2006; Elfenbein & Ambady, 2002; Scherer, Johnstone, & Klasmeyer, 2003). Furthermore, it is possible that developing infant brains are responsive to features of sensory input that are relatively constant across human social environments. For example, although humans may display significant behavioral differences across cultures, at some level, humans might treat neonates similarly. These basic similarities across human behavior, which may escape the attention of adults, could serve as learning cues for infants. Indeed, if one posits powerful learning mechanisms in infancy, then even an infant who is only a few months, weeks, days, or hours old has already had opportunities to be exposed to sensory input from the environment.

Fourth, although nativist theories of emotion suggest that each emotion should be a discrete neural *package*, there has yet to be consistent brain-imaging data that suggest a clear biological signature for any discrete emotion. Barrett and Wager (2006) summarize the ways in which functional neuroimaging studies fail to support biological plausibility for innate emotion systems. For example, one of the most widely cited examples of an emotion–brain pairing is that fear is associated with activation of the amygdala (Murphy, Nimmo-Smith, & Lawrence, 2003; Phan, Wager, Taylor, & Liberzon, 2002).Yet Phan and colleagues (2002) reported that only 60% of studies involving fear showed increased activation in the amygdala, and Murphy and colleagues (2003) reported that only 40% of published functional studies of the amygdala find support for this association. There is good evidence from the animal literature that some fear-related behaviors such as freezing depend on specific nuclei in the amygdala and brainstem (e.g., LeDoux, 2000; Panksepp, 1998). However, none of the behaviors associated with these groups of neurons are associated with any single emotion.

In sum, observation that a behavior appears early in development does not provide sufficient data to conclude that the behavior is innate. It is not clear that people feel or experience emotions similarly across cultures (or even across individuals) or what underlying brain mechanisms might constitute an innate emotion system. As will be discussed later in this chapter, translational research that includes not only typically developing children, but also atypical populations of children and emotional behaviors in nonhuman animals, may help clarify these issues.

NATIVISM AND DOMAIN GENERALITY

The distinction between strong claims of nativism and empiricism is a useful heuristic at one level. Yet these distinctions set up a false dichotomy that does not capture the beliefs of most scientists working in the area of emotional development. Emotion theorists acknowledge that learning occurs over development and few contemporary scientists would maintain that the infant brain has no structure at all. Neurologically healthy children learn to speak, perform numerical computations, attend to faces, recognize inanimate objects, maneuver the physical world, and achieve bipedal locomotion. Therefore, the substantive developmental questions include the following.

1. How can we characterize the initial state of emotion in the human brain prior to sensory experience?
2. How can we characterize is the processes through which that initial state is transformed into mature knowledge and behavior?

Nativistic theories provide a more satisfying response to the first question in that empiricist theories posit the initial state of the infant emotional brain to include only a mechanism for learning. In other words, empiricist theories tend to answer the first issue (initial state) by responding to the second issue (mechanism of change). In this way, it is easy to confound questions about the initial state of the organism with issues about the developmental mechanisms that support change and learning of emotion. Empiricist theories better address the issues of developmental change that hold importance for understanding how to best support, augment, and remediate issues in children's emotional development. In this regard, nativist theories tend to gloss over the ways in which humans can learn so much about the world based upon relatively little evidence and how initial states of knowledge can be expanded into mature representations. It is not the case that nativists see individuals as somehow *fixed*, but it is simply that with so much attention paid to the initial state of the organism, subsequent maturation receives scant attention. Simply put: If everything arrives hard-wired, why and how does change occur? Similarly: Whether or not the infant is born with some rudimentary form of basic emotion, the infant still faces a formidable learning problem in mastering emotional communication.

Given that both nativist and empiricist theories must allow for the infant brain to have some starting point as well as the ability to grow and mature, the differences between the approaches concern the quantity, extensiveness, and type of structures attributed to the initial state of the brain on a continuum. At one end of the continuum, there may be few innate ideas, principles, or mechanisms. These sorts of theories tend to posit very general developmental mechanisms that support learning across numerous domains. Therefore, there is more weight placed on the organizing structure of environmental input combined with a powerful role of sensory and perceptual systems. By contrast, theories at the other end of the spectrum view the brain as highly differentiated, with numerous specialized systems. In these views, the brain is composed of more innate elements that include learning systems that are specific to these particular hypothesized domains of development. Again, however, notice that in this typical kind of characterization of nativist and empiricist approaches, two distinct issues are confounded—namely, the issue of what is innate is confounded with the issue of whether learning mechanisms are specific or domain general.

For the most part, nativist approaches typically posit *modules*, or specialized psychological abilities, that allow us to learn and acquire specific skills. This view, *domain specificity*, is a prominent theoretical position in cognitive science (especially modern cognitive development) that holds that many aspects of cognition are supported by specialized—presumably evolutionarily specified—learning devices often referred to as *modules*. Although the position is typically associated with nativism, it need not be. Domain specificity emerged as a theoretical alternative to empiricist theories that claimed all sorts of learning across domains could be driven by just a few, very general learning devices. One prominent example of a domain-general view includes Jean Piaget's theory of cognitive development (Piaget & Duckworth, 1970). Other domain-general views include behaviorism and the approaches taken by many modern connectionists (Elman et al., 1996). It is important to note, though, that empiricists largely remain open concerning the particulars of the relevant learning algorithms, and they are by no means restricted to the associationist mechanisms historically used by behaviorists.

Proponents of domain specificity argue that domain-general learning mechanisms are unable to overcome the epistemological problems facing learners. Like nativistic theories, domain-specific accounts draw support from the surprising competencies of infants, who are able to reason about things like numeracy, goal-directed behavior, and the physical properties of objects all in the first months of life. Domain-specific theories hold that these competencies are too sophisticated to have been learned via a domain-general process like associative learning, especially over such a short time, given the limitations of infant perceptual, attentional, memory, and motor abilities. The rationale behind domain-specific theories is that evolution equipped humans (and indeed most other species) with specific adaptations designed to overcome persistent problems to be encountered in the environment.

Yet, modularity and nativism are conceptually distinct, and one does not imply the other. For example, a system can become modular (i.e., look specific) through experience if the system's structure is sufficiently plastic. Karmiloff-Smith (1991) put forward a developmental theory that proposes that the brain may become modular through experiences such as social interactions or visual perception. According to this view, modules need not be innate. On the other hand, positing that infants possess complicated learning mechanisms also implies some innate structure. Thus, a learning mechanism that tracks probabilities and contingencies, that is biased to respond to certain features of the environment, or that is preferentially suited to learning some aspects of the environment or treats some aspects of the sensory world as special or privileged would be a system that is innate, but domain general. It is difficult to evaluate various theories in this regard because there is no common agreement about what *counts* as early emotion. Is it a reflex? A small discrete action? An extensive program for action? A bias toward or away from certain features in the environment? For example, an infant can display a *smile* at 1 week of age during REM sleep, at 1 month of age while being stroked, at 2 months of age during social interactions, and at 3 months of age when achieving mastery (such as pulling a string to make music) (Rosenstein & Oster, 1988). If one considers *happiness* to be inherent in the reflexes associated with the random neural activity of REM sleep, then the emotion does appear immediately after birth. However, if the construct of happiness refers to a more social/subjective definition, then the emotion does not appear until much later. In theories of emotion, there is a vagueness or uncertainty about these issues.

The crux of the problem is articulating what counts as early emotion and what drives the changes from these early behaviors into mature, differentiated emotions. Empiricist theories of emotion focus on how developmental change occurs, while underspecifying what gets development rolling. In contrast, nativist theories describe a rich set of emotion building blocks (basic emotions such as anger, happiness, etc.) and then underspecify how early learning and developmental change occurs. The oversimplified version of this view is that we are born with the neural circuitry that supports anger, and we come to have a more differentiated and sophisticated use and understanding of anger as those brain regions grow and form connections with other neural systems underlying processes such as inhibitory control, memory, and so on. This account presupposes that we are born with a system that supports anger and that there is an internal process of change associated with and (maybe) specific to the anger system. Conversely, in most empiricist views—those that are exclusively based upon notions of learning—the processes of developmental change are equally vague. Infants develop more sophisticated perceptual abilities and greater memory capacity, engage in increasingly complex emotional interactions, and somehow change from having periods of undifferentiated arousal or distress to culturally shared understanding and experiences of anger, sadness, joy, disgust, and so on. In sum, the neural mechanisms that humans use to learn about emotion may be no different than those we use to learn to roll sushi or play the piano.

CAN EMOTIONS BE LEARNED?

Because there is little data about the brain mechanisms underlying emotional behaviors, and because observations of children's emotional behaviors are inconclusive about nativism, the heart of this disagreement is the question of what is learnable and what kind of learning the human brain is capable of achieving successfully. The central issue is that the usual arguments advanced in the field of emotional development—that basic emotions are present at birth, that young infants are surprisingly and consistently emotionally competent, and that emotions are similar across cultures—provide an inadequate account of emotional development. For this reason, claims of learnability are central for resolving these issues.

Contemporary approaches to learning and development began with the study of language. Modern linguistics was strongly influenced by Chomsky's observation that language learners make grammatical generalizations that do not appear to be justified by the evidence available to children in the input they hear (Chomsky, 1965). Similar to Hume's argument about causality, Chomsky reasoned that children's generalizations are best explained by innate knowledge. Known as the argument from the *Poverty of the Stimulus*, this position has led to an enduring debate that is central to many of the key issues in cognitive science and human development more broadly. The Poverty of the Stimulus argument is based upon the limited nature of the input children are exposed to, and how much sensory information or evidence could support the complex skills that children master.

In the study of language, the conclusion of this argument is that children must have some innate biases. For example, they might innately favor *structure-dependent rules* (grammatical constructs that operate over phrases and clauses rather than simply over sequences of words). Knowledge about hierarchical structures in grammar could not be learned, according to this argument, because it is never taught, nor is the structure accessible through sensory input. Yet most children learn this quickly. As formulated, the argument based upon the Poverty of the Stimulus is an epistemological problem: The data children receive early in development is indeterminate. Given what we say to children, they would not be able to discern underlying grammatical rules unless they already had some predisposition to know those rules (for a recent example of this argument, see Lidz, Waxman, & Freedman, 2003). The linguistic stimuli that children receive are considered *poor* because there simply is not enough information in perceptual input for a child to learn the system. Simply put, *Poverty of the Stimulus* means that the output observed in the developing child is radically underdetermined by the input the child receives. This also appears to be the case with regard to the type of emotional stimuli that children receive.

There is an indefinite number of alternatives that could be logically consistent with the regularities found in the infant's emotional input. Consider that an infant might observe an adult cry when we are sad, upset, tired, frustrated, hurt, but also when we laugh hard or peel onions; we might cry when talking to others, when watching television, when on the telephone, or when remembering a past event, making the antecedents of the emotion unclear. There are, therefore, many ways in which the emotional learning environment is impoverished. Seyfarth and Cheney (2003a,b) argued that facial and vocal expressions actually have very low *informational value* regarding the internal state of the sender. Smiling faces are usually categorized as happy across cultures (Ekman, Friesen, & Ellsworth, 1972; Russell, 1994). Yet people can smile when they are not happy and can feel happy without smiling. Therefore, a smile does not provide a perfect predictor about the internal state of the sender. The emotion *code* that the developing child must master is further complicated because the nature of emotional signals fluctuates depending upon the persons with whom we are interacting. For example, different types of social interactions will result in laughs with different acoustic properties in the same individual (Devereux & Ginsburg, 2001).

Not surprisingly, although parents often believe that they are able to discern specificity in their own infant's emotional expressions, there is little empirical data to suggest that infants reliably produce emotional expressions with high informational value and referential specificity that map onto discrete emotion categories. One problem is that infants produce configurations of facial behaviors typically identified as *expressions* in situations in which the corresponding emotion is unlikely—by, for example, producing a *sad* facial expression when protesting a sour food (e.g., Camras, 1991; Camras, Lambrecht, & Michel, 1996; Matias & Cohn, 1993). Conversely, infants often fail to produce the predicted set of facial behaviors in situations in which the corresponding emotion is likely (Camras et al., 2002; Hiatt, Campos, & Emde, 1979). In general, it seems that infants have a range of facial behaviors that they use to express negative affect (Camras, Oster, Campos, & Bakeman, 2003) or intensity (Messinger, 2002). Similar findings are apparent in studies of infant crying (Bachorowski & Owren, 2002). Infant cries are very potent signals with salient acoustic properties that help caregivers judge an infant's level of distress and urgency of need, but there is little empirical evidence to support the commonly held notion that infants give distinctive cries unique to eliciting situations—such as when the infant is hungry, scared, tired, or in pain (Gustafson, Wood, & Green, 2000). Instead, what adults are usually able to discern is the intensity of the infant's affect rather than the meaning of the cry (Dinehart, Bolzani, Messinger, & Acosta, 2005). Taken together, this evidence suggests that facial movements and vocal signals do not necessarily display information about the sender's emotional state, even though people routinely perceive those behaviors as coordinated expressions.

Learning to decode emotional signals is also complicated by the fact that no single facial movement or vocal behavior can be associated with a single emotion category. Individual facial muscle movements are indeterminate: Wide eyes may be associated with fear or surprise, an open mouth with happiness, anger, fear, or surprise. Seyfarth and Cheney (2003a,b) refer to this problem as low *referential specificity*. For example, a smile can mean that one feels pleasure (Cacioppo, Berntson, Ernst, & Ito, 2000), embarrassed (Keltner, 1995), contrite (Schneider & Josephs, 1991), subordinate (LaFrance & Hecht, 2000), sexual interest (Mehu, Grammer, & Dunbar, 2007), or is attempting to appease others (Deacon, 1997). Of course, there may be distinctive types of smiles that signal distinctive mental states, but the consistency of such relationships remains to be demonstrated empirically. In general, many communicative behaviors in primates have multiple meanings, depending on their context (de Waal, 2003). At the same time, through this noise, the predictive information conveyed by smiling may well be sufficient to support early learning of emotion. In sum, expressions of emotion are extremely difficult to accurately identify with all contextual clues removed (Wagner, MacDonald, & Manstead, 1986). From a nativist perspective, this state of affairs suggests that emotion expressions would be unlearnable without some innate propensity to process emotions because infants are not able to access the contextual information necessary to interpret these expressions; therefore, an innate mechanism is necessary because most infants are clearly able to master emotion recognition in the absence of positive evidence or learning cues. However, from an empiricist perspective, infants may well be tracking the contextual cues that allow them to learn and interpret emotional signals.

One principle of a dynamic-system theory approach is that learning and development can build upon random occurrences (Camras & Witherton, 2005). Rather than assuming that the infant is learning when he or she sees someone express an emotion, this account holds that the infant begins to track how a random facial configuration such as a smile elicits certain responses from the environment that begin to reinforce the facial behavior. Such an approach can also integrate subjective feeling states. Adult engagement with the infant produces pleasurable feelings in the infant, not because the adult is smiling but simply because the engaged actions make the infant feel good. That feeling good becomes associated with a smile in the sensory environment—or that feeling bad becomes paired with the sound of crying—may emerge much later in learning. Here, the fact that the young infant may not differentiate self from other may facilitate emotion learning.

As adults, we tend to think of emotions as objective and consistent, but it is unlikely that emotions appear that way to an unbiased learner.

Why, for example, should we attend to faces as opposed to fingers when trying to discern another person's subjective feeling state? Why attend to vocal prosody and not hair color or gaze direction? The developing child also must learn to generalize something about the structure of emotions over vast individual differences in other people's manners of expression, facial characteristics, affective styles, as well as across males and females, adults and children, familiar and unfamiliar people. The scope of information that infants must learn to ignore is vast. Each voice has its own timbre, each face its own features and idiosyncrasies, each person a faster or slower or muted or intense style. So many aspects of biological motion are not emotional, yet children quickly learn that a sneer is an emotional communication, whereas a sneeze is not. Moreover, emotions can be present in the environment and have no immediate or salient impact upon the learner. A parent can express extreme anger or hostility toward a gate agent at an airport, but that may not have any direct effect on the interaction between the parent and his infant even moments later. In sum, a critical feature of emotion development—and a basic premise of the Poverty of the Stimulus argument—is that the correct set of patterns is no less simple to learn than other irrelevant or incorrect alternatives.

The general question is whether the data needed to decode emotional meaning are available to the learner. From a nativist perspective, the child could not arrive at the correct behavioral output through sensory-based learning. Since nearly all children do arrive at the correct output, from a nativist perspective this would not be possible without some form of domain-specific knowledge or bias to guide learning. Without some innate core knowledge, learners would have to rely on seemingly random sensory inputs to guide them through a vast array of information in the environment. The general point is that the ultimate goal in emotional development is mastery of signal–meaning pairings. Those signals may be subjective, motoric, or physiological. The deep problem is that no matter how much emotion a learner is exposed to, the various interoceptive and sensory signals cannot cohere and conform to a set of principles if he or she cannot categorize and remember them. That entails keeping track of a vast amount of information and disregarding other sources of information.

On the other hand, the soundness of the Poverty of Stimulus argument can be questioned. First, it is not clear that humans are exposed to features of the environment that are truly *unlearnable*. By analogy, in the study of language, one claim was that linguistic features such as infinite recursion could not be learned without innate grammar. While that may be true in theory, speakers cannot ever produce sentences with infinite recursive structures *in principle*. And even if speakers did produce such sentences, it is not clear that people are able to comprehend sentences with many levels of recursion. While some argue that such an example is best explained by restrictions on working memory rather than language abilities, it remains the case that the linguistic structures people actually produce may well be learnable; this is an empirical question.

Although the emotion data that young children receive have low informational value and referential specificity, is emotion—somehow—learnable through domain-general mechanisms? Do children actually receive enough evidence to learn the patterns of emotions through input alone? It is unclear whether the way to address this question requires a focus on the nature of the input or on the nature of the learning mechanisms available to the child. One way to approach the issue is to examine whether emotion learners do get certain kinds of negative evidence. Indeed, if children begin to form expectations or hypotheses about what might occur in the environment, and subsequent input either matches or does not match their expectations, then that is information that would support learning (Pullum, 1996). In other words, absence of an expectation or pattern is potentially useful negative evidence. Extant theories may also underestimate the probabilistic information in the environment. For example, nonoccurrence of a pairing is also important data for children. While we may smile or laugh for many reasons, we are extremely unlikely to laugh when we are hurt or disgusted. In this manner, there may well be plenty of cues for a savvy emotion learner to begin to use.

Another refutation of the Poverty of the Stimulus argument is the claim that human infants are more powerful learners than many theorists believed. For example, researchers using neural networks and other statistical methods have programmed computers to learn and extract hierarchical structures without negative feedback (see Bates & Elman, 1996; Solan, Ruppin, Horn, & Edelman, 2005). Such general learning mechanisms have been proposed for the ontogenesis of many cognitive abilities such as cross-modal matching, phonetic discrimination, and word segmentation (Kuhl, 1987; Kuhl & Meltzoff, 1982; Saffran, Aslin, & Newport, 1996).

Criticisms of the learning achievements of young infants in these sorts of paradigms are that, while sufficient to solve discrete or artificial problems in the laboratory, these mechanisms are not sufficient to learn complex behaviors in children's real environments. For example, most computational networks are designed to solve a small set of predefined problems (e.g., putting words in the past tense), whereas children have no way of directing their learning so narrowly. These are legitimate concerns that need to be tested. From a developmental perspective, the critical point is that the Poverty of the Stimulus argument is based upon the idea that certain things in the world are not learnable without innate knowledge and domain-specific learning mechanisms. Yet it now appears that more learnable information may be out there in the world than was previously recognized and human infants appear to be more powerful learners than we expected when such theories were developed.

APPLICATION OF THESE ISSUES TO CHILD HEALTH

Ultimately, emotional development is not about philosophical positions regarding the origin of knowledge. It is about what children face as they develop—not universals, evolution, or cross-cultural similarity. What we really need to understand, if we wish to translate basic science into interventions for maladaptive behaviors, is *how* change occurs. How does the individual child break into this social system of communication—what Papoušek and Papoušek have called our first language that enables parent–child communication (Papoušek, Jürgens, & Papoušek, 1992)? My own research has been based on the supposition that there is sufficient evidence in the input for a learner to discern the structure of human emotions and, further, that it is the nature and patterning of this early input that configures the neural circuitry involved in emotion processing. This account suggests that certain properties of the input, namely the salience and predictive validity of certain cues in the environment, are responsible for transitions in emotional development. There are two general points underlying this argument:

1. Early input to infants across families and cultures may be quite similar from the perspective of the developing brain.
2. All biological systems, including emotion, share a need to be responsive to environmental input in order to be adaptive and may therefore share some developmental properties.

Therefore, I consider emotional development as an emergent property resulting from complex learning.

One can consider three aspects of emotional development: the initial state of the infant, the input the infant receives, and the learning processes and cognitive operations that the infant applies to affective input. These components are not independent. For example, the informational content of the input defines the kinds of computations that might be performed and thus the representations that learning mechanisms might use. Therefore, in addition to investigating the initial state of the human infant with regard to emotional abilities, it is also necessary to address the input that learners receive and the learning that takes place early in development. My students and I have attempted to address questions about the emotional input children receive and processes of emotion learning by focusing on the development of children who receive atypical emotional input in the form of inadequate parental care. We attempt to do so in ways that allow developmental comparisons with rodents and nonhuman primates; each species allows exploration of a different level of analysis. Maltreatment of human children is notoriously difficult to define, measure, and investigate empirically. Nevertheless, this phenomenon has provided an important forum for investigating the role of environmental stress, individual differences, and developmental factors in the ontogenesis of social behavior.

Input and Learning: Clues from the Emotional Correlates of Child Maltreatment

Translational research holds tremendous promise for advancing scientific understanding about emotional development and leading to new ideas about clinical interventions. Importantly, many theoretical and practical issues arise in translating between typical and atypical processes and between species. In this section, I provide four examples, employing different kinds of methods, of the ways in which the study of atypical development can help illuminate the mechanisms underlying the learning of emotion and how basic research on emotion promotes better understanding of the ways in which interventions can be tailored to children at risk for emotion-related difficulties. These examples are not exhaustive, but they do highlight the interplay between conceptual issues, basic science, and prevention/intervention in developmental science.

Example 1: Emotional Input Received by Maltreated Children

Related to issues about the nature of the emotional input that children receive, recent work from my laboratory has begun to focus on the nature of maltreated children's input. Parents who physically abuse and/or neglect their children have been characterized by increased hostility, intrusive behaviors, aggressive outbursts, generally negative parenting techniques, and poorly expressed emotions (Bauer & Twentyman, 1985; Camras et al., 1988; Kavanagh, Youngblade, Reid, & Fagot, 1988; Lyons-Ruth & Block, 1996). However, there is little detailed empirical data on these children's expressive environments. We evaluated the facial and vocal expressions of a sample of physically abusive and nonabusive mothers and found that abusive mothers produced atypical and less recognizable expressions of anger (Shackman et al., 2008). For example, physically abusive mothers did not lower and contract their brows as most people do when angry, tended to smile less intensely, and produced lower levels of vocal emotions that lacked variation in pitch. Changes in pitch frequency are important sensory cues that make emotional prosody easier to discern (Bachorowski, 1999). These data suggest that physically abused children may be exposed to less prototypical emotional expressions in their early sensory environments.

The implication of the Shackman and colleagues (2008) study is that whatever kind of developmental mechanism that children use to learn about emotion is likely to be affected by degraded input. Typically, adults exaggerate sensory input to facilitate infant learning. For example, infant-directed speech (*motherese*), which is characterized by a higher fundamental frequency and greater pitch variations, is thought to facilitate infants' language learning (Thiessen, Hill, & Saffran, 2005). Similarly, adults often present infants with high-contrast toys and mobiles to stimulate visual development (Banks, 1980). If maltreated children are exposed to degraded emotional input—meaning that the quality of the signals they receive are less clear, inconsistent, and more difficult to understand—then it is not surprising that emotion learning could be compromised.

Example 2: Input-Related Effects on Sensory Processing and Domain Specificity/Generality

Given that maltreated children may encounter variations in their emotional input, it is possible that children's early experiences alter sensory thresholds for emotion. To explore this possibility as a learning mechanism for emotion, we examined how children categorize emotions. The phenomenon of *categorical perception* occurs when perceptual mechanisms enhance differences between categories at the expense of the ability to detect incremental changes in stimuli within a category (Harnad, 1987). This process is adaptive in that it allows an observer to efficiently assess changes between ecologically meaningful categories (to see that a traffic light has changed from green to yellow; to detect the difference between the pronunciation of a *v* and a *w*) at the cost of noticing subtle changes in a stimulus (such as shades of greens or yellows across individual stoplights, or how individual people pronounce their *v*s). Early demonstrations of categorical perception in the area of speech perception stressed the importance of specialized innate mechanisms (Eimas, Siqueland, Jusczyk, & Vigorito, 1971). However, later investigations revealed that perceptual capacities for speech, as well as other perceptual domains, are learned through experience (Werker & Tees, 1992). It appears that human infants enter the world with general perceptual learning mechanisms that allow them to conduct a preliminary analysis of their environments, but these mechanisms must become tuned to process specific aspects of the infants' environment (Aslin, Jusczyk, & Pisoni, 1998).

When shown facial expressions distributed along a continuum between emotions (e.g., happiness *to* sadness), adults perceive these stimuli as belonging to discrete emotion categories (e.g., happiness *or* sadness) (Young et al., 1997). And category boundaries for familiar and unfamiliar faces can be shifted in adults as a function of frequency of exposure to those faces (Beale & Kiel, 1995). This frequency effect suggests that experience may also play an important role in face perception. To determine if a *frequency* effect for emotions could also be detected, we examined physically abused children's categorical perception of emotional expressions and found that, while all the children we studied perceived emotions in terms of categories (e.g., sad, angry, happy, scared), physically abused children displayed a boundary shift for perceptual categories of anger relative to nonmaltreated children (Pollak & Kistler, 2002). Specifically, physically abused children displayed equivalent category boundaries to nonabused children when discriminating continua of happiness blended into fear and sadness. However, these same children evinced different category boundaries when discriminating angry faces blended into either fear or sadness. These data suggest an effect of learning on the formation of perceptual representations of emotion and, given that categorical perception mechanisms appear to operate similarly across domains and various species (including humans, birds, and chinchillas), that this process may reflect a domain-general learning mechanism subserving emotional development.

Example 3: Input-Driven Cognitive Mechanisms

Children's deployment and control of attention represents another way in which to examine the role of learning in emotional development. The adaptive nature of involuntary attention allocation lies in its ability to quickly alert an organism to a possible danger or other significant event (Sussman, Winkler, & Schröger, 2003). Voluntary allocation of attention toward or away from certain environmental cues is a mechanism that allows children to effectively regulate emotional states (Posner & Rothbart, 1998; Rothbart, Ellis, Rueda, & Posner, 2003). Indeed, a central function of emotion is that it represents a mechanism for alerting an organism to potentially significant events. The emotional salience of the environmental events that capture attentional systems emerges through an organism's learning history (Berti & Schröger, 2003). To examine the ways in which early emotional experience affects voluntary and involuntary attention, we manipulated the task relevance of conflicting affective cues and used event-related potentials (ERPs) to measure physically abused children's cognitive processing. ERPs, which are scalp-derived changes in brain activity over time, are a noninvasive method that is well-suited for studying the neural mechanisms underlying emotion processing in clinical populations of children. Specifically, ERPs allow for the precise temporal measurement of earlier aspects of cognitive processing, which cannot be revealed through techniques such as functional magnetic resonance imaging (fMRI). Of relevance to issues of emotional learning are two specific components of the ERP. One is the P3b, which reflects processes involved in attentional resource allocation, difficulty of stimulus evaluation, the updating of environmental context in working memory, and emotional salience (Keil et al., 2002; Miltner et al., 2005; for discussion, see Pollak & Tolley-Schell, 2004). The second is the N2, associated with cognitive inhibition and regulatory processes (Lamm, Zelazo, & Lewis, 2006; Yeung & Cohen, 2006). In earlier studies (Pollak et al., 1997, 2001) we demonstrated that physically abused children's attention was to facial displays of anger, but not other emotions.

In a more recent study, we extended this research by presenting children with congruent and incongruent facial and vocal emotion expressions while directing their attention toward either the visual or auditory modality. It was important, here, to address questions not only of attention to emotion, but also to examine children's emotion processing more broadly by including vocal expressions of emotion in addition to face processing. Vocal expressions of emotions are particularly important from a developmental perspective in that auditory signals can capture attention from someone who is not already visually attending to the expresser, as is often the case in the communications between infants and toddlers and their caretakers. Despite the salience of auditory cues, Fernald (1993) argued that little attention has been directed toward understanding the role of vocal expressions in emotion perception. Because our previous studies of emotion processing had employed standardized facial stimuli, we also designed this study to use stimuli that depicted children's own parents, with the hypothesis that personalized stimuli might be especially useful for excavating perceptual learning processes.

In general, we found that physically abused children (a) exhibited increased voluntary attention toward both facial and vocal anger cues, (b) were involuntarily drawn to vocal anger cues, and (c) were especially responsive to facial signals of anger from their own parent (Shackman, Shackman, & Pollak, 2007). Physically abused children showed enhanced P3b amplitude when directing their attention to their own mother's facial anger. The groups of abused and control children did not differ when attending to anger posed by unfamiliar adults, or when attending to happy and sad facial expressions posed by either their parent or another adult. Additionally, abused children displayed increased N2 amplitudes when presented with angry distracter cues, suggesting they expended greater effort inhibiting the involuntary processing of task-irrelevant anger. These ERP data suggest that abused children exert more cognitive effort both to engage their attention toward salient anger cues and also to withhold further processing of irrelevant but salient affective cues in the environment, compared to control children.

Example 4: Input-Driven Physiological Mechanisms

In one of our earliest studies, we found that physically abused children perceived angry faces as highly salient relative to other emotions (Pollak et al., 2000). A significant aspect of this study was that we were able to contrast children with different types of maltreatment experience. Physically abused children had experienced *abuse by commission* in that a parent directly injured them. In contrast, neglected children experienced *abuse by omission*—lack of care and responsiveness from parents. Neglected children, who purportedly received less parental support and experience in learning about communicative signals, had difficulty differentiating facial expressions of emotion. Rather than showing global deficits in performance, physically abused children performed well, especially when differentiating angry facial expressions (Pollak et al., 2000). These data suggest that specific kinds of emotional experiences, rather than simply the presence of stress or maltreatment, differentially affect children's emotional functioning. Subsequent studies revealed that institutionally neglected children not only had difficulties differentiating between, and responding to, expressions of emotion but also showed developmentally unusual patterns of formulating selective attachments to caregivers (Wismer Fries & Pollak, 2004).

In a typical social environment, caregivers learn how to recognize and respond to their infants' needs, thereby creating predictable contingencies in the environment; these regularities, in turn, make the infants' environments conducive to further learning (Bigelow & DeCoste, 2003). Another way to address issues of learning in emotional development is to examine the extent to which the neurobiological systems that regulate behaviors such as attachment are dependent upon the social experiences afforded to most infants. With this goal, we studied a sample of children who did not receive the kind of emotionally responsive caregiving typically received by human infants. These children were reared in institutionalized (orphanage) settings, where a prominent lack of emotional and physical contact from caregivers is a consistent adverse feature of the environment.

The specific systems that we explored were the oxytocin (OT) and arginine vasopressin (AVP) neurohypophyseal peptide systems. Research with nonhuman animals suggested that OT and AVP are an integral part of mammalian emotional circuitry (Carter, 1998; Fleming & Corter, 1995; Uvnas-Moberg, 1998; Winslow, Hastings, Carter, Harbaugh, & Insel, 1993). Specifically, these neuropeptides are associated with the emergence of social bonding, parental care, stress regulation, social communication, and emotional reactivity (Insel, 1992; Young & Wang, 2004). OT receptors are part of the neural system of reward circuitry that includes the nucleus accumbens; a critical feature of this system for infant development is that it likely confers a sense of security and protection that makes social interactions rewarding. A growing body of research with rodents suggested that early social experience, through changes in corticotropin-releasing-hormone (CRH), may alter OT and AVP receptor binding (Bester-Meredith & Marler, 2003; Champagne, Diorio, Sharma, & Meaney, 2001). Therefore, we reasoned that early social experience would influence the feedback loops involving social reward circuitry, with developmental implications for stress reactivity and behavioral regulation as the infant matures. Indeed, higher levels of OT are associated with decreases in stress (Lovic & Fleming, 2004).

We found that children who had experienced early institutional neglect had lower overall levels of AVP than family-reared children

(Wismer Fries & Pollak, 2004). These results suggest that social deprivation may inhibit the development of the AVP system. Functionally, central AVP appears to be critical for recognizing familiar individuals, a key component of forming social bonds (Wang & Aragona, 2004). Because emotions are inherently regulatory processes, we evaluated how these neuropeptide systems responded to dynamic social interactions. To do so, we examined hormone levels approximately 20 minutes after children interacted with their mothers. OT levels for family-reared children increased following physical contact with their mothers. Children who experienced early institutional neglect did not show this response following physical contact with their mothers (Wismer Fries & Pollak, 2004). To what extent are the neurobiological mechanisms underlying human emotional behavior dependent upon the social experiences afforded to most infants by their caregivers? These results suggest that a failure to receive species-typical care disrupts the normal development of the OT and AVP systems in young children. Perturbations in this system may interfere with the calming and comforting effects that typically emerge between young children and familiar adults who provide care and protection.

Caveats About Interpreting Studies of Maltreated Children

Important basic science issues in emotion are drawn from studies of nonhuman animals in that invasive methods and experimental manipulations that are not possible or appropriate with humans can be used. At the same time, generalizations about the biological processes underlying emotional behaviors across species require caution for a number of reasons (for full discussion of these issues, see Sanchez & Pollak, in press). Animal models do not always mimic human emotional disorders; brain development, structure, and function are not identical across species; there are chromosomal differences between species; and the actual behaviors exhibited by parents and the way they are received and experienced by offspring are not identical across species. Cross-species comparisons are justified, however, because there may well be common denominators in the roots of emotional functioning across species (Gunnar & Fisher, 2006). One of these may be the role of caregiving, with the effects of poor or inadequate parental nurturance providing critical clues about the mechanisms through which sensory experiences influence emotional development. Indeed, the developmental outcomes of infant maltreatment among nonhuman primates are strikingly similar to those reported in maltreated children (Sanchez et al., 2007).

As discussed earlier in this chapter, most children may develop within relatively typical caregiving environments, making it difficult to fully evaluate the role of early experiences in the configuration of emotion systems. For this reason, the study of maltreated children may be particularly informative. At the same time, studies of clinical or atypical populations cannot harness the staple tool of experimental psychology: random assignment. One caution about using a phenomenon such as child abuse as a way to understand learning mechanisms underlying emotion is the assumption that abuse is the cause, rather than the effect or correlate, of subsequent atypical behavior. It is theoretically possible that heritable factors that co-occur with maltreatment, rather than the experience of being maltreated, are responsible for the behavioral difficulties observed in children. It is also theoretically possible that some individuals carry heritable traits that influence emotional development in ways that increase the likelihood of experiencing maltreatment. In these cases, the study of abused children would be much less informative with regard to understanding the mechanisms of emotional development. Yet converging behavioral genetic data from monkeys and humans highlight the role of postnatal sensory experience in this regard. As in humans, physical abuse in rhesus monkeys has a high prevalence in some family lineages, suggesting intergenerational transmission. However, evidence from rhesus cross-fostering studies suggests that behavioral problems observed in monkeys are due to the postnatal experience of maltreatment rather than genetic heritability (Maestripieri, 2005). Behavioral and molecular genetic analyses also support the view that the experience of abuse has a causal role in the formation of emotional behaviors (Kim-Cohen, 2007). Thus, the phenomenon of child maltreatment is well poised to figure prominently in considerations of the relative contributions of learning in emotional development. In particular, studies of maltreated children (and nonhuman primates) may help excavate the neural learning mechanisms through which sensory experiences influence emotions.

For some scientists, a developmental mechanism might be a behavioral, cognitive, or computational explanation for behavioral change. Increasingly, psychologists are seeking potential neural systems that might account for emotional behaviors. No one level of analysis or type of approach appears to confer an epistemological advantage here, as emotional development occurs at neurophysiological, behavioral, and subjective levels. Still, it is useful to consider the extent to which hypothesized accounts of developmental change are at least biologically plausible. As an example, our findings suggesting perceptual processing differences among abused children are consistent with studies suggesting experiential malleability in the neural circuitry underlying modification of prefrontal neurons (Freedman, Maximilian, & Poggio, 2001). The prefrontal cortex is certainly not the only brain area involved in cognitive tasks as complex as categorization of emotion. Other structures are likely to be relevant to children's emotional functioning such as temporal lobe structures and inferior temporal cortex, both of which may underlie the storage of memories and associations relevant to emotion perception, as well as attentional effects on the fusiform gyrus, implicated in development of face expertise networks (Tomita, Ohbayashi, Nakahara, Hasegawa, & Miyashita, 1999; Wallis, Anderson, & Miller, 2001).

Among the most clinically relevant and consistent findings for abused and neglected children are high levels of anxiety and fear. Studies of isolate-reared monkeys have revealed decreased white matter in parietal and prefrontal cortices as well as alterations in the development of hormone receptors that underlie fearful and anxious behaviors (Sanchez et al., 2007). We (Pollak, Bechner, Vardi, & Curtin, 2005) examined attention regulation in physically abused preschoolers who presented with interpersonal hostility—a situation that predicts abuse in these children's home environments. Autonomic measures such as heart rate and skin conductance were measured in abused and nonabused children while they overheard two unfamiliar adults engage in an argument. The abused children maintained a state of anticipatory monitoring of the environment, from the time the actors began expressing anger throughout the entire experiment—even after the actors had reconciled. This response was quite distinct from that of the nonmaltreated children in the study; the nonmaltreated children showed initial arousal to the expression of anger but were better able to regulate their responses once they determined that it was not personally relevant to them. This type of response to emotional cues in their environments is likely to guide children's social behaviors in ways that are maladaptive. Findings such as these are consistent with a growing body of evidence that indicates that somatic states related to emotion are involved in cognition and learning (Bechara, Tranel, Damasio, & Damasio, 1996; Damasio, 1999; Lo & Repin, 2002). For example, individuals who show stronger somatic marking (larger skin conductance responses; SCRs) also show stronger learning performance (Carter & Pasqualini, 2004). Thus, autonomic arousal in response to threat may initially serve to bias attention toward such salient emotion cues.

Another system potentially linking children's early experiences with subsequent behavior is the limbic hypothalamic pituitary adrenal axis (L-HPA). The L-HPA axis, as well as other afferent and efferent pathways of threat detection and response systems that extend into the prefrontal cortex, is particularly open to modification by experience during early life. The L-HPA system mediates neuroendocrine responses to stress, resulting in the release of steroid hormones from the adrenal gland. These hormones, glucocorticoids, affect a broad array of problems experienced by abused children, including energy mobilization, immune responses, arousal, and cognition (Hart, Gunnar, & Cicchetti, 1995). In a recent study, we found that the degree or severity of neglect experienced by children was associated with long-term regulatory problems of the stress-responsive system (Wismer Fries, Shirtcliff, & Pollak, 2008). Not surprisingly, alterations in pituitary and adrenal function have been associated with illnesses common among previously abused individuals, including depression, anxiety, Posttraumatic Stress Disorder (PTSD), fibromyalgia, hypertension, and immune system suppression (Altemus, Cloitre, & Dhabhar Firdaus, 2003).

Our ERP studies point to some neural mechanisms underlying emotional development. For example, the prefrontally mediated, anterior attentional system appears to track salient properties of target stimuli (Derryberry & Reed, 2001; González, Fuentes, Carranza, & Estévez, 2001; Posner & DiGirolamo, 1998). This may be one of the brain systems affected by maltreatment. Over time, this system may help abused children to learn about the predictive value of anger in a maltreating environment. Yet the enhanced attentional processes that are adaptive in an abusive context may lead to maladaptive behaviors in more normative situations, with aberrant processing of threat cues increasing the child's risk for anxiety. Not surprisingly, the degree of children's attentional differences on our ERP tasks correlates with both the magnitude of abuse the child endured and the child's degree of anxiety symptoms (Shackman et al., 2007). For these reasons, we speculate that the inability to flexibly regulate attention in the presence of threat cues may represent a mechanism by which plasticity in learning confers risk for maladaptation.

FUTURE POSSIBILITIES FOR TRANSLATIONAL APPROACHES

Translational research efforts aimed at understanding the emergence of emotion can meaningfully inform child-oriented interventions. Such research might be aimed at specifying the nature of the emotional input children receive and the mechanisms children use to learn from and respond to their emotional experiences. This type of research would uncover the neurobiological, sensory, and cognitive effects of early experience and thereby help to focus research attention on the precise nature of the problems experienced by children at risk for mental health problems. To illustrate, consider one of the common concerns that mental health professionals frequently observe in children who have endured child abuse and/or neglect: subjective feelings of anxiety, fear, or threat. These feeling states may lead children to any number of developmental pathways. Heightened fear might precipitate mood-regulation problems such as anxiety or depression, somatic and general problems with physical health including immune deficiencies, aggressive responses to perceived feelings of threat or insecurity, or perhaps subclinical feelings of unhappiness that detract from a sense of well-being.

One hypothesized pathway through which children's early experiences might impact sensory thresholds for responding to emotional stimuli may be altered perceptual or attentional processing of emotion (e.g., hypersensitivity to threat-related cues, hyposensitivity to positive or security-related cues). Another pathway might involve the L-HPA system, with its regulatory peptide (corticotropin-releasing hormone, CRH) and cortisol influencing the reciprocal regulatory relationship between the frontal cortex and the amygdala. A third potential pathway could involve functioning of the oxytocin system, which could influence children's developing abilities to feel secure, comforted, and protected. Oxytocin receptors appear to be heavily located in the nucleus accumbens and tightly linked to dopamine systems. These links to reward circuitry suggest that the pleasure and comfort provided by others may be learned or acquired through experience. Thus, atypical development of this reward circuitry may impair the capacity to bind pleasurable human contact with positive emotion states. In addition, oxytocin may help constrain stress responsivity. The more comforted and secure we feel, the harder it may be to become stressed; whereas if we feel unprotected or vulnerable, it is likely easy to trigger a stress response. In this manner, low OT may help account for both the prevalence of attachment-related difficulties as well as frequent observations of cortisol dysregulation and fearful behaviors in abused children.

The general point is that similar emotional outcomes observed in children may be the result of many different kinds of processes, each of which would warrant distinct methods of intervention. Future research that advanced our understanding of the specific primary mechanisms affected in individual children could enlighten development of biologically inspired intervention efforts tailored to address specific processes. Some children might benefit from interventions that emphasize a psychoeducational component wherein children receive explicit instruction in learning to read emotional cues, whereas other children might receive experiences that recalibrate perceptual systems of emotional expressions, and still other children might be taught how to test hypotheses about their interpretation of other people's affect. Other kinds of interventions might focus less on perception of sensory input but promote development of regulatory strategies (see Rothbart and colleagues, this volume). Because perceived stress can influence prefrontal functioning through catecholamine-based and CRH-mediated processes, techniques that help children inhibit medial prefrontal activation could help address fearful behaviors. Development of novel interventions could also focus on oxytocin as outcome measures—for example, by using the healthy functioning of this system to determine response to treatment, or by using basic science data about the functioning of this system to consider the types of social and emotional experiences that could help trigger OT release and be integrated into treatment design. These examples are certainly not meant to be exhaustive. Rather, my intent is merely to speculate about the myriad ways in which advances in basic translational developmental science could spur innovative research into new treatments and how demonstration of effective ways to treat children with emotion-related difficulties could likewise inform our understanding of the basic mechanisms of emotion. Such work is needed to build bridges between basic data that can transform diagnosis, treatment, and the domain of preventive/intervention for children.

CONCLUSION

Understanding the processes through which early social experience affects child development increases the likelihood of developing effective prevention and intervention programs. Studying children who have experienced atypical emotion-learning environments, such as maltreated children, also yields valuable knowledge about fundamental issues in psychological science. These include a focus on the neural circuitry and neurobiological regulation of emotion and their subsequent implications for behavior, as well as understanding adaptations and sequelae of chronic social stress exposure on affective neural circuits—especially during periods of rapid neurobiological change when the brain may be particularly sensitive to contextual or environmental influences. Because existing data have not rendered it possible to reach firm conclusions about whether emotion is innate, we have examined the development of emotion among children whose environments have differed in important ways from a species-typical caregiving environment. The general principle behind these studies is that examining the ways in which the aberrant environments influence biobehavioral development may highlight the nature of the learning mechanisms underlying emotion. Studying this question across species and across typically and atypically developing populations of children may highlight learning mechanisms that may not be obvious when emotional development is unfettered. Ongoing research in this area is focusing on defining and specifying ways in which the environment creates long-term effects on brain and behavior, including potential corrective experiences that might foster recovery of competencies and promote health.

REFERENCES

Altemus, M., Cloitre, M., & Dhabhar Firdaus, S. (2003). Enhanced cellular immune response in women with PTSD related to childhood abuse. *American Journal of Psychiatry*, *160*, 1705–1707.

Aslin, R. N., Jusczyk, P. W., & Pisoni, D. B. (1998). Speech and auditory processing during infancy: Constraints on and precursors to language. In W. Damon, D. Kuhn, & R. S. Siegler (Eds.), *Handbook of child psychology: Vol. 2. Cognition, perception, and language* (pp. 147–198). New York: Wiley.

Bachorowski, J. A. (1999). Vocal expression and perception of emotion. *Current Directions in Psychological Science*, *8*, 53–57.

Bachorowski, J. A., & Owren, M. J. (2002). Vocal acoustics in emotional intelligence. In L. F. Barrett & P. Salovey (Eds.), *The wisdom in feeling: Psychological processes in emotional intelligence* (pp. 11–36). New York: Guilford.

Banks, M. S. (1980). The development of visual accommodation during early infancy. *Child Development*, *51*, 646–666.

Barrett, L. F. (2006). Are emotions natural kinds? *Perspectives on Psychological Science*, *1*, 28–58.

Barrett, L. F., & Wager, T. D. (2006). The structure of emotion: Evidence from neuroimaging studies. *Current Directions in Psychological Science*, *15*, 79–83.

Bates, E., & Elman, J. (1996). Learning rediscovered. *Science*, *274*, 1849–1850.

Bauer, W. D., & Twentyman, C. T. (1985). Abusing, neglectful, and comparison mothers' responses to child-related and non-child-related stressors. *Journal of Consulting and Clinical Psychology*, *53*, 335–343.

Beale, J. M., & Keil, F. C. (1995). Categorical effects in the perception of faces. *Cognition*, *57*, 217–239.

Bechara, A., Tranel, D., Damasio, H., & Damasio, A. R. (1996). Failure to respond autonomically to anticipated future outcomes following damage to prefrontal cortex. *Cerebral Cortex*, *6*, 215–225.

Berti, S., & Schröger, E. (2003). Working memory controls involuntary attention switching: Evidence from an auditory distraction paradigm. *European Journal of Neuroscience, 17*, 1119–1122.

Bester-Meredith, J. K., & Marler, C. A. (2003). Vasopressin and the transmission of paternal behavior across generations in mated, cross-fostered *Peromyscus* mice. *Behavioral Neuroscience, 117*, 455–463.

Bigelow, A. E., & DeCoste, C. (2003). Sensitivity to social contingency from mothers and strangers in 2-, 4-, and 6- month-old infants. *Infancy, 4*, 111–140.

Bowlby, J. (1988). *A secure base: Parent–child attachment and healthy human development.* New York: Basic Books.

Buck, R. (1999). The biological affects: A typology. *Psychological Review, 106*, 301–336.

Bullock, M., & Russell, J. A. (1984). Preschool children's interpretation of facial expressions of emotion. *International Journal of Behavioral Development, 7*, 193–214.

Cacioppo, J. T., Berntson, G. G., Ernst, J. M., & Ito, T. A. (2000). Social neuroscience. In A. E. Kazdin (Ed.), *Encyclopedia of psychology: Vol. 7* (pp. 353–355). Washington, DC: APA.

Campos, J. J. (1996). The functionalist approach to emotion: Implications for emotional development. *Infant Behavior and Development, 19*, 154.

Campos, J. J., Mumme, D. L., Kermoian, R., & Campos, R. G. (1994). A functionalist perspective on the nature of emotion. *Monographs of the Society for Research in Child Development*, 59, 284–303.

Camras, L. A. (1991). The development of emotion knowledge. *PsycCRITIQUES*, 36, 491–492.

Camras, L., Ribordy, S., Hill, J., Martino, S., Spaccarelli, S., & Stefani, R. (1988). Recognition and posing of emotional expressions by abused children and their mothers. *Developmental Psychology, 24*(6), 776–781.

Camras, L. A., Meng, Z., Ujiie, T., Dharamsi, S., Miyake, K., Oster, H., et al. (2002). Observing emotion in infants: Facial expression, body behavior, and rater judgments of responses to an expectancy-violating event. *Emotion, 2*, 179–193.

Camras, L. A., Oster, H., Campos, J. J., & Bakeman, R. (2003). Emotional facial expressions in European-American, Japanese, and Chinese infants. In P. Ekman, J. J. Campos, R. J. Davidson, & F. B. M. de Waal (Eds.), *Emotions inside out: 130 years after Darwin's "the expression of the emotions in man and animals"* (pp. 135–151). New York: New York University Press.

Camras, L. A., & Witherton, D. A. (2005). Development as self-organization: New approaches to the psychology and neurobiology of development. *Developmental Review, 25*, 328–350.

Carey, R. J. (1985). Lateralized decrease in self-stimulation induced by haloperidol in rats with unilateral 6-hydroxydopamine lesions. *Behavioural Brain Research, 18*, 215–222.

Caron, R. F., Caron, A. J., & Myers, R. S. (1985). Do infants see emotional expressions in static faces? *Child Development, 56*, 1552–1560.

Carter, C. S. (1998). Neuroendocrine perspectives on social attachment and love. *Psychoneuroendocrinology, 23*, 779–818.

Carter, S., & Pasqualini, M. C. S. (2004). Stronger autonomic response accompanies better learning: A test of Damasio's somatic marker hypothesis. *Cognition & Emotion, 18*, 901–911.

Champagne, F., Diorio, J., Sharma, S., & Meaney, M. J. (2001). Naturally occurring variations in maternal behavior in the rat are associated with differences in estrogen-inducible central oxytocin receptors. *Proceedings of the National Academy of Science, USA, 122*, 12736–12741.

Chomsky, N. (1965). *Aspects of the theory of syntax*. Cambridge, MA: MIT Press.

Chomsky, N. (2003). Review of verbal behavior by B. F. Skinner. In M. P. Munger (Ed.), *The history of psychology: Fundamental questions* (pp. 408–429). New York: Oxford University Press. (Original work published 1959.)

Cosmides, L., & Tooby, J. (2000). Evolutionary psychology and emotions. In M. Lewis & J. Haviland-Jones (Eds.), *Handbook of emotions* (pp. 91–115). New York: Guilford.

Damasio, A. (1999). *The feeling of what happens: Body and emotion in the making of consciousness*. Fort Worth, TX: Harcourt College Publishers.

Darwin, C. (1965). *The expression of the emotions in man and animals*. London: John Murray. (Work originally published 1872.)

Deacon, S. A. (1997). Intercountry adoption and the family life cycle. *American Journal of Family Therapy, 25*, 245–260.

DeCasper, A. J., & Spence, M. J. (1986). Prenatal maternal speech influences newborns' perception of speech sounds. *Infant Behavior and Development, 9*, 133–150.

Dehaene, S., & Cohen, L. (1997). Cerebral pathways for calculation: Double dissociation between rote verbal and quantitative knowledge of arithmetic. *Cortex, 33*, 219–250.

Derryberry, D., & Reed, M. A. (2001). A multidisciplinary perspective on attentional control. In C. L. Folk & B. S. Gibson (Eds.), *Attraction, distraction and action: Multiple perspectives on attentional capture* (pp. 325–347). New York: Elsevier Science.

Devereux, P. G., & Ginsburg, G. P. (2001). Sociality effects on the production of laughter. *Journal of General Psychology, 128*, 227–240.

De Waal, F. B. M. (2003). Darwin's legacy and the study of primate visual communication. *Annals of the New York Academy of Sciences, 1000*, 7–31.

Dimberg, U., Thunberg, M., & Elmehed, K. (2000).Unconscious facial reactions to emotional facial expressions. *Psychological Science, 11*, 86–89.

Dinehart, L., Bolzani, H., Messinger, D., & Acosta, S. I. (2005). Adult perceptions of positive and negative infant emotional expressions. *Infancy*, 8, 279–303.

Eibl-Eibesfeldt, I. (1972). Similarities and differences between cultures in expressive movements. In R. A. Hinde (Ed.), *Non-verbal communication*. Cambridge, UK: Cambridge University Press.

Eimas, P. D., Siqueland, E. R., Jusczyk, P., & Vigorito, J. (1971). Speech perception in infants. *Science, 171*, 303–306.

Ekman, P. (1972). Universal and cultural differences in facial expressions of emotion. Nebraska Symposium on Motivation. 1971, pp. 207–83.

Ekman, P. (1973). Universal facial expressions in emotion. *StudiaPsychologica, 15*, 140–147.

Ekman, P. (1992). Are there basic emotions? *Psychological Review*, 99, 550–553.

Ekman, P. (1994). Strong evidence for universals in facial expressions: A reply to Russell's mistaken critique. *Psychological Bulletin, 115*, 268–287.

Ekman, P. (1999). Basic emotions. In T. Dalgleish & M. J. Power (Eds.), *Handbook of cognition and emotion* (pp. 45–60). New York: Wiley.

Ekman, P., Campos, J. J., Davidson, R. J., & de Waal, F. B. M. (2003). *Emotions inside out: 130 years after Darwin's "The expression of the emotions in man and animals."* New York: New York University Press.

Ekman, P., Friesen, W. V., & Ellsworth, P. (1972). *Emotion in the human face: Guidelines for research and an integration of findings*. Oxford, UK: Pergamon Press.

Elfenbein, H. A., & Ambady, N. (2002). Is there an in-group advantage in emotion recognition? *Psychological Bulletin, 128*, 243–249.

Elman, J. L., Bates, E. A., Johnson, M. H., Karmiloff-Smith, A., Parisi, D., & Plunkett, K. (1996). *Rethinking innateness: A connectionist perspective on development*. Cambridge, MA: MIT Press.

Fernald, A. (1993). Approval and disapproval: Infant responsiveness to vocal affect in familiar and unfamiliar languages. *Child Development*, 64, 657–674.

Fleming, A. S., & Corter, C. M. (1995). Psychobiology of maternal behavior in nonhuman mammals. In M. H. Bornstein (Ed.), *Handbook of parenting: Biology and ecology of parenting: Vol. 2.* (pp. 59–85). Hillsdale, NJ: Erlbaum.

Fox, N. A., & Davidson, R. J. (1988). Patterns of brain electrical activity during facial signs of emotion in 10-month-old infants. *Developmental Psychology, 24*, 230–236.

Freedman, D. J., Maximilian, R., & Poggio, T. (2001). Categorical representations of visual stimuli in the primate prefrontal cortex. *Science, 291*, 312–316.

Fridlund, A. J. (1994). *Human facial expression: An evolutionary view.* San Diego, CA: Academic Press.

Gergely, G., & Csibra, G. (2003). Teleological reasoning in infancy: The naïve theory of rational action. *Trends in Cognitive Sciences, 7*, 287–292.

Gonzalez, C., Fuentes, L. J., Carranza, J. A., & Estevez, A. F. (2001). Temperament and attention in the self-regulation of 7-year-old children. *Personality & Individual Differences, 30*, 931–946.

Gunnar, M. R., & Fisher, P. A. (2006). Bringing basic research on early experience and stress neurobiology to bear on preventive interventions for neglected and maltreated children. *Development and Psychopathology, 18*, 651–677.

Gustafson, G. E., Wood, R. M., & Green, J. A. (2000). Can we hear the causes of infants' crying? In R. G. Barr, B. Hopkins, & J. A. Green (Eds.), *Crying as a sign, a sympton, & a signal: Clinical emotional and developmental aspects of infant and toddler crying* (pp. 8–22). New York: Cambridge University Press.

Harnad, S. (1987). *Categorical perception.* New York: Cambridge University Press.

Hart, J., Gunnar, M., & Cicchetti, D. (1995). Salivary cortisol in maltreated children: Evidence of relations between neuroendocrine activity and social competence. *Development and Psychopathology, 7*, 11–26.

Haviland, J. M., & Lelwica, M. (1987). The induced affect response: 10-week-old infants' responses to three emotion expressions. *Developmental Psychology, 23*, 97–104.

Hiatt, S. W., Campos, J. J., & Emde, R. N. (1979). Facial patterning and infant emotional expression: Happiness, surprise, and fear. *Child Development, 50*, 1020–1035.

Hodgson, D. M., & Coe, C. L. (2006). *Perinatal programming: Early life determinants of adult health and disease.* London: Taylor & Francis Press.

Hume, D. (1902). An inquiry concerning human understanding. In L. A. Selby-Bigge (Eds.), *Enquiries concerning the human understanding and concerning the principles of morals.* Oxford, UK: Oxford University Press. (Original work published 1748.)

Insel, T. R. (1992). Oxytocin-A neuropeptide for affiliation: Evidence from behavioral, receptor autoradiographic, and comparative studies. *Psychoneuroendocrinology, 17*, 3–35.

Izard, C. E. (1971). *The face of emotion.* East Norwalk, CT: Appleton-Century-Crofts.

Izard, C. E. (1977). *Human emotions.* New York: Plenum

Izard, C. E. (1978). Emotions as motivations: An evolutionary-developmental perspective. *Nebraska Symposium on Motivation, 26*, 163–200.

Izard, C. E. (1984). Emotions without feelings? *PsycCRITIQUES, 29*, 457–459.

Izard, C. E. (1991). Assessing emotion. *PsycCRITIQUES, 36*, 578–578.

Izard, C. E. (1993). Four systems for emotion activation: Cognitive and noncognitive processes. *Psychological Review, 100*, 68–90.

Izard, C. E. (1997). Emotions and facial expressions: A perspective from differential emotions theory. In J. A. Russell & J. M. Fernández-Dols (Eds.), *The psychology of facial expression* (pp. 57–77). New York: Cambridge University Press.

Izard, C. E., Hembree, E. A., & Huebner, R. R. (1987). Infants' emotion expressions to acute pain: Developmental change and stability of individual differences. *Developmental Psychology, 23*, 105–113.

Izard, C. E., & Malatesta, C. Z. (1987). Perspectives on emotional development I: Differential emotions theory of early emotional development. In J. D. Osofsky (Ed.), *Handbook of infant development* (2nd ed., pp. 494–554). Oxford, UK: Wiley.

Izard, C. E., Youngstrom, E. A., Fine, S. E., Mostow, A. J., & Trentacosta, C. J. (2006). Emotions and developmental psychopathology. In D. Cicchetti & D. J. Cohen (Eds.), *Developmental psychopathology: Vol 1. Theory and method* (2nd ed., pp. 244–292). Hoboken, NJ: Wiley.

Johnson-Laird, P. N., & Oatley, K. (1992). Basic emotions, rationality, and folk theory. *Cognition & Emotion*, 6, 201–223.

Kahana-Kalman, R., & Walker-Andrews, A. S. (2001). The role of person familiarity in young infants' perception of emotional expressions. *Child Development, 72*, 352–369.

Kant, I. (1902). *Critique of pure reason. Trans. J. M. D. Meiklejohn.* London: Henry G. Bohn.

Kanwisher, N. (2000). Domain specificity in face perception. *Nature Neuroscience, 3*, 759–763.

Karmiloff-Smith, A. (1991). Beyond modularity: Innate constraints and developmental change. In S. Carey & R. Gelman (Eds), *The epigenesis of mind: Essays on biology and cognition* (pp. 171–198). Hillsdale, NJ: Erlbaum.

Kavanagh, K. A., Youngblade, L., Reid, J. B., & Fagot, B. I. (1988). Interactions between children and abusive versus control parents. *Journal of Clinical Child Psychology, 17*, 137–142.

Keil, A., Bradley, M. M., Hauk, O., Rockstroh, B., Elbert, T., & Lang, P. J. (2002). Large-scale neural correlates of affective picture processing. *Psychophysiology, 39*, 641–649.

Keltner, D. (1995). Signs of appeasement: Evidence for the distinct displays of embarrassment, amusement, and shame. *Journal of Personality and Social Psychology*, 68, 441–454.

Keltner, D., & Haidt, J. (2001). Social functions of emotions. In T. J. Mayne & G. A. Bonanno (Eds.), *Emotions: Currrent issues and future directions* (pp. 192–213). New York: Guilford.

Kim-Cohen, J. (2007). Resilience and developmental psychopathology. *Child and Adolescent Psychiatric Clinics of North America, 16*, 271–283.

Klinnert, M. D., Emde, R. N., Butterfield, P., & Campos, J. J. (1986). Social referencing: The infant's use of emotional signals from a friendly adult with mother present. *Developmental Psychology, 22*, 427–432.

Kuhl, P. K. (1987). The special-mechanisms debate in speech research: Categorization tests on animals and infants. In S. Harnad (Ed.), *Categorical perception: The groundwork of cognition* (pp. 355–386). New York: Cambridge University Press.

Kuhl, P. K., & Meltzoff, A. N. (1982). The bimodal perception of speech in infancy. *Science, 218*, 1138–1141.

LaFrance, M., & Hecht, M. A. (2000). Gender and smiling: A meta-analysis. In A. H. Fischer (Ed.), *Gender and emotion: Social psychological perspectives* (pp. 118–142). New York: Cambridge University Press.

Lamm, C., Zelazo, P. D., & Lewis, M. D. (2006). Neural correlates of cognitive control in childhood and adolescence: Disentangling the contributions of age and executive function. *Neuropsychologia, 44*, 2139–2148.

Langer, S. K. (1967). *Mind: An essay on human feeling: I*. Oxford, UK: Johns Hopkins Press.

LeDoux, J. E. (2000). Emotion circuits in the brain. *Annual Review of Neuroscience, 23*, 155–184.

Leslie, A. M. (1987). Pretense and representation: The origins of "Theory of Mind." *Psychological Review, 94*, 412–426.

Leslie, A. M., & Keeble, S. (1987). Do six-month-old infants perceive causality? *Cognition, 25*, 265–288.

Levenson, R. W. (2003a). Blood, sweat, and fears: The autonomic architecture of emotion. In P. Ekman, J. J. Campos, R. J. Davidson, & F. B. M. de Waal (Eds.), *Emotions inside out: 130 years after Darwin's "The expression of the emotions in man and animals"* (pp. 348–366). New York: New York University Press.

Levenson, R. W. (2003b). For distinguished contributions to psychophysiology: Arne Ohman. *Psychophysiology, 40*, 317–321.

Lewis, M., Ramsay, D. S., & Sullivan, M. W. (2006). The relation of ANS and HPA activation to infant anger and sadness response to goal blockage. *Developmental Psychobiology, 48*, 397–405.

Lidz, J., Waxman, S., & Freedman, J. (2003). What infants know about syntax but couldn't have learned: Experimental evidence for syntactic structure at 18 months. *Cognition, 89*, B65–B73.

Lo, A. W., & Repin, D. V. (2002). The psychophysiology of real-time financial risk processing. *Journal of Cognitive Neuroscience, 14*, 323–339.

Locke, J. (1709). *An Essay concerning human understanding*. Edinburgh, UK: A. Donaldson.

Lovic, V., & Fleming, A. S. (2004) Artificially-reared female rats show reduced prepulse inhibition and deficits in the attentional set shifting task—reversal of effects with maternal-like licking stimulation. *Behavioural Brain Research, 148*, 209–219.

Lundqvist, D., & Öhman, A. (2005). Emotion regulates attention: The relation between facial configurations, facial emotion, and visual attention. *Visual Cognition, 12*, 51–84.

Lyons-Ruth, K., & Block, D. (1996). The disturbed caregiving system: Relations among childhood trauma, maternal caregiving, and infant affect and attachment. *Infant Mental Health Journal, 17*, 257–275.

Maestripieri, D. (2005). Gestural communication in three species of macaques (*Macaca mulatta, M. nemestrina, M. arctoides*): Use of signals in relation to dominance and social context. *Gesture, 5*, 57–73.

Matias, R., & Cohn, J. F. (1993). Are max-specified infant facial expressions during face-to-face interaction consistent with differential emotions theory? *Developmental Psychology, 29*, 524–531.

Mehler, J., Jusczyk, P., Lambertz, G., & Halsted, N. (1988). A precursor of language acquisition in young infants. *Cognition, 29*, 143–178.

Mehu, K., Grammer, R., & Dunbar, R. I. M. (2007). Smiles when sharing. *Evolution and Human Behavior, 28*, 415–422.

Messinger, D. S. (2002). Positive and negative infant facial expressions and emotions. *Current Directions in Psychological Science, 11*, 1–6.

Miltner, W. H. R., Trippe, R. H., Krieschel, S., Gutberlet, I., Hecht, H., & Weiss, T. (2005). Event-related brain potentials and affective responses to threat in spider/snake-phobic and non-phobic subjects. *International Journal of Psychophysiology, 57*, 43–52.

Montague, D. P. F., & Walker-Andrews, A. S. (2002). Mothers, fathers, and infants: The role of person familiarity and parental involvement in infants' perception of emotion expressions. *Child Development, 73*, 1339–1352.

Morton, J., & Johnson, M. H. (1991). A two-process theory of infant face recognition. *Psychological Review*, 98, 164–181.

Murphy, F. C., Nimmo-Smith, I., & Lawrence, A. D. (2003). Functional neuroanatomy of emotions: A meta-analysis. *Cognitive, Affective & Behavioral Neuroscience, 3*, 207–233.

Öhman, A., & Mineka, S. (2001). Fears, phobias, and preparedness: Toward an evolved module of fear and fear learning. *Psychological Review, 108*, 483–522.

Ortony, A., & Turner, T. J. (1990). What's basic about basic emotions? *Psychological Review*, 97, 315–331.

Panksepp, J. (1998). *Affective neuroscience: The foundations of human and animal emotions*. New York: Oxford University Press.

Panksepp, J. (2000). *The neurodynamics of emotions: An evolutionary-neurodevelopmental view*. In M. D. Lewis & I. Granic (Eds.), *Emotion, development, and self-organization: Dynamic systems approaches to emotional development* (pp. 236–264). New York: Cambridge University Press.

Papoušek, H., Jürgens, U., & Papoušek, M. (1992). *Nonverbal vocal communication: Comparative and developmental approaches*. New York: Cambridge University Press.

Phan, K. L., Wager, T. D., Taylor, S. F., & Liberzon, I. (2002). Functional neuroanatomy of emotion: A meta-analysis of emotion activation studies in PET and fMRI. *Neuroimage, 16*, 331–348.

Piaget, J. (1970). *Genetic epistemology*. Trans. E. Duckworth. New York: Columbia University Press.

Plutchik, R. (1982). A psychoevolutionary theory of emotions. *Social Science Information/sur Les Sciences Sociales, 21*, 529–553.

Pollak, S., Cicchetti, D., Hornung, K., & Reed, A. (2000). Recognizing emotion in faces: Developmental effects of child abuse and neglect. *Developmental Psychology*, 36(5), 679–688.

Pollak, S., Cicchetti, D., Klorman, R., & Brumaghim, J. (1997). Cognitive brain event-related potentials and emotion processing in maltreated children. *Child Development*, 68(5), 773–787.

Pollak, S., & Fries, A. (2001). Perceptual asymmetries reflect developmental changes in the neuropsychological mechanisms of emotion recognition. *Emotion*, *1*(1), 84–98.

Pollak, S. D., & Kistler, D. J. (2002). Early experience is associated with the development of categorical representations for facial expressions of emotion. *Proceedings of the National Academy of Sciences USA*, 99, 9072–9076.

Pollak, S. D., Vardi, S., Bechner, A. M. P., & Curtin, J. J. (2005). Physically abused children's regulation of attention in response to hostility. *Child Development*, *76*, 968–977.

Pollak, S. D., & Tolley-Schell, S. A. (2004). *Attention, emotion, and the development of psychopathology*. New York: Guilford Press.

Posner, M. I., & DiGirolamo, G. J. (1998). Executive attention: Conflict, target detection, and cognitive control. In R. Parasuraman (Ed.), *Attentive brain* (pp. 401–423). Cambridge, MA: MIT Press.

Posner, M. I., & Rothbart, M. K. (1998). Attention, self-regulation and consciousness. *Philosophical Transactions of the Royal Society of London: Series B. Biological Sciences*, *353*, 1915–1927.

Pullum, G. K. (1996). Learnability, hyperlearning, and the poverty of the stimulus. In J. Johnson, M. L. Juge, & J. L. Moxley (Eds.), *Proceedings of the 22nd Annual Meeting: General session and parasession on the role of learnability in grammatical theory* (pp. 498–513). Berkeley, CA: Berkeley Linguistics Society.

Putnam, H. (1967). The "innateness hypothesis" and explanatory models in linguistics. *Synthese*, *17* (1), 12–22.

Rosenstein, D., & Oster, H. (1988). Differential facial responses to four basic tastes in newborns. *Child Development*, 59, 1555–1568.

Rothbart, M. K., Ellis, L. K., Rueda, M. R., & Posner, M. I. (2003). Developing mechanisms of temperamental effortful control. *Journal of Personality*, *71*, 1113–1143.

Russell, J. A. (1994). Is there universal recognition of emotion from facial expressions? A review of the cross-cultural studies. *Psychological Bulletin*, *115*, 102–141.

Russell, J. A., & Bullock, M. (1986). On the dimensions preschoolers use to interpret facial expressions of emotion. *Developmental Psychology*, *22*, 97–102.

Russell, J. A., & Paris, F. A. (1994). Do children acquire concepts for complex emotions abruptly? *International Journal of Behavioral Development*, *17*, 349–365.

Saffran, J., Aslin, R., & Newport, E. (1996). Statistical learning by 8-month-old infants. *Science, 274*(5294), 1926–1928.

Sanchez, M. M., Alagbe, O., Felger, J. C., Zhang, J., Graff, A. E., Grand, A. P., et al. (2007). Activated p38 MAPK is associated with decreased CSF 5-HIAA and increased maternal rejection during infancy in rhesus monkeys. *Molecular Psychiatry, 12*, 895–897.

Sanchez, M. M., and Pollak, S. D. (In press). Socio-emotional development following early abuse and neglect: Challenges and insights from translational research. de Haan, M., and Gunnar, M. R. (Eds). *Handbook of Developmental Social Neuroscience*. Guilford Press.

Scherer, K. R., Johnstone, T., & Klasmeyer, G. (2003). Vocal expression of emotion. In R. J. Davidson, K. R. Scherer, & H. H. Goldsmith (Eds.), *Handbook of affective sciences*. Oxford, UK: Oxford University Press.

Schneider, K., & Josephs, I. (1991). The expressive and communicative functions of preschool children's smiles in an achievement-situation. *Journal of Nonverbal Behavior, 15*, 185–198.

Schopenhauer, A. (1928). *The philosophy of Schopenhauer.* Ed. I. Edman. New York: The Modern Library.

Seyfarth, R. M., & Cheney, D. L. (2003a). Meaning and emotion in animal vocalizations. In P. Ekman, J. J. Campos, R. J. Davidson, & F. B. M. de Waal (Eds.), *Emotions inside out: 130 years after Darwin's "The expression of the emotions in man and animals"* (pp. 32–55). New York: New York University Press.

Seyfarth, R. M., & Cheney, D. L. (2003b). Signalers and receivers in animal communication. *Annual Review of Psychology, 54*, 145–173.

Shackman, J. E., Fatani, S., Camras, L. A., Berkowitz, M. J., Bachorowski, J. A., & Pollak, S. D. (2008). Emotion expression among abusive mothers is associated with their children's emotion processing. Manuscript under review.

Shackman, J. E., Shackman, A. J., & Pollak, S. D. (2007). Physical abuse amplifies attention to threat and increases anxiety in children. *Emotion, 7*, 838–852.

Solan, Z., Ruppin, E., Horn, D., & Edelman, S. (2005). Evolution of language diversity: Why fitness counts. In M. Tallerman (Ed.), *Language origins: Perspectives on evolution* (pp. 357–371). New York: Oxford University Press.

Sorce, J. F., Emde, R. N., Campos, J. J., & Klinnert, M. D. (1985). Maternal emotional signaling: Its effect on the visual cliff behavior of 1-year-olds. *Developmental Psychology, 21*, 195–200.

Spelke, E. S. (1999). Innateness, learning and the development of object representation. *Developmental Science, 2*, 145–148.

Spelke, E. S., & Kinzler, K. D. (2007). Core knowledge. *Developmental Science, 10*, 89–96.

Spinoza, B. (1957). *The road to inner freedom.* New York: Philosophical Library. (Original work published 1677.)

Sussman, E., Winkler, I., & Schröger, E. (2003). Top-down control over involuntary attention switching in the auditory modality. *Psychonomic Bulletin & Review, 10,* 630–637.

Thiessen, E. D., Hill, E. A., & Saffran, J. R. (2005). Infant-directed speech facilitates word segmentation. *Infancy, 7,* 53–71.

Tomita, H., Ohbayashi, M., Nakahara, K., Hasegawa, I., & Miyashita, Y. (1999). Top-down signal from prefrontal cortex in executive control of memory retrieval. *Nature, 401,* 699–701.

Tomkins, S. S. (1963). *Affect imagery consciousness, 2: The negative affects.* New York: Tavistock/Routledge.

Turati, C. (2004). Why faces are not special to newborns: An alternative account of the face preference. *Current Directions in Psychological Science, 13,* 5–8.

Uvnas-Moberg, K. (1998). Oxytocin may mediate the benefits of positive social interactions and emotions. *Psychoneuroendocrinology, 23,* 819–835.

Wagner, H. L., MacDonald, C. J., & Manstead, A. S. (1986). Communication of individual emotions by spontaneous facial expressions. *Journal of Personality and Social Psychology, 50,* 737–743.

Wallis, J. D., Anderson, K. C., & Miller, E. K. (2001). Single neurons in prefrontal cortex encode abstract rules. *Nature, 411,* 935–956.

Wang, Z., & Aragona, B. J. (2004). Neurochemical regulation of pair bonding in male prairie voles. *Physiology and Behavior, 83,* 319–328.

Werker, J. F., & Tees, R. C. (1992). The organization and reorganization of human speech perception. *Annual Review of Neuroscience, 15,* 377–402.

Widen, S. C., & Russell, J. A. (2003). A closer look at preschoolers' freely produced labels for facial expressions. *Developmental Psychology, 39,* 114–128.

Winslow, J. T., Hastings, N., Carter, C. S., Harbaugh, C. R., & Insel, T. R. (1993). A role for central vasopressin in pair bonding in monogamous prairie voles. *Nature, 365,* 545–548.

Wismer Fries, A. B., & Pollak, S. D. (2004). Emotion understanding in postinstitutionalized Eastern European children. *Development and Psychopathology, 16,* 355–369.

Wismer Fries, A. B., Shirtcliff, E. A., & Pollak, S. D. (2008). Neuroendocrine dysregulation following early social deprivation in children. *Developmental Psychobiology, 50*(6), 588–599.

Xu, F., Spelke, E. S., & Goddard, S. (2005). Number sense in human infants. *Developmental Science, 8,* 88–101.

Yeung, N., & Cohen, J. D. (2006). The impact of cognitive deficits on conflict monitoring: Predictable dissociations between the error-related negativity and N2. *Psychological Science*, *17*, 164–171.

Young, A. W., Rowland, D., Calder, A. J., Etcoff, N. L., Seth, A., & Perret, D. I. (1997). Facial expression megamix: Tests of dimensional and category accounts of emotion recognition. *Cognition*, *63*, 271–313.

Young, L. J., & Wang, Z. (2004). The neurobiology of pair bonding. *Nature Neuroscience*, *7*, 1048–1054.

Zink, C. F., Tong, Y., Chen, Q., Bassett, D. S., Stein, J. L., & Meyer-Lindenberg, A. (2008). Know your place: Neural processing of social hierarchy in humans. *Neuron*, *58*, 273–283.

CHAPTER

7

What Are Little Boys Made Of? Snips and Snails and Puppy Dog Tails

Etiological Bases of Conduct Disorder and Related Conduct Problems

Elena L. Grigorenko

". . . 2,319,258 adults were held in U.S. prisons or jails at the start of 2008—one out of every 99.1 adults, and more than any other country in the world" (CNN, 2008). Rates of incarceration vary by ethnic groups. Based on data from the U.S. Department of Justice (2006, 1 in 36 Hispanic and 1 in 15 Black adults (and 1 in 9 between the ages of 20 and 34) are jailed (Liptak, 2008). The financial expenses associated with the U.S. prison system are gigantic, amounting, in 2007, to $49 billion—a sum that is six times greater than expenditures for higher education (CNN, 2008). The United States is reported to be the world's leader in

Preparation of this chapter was supported by funds from the American Psychological Foundation and by funds from the State of Connecticut (Judicial Branch, Contract SO1271) to Elena L. Grigorenko. I am thankful to Ms. Lyn Long and Ms. Mei Tan for their editorial assistance.

incarceration, both with regard to the size of its general population[1] and to the number of inmates per capita.[2]

Another aspect of these statistics is the cost of crime to its victims. According to 2005 statistics from the U.S. Bureau of Justice (U.S. Department of Justice, n.d.a), U.S. residents age 12 or older were the victims of approximately 23 million crimes, with the overwhelming majority of them property crimes (77%) or personal thefts (1%), and one-fourth (~22%) crimes of violence (19.8%—rape or sexual assault; 19.8%—assault with injury; 59.3%—robberies; and 1.1%—murders). Translated into financial terms, the annual damage associated with crime is estimated in billions of dollars (e.g., in 1992 crime victims lost $17.6 billion in direct costs; U.S. Department of Justice, 1994).

Thus, on both sides of the fence, the burden of crime for victims and perpetrators who, paradoxically, often join in experiences of trauma, broken lives, and shattered futures, is substantial. Further stratification of both the crime perpetrators and the prison population reveals that across all types of crimes, 67.5% of offenders are rearrested within 3 years; the rearrest rate for violent offenders is estimated at 59.6% (U.S. Department of Justice, n.d.b). These data, arguably, indicate that a significant amount of crime is committed by a fairly limited group of individuals; indeed, although there are no specific statistics, isolated studies indicate that a large portion of all crimes (up to 50%) appears to be committed by a relatively small number of individuals, perhaps as small as 10% (Wolfgan, Figlio, & Sellin, 1972). Yet, there is a substantial number of individuals who engage in the desistance process, diverting from crime in the course of life trajectories; in fact, desisting and aging out of crime appear to be a common rule rather than an exception (Sampson & Laub, 2005). The complex dynamics of predisposition for criminal behavior, engagement in criminal acts, and possible commitment to or diversion from criminal behavior throughout the lifespan is directly related to the question of the etiology of crime.

---

[1] China, with its general population of ~1,321,851,888, has ~1,500,000 million people behind bars, where the U.S., with its general population of ~301,139,947 has ~2,300,000 people behind bars.

[2] U.S.'s estimates are 750 per 100,000 people, with its closest rivals being Russia, at 628 per 100,000, and other countries or members of the former Soviet bloc.

The task of understanding the etiology of criminal behavior has been central to many scientific disciplines, including psychology. In her recent review article, Terrie Moffitt (Moffitt, 2005) carried out a comprehensive survey of the psychological, behavior-genetic, and genetic literature on antisocial behavior and concluded that the manifestation and duration of antisocial behavior is driven by substantial and dynamic interactive cocontributions of genetic and environmental factors that are often difficult to disentangle. Yet, although this argument is valid in the context of establishing causality and of attempting to unfold complex layers of risk for antisocial behavior, it is important to perform an *act of artificial separation* of genes and environments for at least two reasons: (a) to exercise skills in healthy reductionism that are crucial for untangling complex etiological networks underlying human behaviors, and (b) to formulate an informed and clear message with regard to the etiology of antisocial behavior for practitioners working with individuals with conduct problems and with the general public.

Thus, contextualized within the framework of *healthy reductionism*[3], the following discussion is structured as follows. First, the so-called "main" effects of environments and genes on the manifestation of conduct problems are discussed. The question that underlies this portion of the chapter makes an inquiry into environmental and genetic risk factors that, when considered in isolation at least seemingly are associated with heightened likelihood for antisocial behaviors. Second, various interactive effects are considered. The discussion in that section is structured around interactive effects of environmental risk factors; interactive effects of genetic risk factors; and interactive effects of genetic and environmental risk factors. Third, in the spirit of translational research, I attempt to summarize this overview with a few statements of relevance to practitioners working with individuals who have demonstrated antisocial behavior and with the lay public.

---

[3] In contrast to what Dennett called "greedy reductionism:" ". . . in their zeal to explain too much, too fast, scientists and philosophers often underestimate the complexity, trying to skip whole layers or levels of theory in their rush to fasten everything securely to the foundation" [(Dennett, 1995) pp. 82–83].

GENERAL CONSIDERATIONS

Before engaging in this discussion, I would like to clarify three important aspects of this review. First, this review is primarily focused on male juvenile offenders with criminal records. Second, although not exclusively, a vast majority of these individuals meet the criteria for the diagnosis of Conduct Disorder (CD). One of the subtypes of CD that connects it with antisocial behavior (and Antisocial Personality Disorder) through the life-course is a persistent pattern of aggressive and violent behavior. The main characteristics of this *connecting* or *connected* subtype of CD are: (a) early onset, typically before the age of 10; (b) early precursors of CD expressed by aggressive behaviors evident by 2 to 3 years of age; (c) a significantly higher likelihood (10–15 times) that CD will be developed by boys than girls; (d) a lifetime course. Thus, this literature review is not comprehensive, but is biased by these constraints: gender (i.e., males) and the presence of early offences (i.e., juvenile criminal records). Third, in this review I omit a discussion of psychological indicators that capture traits predisposing an individual for violence. Although references are made to temperament, personality, and cognitive indicators traditionally associated with antisocial behavior and violence, these references are cursory. The review is focused on the dichotomy of environmental and genetic influences in an effort to raise important questions about the relationships between *risky* environments and *risky* genes. Thus, although this overview, like many others, presents data from both schools of thought on the causes of crime—one focused on the role of individual differences and the other focused on structural and contextual variables that predispose an individual to violence—this review primarily focuses on individual differences raising from the coaction of environments and genes.

IN SEARCH OF *MAIN EFFECTS*

As previously indicated, for the purposes of this review I utilize the tradition of separating environmental and genetic risk forces as they pertain to the etiology of antisocial behavior, Conduct Disorder, and juvenile delinquency. Correspondingly, the following literature is summarized under the subheadings of Environmental and Genetic risk factors.

Risky Environments

Antisocial behavior is defined in contrast to prosocial or social-values-oriented behavior; thus, its definitions always include an orientation toward and inclusion of social principles, values, and norms and a society's capacity to install, support, and promote them. There are multiple models in the literature that investigate the emergence of antisocial behaviors in the context of relationships between an individual and society (e.g., [Glueck & Glueck, 1968; Hirschi, 1969]). One such model differentiates these relationships into age-specific bands, arguing that through these intrapersonal bands maturing individuals accept and internalize their ties to each other and society (Sampson & Laub, 1990, 1993). Specifically, this model, referred to as a *revised age-graded theory of informal social control* (Sampson & Laub, 2005), stresses the importance of parents (i.e., parenting styles and attachment characteristics), peers, religion, and the school system in childhood and adolescence; the importance of participation in vocational training, military service, higher education, and the labor force; as well as the importance of forming family and other close relationships and participating in social and religious institutions in young adulthood.

Neighborhoods and Schools

A variety of sociodemographic characteristics appear to be predictive of conduct problems (Shaw, Bell, & Gilliom, 2000). More juvenile crime is associated with innercity areas characterized by dilapidation, hostility, disorganization, and high residential mobility (Kroneman, Loeber, & Hipwell, 2004; Sampson, Raudenbush, & Earls, 1997). Moreover, risky neighborhoods have been reported to amplify the impact of individual predispositions on delinquent conduct (Lynam et al., 2000). In addition, levels of neighborhood poverty are positively associated with other behavior indicators that themselves are risk factors for conduct problems (e.g., teenage pregnancy, high-school drop-out; (Brooks-Gunn, Duncan, Klebanov, & Sealand, 1993; Sommers & Baskin, 1994). However, it appears that direct influences of risky neighborhoods are modified by characteristics of the community itself (Browning, Feinberg, & Dietz, 2004) and by family variables (Gorman-Smith, Tolan, Zelli, &

Huesmann, 1996). In addition, children and youth with antisocial behavior tend to come, disproportionately, from low socioeconomic status (SES) neighborhoods (Offord, Alder, & Boyle, 1986) and minority backgrounds (Chapman, Desai, Falzer, & Borum, 2006; Kilgore, Snyder, & Lentz, 2000). Moreover, children with antisocial behavior tend to attend schools characterized by high rates of crime, problematic relationships between faculty and students, and high levels of environmental risk (DeWit et al., 2000; Hadley-Ives, Stiffman, Elze, Johnson, & Dore, 2000; Kilgore et al., 2000; Loukas & Robinson, 2004; Shafii & Shafii, 2003). There is also evidence that, on the contrary, schools with well-formulated, consistent, and sustained rules are characterized by low rates of students' delinquent behaviors (D. C. Gottfredson, 2001; G. D. Gottfredson, Gottfredson, Payne, & Gottfredson, 2005).

Family

Low SES, parental unemployment, low parental education, and dependency on welfare benefits have been reported to be associated with antisocial behavior and conduct problems in juveniles (Velez, Johnson, & Cohen, 1989). Low SES (e.g., welfare status) is not only characteristic of children with CD as a group (Loeber, Green, Keenan, & Lahey, 1995), but it is also associated with an earlier onset of the disorder (Loeber, Farrington, Stouthamer-Loeber, & Van Kammen, 1998). These relationships, however, appear to be of a complex nature, with the general link between SES and delinquency, in particular, being conditioned on family social practices (Dodge, Pettit, & Bates, 1994).

In addition, family size (Farrington, 1992, 1993; Newson, Newson, & Adams, 1993), birth order (Warren, 1966), and sibling influences (Reiss & Farrington, 1994) have been reported to be associated with antisocial behaviors, delinquency, and conduct problems. However, these associations also appear to be multifaceted and need further investigation (Cote, Earls, & Lalumiere, 2002).

Although the factors mentioned are important, the bulk of literature linking family variables and juvenile delinquency is clustered into three main groups: (a) child-rearing, especially maltreatment and abuse; (b) marital conflicts and family structure; and (c) individual characteristics of parents as a source of both genetic and environmentally negative influences. These three bodies of literature are quite substantial and cannot be comprehensively reviewed here. Correspondingly, only selective findings are highlighted.

With regard to child-rearing practices, parental rejection (McCord, 1979; Robins, 1978), harsh or punitive discipline (Haapasalo & Pokela, 1999), and reduced or absent parental supervision (Stern & Smith, 1999) are considered to be reliable predictors of juvenile delinquency. Early child maltreatment (Smith & Thornberry, 1995), physical abuse (Malinosky-Rummell & Hansen, 1993), sexual abuse (Feiring, Miller-Johnson, & Cleland, 2007), and psychological abuse (Haapasalo & Moilanen, 2004) all predict later delinquency. Parenting practices resulting in child maltreatment are of great cost to society: Their total costs are estimated at $20 billion direct (Bess, 2002) and over $69 billion indirect per year (Fromm, 2001).

Domestic violence and parental conflict are also reliable predictors of delinquent behaviors (Buehler, Anthony, Krishnakumar, & Stone, 1997). Incomplete family structure (Fergusson, Horwood, & Lynskey, 1994; Velez et al., 1989), divorce (Kolvin, Miller, Fleeting, & Kolvin, 1988), and bad marital relationships (Cui, Donnellan, & Conger, 2007) are all considered to be risk factors for delinquency with their independent, direct predictive powers, but none of these effects are deterministic and there is evidence for modification of the impact by various protective factors (Hart, O'Toole, Price-Sharps, & Shaffer, 2007). Of note are also multifarious reciprocal relationships between the child-rearing environment and child problem behavior, so that growth in conduct problems in children appears to be impacting subsequent parental behaviors (Patrick, Snyder, Schrepferman, & Snyder, 2005; Stattin & Kerr, 2000).

Last, but not least, specific characteristics of parents themselves are reliably predictive of delinquent outcomes (Lipsey & Derzon, 1998). First and foremost, specific forms of psychopathology in parents are predictive of these types of psychopathology in children. Thus, parents with Antisocial Personality Disorder (Frick et al., 1992) and various conduct problems (Faraone, Biederman, Keenan, & Tsuang, 1991; Lahey et al., 1988; Lipsey & Derzon, 1998) tend to have children demonstrating delinquent behaviors. Second, there is a substantial amount of crossover in familial transmission of psychopathology. Specifically, psychiatric conditions such as substance abuse (Loeber et al., 1995) and maternal depression (Dumas & Wahler, 1985; Loeber et al., 1998; Zahn-Waxler, Iannotti, Cummings, & Denham, 1990) are associated with conduct problems in children.

Peers

The tradition of considering peer influences in the early onset of antisocial behavior extends itself to the classic sociological paradigm of *symbolic interactionism*, which, in the framework of social learning theory (Akers, 1998), asserts that criminal behavior arises as a product of a learning process based on interactions in close peer networks (Sutherland, 1947). There is a substantial amount of data supporting this assertion and indicating, specifically, that having delinquent peers is, indeed, one of the strongest correlates of juvenile delinquency (Dishion & Patterson, 2006; Elliott & Menard, 1996; Haynie, 2001; Keena, Loeber, Zhang, & Stouthamer-Loeber, 1995; Patterson, Capaldi, & Bank, 1991; Warr, 2002), although the strength of association varies depending on the level of internal and external constraints (Cass, 2007; Piquero, Gover, MacDonald, & Piquero, 2005) and the quality of the friendships (Piehler & Dishion, 2007).

Along with the literature on delinquent peer pressure as one of the main correlates of criminal juvenile activity, there is a growing body of literature on other risk and protective factors associated with the ability to submit to or resist peer pressure. Among the risk factors are those such as chaotic and disorganized school environments (Payne, Gottfredson, & Gottfredson, 2003), poor teacher-student relationships (Welsh, Greene, & Jenkins, 1999), low school adjustment and attachment, lack of interest in and engagement with extra-curricular activities, and the absence of positive mentor-like authorities (Osgood, Wilson, O'Malley, Bachman, & Johnston, 1996). Among the protective factors are strong moral values (Akers, 1998), strong social ties to family members and nondelinquent peers (Heimer & De Coster, 1999), disapproval of criminality (Mears, Ploeger, & Warr, 1998), and the quantity and quality of parent monitoring (Svensson, 2003).

It is notable that many researchers comment on the complex nature of these relationships, which exhibit multiple reciprocal connections as well as cumulative (both additive and interactive) effects associated with the enhanced impact of multiple factors if they occur simultaneously, whether in risky or protective contexts (Lansford, Criss, Pettit, Dodge, & Bates, 2003; Liu, 2004; Simons, Chao, Conger, & Elder, 2001).

Risky Genes

There are many ways to seek evidence of genetic involvement in the manifestation of complex human behaviors. The two most widely used methods, however, are: (a) a whole-genome search of the regions harboring potential gene-candidates for a disorder or a behavior, in which the genome is covered with a large set of highly polymorphic, multi-allelic (so-called short tandem repeat polymorphisms, or STRP) or di-allelic (so-called single nucleotide polymorphisms, or SNP) markers; and (b) an investigation of specific gene-candidates, in which a particular gene is selected on the basis of an a priori hypothesis, and the involvement of this gene with a particular phenotype is tested with means of inferential statistics. Both methods are aimed at investigating the relevance of the structural variation in DNA and genes to individual differences in behavior. With the first method, researchers scan the whole genome in an attempt to identify a limited number of regions that appear to be cosegregating among relatives with the same disorder and then investigate these regions, trying to identify specific genes that contribute to the disorders. With the second method, researchers capitalize on ideas developed in animal research or pharmacological research and attempt to investigate genetic variability in a gene hypothesized to be relevant to the disorder of interest. The first method utilizes both linkage and association approaches, whereas the second method uses only the association paradigm (see Table 7.1).

Regions in the Genome

Currently, there is only one whole-genome scan for genes influencing CD (Dick et al., 2004). This study, however, has one distinct feature—the probands in this study were identified postfactum. Specifically,

Table 7.1 Molecular-Genetic Designs Used in Genetic Studies of Complex Traits Such as Conduct Problems

Study Type	Function	Design (units of analyses)	Outcome
Linkage Study	Permits geneticists to track patterns of inheritance of specific genetic variants or larger chunks of genetic materials (e.g., chromosomal pieces or regions) within families	Uses related people only, i.e., family members: extended, nuclear, or pairs of any degree of relatedness (parents and children, siblings, cousins, and so on)	Establishes a link between a disorder or trait (i.e., a phenotype) and a particular location in the genome that can be subsequently investigated for an association with specific genes harbored in this location
Association Study	Allows geneticists to investigate connections in the general population between a particular variant in a particular gene (e.g., a variant that alters a production of a particular protein) and the disorder or trait of interest by detecting a statistical correlation between the two	Uses related and unrelated people Related people: Family members (see above) Unrelated people: Cases (people with the phenotype of interest) and Controls (people who matched to the Cases on a number of important parameters, e.g., ethnicity, gender, age, exposure to a particular type of environment, but do not have the phenotype of interest)	Identifies a specific genetic factor (a genetic variant) associated with the manifestation of the phenotype of interest

in typical whole-genome scans, a sample of participants is ascertained through a proband who possesses a disorder of interest. After such probands are identified, their relatives are included in the study. In this particular case, the probands were identified through a different study for a different phenotype—specifically, the phenotype of alcoholism used in the Collaborative Study on the Genetics of Alcoholism (COGA). Thus, alcoholic probands were recruited and their family members were invited to participate. All consenting participants older than 18 were administered a semistructured clinical assessment that permitted a retrospective diagnosis of CD; this phenotype was then used in subsequent analyses. The results of this genome scan identified six regions of the genome, for both categorical and continuous phenotypes, which produced suggestive but not, strictly speaking, statistically significant results. These regions were 19p13.12 and 19q12, 2p11.2, 12q13.13, 3q12.3, and 1q32.1[4]. The findings suggest that one or more of these regions might harbor genes linked to the development of CD.

Candidate Genes

Research with humans and with animal models has identified a number of likely types of proteins that are associated with antisocial behavior. Correspondingly, there is research on the sources of genetic variation that are associated with variations in these proteins. Thus, the following groups of genes have been investigated as the structural genetic bases for antisocial behavior: (a) neurotransmitters and (b) "other" genes.

Neurotransmitter signaling pathways. When neurotransmitter signaling pathways are studied, a number of proteins establishing such pathways should be considered. First, there are the specific neurotransmitter ligands themselves (e.g., dopamine—DA, serotonin—5-HTT, gamma (γ)-aminobutyric acid—GABA). Second, for a postsynaptic signal to originate, it should be received by a particular protein known as a *receptor*. There are ligand-specific, committed receptors (e.g., dopamine has five types of different receptors, $DRD_{1\text{-}5}$) and receptors able to bind one or more types of ligands. Third, there are proteins that are needed to transport the remaining ligand from the neuronal cleft; these proteins are called *transporters* and, once again, there could be neurotransmitter-exclusive or multifunctional transporters. Finally, there are molecules that participate in both the synthesis and degradation of

---

[4]To acknowledge specifics of chromosomal architecture, a special nomenclature was introduced. In this nomenclature, the first number indicates the number of a particular chromosome (e.g., 1), the letter signifies a particular chromosomal arm (*p* for short, and *q* for long arms; e.g., 1q points to the long arm of chromosome 1), and subsequent numbers designate a specific cytological band in which a marker or a signal of interest resides (e.g., 1q32.1, where 32.1 is a specific cytological location on the long arm of chromosome 1).

neurotransmitters (e.g., monoamine oxidase, which is a protein that metabolizes serotonin, dopamine, and norepeniphrine). All these systems of genes and proteins are naturally interactive, since they assemble pathways engaged in the transmission of the neural signal.

To illustrate, consider an example of interactive events characteristic of dopamine transmission. In brief, DA activates the five types of dopamine receptors ($DRD_{1\text{-}5}$), each of which is controlled by its own genes. The D_4 receptor is controlled by the gene DRD_4. Variation (i.e., polymorphic allelic differences in the population) in DRD_4 has been associated with externalizing and antisocial behaviors (Bakermans-Kranenburg & van Ijzendoorn, 2006; Faraone, Doyle, Mick, & Biederman, 2001; Holmes et al., 2002; Munafò, Yalcin, Willis-Owen, & Flint, in press; Young et al., 2002). In addition, polymorphisms in the genes coding for two other receptors, D_2 and D_5, were associated with antisocial behavior in alcoholism (Lu, Lee, Ko, & Lin, 2001) and antisociality (Vanyukov, Moss, Kaplan, Kirillova, & Tarter, 2000), respectively. In synaptic clefts, DA is deactivated by reuptake via its transporter, the protein coded by the *DAT1* (also known as *SLC6A3*[5]) gene. There is evidence that genetic variation in this gene might be related to the manifestation of behavior problems (Kuikka et al., 1998; Yang et al., 2007). DA is broken down by catechol-O-methyl transferase (encoded by the *COMT* gene) and monoamine oxidase (controlled by *MAO-A* and *MAO-B* genes), and is metabolized to norepinephrine by dopamine beta-hydroxylase precursor (encoded by the *DβH* gene). There are substantial bodies of literature connecting *COMT* (Craddock, Owen, & O'Donovan, 2006; Thapar et al., 2005), *MAO-A* (Kim-Cohen et al., 2006), *MAO-B* (Oreland, Nilsson, Damberg, & Hallman, 2007), and *DβH* (Cubells & Zabetian, 2004) to psychopathology in general and conduct problems in particular. Finally, the activity of DA-converting enzymes is itself controlled by genes. For example, monoaminergic activity is regulated, among other things, by a transcription factor AP-2 beta (Berggard, Damberg, &

---

[5] There is a consistent nomenclature for genes coding for proteins functioning as neurotransmitters. All such genes have the *SLC6* (solute carrier family 6) abbreviation in them and then a letter indicating type and number of the associated protein (e.g., A3).

Oreland, 2005; Damberg, Eller, Tonissaar, Oreland, & Harro, 2001), encoded by the *TFAPβ2* gene. Genetic variation in *TFAPβ2* has been associated with behaviors engaging monoaminergic mechanisms (Damberg, 2005).

As evident from the preceding paragraph, the literature has numerous examples connecting criminality itself and its behavioral correlation features (e.g., aggression) to structural polymorphic genetic markers. In addition to the structural genetic variation that is associated with the turnover of dopamine, polymorphisms in a number of other neurotransmitter-related genes were associated with antisocial behaviors and related traits. For example, specific variants in the serotonin transporter gene, *5-HTT* (or *SLC6A4*), have been associated with violent behavior (Retz, Retz-Junginger, Supprian, Thome, & Rosler, 2004), conduct disorder (Cadoret et al., 2003; Sakai et al., 2006), behavior disinhibition (Twitchell et al., 2001), antisocial behavior in alcoholism (Ishiguro et al., 1999), and violent suicide (Courtet et al., 2001). In addition, polymorphisms in other serotonin (5-HTT) or serotonin-related genes, the gene coding for tryptophan hydroxylase (TPH1), a protein participating in the biosynthesis of serotonin (Hill et al., 2002), and serotonin receptor genes (*HTR1B* [(Soyka, Preuss, Koller, Zill, & Bondy, 2004) and *HTR2A* (Hill et al., 2002) were shown statistically significantly or suggestively to be associated with antisocial behavior in alcoholism.

Conduct disorder has also been associated with one of many γ-aminobutyric acid (GABA) receptor proteins, a receptor A_2 (*GABRA2*); this finding was obtained on the same sample as described previously—the COGA sample (Dick et al., 2006). In addition, using a principal component analyses of a number of variables indicative of externalizing behaviors, the same group, using almost the same sample of individuals, reanalyzed markers obtained through their previous genome scan (see previous) and identified an additional region of interest, 7q21.11–7q33. Having explored this region, they established an association between this combined externalizing factor and polymorphisms in the muscarinic acetylcholine receptor M_2 gene (*CHRM2*).

Finally, externalizing symptoms have been associated with genetic variability in adrenergic neurotransmission. Specifically, a single polymorphism in the gene *ADRA2A*, coding for one of the adrenergic receptor proteins[6], was found to be associated with Oppositional Defiant Disorder, CD, and other disorders (Comings, Gonzalez, Cheng Li, & MacMurray, 2003).

Other genes. Only a limited number of studies have investigated structural variability in genes other than those directly related to the neuronal signaling. One such study, based on specific hypotheses generated in the animal literature, investigated polymorphisms in one of the protein kinases, C (PKC), an enzyme that has the capacity to regulate other proteins by chemically adding phosphate groups to them (i.e., phosphorylating them). There are three large subtypes of PKCs, α, β, and γ—all expressed in different tissues and having different functions. PKC-γ is present solely in the brain (abundant in the cerebellum, hippocampus, and cerebral cortex) and spinal cord and has been reported (as summarized in [Schlaepfer et al., 2007]) to be engaged in such functions as synaptic formation, long-term potentiation and depression, and modulation of neurostransmitter receptors (e.g., $GABA_A$). A group of researchers associated genetic variability in the gene, coding for PKC-γ (*PRKCG*) with behavior disinhibition (Schlaepfer et al., 2007).

Because of the predominance of males among individuals demonstrating antisocial behavior, researchers have investigated the genes located on the X chromosome. In particular, the variation in the androgen receptor gene (*AR*)—a gene that codes for the protein that functions as a steroid-hormone activated transcription factor—has been associated with externalizing (conduct and oppositional defiant) disorders (Comings, Chen, Wu, & Muhleman, 1999).

Comments on Main Effects

In sum, the literature contains long laundry lists of risk factors that, in abstract terms, can be separated into environmental and genetic factors. Clearly, such a separation is artificial in many respects. For example, although parents create environments for their children, they also

---

[6] These proteins are functional in the regulation of neurotransmitter release from sympathetic nerves and from adrenergic neurons in the central nervous system.

pass along genes to their children, thus forming multiway associations between their genes that predispose them for particular behaviors (e.g., antisocial behaviors) and particular parenting styles (e.g., neglect and abuse), as well as between their genes and the genes they have passed along to their children (e.g., risk genes for CD), so that children's genes, in turn, can trigger particular reactions from their parents (e.g., harsh discipline in response to disobedience), and so forth. In other words, these associations soon become quite difficult to disentangle; collectively, they form the bioecological texture of delinquency.

Yet, as indicated previously, the factors discussed in this section of the chapter were searched for and discovered in the context of the quest for main effects predictive of delinquency outcomes. As is always the case in the social sciences, the studies of predictors for delinquency have generated some "good leads" (Rutter, Caspi, & Moffitt, 2003), but they are far from being decisive or deterministic in terms of their findings' etiological or interventional power. Recently, in addition to designs enabling inquiries into main effects, a number of different designs have emerged that permit an a priori investigation of the interaction of environments and genes. Studies conducted within the framework of these designs are briefly commented on in the following.

IN SEARCH OF INTERACTION EFFECTS

Here the word *interaction* is used in its broadest sense, as a "reciprocal action, effect, or influence" (Webster's New Universal Unabridged Dictionary, 1996, p. 992). In other words, an *interaction* is registered when two people, objects, factors, or events (i.e., *interaction agents*) have an effect on each other. This effect might result in some emergent phenomena, which cannot be attributed to either of the interaction agents solely but require the co-occurrence (often in space and time, but other types are possible) of the agents of interaction. In other words, interactions assume an accumulation of nonlinear factors that result in the manifestation of a previously unforeseen outcome. The following discussion examines three types of interactions: (a) between various environmental factors; (b) between various genetic factors; and (c) between environmental and genetic factors.

Environment–Environment Interactions

There are numerous studies that were designed to bring together different environmental effects that had previously been considered in isolation. For example, both family and school factors are important, and the literature indicates differential developmental outcomes when family and schooling indicators are considered interactively. Specifically, there is evidence in the literature that learning gains as conditioned by school sizes are greater for students from disadvantaged families than families with higher incomes (Lee & Smith, 1997). There is also evidence of nonlinear relationships between social capital at home and students' abilities to benefit from social capital at school (Crosnoe, 2004).

Similarly, the importance of the interaction between indicators of family and peer environments has been shown to be important (Simons et al., 2001). Specifically, although there was no direct association between oppositional/defiant behavior during childhood and a trajectory of increasing involvement with deviant peers and delinquency during adolescence, early oppositional/defiant behavior undermined effective parenting practices. Lack of positive parenting, consequently, predicted an increased engagement with deviant peers and delinquency during adolescence. Interaction effects also appear to be important for the activation of protective factors. Specifically, it has been shown that problems in the parent-child relationship can be countered by positive affiliation and support from friends, relatives, and other significant adults (Call & Mortimer, 2001). There is evidence in the literature that such family factors as low cohesion are differentially associated with low social competence and self-worth only in adolescents without a best friend (Gauze, Bukowski, Aquan-Assee, & Sippola, 1996). Likewise, high-quality friendship was reported to be a protective factor negating the association between child abuse and subsequent low self-esteem (Bolger, Patterson, & Kupersmidt, 1998). Thus, it is possible that co-occurrence of specific peer relationships, whether dyadic (Buhrmester & Furman, 1987; Laub, Nagin, & Sampson, 1998) or group (Ladd, 2006; Lansford et al., 2003), and early negative family experience can differentiate behavioral outcomes in an interactive manner (Criss, Pettit, Bates, Dodge, & Lapp, 2002).

Although the literature on CD does not yet contain plentiful examples of interactions between environmental factors, there is strengthening support for the use of statistical models that are capable of capturing nonlinear interactions (Ousey & Wilcox, 2007). This argument is particularly strong in sociology and criminology (Agnew, Brezina, Wright, & Cullen, 2002; Agnew & Raskin White, 1992; Sampson & Laub, 1993), where the research shows that what were previously perceived as deterministic *main effect* variables appear to demonstrate time- and context-sensitivity, rising and falling in their importance during particular developmental stages of the life span.

Gene–Gene Interactions

Similar to the nonlinear accumulation of environmental factors that differentiate pathways of engagement with and desistance from criminal behaviors, it is possible to hypothesize that there might be nonlinear interactions between various genetic variants (*epistatic interactions*) predisposing for the manifestation of conduct problems. There is a large amount of literature on the role of epistatic interaction in medicine, especially in studies of cancer (Fijneman, 2005). Research on the concept of gene–gene interaction is still limited (Comings, Gade-Andavolu, Gonzalez, Wu, Muhleman, Blake, Chiu et al., 2000; Comings, Gade-Andavolu, Gonzalez, Wu, Muhleman, Blake, Dietz et al., 2000; Grigorenko et al., 2008), but it testifies to the substantial importance of such interactions for the understanding of the genetic texture of predisposition for antisocial behaviors.

It is possible that an accumulation of risk factors (e.g., copresence of structural DNA polymorphisms each of which has been associated with CD) might result in the formation of nonlinear higher-order effects of importance to the development and manifestation of conduct problems. Again, pointing to the medical literature, it appears that the coexistence of such *risky* genetic variants is not characterized by simple additive effects, but rather by various nonlinear outcomes.

Gene–Environment Interactions

Recently, the field has seen a surge of studies investigating interactions between genes (or specific genetic variants called *alleles*) and environments. The essence of gene–environment interaction is to capture differences in susceptibility to specific environments that are related to differences in genotypes. Although the hypothesis of the importance of these interactions was formulated long ago (Cadoret, Cain, & Crowe, 1983; Cloninger, Sigvardsson, Bohman, & von Knorring, 1982), the field has only recently begun to systematically test it with both measured genetic variants and measured environments. This line of inquiry was triggered by a study that investigated the interaction that arises from the presence of the risky genetic variant in the promoter[7] region of the MAO-A gene and the presence of child maltreatment in a large sample of males (Caspi et al., 2002). The results showed the differentiation between the developmental outcomes: A combination of the low-MAO-A allele and severe maltreatment characterized the child-abuse group, with 85% of the participants demonstrating some antisocial outcomes; the other study groups (low- versus high-MAO-A allele versus no or probable maltreatment) did not show the frequency nearly as high. This initial study was well received and a chain of studies followed, both attempting to replicate the original finding and to apply the methodology to other risk genes and other risk environments. Thus, in addition to numerous studies of the MAO-A promoter variant and maltreatment (for a review see [Kim-Cohen et al., 2006]), there are also other studies investigating different interactions with regard to the outcome of antisocial behavior. Specifically, there is evidence that differentiates the outcome of depression in maltreated children with regard to the promoter variant in the serotonin transporter gene (*5-HTT*) and the availability and quality of social support (Kaufman et al., 2004). There is also evidence for the role of the interaction between the *COMT* variants (val158met) and birth weight (Langley & Thapar, 2006). In addition, it has been shown that the presence/absence of specific alleles in the dopamine transporter gene (*DAT1* or *SLC6A3*) and the presence/absence of maternal rejection differentiates depression outcomes in incarcerated juvenile offenders (Haeffel et al., 2008).

---

[7] A regulatory region of DNA generally located upstream of a gene (i.e., outside of the gene, prior to its first coding unit); this region generally promotes transcription of the gene.

The amount of studies of gene–environment investigations is mushrooming (for an illustration, see the special issue on gene–environment interaction published by *Development and Psychopathology*, Vol. 19, 2007), but the texture of the results varies. There are many positions in the literature, interpreting the variability and the range of results of gene–environment interactions as largely statistical artifacts (Eaves, 2006), to references to plausible small effect sizes (Salanti, Higgins, & White, 2006) and the imprecision of the methodology used in these studies (Wallace, 2006). Yet, the very premise of these types of research makes infinite sense, since it differentiates the behavioral expression of specific genetic risk factors in the context of specific risk environments.

Comments on Interaction Effects

In sum, it appears that, in addition to considering long-standing main effects of environmental and genetic risk factors, the field needs to be aware of and proactive toward interaction effects. Might these effects eventually result in individualized treatment of antisocial behavior similar to the idea of individualized medicine now widely discussed? Might we ever test for high-risk genetic variants early in life and attempt negating their potential negative influence in the presence of a particular environmental trigger by eliminating this trigger? It is possible, but it would require that a combination of both behavioral and pharmacological approaches be developed and tested in combination and collaboration. There are interesting studies going on that investigate the differentiation of the impacts of intervention depending on the genotype of the intervention recipient, but it will take time for that literature to be refined.

Comments on Mixture Models

It was stated at the beginning of the chapter that the differentiation of main effects of environments and genes is, of course, a simplification, although often a helpful one in the context of attempting to decompose complex etiological forces resulting in the manifestation of conduct problems. Currently, there are a number of theoretical models capturing the nonlinear, interactive, and transactional nature of such etiological forces. Most (if not all) of these models are grounded in a developmental psychopathology framework (Cicchetti & Rogosch, 2002). The main feature of this framework is the realization that the manifestation of psychopathology is not a predetermined (either by environments/events or by genes) outcome, but rather an emergent phenomenon produced by the dynamic system connecting the individual and his or her internal and external contexts (Cicchetti & Rogosch, 2002; Sameroff, 2001). This framework stresses the fluidity of development, both the integration and disintegration of psychological functions within and across domains and contexts (Rutter & Sroufe, 2000), evolutionary nature and the transformation of these functions in the course of development (Cicchetti & Sroufe, 2000), and the interlocking nature of development that makes impossible its neat separation into its biological, psychological, and social contextual systems. Development itself here is viewed as quilted from a number of age- and stage-specific tasks, and these tasks arrange themselves into a hierarchical system so that every past or current success/failure predicts, to a certain degree, most future successes/failures (Cicchetti, 1993; Cicchetti & Rogosch, 2002). Of note also is the differentiation of risk, promotive, and protective processes or factors. *Risk factors* are factors associated with an increased probability of negative outcome(s). The processes that moderate the impact of the risk factors are typically referred to as *promotive factors* and *protective factors* (Sameroff, Bartko, Baldwin, Baldwin, & Seifer, 1998). *Promotive factors* tend to increase the probability of positive outcome(s); they are typically linked to the development of competencies and prosocial behavior (Luthar, Cicchetti, & Becker, 2000) or the desistance of negative behaviors or remission of disorders. *Protective factors* tend to decrease the probability of negative outcome(s) (Kraemer, Stice, Kazdin, Offord, & Kupfer, 2001; Masten, 2007; Masten & Garmezy, 1985; Masten & Obradovic, 2006).

One additional consideration here is that developmental outcomes are often characterized by the presence of *just the right proportion* of different forces shaping such an outcome. Development can be, at least to some degree, captured by a mixture model, where the outcome does not depend on the *amount* of a developmental event (e.g., harsh parenting), but rather on the fraction of each of the developmental events in the current *mixture* of events constituting the texture of life (and the development) of a particular person. In other words, as discussed previously, early maltreatment per se is not deterministically linked to psychopathology, but it can be linked to psychopathology where the mixture of other developmental events at a particular developmental stage was such that early maltreatment was weighted more (e.g., when that person had no extended supportive social network of positive friendship) or less (e.g., when such a network of friends was available). The amount of determinism appears to be even less so when random events (such as meeting a future spouse or breaking a leg), which can *shake* the existing dynamic system and propel its self-organization, appear. Neither protective nor risky factors are fixed to be such and they can neglect or switch their roles and nature at different stages of development.

One illustration of such a dynamic system arises from the development of the innate immune response. For the immune system to develop properly, the child needs to experience *dirt* early in life. The hygienic elimination of triggers of autoimmune response (e.g., animal and earth dirt in houses) has resulted in the development of a substantial portion of children of this generation whose immune responses are jeopardized. The maturation of the immune system can also be captured by a mixture model—it is not the shared presence of the triggers of the immune response that is important; it is the right dosage of these triggers so that the system is challenged and the impetus for its development is in place, but it is not overwhelmed to the point of malfunctioning before maturing. Considerations of these delicate dynamics of development are central for theorizing within the context of developmental psychopathology.

It appears that, with regard to the manifestation of CD among male juvenile offenders, mixture models revealing predisposing versus prohibiting ratios of risky, promotive, and protective factors (which can be labeled as environmental or genetic) might serve as one of the many helpful operationalizations of the complex etiological dynamics of the development of this disorder.

SUMMARY THOUGHTS

Years of research into the etiology of antisocial behavior have resulted in the identification of a substantial number of risk factors that are, interpretively, referred to as *environmental factors*. Although the timeline associated with genetic research into the etiological bases of delinquency is far shorter than that of environmental risk factors, this research has also quite fruitfully identified various genetic vulnerability agents that predispose their carriers for negative behavioral outcomes. Finally, the last few years of research—specifically, since the landmark 2002 *Science* paper by Caspi and colleagues (Caspi et al., 2002)—have triggered a new line of investigation into interactive effects that potentially underlie the etiology of conduct disorders. Along with this investigation, there is new and renewed interest in both gene–gene and environment–environment interaction effects. The current state of the field can be summarized as follows:

1. There are no *main effects*, either environmental or genetic, that deterministically define an outcome of antisocial behavior.
2. There are multiple environmental and genetic risk factors that appear to heighten the likelihood of the manifestation of antisocial behavior.
3. Although both environmental and genetic risk factors might function additively, there appears to be a substantial presence of nonlinear interaction effects. These effects are thought to be small in magnitude but quite important in substance.
4. The presence of these interactive effects does not negate policy orientations toward the development of intervention approaches that can work for at least a portion, although desirably a substantial portion, of children with conduct problems.

All in all, the field is making huge strides in understanding the etiology of Conduct Disorder in childhood and its links to Antisocial Personality Disorder in adulthood. The majority of the work, especially the work presented in this chapter, is made with regard to the development of CD in males. It is clear, however, that, whatever little boys with conduct disorders are made of, there must be ways to prevent the manifestation of serious antisocial behavior by administering interventions that are based on the field's understanding of the risk factors both within and outside these boys to mitigate the negative influence of these factors. I wish that dealing with these risk factors were as easy as removing snips, snails, and puppy dog tails from little boys' pockets. It is, clearly, not so easy, but there is evidence that it is possible.

REFERENCES

Agnew, R., Brezina, T., Wright, J. P., & Cullen, F. T. (2002). Strain, personality traits, and delinquency: Extending general strain theory. *Criminology*, *40*, 43–72.

Agnew, R., & Raskin White, H. (1992). An empirical test of general strain theory. *Criminology*, *30*, 475–499.

Akers, R. L. (1998). *Social learning and social structure: A general theory of crime and deviance*. Boston: Northeastern University Press.

Bakermans-Kranenburg, M. J., & van Ijzendoorn, M. H. (2006). Gene-environment interaction of the dopamine D4 receptor (*DRD4*) and observed maternal insensitivity predicting externalizing behavior in preschoolers. *Developmental Psychobiology*, *48*, 406–409.

Berggard, C., Damberg, M., & Oreland, L. (2005). Brainstem levels of transcription factor AP-2 in rats are changed after treatment with phenelzine, but not citalopram. *BMC Pharmacology*, *5*, 1.

Bess, R. (2002). *The cost of protecting vulnerable children. Caring for children: Facts and perspectives*. Washington, DC: The Urban Institute.

Bolger, K., Patterson, C., & Kupersmidt, J. (1998). Peer relationships and self-esteem among children who have been maltreated. *Child Development*, *69*, 1171–1197.

Brooks-Gunn, J., Duncan, G. J., Klebanov, P. K., & Sealand, N. (1993). Do neighborhoods influence child and adolescent development? *American Journal of Sociology*, *99*, 353–395.

Browning, C. R., Feinberg, S. L., & Dietz, R. D. (2004). The paradox of social organization: Networks, collective efficacy, and violent crime in urban neighborhoods. *Social Forces*, *83*, 503–534.

Buehler, C., Anthony, C., Krishnakumar, A., & Stone, G. (1997). Interparental conflict and youth problem behaviors: A meta-analysis. *Journal of Child and Family Studies*, *6*, 223–247.

Buhrmester, D., & Furman, W. (1987). The development of companionship and intimacy. *Child Development*, *58*, 1101–1113.

Cadoret, R. J., Cain, C. A., & Crowe, R. R. (1983). Evidence for gene-environment interaction in the development of adolescent antisocial behavior. *Behavior Genetics*, *13*, 301–310.

Cadoret, R. J., Langbehn, D., Caspers, K., Troughton, E. P., Yucuis, R., Sandhu, H. K., et al. (2003). Associations of the serotonin transporter promoter polymorphism with aggressivity, Attention Deficit, and Conduct Disorder in an adoptee population. *Comprehensive Psychiatry, 44*, 88–101.

Call, K. T., & Mortimer, J. T. (2001). *Arenas of comfort in adolescence: A study of adjustment in context.* Mahwah, NJ: Erlbaum.

Caspi, A., McClay, J., Moffitt, T. E., Mill, J., Martin, J., Craig, I. W., et al. (2002). Role of genotype in the cycle of violence in maltreated children. *Science, 297*, 851–854.

Cass, A. I. (2007). Routine activities and sexual assault: An analysis of individual- and school-level factors. *Violence and Victims, 22*, 350–366.

Chapman, J. F., Desai, R. A., Falzer, P. R., & Borum, R. (2006). Violence risk and race in a sample of youth in juvenile detention: The potential to reduce disproportionate minority confinement. *Youth Violence and Juvenile Justice, 4*, 170–184.

Cicchetti, D. (1993). Developmental psychopathology: Reactions, reflections, projections. *Developmental Review, 13*, 471–502.

Cicchetti, D., & Rogosch, F. A. (2002). A developmental psychopathology perspective on adolescence. *Journal of Consulting and Clinical Psychology, 70*, 6–20.

Cicchetti, D., & Sroufe, L. A. (2000). The past as prologue to the future: The times, they've been a changin'. *Development and Psychopathology, 12*, 255–264.

Cloninger, C. R., Sigvardsson, S., Bohman, M., & von Knorring, A. L. (1982). Predisposition to petty criminality in Swedish adoptees. II. Cross-fostering analysis of gene-environment interaction. *Archives of General Psychiatry, 39*, 1242–1247.

CNN. (2008). *Report: 1 percent of U.S. adults behind bars.* Retrieved May 12, 2008, from http://www.cnn.com/2008/CRIME/02/28/prison.population.ap/index.html

Comings, D. E., Chen, C., Wu, S., & Muhleman, D. (1999). Association of the androgen receptor gene (AR) with ADHD and Conduct Disorder. *Neuroreport, 10*, 1589–1592.

Comings, D. E., Gade-Andavolu, R., Gonzalez, N., Wu, S., Muhleman, D., Blake, H., Chiu, H., et al. (2000). Multivariate analysis of associations of 42 genes in ADHD, ODD and Conduct Disorder. *Clinical Genetics, 58*, 31–40.

Comings, D. E., Gade-Andavolu, R., Gonzalez, N., Wu, S., Muhleman, D., Blake, H., Saucier, G., et al. (2000). Comparison of the role of dopamine, serotonin, and noradrenaline genes in ADHD, ODD and Conduct Disorder: Multivariate regression analysis of 20 genes. *Clinical Genetics, 57*, 178–196.

Comings, D. E., Gonzalez, N. S., Cheng Li, S. C., & MacMurray, J. (2003). A "line item" approach to the identification of genes involved in polygenic behavioral disorders: The adrenergic alpha2A (ADRA2A) gene. *American Journal of Medical Genetics: Part B, Neuropsychiatric Genetics, 118*, 110–114.

Cote, K., Earls, C. M., & Lalumiere, M. L. (2002). Birth order, birth interval, and deviant sexual preferences among sex offenders. *Sexual Abuse: Journal of Research and Treatment, 14*, 67–81.

Courtet, P., Baud, P., Abbar, M., Boulenger, J. P., Castelnau, D., Mouthon, D., et al. (2001). Association between violent suicidal behavior and the low activity allele of the serotonin transporter gene. *Molecular Psychiatry, 6*, 338–341.

Craddock, N., Owen, M. J., & O'Donovan, M. C. (2006). The catechol-O-methyl transferase (COMT) gene as a candidate for psychiatric phenotypes: Evidence and lessons. *Molecular Psychiatry, 11*, 446–458.

Criss, M. M., Pettit, G., Bates, J., Dodge, K., & Lapp, A. (2002). Family adversity, positive peer relationships, and children's externalizing behavior: A longitudinal perspective on risk and resilience. *Child Development, 74*, 1220–1237.

Crosnoe, R. (2004). Social capital and the interplay of families and schools. *Journal of Marriage and Family, 66*, 267–280.

Cubells, J. F., & Zabetian, C. P. (2004). Human genetics of plasma dopamine beta-hydroxylase activity: Applications to research in psychiatry and neurology. *Psychopharmacology, 174*, 463–476.

Cui, M., Donnellan, M. B., & Conger, R. D. (2007). Reciprocal influences between parents' marital problems and adolescent internalizing and externalizing behavior. *Developmental Psychology, 43*, 1544–1552.

Damberg, M. (2005). Transcription factor AP-2 and monoaminergic functions in the central nervous system. *Journal of Neural Transmission, 112*, 1281–1296.

Damberg, M., Eller, M., Tonissaar, M., Oreland, L., & Harro, J. (2001). Levels of transcription factors AP-2alpha and AP-2beta in the brainstem are correlated to monoamine turnover in the rat forebrain. *Neuroscience Letters, 313*, 102–104.

Dennett, D. C. (1995). *Darwin's dangerous idea: evolution and the meanings of life*. New York: Touchstone.

DeWit, D. J., Offord, D. R., Sanford, M., Rye, B. J., Shain, M., & Wright, R. (2000). The effect of school culture on adolescent behavioral problems: Self-esteem, attachment to learning, and peer approval of deviance as mediating mechanisms. *Canadian Journal of School Psychology, 16*, 15–38.

Dick, D. M., Bierut, L., Hinrichs, A., Fox, L., Bucholz, K. K., Kramer, J., et al. (2006). The role of GABRA2 in risk for Conduct Disorder and alcohol and drug dependence across developmental stages. *Behavior Genetics, 36*, 577–590.

Dick, D. M., Li, T. K., Edenberg, H. J., Hesselbrock, V., Kramer, J., Kuperman, S., et al. (2004). A genome-wide screen for genes influencing Conduct Disorder. *Molecular Psychiatry, 9*, 81–86.

Dishion, T. J., & Patterson, G. R. (2006). The development and ecology of antisocial behavior in children and adolescents. In D. Cicchetti & D. J. Cohen (Eds.), *Developmental psychopathology: Vol 3, Risk, disorder, and adaptation* (pp. 503–541). Hoboken, NJ: Wiley.

Dodge, K. A., Pettit, G. S., & Bates, J. E. (1994). Socialization mediators of the relation between socioeconomic status and child conduct problems. *Child Development, 65*, 649–665.

Dumas, J. E., & Wahler, R. G. (1985). Indiscriminate mothering as a contextual factor in aggressive-oppositional child behavior: "Damned if you do and damned if you don't". *Journal of Abnormal Child Psychology, 13*, 1–17.

Eaves, L. J. (2006). Genotype x environment interaction in psychopathology: Fact or artifact? *Twin Research and Human Genetics, 9*, 1–8.

Elliott, D. S., & Menard, S. (1996). Delinquent friends and delinquent behavior: Temporal and developmental patterns. In J. D. Hawkins (Ed.), *Delinquency and crime: Current theories* (pp. 28–67). New York: Cambridge University Press.

Faraone, S. V., Biederman, J., Keenan, K., & Tsuang, M. T. (1991). Separation of DMS-III Attention-Deficit Disorder and Conduct Disorder: Evidence from a family-genetic study of American child psychiatric patients. *Psychological Medicine, 21*, 109–121.

Faraone, S. V., Doyle, A. E., Mick, E., & Biederman, J. (2001). Meta-analysis of the association between the 7-repeat allele of the dopamine D4 receptor gene and AttentionDeficit/Hyperactivity Disorder. *American Journal of Psychiatry, 158*, 1052–1057.

Farrington, D. P. (1992). *Explaining the beginning, progress, and ending of antisocial behavior from birth to adulthood.* In J. McCord (Ed.), *Facts, frameworks, and forecasts* (pp. 253–286). New Brunswick, NJ: Transaction Publishers.

Farrington, D. P. (1993). Childhood origins of teenage antisocial behavior and adult social dysfunction. *Journal of the Royal Society of Medicine, 86*, 13–17.

Feiring, C., Miller-Johnson, S., & Cleland, C. M. (2007). Potential pathways from stigmatization and internalizing symptoms to delinquency in sexually abused youth. *Child Maltreatment, 12*, 220–232.

Fergusson, D. M., Horwood, L. J., & Lynskey, M. T. (1994). Parental separation, adolescent psychopathology, and problem behaviors. *Journal of the American Academy of Child & Adolescent Psychiatry, 33*, 1122–1131.

Fijneman, R. J. (2005). Genetic predisposition to sporadic cancer: How to handle major effects of minor genes? *Cellular Oncology, 27*, 281–292.

Frick, P. J., Lahey, B. B., Loeber, R., Stouthamer-Loeber, M., Christ, M. A. G., & Hanson, K. (1992). Familial risk factors to Oppositional Defiant Disorder and Conduct Disorder: Parental psychopathology and maternal parenting. *Journal of Consulting and Clinical Psychology, 60*, 49–55.

Fromm, S. (2001). *Total estimated costs of child abuse and neglect in the United States*. Chicago: Prevent Child Abuse America.

Gauze, C., Bukowski, W., Aquan-Assee, J., & Sippola, L. (1996). Interactions between family environment and friendship and associations with self-perceived well-being during adolescence. *Child Development, 67*, 2201–2216.

Glueck, S., & Glueck, E. (1968). *Delinquents and nondelinquents in perspective*. Cambridge, MA: Harvard University Press.

Gorman-Smith, D., Tolan, P. H., Zelli, A., & Huesmann, L. R. (1996). The relation of family functioning to violence among inner-city minority youths. *Journal of Family Psychology, 10*, 115–129.

Gottfredson, D. C. (2001). *Schools and delinquency*. New York: Cambridge University Press.

Gottfredson, G. D., Gottfredson, D. C., Payne, A. A., & Gottfredson, N. C. (2005). School climate predictors of school disorder: Results from a National Study of Delinquency Prevention in Schools. *Journal of Research in Crime and Delinquency, 42*, 412–444.

Grigorenko, E. L., DeYoung, C. G., Getchell, M., Haeffel, G. J., af Klinteberg, B., Koposov, R. A., et al. (2008). *Serious conduct problems and variation in dopaminergic genes*. Unpublished manuscript.

Haapasalo, J., & Moilanen, J. (2004). Official and self-reported childhood abuse and adult crime of young offenders. *Criminal Justice and Behavior, 31*, 127–149.

Haapasalo, J., & Pokela, E. (1999). Child-rearing and child abuse antecedents of criminality. *Aggression and Violent Behavior, 4*, 107–127.

Hadley-Ives, E., Stiffman, A. R., Elze, D., Johnson, S. D., & Dore, P. (2000). Measuring neighborhood and school environments: Perceptual and aggregate approaches. *Journal of Human Behavior in the Social Environment, 3*, 1–28.

Haeffel, G. J., Getchell, M., Koposov, R. A., Yrigollen, C. M., Deyoung, C. G., Klinteberg, B. A., et al. (2008). Association between polymorphisms in the dopamine transporter gene and depression: Evidence for a gene-environment interaction in a sample of juvenile detainees. *Psychological Science*, *19*, 62–69.

Hart, J. L., O'Toole, S. K., Price-Sharps, J. L., & Shaffer, T. W. (2007). The risk and protective factors of violent juvenile offending: An examination of gender differences. *Youth Violence and Juvenile Justice*, *54*, 367–384.

Haynie, D. L. (2001). Delinquent peers revisited: Does network structure matter? *American Journal of Sociology*, *106*, 1013–1057.

Heimer, K., & DeCoster, S. (1999). The gendering of violent delinquency. *Criminology*, *37*, 277–317.

Hill, E. M., Stoltenberg, S. F., Bullard, K. H., Li, S., Zucker, R. A., & Burmeister, M. (2002). Antisocial alcoholism and serotonin-related polymorphisms: Association tests. *Psychiatric Genetics*, *12*, 143–153.

Hirschi, T. (1969). *Causes of delinquency*. Berkeley: University of California Press.

Holmes, J., Payton, A., Barrett, J., Harrington, R., McGuffin, P., Owen, M., et al. (2002). Association of DRD4 in children with ADHD and comorbid conduct problems. *American Journal of Medical Genetics*, *114*, 150–153.

Ishiguro, H., Saito, T., Akazawa, S., Mitushio, H., Tada, K., Enomoto, M., et al. (1999). Association between drinking-related antisocial behavior and a polymorphism in the serotonin transporter gene in a Japanese population. *Alcoholism: Clinical & Experimental Research*, *23*, 1281–1284.

Kaufman, J., Yang, B. Z., Douglas-Palumberi, H., Houshyar, S., Lipschitz, D., Krystal, J. H., et al. (2004). Social supports and serotonin transporter gene moderate depression in maltreated children. *Proceedings of the National Academy of Sciences of the USA*, *101*, 17316–17321.

Keena, K., Loeber, R., Zhang, Q., & Stouthamer-Loeber, M. (1995). The influence of deviant peers on the development of boys' disruptive and delinquent behavior: A temporal analysis. *Development and Psychopathology*, *7*, 715–726.

Kilgore, K., Snyder, J., & Lentz, C. (2000). The contribution of parental discipline, parental monitoring, and school risk to early-onset conduct problems in African American boys and girls. *Developmental Psychology*, *36*, 835–845.

Kim-Cohen, J., Caspi, A., Taylor, A., Williams, B., Newcombe, R., Craig, I. W., et al. (2006). MAOA, maltreatment, and gene–environment interaction predicting children's mental health: New evidence and a meta-analysis. *Molecular Psychiatry*, *11*, 903–913.

Kolvin, I., Miller, F. J., Fleeting, M., & Kolvin, P. A. (1988). Social and parenting factors affecting criminal-offence rates: Findings from the Newcastle Thousand Family Study (1947–1980). *British Journal of Psychiatry*, *152*, 80–90.

Kraemer, H. C., Stice, E., Kazdin, A., Offord, D., & Kupfer, D. (2001). How do risk factors work together? Mediators, moderators, and independent, overlapping, and proxy risk factors. *American Journal of Psychiatry*, *158*, 848–856.

Kroneman, L., Loeber, R., & Hipwell, A. E. (2004). Is neighborhood context differently related to externalizing problems and delinquency for girls compared with boys? *Clinical Child and Family Psychology Review*, *7*, 109–122.

Kuikka, J. T., Tiihonen, J., Bergstrom, K. A., Karhu, J., Rasanen, P., & Eronen, M. (1998). Abnormal structure of human striatal dopamine re-uptake sites in habitually violent alcoholic offenders: A fractal analysis. *Neuroscience Letters*, *253*, 195–197.

Ladd, G. W. (2006). Peer rejection, aggressive or withdrawn behavior, and psychological maladjustment from ages 5 to 12: An examination of four predictive models. *Child Development*, *77*, 822–846.

Lahey, B. B., Hartdagen, S. E., Frick, P. J., McBurnett, K., Connor, R., & Hynd, G. W. (1988). Conduct Disorder: Parsing the confounded relation to parental divorce and antisocial personality. *Journal of Abnormal Psychology*, *97*, 334–337.

Langley, K., & Thapar, A. (2006). COMT gene variant and birth weight predict early-onset antisocial behavior in children with Attention-Deficit/Hyperactivity Disorder. *Directions in Psychiatry*, *26*, 219–225.

Lansford, J. E., Criss, M. M., Pettit, G. S., Dodge, K. A., & Bates, J. E. (2003). Friendship quality, peer group affiliation, and peer antisocial behavior as moderators of the link between negative parenting and adolescent externalizing behavior. *Journal of Research on Adolescence*, *13*, 161–184.

Laub, J., Nagin, D., & Sampson, R. (1998). Trajectories of change in criminal offending: Good marriages and the desistance process. *American Sociological Review*, *63*, 225–238.

Lee, V. E., & Smith, J. B. (1997). High school size: Which works best and for whom? *Educational Evaluation and Policy Analysis*, *19*, 205–227.

Lipsey, M. W., & Derzon, J. H. (1998). Predictors of violent or serious delinquency in adolescence and early adulthood: A synthesis of longitudinal research. In R. Loeber & D. P. Farrington (Eds.), *Serious & violent juvenile offenders: Risk factors and successful interventions* (pp. 86–105). Thousand Oaks, CA: Sage Publications.

Liptak, A. (2008, February 28, 2008). 1 in 100 U.S. adults behind bars, new study says. *The New York Times*.

Liu, R. X. (2004). Parent-youth conflict and school delinquency/cigarette use: The moderating effects of gender and associations with achievement-oriented peers. *Sociological Inquiry*, *74*, 271–297.

Loeber, R., Farrington, D. P., Stouthamer-Loeber, M., & Van Kammen, W. B. (1998). *Antisocial behavior and mental health problems: Explanatory factors in childhood and adolescence*. Mahwah, NJ: Lawrence Erlbaum.

Loeber, R., Green, S. M., Keenan, K., & Lahey, B. B. (1995). Which boys will fare worse? Early predictors of the onset of Conduct Disorder in a six-year longitudinal study. *Journal of the American Academy of Child & Adolescent Psychiatry, 34*, 499–509.

Loukas, A., & Robinson, S. (2004). Examining the moderating role of perceived school climate in early adolescent adjustment. *Journal of Research on Adolescence, 14*, 209–233.

Lu, R. B., Lee, J. F., Ko, H. C., & Lin, W. W. (2001). Dopamine D2 receptor gene (DRD2) is associated with alcoholism with Conduct Disorder. *Alcoholism: Clinical & Experimental Research, 25*, 177–184.

Luthar, S. S., Cicchetti, D., & Becker, B. (2000). The construct of resilience: A critical evaluation and guidelines for future work. *Child Development, 71*, 543–562.

Lynam, D. R, Caspi, A., Moffitt, T. E., Wikstrom, P.-O., Loeber, R., & Novak, S. (2000). The interaction between impulsivity and neighborhood context on offending: The effects of impulsivity are stronger in poorer neighborhoods. *Journal of Abnormal Psychology, 109*, 563–574.

Malinosky-Rummell, R., & Hansen, D. J. (1993). Long-term consequences of childhood physical abuse. *Psychological Bulletin, 114*, 68–79.

Masten, A. S. (2007). Resilience in developing systems: Progress and promise as the fourth wave rises. *Development and Psychopathology, 19*, 921–930.

Masten, A. S., & Garmezy, N. (1985). Risk, vulnerability, and protective factors in developmental psychopathology. In B. B. Lahey & A. E. Kazdin (Eds.), *Advances in clinical child psychology: Vol. 8* (pp. 1–52). New York: Plenum Press.

Masten, A. S., & Obradovic, J. (2006). Competence and resilience in development. *Annals of the New York Academy of Sciences, 1094*, 13–27.

McCord, J. (1979). Some child-rearing antecedents of criminal behavior in adult men. *Journal of Personality and Social Psychology, 37*, 1477–1486.

Mears, D. P., Ploeger, M., & Warr, M. (1998). Explaining the gender gap in delinquency: Peer influence and moral evaluations of behavior. *Journal of Research in Crime and Delinquency, 35*, 251–266.

Moffitt, T. E. (2005). The new look of behavioral genetics in developmental psychopathology: Gene-environment interplay in antisocial behaviors. *Psychological Bulletin, 131*, 533–554.

Munafò, M. R., Yalcin, B., Willis-Owen, S. A., & Flint, J. (2008). Association of the dopamine D4 receptor (DRD4) gene and approach-related personality traits: Meta-analysis and new data. *Biological Psychiatry, 163*, 197–206.

Newson, J., Newson, E., & Adams, M. (1993). The social origins of delinquency. *Criminal Behavior and Mental Health, 3*, 19–29.

Offord, D. R., Alder, R. J., & Boyle, M. H. (1986). Prevalence and sociodemographic correlates of Conduct Disorder. *American Journal of Social Psychiatry*, 6, 272–278.

Oreland, L., Nilsson, K., Damberg, M., & Hallman, J. (2007). Monoamine oxidases—activities, genotypes and the shaping of behaviour. *Journal of Neural Transmission, 114*, 817–822.

Osgood, D. W., Wilson, J. K., O'Malley, P. M., Bachman, J. G., & Johnston, L. D. (1996). Routine activities and individual deviant behavior. *American Sociological Review, 61*, 635–655.

Ousey, G. C., & Wilcox, P. (2007). The interaction of antisocial propensity and life-course varying predictors of delinquent behavior: Differences by method of estimation and implications for theory. *Criminology, 45*, 313–354.

Patrick, M. R., Snyder, J., Schrepferman, L. M., & Snyder, J. (2005). The joint contribution of early parental warmth, communication and tracking, and early child conduct problems on monitoring in late childhood. *Child Development, 76*, 999–1014.

Patterson, G. R., Capaldi, D., & Bank, L. (1991). An early starter model for predicting delinquency. In D. J. Pepler & K. H. Rubin (Eds.), *The development and treatment of childhood aggression* (pp. 139–168). Hillsdale, NJ: Lawrence Erlbaum.

Payne, A. A., Gottfredson, D. C., & Gottfredson, G. D. (2003). Schools as communities: The relationship among communal school organization, student bonding, and school disorder. *Criminology, 41*, 749–777.

Piehler, T. F., & Dishion, T. J. (2007). Interpersonal dynamics within adolescent friendships: Dyadic mutuality, deviant talk, and patterns of antisocial behavior. *Child Development, 78*, 1611–1624.

Piquero, N. L., Gover, A. R., MacDonald, J. M., & Piquero, A. R. (2005). The influence of delinquent peers on delinquency: Does gender matter? *Youth & Society, 36*, 251–275.

Reiss, A. J. J., & Farrington, D. P. (1994). Advancing knowledge about co-offending: Results from a prospective longitudinal survey of London males. In D. P. Farrington (Ed.), *Psychological explanations of crime* (pp. 315–350). Brookfield, VT: Dartmouth Publishing.

Retz, W., Retz-Junginger, P., Supprian, T., Thome, J., & Rosler, M. (2004). Association of serotonin transporter promoter gene polymorphism with violence: Relation with personality disorders, impulsivity, and childhood ADHD psychopathology. *Behavioral Sciences & the Law*, *22*, 415–425.

Robins, L. N. (1978). Sturdy childhood predictors of adult antisocial behaviour: Replications from longitudinal studies. *Psychological Medicine*, 8, 611–622.

Rutter, M., Caspi, A., & Moffitt, T. E. (2003). Using sex differences in psychopathology to study causal mechanisms: Unifying issues and research strategies *Journal of Child Psychology & Psychiatry & Allied Disciplines*, *44*, 1092–1115.

Rutter, M., & Sroufe, L. A. (2000). Developmental psychopathology: Concepts and challenges. *Development and Psychopathology*, *12*, 265–296.

Sakai, J. T., Young, S. E., Stallings, M. C., Timberlake, D., Smolen, A., Stetler, G. L., et al. (2006). Case-control and within-family tests for an association between Conduct Disorder and 5HTTLPR. *American Journal of Medical Genetics: Part B, Neuropsychiatric Genetics*, *141*, 825–832.

Salanti, G., Higgins, J. P., & White, I. R. (2006). Bayesian synthesis of epidemiological evidence with different combinations of exposure groups: Application to a gene-gene-environment interaction. *Statistics in Medicine*, *25*, 4147–4163.

Sameroff, A. J. (2001). Developmental systems and psychopathology. *Development and Psychopathology*, *12*, 297–312.

Sameroff, A. J., Bartko, W. T., Baldwin, A., Baldwin, C., & Seifer, R. (1998). Family and social influences on the development of child competence. In M. Lewis & C. Feiring (Eds.), *Families, risk, and competence* (pp. 161–185). Mahwah, NJ: Lawrence Erlbaum.

Sampson, R. J., & Laub, J. H. (1990). Crime and deviance over the life course: The salience of adult social bonds. *American Sociological Review*, *55*, 609–627.

Sampson, R. J., & Laub, J. H. (1993). *Crime in the making: Pathways and turning points in life*. Cambridge, MA: Harvard University Press.

Sampson, R. J., & Laub, J. H. (2005). A life-course view of the development of crime. *Annals of the American Academy of Political and Social Science*, *602*, 12–45.

Sampson, R. J., Raudenbush, S. W., & Earls, F. (1997). Neighborhoods and violent crime: A multilevel study of collective efficacy. *Science*, *277*, 918–924.

Schlaepfer, I. R., Clegg, H. V., Corley, R. P., Crowley, T. J., Hewitt, J. K., Hopfer, C. J., et al. (2007). The human protein kinase C gamma gene (PRKCG) as a susceptibility locus for behavioral disinhibition. *Addiction Biology, 12*, 200–209.

Shafii, M., & Shafii, S. L. (2003). School violence, depression, and suicide. *Journal of Applied Psychoanalytic Studies, 5*, 155–169.

Shaw, D. S., Bell, R. Q., & Gilliom, M. (2000). A truly early starter model of antisocial behavior revisited. *Clinical Child and Family Psychology Review, 3*, 155–172.

Simons, R. L., Chao, W., Conger, R. D., & Elder, G. H., Jr. (2001). Quality of parenting as mediator of the effect of childhood defiance on adolescent friendship choices and delinquency: A growth curve analysis. *Journal of Marriage & Family, 63*, 63–79.

Smith, C. A., & Thornberry, T. P. (1995). The relationship between childhood maltreatment and adolescent involvement in delinquency. *Criminology, 33*, 451–481.

Sommers, I., & Baskin, D. R. (1994). Factors related to female adolescent initiation into violent street crime. *Youth & Society, 25*, 468–489.

Soyka, M., Preuss, U. W., Koller, G., Zill, P., & Bondy, B. (2004). Association of 5-HT1B receptor gene and antisocial behavior in alcoholism. *Journal of Neural Transmission, 111*, 101–109.

Stattin, H., & Kerr, M. (2000). Parental monitoring: A reinterpretation. *Child Development, 71*, 1072–1085.

Stern, S. B., & Smith, C. A. (1999). Reciprocal relationships between antisocial behavior and parenting: Implications for delinquency intervention. *Families in Society, 80*, 169–181.

Sutherland, E. H. (1947). *Criminology*. Philadelphia: Lippincott.

Svensson, R. (2003). Gender differences in adolescent drug use: The impact of parental monitoring and peer deviance. *Youth & Society, 34*, 300–329.

Thapar, A., Langley, K., Fowler, T., Rice, F., Turic, D., Whittinger, N., et al. (2005). Catechol O-methyltransferase gene variant and birth weight predict early-onset antisocial behavior in children with Attention-Deficit/Hyperactivity Disorder. *Archives of General Psychiatry, 62*, 1275–1278.

Twitchell, G. R., Hanna, G. L., Cook, E. H., Stoltenberg, S. F., Fitzgerald, H. E., & Zucker, R. A. (2001). Serotonin transporter promoter polymorphism genotype is associated with behavioral disinhibition and negative affect in children of alcoholics. *Alcoholism: Clinical & Experimental Research, 25*, 953–959.

U.S. Department of Justice. (n.d.a). *Criminal victimization*. Retrieved May 12, 2008, from http://www.ojp.usdoj.gov/bjs/cvictgen.htm

U.S. Department of Justice. (n.d.b). *Reentry trends in the U.S.: Recidivism.* Retrieved May 12, 2008, from http://www.ojp.usdoj.gov/bjs/reentry/recidivism.htm

U.S. Department of Justice. (1994). *The costs of crime to victims: Crime data brief.* Retrieved May 12, 2008, from http://www.ojp.usdoj.gov/bjs/pub/ascii/coctv.txt

Vanyukov, M. M., Moss, H. B., Kaplan, B. B., Kirillova, G. P., & Tarter, R. E. (2000). Antisociality, substance dependence, and the DRD5 gene: A preliminary study. *American Journal of Medical Genetics, 96,* 654–658.

Velez, C. N., Johnson, J., & Cohen, P. (1989). A longitudinal analysis of selected risk factors for childhood psychopathology. *Journal of the American Academy of Child & Adolescent Psychiatry, 28,* 861–864.

Wallace, H. M. (2006). A model of gene-gene and gene-environment interactions and its implications for targeting environmental interventions by genotype. *Theoretical Biology & Medical Modelling, 3,* 35.

Warr, M. (2002). *Companions in crime.* New York: Cambridge University Press.

Warren, J. R. (1966). Birth order and social behavior. *Psychological Bulletin, 65,* 38–49.

Welsh, W. N., Greene, J. R., & Jenkins, P. H. (1999). School disorder: The influence of individual, institutional, and community factors. *Criminology, 37,* 73–115.

Wolfgan, M. E., Figlio, R. M., & Sellin, T. (1972). *Delinquency in a birth cohort.* Chicago: University of Chicago Press.

Yang, B., Chan, R. C., Jing, J., Li, T., Sham, P., & Chen, R. Y. (2007). A meta-analysis of association studies between the 10-repeat allele of a VNTR polymorphism in the 3'-UTR of dopamine transporter gene and Attention-Deficit/Hyperactivity Disorder. *American Journal of Medical Genetics: Part B, Neuropsychiatric Genetics, 144,* 541–550.

Young, S. E., Smolen, A., Corley, R. P., Krauter, K. S., DeFries, J. C., Crowley, T. J., et al. (2002). Dopamine transporter polymorphism associated with externalizing behavior problems in children. *American Journal of Medical Genetics, 114,* 144–149.

Zahn-Waxler, C., Iannotti, R. J., Cummings, E. M., & Denham, S. (1990). Antecedents of problem behaviors in children of depressed mothers. *Development and Psychopathology, 2,* 271–291.

CHAPTER

8

Translational Issues in the Development and Prevention of Children's Early Conduct Problems

Challenges in Transitioning From Basic to Intervention Research

Daniel S. Shaw

This chapter provides an example of a roadmap for conducting translational research for researchers currently engaged in basic research on developmental and clinical issues for children. As indicated by the theme of this volume, there is a need for basic researchers to transfer the focus of their efforts to more applied outcomes, including

I wish to express my appreciation for the many collaborators who made this research possible, including Drs. Richard Bell, Joan Vondra, Thomas Dishion, Frances Gardner, and Melvin Wilson, as well as the staffs and participants of the Pitt Mother & Child Projects and the Early Steps Projects. Support for this research was provided to the author by grants 50907 and 62921 from the National Institute of Mental Health, and grant 016110 from the National Institute on Drug Abuse. I also wish to thank Dr. Anne Gill and Ms. Heather Gross for providing feedback on an initial draft of the manuscript.

preventive interventions and clinical treatments that address suboptimal developmental outcomes and clinical disorders. The recent emphasis on translational research is both an exciting and an intimidating prospect for researchers whose primary interests have been directed toward studying individual differences in normative outcomes among relatively low-risk populations or clinical outcomes among high-risk populations. It is a formidable challenge to spend several years attempting to identify reliable precursors of clinically meaningful child outcomes; however, it is a challenge of a different kind to generate an intervention based on these findings that is both usable and effective in addressing or preventing child problem behavior. The current chapter provides an example of one such research program that began by identifying developmental precursors of children's early conduct problems and subsequently used findings from this longitudinal research to adapt an already-existing intervention to prevent the development of children's early conduct problems.

Part One of the chapter describes an overview of the issues faced in conducting translational research on conduct problems in early childhood, including the dual challenges of providing data on developmental pathways leading to child problem behavior and developing an intervention that is both feasible and effective. Part Two reviews the specific basic program of research that laid the groundwork for developing our intervention—the Pitt Mother & Child Project. Part Three describes the adaptation and development of the intervention—the Early Steps Project—and an evaluation of its efficacy. Finally, Part Four is devoted to summarizing the current status of the program of research and remaining challenges.

PART ONE: PATHWAYS TO TRANSLATIONAL RESEARCH IN EARLY CHILDHOOD

Developing a Knowledge Base About a Child Problem Behavior

The challenges for establishing a developmentally informed program of translational research are somewhat daunting. Indeed, validating a developmental trajectory of a problem behavior or developing an effective intervention to prevent the onset of a problem behavior in one person's career would be considered a commendable achievement. The first prerequisite for meeting this challenge is to have a sufficient knowledge base to understand the developmental course of the targeted problem behavior (Conduct Problems Prevention Research Group, 1999). Implicit in this first goal is to identify the mechanisms underlying associations between risk factors and the target problem behavior. Ideally, such research would be carried out using prospective, longitudinal designs to identify reliable associations between hypothesized risk factors and later child problem behavior. Some researchers spend careers conceptualizing, testing, and refining models for specific types of child problem behavior and ensuring their findings' generalizability across gender, culture and ethnicity, socioeconomic status, and community type. Depending on the expression and stability of the problem behavior in question, this might take 5 to 10 or even more years to initially identify reliable correlates of the problem behavior and follow their course across developmental stages to the age period when the behavior has been shown to be relatively stable over time. For example, in the study of children's conduct problems, a large percentage of early starters can be identified in early childhood when similar types of problem behaviors initially become manifest. In contrast, clinically meaningful levels of depressive symptoms are relatively uncommon before age 8 for most children, making it more difficult to trace depression's development and correlates prior to formal school entry.

In addition, most of our models of child problem behavior are necessarily incomplete given the complexity of developmental psychopathology in general and the principles of equifinality and multifinality in particular (Cicchetti & Rogosch, 1996). *Equifinality* suggests that there are multiple pathways leading to the same child outcome and *multifinality* highlights the fact that many children with similar profiles at one point in time often demonstrate divergent longitudinal trajectories in adjustment. Part of the reason for such divergence involves variation in culture, gender, and biological markers that are often not rigorously tested or understood to the extent of other indicators of social risk (e.g., parenting). Despite the complexity of factors related to child development and the substantive and methodological limitations of existing research, at some point researchers need to get beyond the statement "more research is needed" and make the transition to intervention. Note that the data sets used to inform the current intervention also were incomplete in accounting for all cultural and biological variation. Despite including a large sample of predominantly low-income, ethnically diverse toddlers followed from infancy through adolescence, the sample was limited by its inclusion of only boys and families living in a predominantly urban environment. Although approximately 40% of families were African American, few were of Latino or other cultural descent. Finally, the study did not have a genetically informed design, albeit DNA is currently being collected to examine genetic and gene by environment effects.

Development of Interventions to Address a Specific Problem Behavior

A second prerequisite for translating the findings of basic research to the domain of prevention and intervention is developing an intervention that successfully reduces the problem behavior of interest. Again, many prevention or clinical scientists spend their entire careers conceptualizing, developing, and refining an intervention; expanding its breadth of coverage to address variations in children's developmental status, gender, and cultural issues over time; as well as issues pertaining to training fidelity and variations in therapist qualifications for successful implementation of the program. These many and varied challenges should not stop basic researchers from working to develop an intervention based on their research findings; however, they should be aware of the inherent complexities of validating an intervention's efficacy initially and, if they are fortunate enough to do so, the many follow-up issues that will emerge. For example, Webster-Stratton (1985) began working with preschool-age children whose parents were seeking assistance for child externalizing problems in clinical settings, but they became more interested in conducting preventive interventions in community samples of children identified as at risk in Head Start or elementary school settings. Olds (2002) initially tested his nurse practitioner home-visitation model in a largely rural setting in upstate New York with predominantly Caucasian families, but he has subsequently conducted trials in two large urban areas (Memphis and Denver) with ethnically diverse families. In addition, while the first two trials were conducted using nurses, he also tested the use of paraprofessionals in implementing the program. Forgatch's parent-management treatment program (Forgatch, Patterson, & DeGarmo, 2005) was initially developed and tested for families recently experiencing a divorce, but it has been adapted and refined for children showing problem behavior regardless of the family's structural context. In addition, Forgatch has devoted significant energy to the issue of training fidelity and found it to mediate the effectiveness of the intervention across American and Norwegian samples. Finally, and relevant to the current intervention, Dishion and Kavanagh (2003) developed the Family Check Up for adolescents showing problem behavior, and they gradually adapted the model for both school-age children and toddlers.

The Chasm Between Identification of Problem Behavior and Engaging Families

The magnitude and complexity of developing and refining an intervention cannot be underestimated. Some basic researchers may desire to pursue the development of their own intervention independently or with only intermittent consultation from experts, and this might be feasible in instances when the scope of the intervention is narrow (e.g., addressing improvements in specific behavior such as sleep) and/or the basic researcher already has some clinical expertise (e.g., practicing psychologist, psychiatrist, or pediatrician). However, it can be helpful to collaborate with an interventionist who has previous experience and expertise in developing similar types of programs *and* testing their efficacy. In the case of the intervention developed for the current project, the Early Steps Project, although the author is an experienced family therapist, a collaboration was sought with Dr. Thomas Dishion, who spent several years developing and refining an intervention model to address child problem behavior.

A third component of translational research is especially relevant for those wishing to develop a preventive intervention: identifying children at high risk for developing the targeted child problem behavior. This issue may be less salient for interventionists studying problem behaviors for which families typically seek services in mental health clinics, thereby ensuring identification of appropriate children. In such cases, the problem behavior typically causes sufficient functional impairment and distress for children, caregivers, and teachers that parents are often referred for services for these problems (e.g., Autism Spectrum Disorder, Attention-Deficit/Hyperactivity Disorder). However, based on the premise that child behavior may be more malleable in early versus later childhood (Dishion & Patterson, 1992), several investigators have invested resources in developing preventive interventions in early childhood and even earlier during the prenatal period (Olds, 2002; Baydar, Reid, & Webster-Stratton, 2003).

Research on the precursors of child conduct problems has identified a plethora of child, family, and community risk factors associated with early starting problem behavior, providing the field with a fairly refined representation of risk factors associated with early starting trajectories of conduct problems (e.g., Aguilar, Sroufe, Egeland, & Carlson, 2000; Campbell et al., 1996; Moffitt & Caspi, 2001; Shaw, Gilliom, Ingoldsby, & Nagin, 2003). Nonetheless, identifying young children at risk for problematic trajectories and motivating families to seek assistance for child problem behavior are not synonymous. As discussed later, only a small minority of families with children showing elevated conduct problems in early childhood may decide to *take advantage* of available services. This reluctance to engage in services might be influenced by a few factors. First, if the family with such a child is from a lower socioeconomic strata, they may distrust government services in general and mental health services in particular, as their previous contacts with government agencies and researchers may have been unpleasant and aversive. When these families are from minority groups who have a history of mistreatment by researchers, this distrust might be further amplified. For example, more than one African American family in our basic research program was aware of the Tuskegee study that failed to treat African American adults with syphilis over the course of 4 decades (Corbie-Smith, 1999).

A second type of resistance that parents often express for engaging in preventive interventions for children's *early* conduct problems, especially when *early* means children under the age of 2, is their belief that their child will *grow out of* his or her disruptive behavior. In many cases, parent's perceptions will be correct, as rates of disruptive and oppositional behavior wane between the ages of 2 and 5, thus validating their intuition. Nonetheless, parental beliefs do not coincide with our longitudinal data, which suggest that correlates of later conduct problems can be identified prior to age 2—an issue we revisit later in the chapter.

A third issue influencing engagement pertains to vehicles for identifying very young children at risk for early conduct problem trajectories. The pediatrician's office is an important point of entry in identifying children at early risk for problem outcomes, but to use this entry point requires that families have regular contact with a primary care physician. When the intervention is designed to target families on the lower end of the socioeconomic scale, this point of entry is not practicable as many low-income families do not have health insurance or a primary care physician. Currently, educational enrichment programs for young children, such as Early Head Start and Head Start, offer points of contact for engaging low-income children and their families. In our own research, we have utilized the Women, Infants, and Children Nutritional Supplement Programs (WIC) for this purpose. Similar to Headstart, WIC is a federally funded program whose mandate is to promote young children's health, primarily through providing funds for parents of children from birth to age 5 to purchase nutritional foods. WIC also has a history of promoting prevention by supporting immunization and breastfeeding programs, as well as psychosocial programs such as Olds's nurse home-visitation program and now our Early Steps Program.

A fourth issue that can often hinder family engagement in preventive interventions is the intervention's fit to actual families' needs. The intervention's user-friendliness will be evaluated by potential families on several dimensions. First, is the intervention carried out in a place that is convenient for families to attend? As low-income families may initially have ambivalent or distrustful feelings about service providers in general and mental health professionals in particular, such fears may be exacerbated by having to meet with professionals outside of their communities or neighborhoods. There are also practical concerns such as childcare issues for the target child and siblings as well as the affordability of transportation and parking costs. Many of these issues can be attenuated by making the intervention more accessible for families.

For example, Cunningham and associates (Cunningham, Bremner, & Boyle, 1995) convene parent groups for children with ADHD and other disruptive problem behavior in community settings near families' homes. In trials of our Early Steps Project, families are given the option of having the therapist come to their homes, accompanied by staff who attend to childcare needs. If families feel uncomfortable about having visitors in their homes or therapists find that conditions in the home make it difficult for meetings (e.g., too many unplanned interruptions), we meet at our offices or at a coffee shop close to the family's home, with transportation provided to the family if needed. The choice of the meeting place is given to the parent, meeting where he or she is most comfortable.

PART TWO: THE BASIC PROGRAM OF RESEARCH: THE GENESIS OF THE PITT MOTHER & CHILD PROJECTS

The goal of our basic research program was to identify developmental precursors of antisocial behavior, with the dual agenda of advancing understanding of pathways leading to early starting conduct problems and identifying targets for future preventive interventions (Shaw & Bell, 1993). The study of antisocial behavior in childhood was deemed important because of the direct cost of such behavior to society—not only in terms of damaged property and disruption of normal patterns of living, but also because of the difficulty of treating delinquent youth and the potential emergence of later adult criminality and other serious disorders such as substance abuse (Moffitt & Caspi, 2001; Shaw, Bell, & Gilliom, 2000). Moreover, *early starters*, youth who show a persistent and chronic trajectory of antisocial behavior from early childhood to adulthood, represent approximately 6% of the population yet are responsible for almost half of adolescent crime and three-fourths of violent crimes (Offord, Boyle, & Racine, 1991). Despite the plethora of research on the treatment of antisocial behavior in childhood, efforts to prevent its development have proven to be difficult (Conduct Problems Prevention Research Group, 1999). It was believed that the limited success of effective treatment of conduct problems among school-age children and adolescents was due to an inability to fully understand either the developmental trajectories leading to the disorder or the most appropriate content and timing of the intervention. As an example, past research on treatment of conduct problems has shown that interventions implemented prior to school age have a higher probability of success than those implemented later (Dishion & Patterson, 1992). In response to the need to more fully understand the origins of early conduct problems (Moffitt, Caspi, Dickson, Silva, & Stanton 1996; Patterson, Capaldi, & Bank, 1991), Shaw and Bell (1993) proposed a bridging model of early conduct problems beginning in early childhood.

Initial Bridging Model of Antisocial Behavior and the Focus on the Toddler Period

The goal of the bridging model was to integrate theory and normative empirical work on young children's development with studies of correlates of older children's conduct problems. The work of several investigators figured prominently in the development of the bridging model. At a broad level, Hirschi's (1969) social control theory provided a mechanism from which to understand parental influence, as the antisocial child's lack of self-control was postulated to emerge from his inability to form an attachment to parents in early development. Sroufe's (1983) conceptualization and application of attachment theory to early conduct problems was also instrumental, describing how avoidant working models are formed during infancy and demonstrating how they predisposed children to show later noncompliant and hostile acting-out behavior (Erickson, Sroufe, & Egeland, 1985). Greenberg and Speltz's (1988) cognitive-affective model, also conceptualized from an attachment perspective, provided specific examples of how parent-child interchanges from ages 2 to 4 would lead to early disruptive behavior based on the dyad's inability to form a goal-corrected partnership. Finally, Patterson's (1982) model of coercion applied principles from social learning theory to explain how patterns of family interaction might produce conduct problems in school-age children, a model adapted and validated in early childhood by Martin (1981). Martin's work provided the critical empirical link by uncovering longitudinal associations between unresponsive caregiving and coercive parent–child interaction, thereby establishing a bridge between attachment and social learning models.

Implicit in this approach is a focus on early childhood, and particularly on the transition from infancy to the toddler period, which is marked by the highest rates of aggressive and noncompliant behaviors in the life course (Shaw, Bell, & Gilliom, 2000; Tremblay et al., 1999). These atypically high levels of disruptive behaviors have been attributed to a confluence of multiple biological and social factors, as the toddler years represent a time of marked change for children in terms of cognitive, emotional, and physical maturation. Despite growth in all of these areas, children's developing cognitive abilities are not well matched to the challenges afforded by their newfound physical mobility. Their new mobility permits children to ambulate quickly but without the cognitive appreciation to anticipate the consequences of violating others' personal space, understand the principles of electricity or gravity, or consider the potential hazards of straying too far from caregivers in novel settings (e.g., shopping malls). Thus, toddlers require proactive involvement and monitoring to literally keep them out of harm's way (Gardner, Sonuga-Barke, & Sayal, 1999). For parents dealing with this transformation (Shaw, Bell, & Gilliom, 2000), the nature of the parent–child relationship changes from a focus on responsivity and sensitivity to the immobile infant's emotional needs to monitoring a mobile and naive toddler. As a result of this shift, parental pleasure in child-rearing has been shown to decrease from the first to the second years (Fagot & Kavanagh, 1993). Using the social learning model of Patterson (1982) and attachment models of Sroufe and Fleeson (1986), we hypothesized that this period of developmental transition might be critical for determining how normative increases in disruptive behavior are either attenuated or amplifed by individual differences in child, parent, and family risk factors, as well as more distal community-level factors of cumulative adversity.

Methodologically, in developing the model we adopted and integrated the reciprocal effects model of Bell (1968) and the transactional perspective of Sameroff and Chandler (1975). We also considered it critical to incorporate the normal cognitive and emotional changes that children undergo from infancy to school entry. Thus, our framework considered (a) ongoing influences that parents and children have on each other (Bell, 1968) and (b) the previous behavior of both parents and children in accounting for their later behavior (Sameroff & Chandler, 1975) within the context of children's rapidly evolving development. As is evident from our use of several theoretical frameworks, the model attempted to integrate previous perspectives on developmental psychopathology. The novelty of this bridging model rests primarily on its ability to synthesize perspectives from disparate theoretical frameworks and different developmental periods to provide a cohesive framework for understanding processes leading to the antecedents of conduct problems in early childhood.

The bridging model was originally targeted for young boys from low-income families, capitalizing on the greater risk of serious conduct problems among males from impoverished settings and the more developed research base on the emergence of boys' externalizing disorders. More details regarding the developmental model can be found in Shaw and colleagues (Shaw & Bell, 1993; Shaw, Bell, & Gilliom, 2000), but they are summarized here. The approach was consistent with the observations of earlier investigators taking a developmental perspective toward childhood psychopathology (Renken, Egeland, Marvinney, Mangelsdorf, & Sroufe, 1989), in that early conduct problems are generated as a result of transactions between children and their environments over time (Patterson, 1982; Sameroff & Chandler, 1975). Particularly during early childhood, it was believed to be important to take into account transformations that occur in both child and parent behaviors as the child matures. For example, temperamentally difficult infants might be more noncompliant as toddlers, compared to easy infants. Moreover, parents who show low levels of responsivity during infancy and lower levels of positivity during the toddler period in facing the challenges of the "terrible twos" would be expected to lead to more acrimonious parent–child interactions and higher rates of child disruptive behavior during the toddler and preschool periods. In addition to child and parent behaviors, it was also necessary to consider the potential effects of stressors within and outside the family that compromise the quality of the caregiving environment, including maternal depression and social support, as well as neighborhood quality. In particular, the role of maternal depression was emphasized, given its consistent link to both caregiving quality and child maladaptive outcomes (Beardslee, Versage, & Gladstone, 1998; Belsky, 1984; Conger, Patterson, & Ge, 1995; Marchand, Hock, & Widaman, 2002).

Methods and Findings From the Pitt Mother and Child Projects

In the Pitt Mother and Child Project (PMCP), data from two cohorts of children studied from infancy through adolescence have been analyzed to examine normative developmental issues and basic tenets of the bridging model. However, for purposes of the current chapter, findings will be limited to Cohort II because it was larger (310 participants versus 100 participants in Cohort I), included intensive assessments, and followed children through adolescence. Cohort II is a sample of 310 boys recruited prior to 18 months of age and, at present, followed through age 17 years (Shaw et al., 1998; Shaw, Bell, & Gilliom, 2000).

For both cohorts, the source for subject recruitment was low-income families with male infants who used the Allegheny County's WIC program in the Pittsburgh metropolitan area (Shaw et al., 2003). Throughout the Pittsburgh metropolitan area, 310 participants were recruited from WIC sites over the course of 2 years. At the time of the first assessment, when infants were 1.5 years old, mothers ranged in age from 17 to 43 years (M = 28 years). Of the sample, 53% were Caucasian, 36% were African American, 5% were biracial, and 6% were other (e.g., Hispanic). At the 1.5 year visit, 65% of mothers were either married or living with a partner, 26% were single, 7% were divorced, and 2% were in other living arrangements. Mean per capita family income was $2,892 per year and the mean Hollingshead socioeconomic-status score was 24.8, indicative of an unskilled, working-class sample.

Retention of the families has been high over the study's duration, averaging 90 to 96% when children were between ages 2 and 6, and 85 to 91% between ages 8 and 15 (i.e., 89% at age 15). In addition, no selective attrition effects at age 15 have been found for child problem behavior or socioeconomic characteristics at assessments when children were ages 1.5, 2, or 3.5.

As the primary focus has been the identification of factors in early childhood associated with school-age and adolescent antisocial behavior, the description of procedures focuses on observational procedures and questionnaires that were administered when children were between the ages of 1.5 and 2, with similar procedures used at ages 3.5 and 5. Throughout the study, there has been a focus on identifying developmentally critical constructs using multiple methods and informants. For example, at ages 1.5 and 2, assessments included structured parent–child interactive tasks, free play, and maternal interviews. Assessment tasks were selected to vary in stress level so that mother and child behavior could be observed across a broad spectrum of conditions, from which observations of negative emotionality and disruptive behavior were rated. The age-2 laboratory visit was preceded by a 1.5-hour home visit (i.e., occurring on the same day) to observe the quality of the home environment and parent–child interaction during structured tasks and during an interview with the mother. As part of both laboratory visits, mothers completed inventories about risk factors that might compromise parenting quality (Belsky, 1984) or directly affect child adjustment, including such domains as maternal depressive symptoms (Beck et al., 1988), daily parenting hassles (Crnic & Greenberg, 1990), maternal social support (Crnic, Greenberg, Ragozin, Robinson, & Basham, 1983), and neighborhood quality. In addition to observing parents interacting with their children in the home setting during unstructured interactions, mother–son dyads were observed during teaching and cleanup tasks, from which ratings of both rejecting and positive parenting were made.

Identification of Risk Factors Associated With Child and Adolescent Antisocial Behavior

To identify risk factors associated with conduct problems in middle childhood and more serious forms of antisocial behavior during adolescence, several approaches have been used to analyze the PMCP, including both variable- and person-oriented methods, using parent, teacher, and youth reports of child conduct problems and antisocial behaviors. Although parents often have more contact with children than other adults during early childhood and thus we consider their reports to be critical especially during the first 5 years, it is also important to see if parental reports are validated in contexts outside of the home. This issue is magnified by the use of parental report for many of our early predictors of child problem behavior (e.g., maternal depression). It is also quite possible that even if parental reports of child behavior in the home are accurate, child disruptive behavior might be limited to the home environment. Therefore, after school entry we rely heavily on teacher reports of child disruptive behavior during middle childhood, as well as youth themselves during adolescence when most antisocial activities become covert because of the potential consequences of being apprehended for engaging in more serious forms of antisocial behavior (e.g., physical or sexual assault, drug dealing).

Based on our model, our focus was on three primary risk factor domains: (a) early forms of child disruptive behavior, (b) both negative and positive dimensions of parenting, and (c) risk factors that could compromise parenting (e.g., maternal depression, social support) or directly compromise child functioning. In addition, with our focus on families living in poverty, we were also concerned with the cumulative impact that living in the context of multiple stressors might have for the development and persistence of conduct problems (Rutter et al., 1975; Shaw, Vondra, Dowdell Hommerding, Keenan, & Dunn, 1994). In addition, we were especially interested in factors that were validated across reporter, time, and context. Thus, most of the following findings rely on predictor variables that were initially assessed using observational methods or parental reports in early childhood and later measures of child disruptive behavior assessed using teacher or youth reports, and in some cases corroborated by parental report.

In the first study of this type to examine how early risk factors were related to school-age conduct problems, cluster analysis was used to identify groups of families who shared characteristics across four domains: child characteristics, maternal parenting behavior, family context, and sociodemographic characteristics (Campbell, Shaw, & Gilliom, 2000; Shaw, Bell, & Gilliom, 2000).We then examined how such groups of children fared on measures of conduct problems according to both parents and teachers at school age. Importantly, this study compared findings from our community sample of low-income, ethnically diverse infants with those of Susan Campbell's predominantly middle-class, European American (EA) preschoolers identified on the basis of ADHD symptoms. In both samples, the children who showed the most consistent pattern of conduct problems at school age (age 6 in the Shaw sample, age 9 in the Campbell sample) were marked by elevated rates of risk factors across child, parent, family, and sociodemographic domains. At the time of the study entry (age 1.5 in the Shaw sample, age 3 to 4 in the Campbell sample), in both cohorts the multiple risk group demonstrated elevated hyperactivity and aggression, more negative and less positive parenting, and higher rates of maternal depressive symptoms, stressful life events, and sociodemographic risk than families in clusters with fewer risk factors (e.g., no-risk group, child-risk-only group). In both samples, echoing the findings of Rutter (Rutter et al., 1975) and others (Ackerman, Kogos, Youngstrom, Schoff, & Izard, 1999; Sameroff, Seifer, & Bartko, 1997), children in the multiple-risk group were observed to show the most disruptive behaviors at study entry and display more conduct problems and lower social competence at follow-up relative to other risk groups.

As children in the PMCP reached age 8 and frequencies of psychiatric diagnoses of disruptive behavior increased, we were able to look back at risk factors in early childhood that discriminated clinically meaningful problems at school age (Shaw, Gilliom, & Giovannelli, 2000). The Kiddie-Schedule for Affective Disorders–Epidemiologic Version (K-SADS-E; Puig-Antich, et al., 1980) was administered to mothers to derive diagnoses of DSM-IV disruptive disorders. Teachers completed the Teacher Report Form (Achenbach, 1991) at age 8, from which scores greater than or equal to the 90th percentile on the Aggression factor were used to establish clinical impairment. Children who met criterion for Oppositional Defiant Disorder (ODD), Conduct Disorder (CD), and/or Attention-Deficit/Hyperactivity Disorder (ADHD) at age 8 were again marked by early problem behaviors and multiple family risk factors (e.g., maternal depression, low social support, poor parenting) that were evident in the second year of life. However, because many of the measures of early child and family functioning were derived from maternal report, the sole exception being observed high rejecting and low positive parenting, it was important to corroborate the results using teacher reports.

The first surprise was that maternal reports of infant negative emotionality and age 2 externalizing problems were *not* related to clinically meaningful conduct problems at school age as rated by teachers. As seen

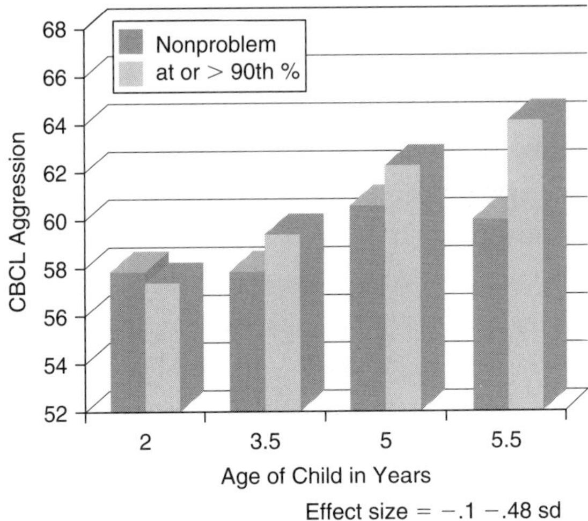

Figure 8.1 Trajectories Leading to Clinically-Elevated Scores on TRF Aggression at Age 8: CBCL Aggression at Ages 2, 3.5, 5, and 5.5.

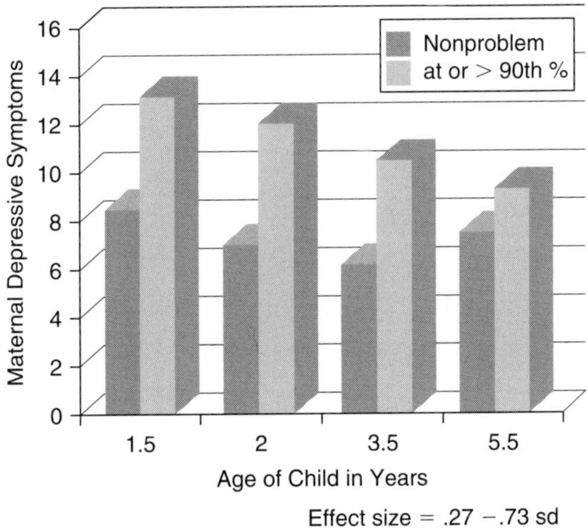

Figure 8.2 Trajectories Leading to Clinically-Elevated Scores on TRF Aggression at Age 8: Maternal Depressive Symptoms at Ages 1.5, 2, 3.5, and 5.5.

in Figure 8.1, boys who were later identified by teachers as being at or above the 90th percentile on aggressive behavior were not distinguished by parent reports at age 2 (d = –.1) and only became reliably discriminated by age 5.5 (d = .48). Although somewhat surprising, this finding has been replicated by others (e.g., Aguilar et al., 2000; Moffitt & Caspi, 2001). However, as shown in Figure 8.2 for maternal depressive symptoms and consistent with our focus on contextual factors, teacher-identified aggressive children were more likely to live in families characterized by high rates of rejecting and low rates of positive parenting, parenting hassles, maternal depression, neighborhood dangerousness, and low social support when children were 1.5 to 2 years old. Effect sizes were in the moderate to high range, spanning from .5 for parenting to .73 and .80 for maternal depressive symptoms and low social support, respectively.

Using Nagin's (2005) semiparametric modeling procedures to discriminate children following persistently high trajectories of conduct problems from ages 2 to 8, again observations of both caregiving quality and maternal reports of depressive symptoms discriminated children showing persistent trajectories of conduct problems (Shaw et al., 2003). In addition, one observed child factor discriminated maternal reports of child problem behavior: behavioral inhibition. Children who showed high levels of fear*less*ness in a behavioral inhibition task were found to have high levels of conduct problems from ages 2 to 8. These findings provided a child variable that had been theorized about but lacked empirical validation in our earlier studies of school-age problem behavior.

Recently, we have extended these analyses to ages 11 to 12 and 15 using the same measures of rejecting/positive parenting and maternal depressive symptoms as predictors of antisocial behavior, drug use, and sexual activity based on teacher and youth reports at ages 11 to 12 and youth reports at age 15 (Shaw & Gross, 2008). As shown in Figure 8.3, the same observations of rejecting/positive parenting at age 2 used to discriminate parent and teacher reports of clinically meaningful conduct problems at age 8 continued to discriminate teacher and youth reports of more serious forms of antisocial behavior at ages 11 to 12 and 15, including such items as school expulsion, engagement in unprotected sex, and arrest. In addition, at age 15, maternal depressive symptoms at ages 1.5 to 2 were also found to significantly correlate with age-15 youth reports of theft; having unprotected sex; carrying, threatening, or using a weapon; gang membership; marijuana use; and arrest (all $p < .05$). These analyses suggest that for boys, two potentially modifiable early risk factors—caregiving quality and maternal depression—predicted serious

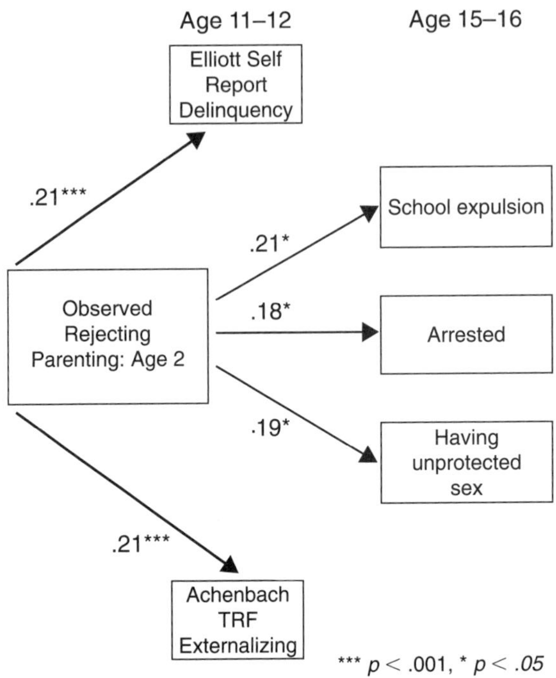

Figure 8.3 Associations between Observed Rejecting Parenting at age 2 and youth and teacher reports of antisocial behavior at ages 11-12 and 15-16: Pitt Mother & Child Project.

antisocial behavior, drug use, and risky sexual behavior across time, context, and informant.

These longitudinal findings suggest intervention targets, with certain caveats. First, we would need to be careful about using them to designate targets of intervention in groups different from those in the study: lower income boys of primarily European American and African American descent. Second, they are correlational, thus it is possible that unmeasured factors correlated with maternal depression and parenting behavior might be the actual causal factors in our findings. If so, then we might intervene effectively to alter maternal depression and parental caregiving and still find no impact on child-conduct trajectories. Of course, this is why translational research is not solely applied science—it is also important for the basic science of child development. Translational research allows us to put our theories to the test. Finally, although we found only one aspect of child temperament to be predictive (i.e., fearlessness), heritable child characteristics we did not measure might mediate or moderate effects of early parenting and maternal depression on conduct trajectories (see Caspi et al., 2002). This last concern has led us to recently collect DNA so we can examine gene and gene by environment effects in the PMCP.

Research Findings From the PMCP and Implications for Intervention

The results from the PMCP suggest that young boys' pathways leading to serious conduct problems and more serious forms of antisocial behavior *across* context are marked by multiple risk factors across child, parenting, and community domains; and in fact, prior to age 2, merely perceiving one's child as difficult or behaviorally disruptive was not predictive of later conduct problems at school according to teacher reports. Our confidence in these findings was bolstered by the consistency of other investigative teams studying the early antecedents of conduct problems (Renken et al., 1989), including the collaborative study with Campbell and colleagues (Campbell, Shaw, & Gilliom, 2000). The results suggested potentially malleable targets for preventive interventions for young children from low-income environments, including parenting, maternal well-being, and other factors that compromise both parenting and maternal well-being, as well as the accumulation of these stressors in the children's ecology. In developing our intervention, we also took seriously the reservations of others who have tried to intervene with high-risk families and failed because they neglected to address contextual factors (Kazdin, 1995). Salvador Minuchin, the founder of structural family therapy, gave up working with low-income, high-risk families because he concluded it was analogous to putting Band-Aids on people who require surgery (Malcolm, 1978). In addition, there was also an imperative to expand and test the model's validity with other populations, including female children, families living in rural and suburban communities, and those from other cultural groups than Caucasian and African American. To accomplish this goal, collaborations were initiated with other clinical researchers with expertise in these domains and access to ethnically diverse populations living in rural and suburban communities.

Motivation for change is another issue that has been addressed only indirectly in the PMCP that is especially salient for those interested in preventive interventions. As noted earlier, it is one challenge to identify potentially modifiable risk factors associated with pathways to conduct problems; it is another type of challenge to engage families with young children showing problematic behavior or adults reporting low levels of well-being to seek assistance. This issue was brought home in the early phases of the PMCP, in which clinical referrals were made to nearly 50% of our families based on elevated levels of child conduct problems and/or maternal depression when children were ages 1.5 and 2. As the author was concurrently serving as the Director of the Psychology Department's in-house mental health clinic and leading the clinic's family therapy team where intervention services were being offered at $2 per session, it was possible to monitor how many families called the clinic for services over a 2-year period. Only 3 of the 148 families (2%) referred for services contacted the clinic, suggesting that more than longitudinal data on risk factors for antisocial behavior would be needed to successfully engage families in a preventive intervention. Missing from our traditional interventions (even at $2 an hour) were more user-friendly methods to meet family's logistic challenges (e.g., seeing families at their homes, providing child care during intervention) *and* enhancing parents' motivation to change their behavior for the welfare of their children.

PART THREE: DEVELOPMENT OF FAMILY-BASED PREVENTIVE INTERVENTION FOR TODDLERS: THE FAMILY CHECK UP

For several years, the author contemplated how best to fill the deep chasm between our knowledge base of risk factors associated with early starting conduct problems and current intervention practices for primarily older children and adolescents (e.g., Henngeler & Bourdin, 1990; Forgatch et al., 2005). In many of these cases, parents had been motivated to change because of feared consequences for their children, such as being removed from a mainstream classroom or school. For adolescents, there was the consequence of incarceration that motivated investment in treatment. For families with young children, the consequences for parents were typically limited to managing their children at home. Nonetheless, knowing that the "terrible twos" were often a time of distress for parents and having a research base to show parents that proximal factors in the child's ecology may be important in determining the course of children's trajectories, there was potential ammunition for motivating change.

The author was not alone in his concerns, as motivation or resistance to change had become a common theme for prevention scientists studying the development and effectiveness of family-based interventions. For example, resistance to change had been programmatically studied by Patterson and Chamberlain (1994). In general, therapist training in developing collaborative relationships with parents and working through motivation issues in therapy is a key to the change of parenting practices (Shaw, Dishion, Supplee, Gardner, & Arnds, 2006). Miller and colleagues developed the technique of motivational interviewing to encapsulate the therapist–client dynamics that are most likely to result in productive change. For example, the Drinker's Check Up is a direct application of motivational interviewing designed to promote change in adults who drink heavily (Miller & Rollnick, 2002). Two of the key strategies of the Drinker's Check Up are to use assessment data in a feedback interview to elicit interactions between the client and therapist that influence change and to provide the client with a flexible menu of strategies to achieve reductions in drinking. Several studies reveal that random assignment to the brief Drinker's Check Up is as effective as 28 days of costly inpatient treatment for reducing problem drinking in adults (Miller & Rollnick, 2002).

Inspired by the work of Miller and colleagues on motivational interviewing, Dishion and Kavanagh (2003) developed the Family Check Up (FCU) to serve as the foundation of an ecological approach to child and family interventions. The FCU is a first step in a menu of empirically supported child and family interventions designed to reduce problem behavior and promote emotional well-being in children and families.

Thus, the intellectual prayers of the author were answered in 1999 upon meeting Dr. Dishion and learning about the FCU. Dr. Dishion previously focused on using the FCU with adolescents and youth transitioning to adolescence and had recently begun to develop methods for applying the FCU to problem behavior in younger children.

This collaboration also initially included colleague Dr. Frances Gardner. Dr. Gardner had also been conducting basic research on the contributions of positive and proactive parenting in the development of preschoolers' conduct problems. Whereas the author's previous basic research focused on negative dimensions of parenting, such as rejecting and harsh discipline methods, and some positive aspects of caregiving, including responsiveness and involvement, Dr. Gardner's focus on proactive dimensions extended our frame of reference on parenting to include positive behaviors that prevent the occurrence of coercive parent-child interactions. By focusing on how parents can anticipate problematic situations (e.g., bringing toys for children to play with in the supermarket or on long car trips) or provide structure for children through scaffolding and proactive involvement, parents can avoid getting into situations that are often unpleasant for both them and their children (Gardner et al., 1999).

The Family Check Up for Toddlers

In many ways, the FCU model differs from traditional clinical models and practice, especially the salience of assessment and the emphasis on motivating change (Gill, Hyde, Shaw, Dishion, & Wilson, in press). In contrast to the standard clinical model, the FCU is based on a health-maintenance model, which explicitly promotes periodic contact with families (yearly at a minimum) over the course of key developmental transitions. Whereas traditional clinical models are activated in response to clinical pathology, the health-maintenance model involves periodic contact between client and provider to promote health and proactively prevent problems. Examples of health-maintenance models include the use of semiannual cleanings in dentistry and well-baby check-ups in pediatrics.

The FCU also differs from traditional clinical practice with its explicit focus on providing a comprehensive assessment of child and family functioning. Data obtained from assessments are shared with families in feedback sessions to enhance their motivation for change (Miller & Rollnick, 2002). Feedback sessions are often followed by the introduction of family management techniques (Forgatch et al., 2005) to achieve change in parenting and child problem behavior. The comprehensive assessment essentially drives the intervention, providing detailed information about domains of child (e.g., negative emotionality), family (e.g., parental depression, marital quality), and community-level (e.g., neighborhood dangerousness) risk factors that past research has shown to be directly related to the development of early onset conduct problems (Shaw et al., 2006). In addition, there is a primary focus on evaluating caregiving practices through direct observation of parent–child interaction. In the case of the FCU for toddlers, this task is accomplished by having parent–child dyads participate in a series of structured (e.g., clean-up and teaching tasks) and semistructured (e.g., preparing a meal) tasks commonly used in social development research with young children. The FCU is also *ecological* in its emphasis on improving children's adjustment across settings by motivating positive parenting practices and thereby reducing the frequency of situations that would elicit coercive parent–child interactions and the use of harsh, rejecting caregiving. Moreover, the comprehensive assessment allows tailoring and adaptation, in that the intervention is *fit* to the family's circumstances and their desires for more or less or different forms of treatment.

The FCU utilizes two main components to facilitate change: motivational interviewing and family management practices (Gill et al., in press). As noted previously, the motivational interviewing component is based on Miller and Rollnick's work (2002) using the Drinker's Check Up, in which assessment data regarding the negative consequences of alcohol abuse on individuals' work and family lives are shared in a feedback interview with clients. In working with families of young children, the FCU feedback session is designed to elicit motivation for the parent(s) to change problematic behaviors in the child, which is often achieved by modifying parenting behavior (Forgatch et al., 2005) or aspects of the caregiving context that compromise parenting quality. While motivational interviewing was developed for adult drinkers, Dishion and Kavanagh (2003) initially used the FCU for families with adolescents showing problem behaviors. Complier Average Causal Effect models indicated that motivation interviewing was the key component of the intervention linked to long-term reductions in substance use and antisocial behavior (Connell, Dishion, Yasui, & Kavanagh, 2007).

After addressing motivation, the FCU provides options for follow-up intervention. The therapist may give referrals for help with problems outside of parenting; however, the core of most interventions with young children focuses on family management issues. This component includes a collective set of parenting skills, commonly referred to as *Parent Management Training*, based on social learning principles of reinforcement and modeling (Forgatch et al., 2005; Patterson, 1982). Parent Management Training has been consistently associated with improvement in parenting and subsequent reductions in child problem behavior, particularly conduct problems (Bullock & Forgatch, 2005; Patterson, Reid, & Dishion, 1992), and has been formally deemed an *empirically supported treatment* (Chambless & Ollendick, 2001). In the FCU, parent management techniques can be applied to the specific behavior problems highlighted by the comprehensive assessment.

Empirically Validating the Family Check Up: The Early Steps Projects

Beginning in 1999, with colleagues Dishion and Gardner and informed by the data collected as part of the PMCP, the FCU was initially tested for families with toddler boys at risk for early starting conduct problems. Using previously discussed longitudinal data from the PMCP regarding the predictive validity of such factors as child fearlessness, parenting, maternal depression, and social support, as well as incorporating findings from Gardner and colleagues' (1999) work on proactive dimensions of positive parenting, initial screening and more intensive assessment protocols were designed to assess these domains, as well as different facets of child problem behaviors (e.g., observed and parent-reported aggression, oppositional behavior). WIC was chosen as the target site for recruiting families based on the author's success in using this source in his basic research to identify low-income children at risk for developing serious antisocial behavior. WIC was also selected because it was an existing federal service program for low-income families. Thus, if the intervention was found to be successful, it offered the possibility of administering the program at WIC agencies not only in Pittsburgh, but across the country. Pittsburgh was selected as the site for the pilot study because of the author's existing ties with local WIC administrators. To further enhance parental engagement, families were given the option of having intervention sessions conducted at their homes or the lab, with most families choosing the home; therefore, all assessments were conducted in the family homes. Therapists were labeled as *parent consultants* to denote their expert status and make engagement more promising and less *shrink-like*.

As many boys in the PMCP demonstrated average to above-average adjustment despite coming from low socioeconomic backgrounds and, in some cases, living in suboptimal neighborhoods, a gating procedure was instituted to increase the probability of identifying toddlers with a high risk for developing early conduct problems based on risk factors identified in the PMCP and by other researchers (e.g., Bates, Maslin & Frankel, 1985; Nagin & Tremblay, 1999; Renken et al., 1989; Wakschlag & Hans, 1999). Screening factors identified by other researchers included child negative emotionality (Bates), maternal substance use (Wakschlag), and teen parent status (Nagin). Note that child conduct problems were included in the screening as a risk factor at age 2, despite not being found to reliably discriminate conduct problems at age 8 according to teacher reports (Shaw, Bell, & Gilliom, 2000), to provide *ammunition* for parent consultants to use in motivating parents to address child problem behavior. In fact, parent perceptions of child conduct problems were found to be fairly stable over time in the PMCP, with 88% of parents who viewed their children at or above the 90th percentile on the CBCL Aggression scale at age 2 reporting their children to show clinically elevated levels of Aggression at age 5 (Shaw, Gilliom, & Giovannelli, 2000). These findings mirror the findings of other researchers studying the stability of *parent* perceptions of child conduct problems from the toddler to preschool or early school-age periods (e.g., Campbell, 1990; Jersild & Markey, 1935; Richman, Stevenson, & Graham, 1982). Thus, risk criteria for recruitment were defined as at or above one standard deviation above normative averages on several screening measures within the following three domains: (a) child behavior (conduct problems, high-conflict relationships with adults), (b) family problems (maternal depression, daily parenting challenges, substance use problems, teen parent status), and (c) sociodemographic risk (low education achievement and low family income using WIC criterion).

The Early Steps Pilot Study was limited to boys because much of the data on children's early risk factors for later conduct problems had been limited to boys including the PMCP. In the pilot study, we targeted children between the ages of 1.75 and 2.50, balancing our ability to predict later conduct problems (i.e., as early as 18 months) with parents' openness to address child problem behaviors for children as young as 18 months. In the end, parents were approached at WIC sites and invited to participate if they had a son between 1.75 and 2.50 years of age and met the study criteria by having socioeconomic, family, and/or child risk factors for future behavior problems. Based on these criteria, the demographic characteristics of the Early Steps Pilot Study reflected those of a low socioeconomic status, urban sample, with the average family income being $15,374 per year (SD = $8,754), 66.6% of the sample having a high school education or less; the majority of the sample being African American (48.3%) or biracial (11.7%); and 55% being single and never married (50%) or separated, divorced, or widowed (5%).

Results from the Early Steps Pilot Study. The initial Early Steps Project involved 120 high-risk families recruited from multiple WIC clinics in the Pittsburgh metropolitan area, with half of the sample being randomly assigned to the FCU and the other half of the sample followed passively during yearly assessments from ages 2 to 4. There were several advantages to having a small pilot intervention study before embarking on the Early Steps–Multisite (ES-M) Study. First, it provided an opportunity to test the intervention for its cultural sensitivity and developmental appropriateness. Second, it provided an experiential basis for preparing manuals describing the range of services. Third, it allowed us to examine parents' receptivity to addressing child conduct problems in early childhood, in general, and specifically prior to age 2.

So far, we have two published reports based on these pilot data. In the first, Shaw and colleagues (2006) found significant intervention effects on observed parent involvement and the boys' problem behaviors by preschool. Specifically, using an intention-to-treat analysis in which all families assigned to the intervention group were compared to families assigned to the control group regardless of their actual contact with parent consultants, caregivers randomly assigned to the intervention condition were shown to maintain high levels of involvement with their young child from ages 2 to 4, whereas control families decreased their level of involvement, as observed by home visitors. Similarly, parent ratings of problem behavior on the Child Behavior Checklist (destructive factor) showed decreases for the intervention group relative to the control group at age 3. In addition, for children with a high-risk profile of high child fearlessness and maternal depression at age 2, intervention effects on child conduct problems were evident at age 4. In the second paper, Gardner, Shaw, Dishion, Supplee, and Burton (2007) examined direct observations of family interaction and found that parents in the intervention group used more proactive and positive parenting at child-age 3 than did the control group. Furthermore, increases in proactive parenting also predicted decreases in child problem behavior. These intervention gains were accomplished with an average of 3.27 sessions (SD = 2.34), including the get-to-know-you and feedback sessions as two of these meetings, and with only one dose of the intervention. Thus, the pilot study was largely successful in several areas: engaging families with toddlers at high risk for early starting conduct problems, identifying malleable intervention targets (parent involvement, proactive parenting), and providing preliminary data in support of the intervention reducing young children's problem behaviors. In addition, despite the relative brevity of the intervention and only one dose, 2 years later, intervention effects were evident for families with risk profiles (high child fearlessness and high maternal depression at age 2) that were comparable to the profiles of the highest risk families in the PMCP.

The Early Steps Pilot Study also was critical in providing data about parental engagement in the intervention. Essentially, our goal was to recruit low-income families with a toddler demonstrating high rates of conduct problems and other family and socioeconomic risk factors into a family-based intervention, for which the author's efforts had proved largely futile in the PMCP. In contrast, 92% of families randomly assigned to the intervention group in the Early Steps Pilot Study engaged in the intervention, as indicated by meeting with parent consultants for at least a get-to-know-you and a feedback session. Second, we learned that parents with children under the age of 2 were reticent to address children's conduct problems even in cases in which they were concerned about the child's behavior because of their conviction that the child would "grow out of it." These data prompted us to move the recruitment period back from 1.75 to 2.0 years in our next study despite data from the PMCP that we could comparably predict later child behavior from age 1.5 or 1.75 as well as from age 2. Third, we found no dose response for the intervention (Shaw et al., 2006), as the number of sessions that families met with parent consultants was unrelated to the magnitude of reductions in child conduct problems. There are several plausible explanations for the lack of a dose response. For example, although a greater contact with parent consultants would be expected to be associated with greater reductions in child problem behavior, it is sometimes the case that families facing higher levels of social and emotional adversity stay in treatment longer without significant improvements in child behavior because of the chaotic and stressful nature of these families' lives. However, an alternative explanation, and one consistent with the premise of motivational interviewing, is that parents can make the changes themselves if properly motivated. We kept these findings and questions in mind as we sought to expand the scope of the intervention in our next and more ambitious trial.

Despite these important findings, the Early Steps Pilot Study was limited by its relatively small sample size, the use of only male children from European American and African American ethnic backgrounds recruited from one urban community, and the limited dose of intervention services offered to the families. In reference to the limited dosage of the intervention, it was expected that, from the perspective of a health-maintenance model, repeated dosages of the FCU would be associated with longer-lasting and broader gains in both child behavior and parenting. At a psychological level, it was also believed that repeated contact with the same parent consultant might promote parental support and confidence in their abilities, based on the knowledge that an expert in child mental health was watching out for the welfare of his or her child and family during the early childhood years. Finally, although intervention gains were found for both child conduct problems and positive parenting, our theoretical perspective suggested that intervention effects should be mediated by changes in family processes—most notably parenting, which was only partially supported in the Early Steps Pilot Study (Gardner et al., 2007).

The Early Steps Multisite Study

The Early Steps Multisite Study was initiated to remedy many of the limitations of the Early Steps Pilot Study. First, the sample included equal numbers of boys *and* girls. Second, the size was expanded to include 731 at-risk families, half of whom were randomly assigned to the FCU versus WIC, as usual. Third, the families were recruited from three geographically and culturally unique regions, including metropolitan Pittsburgh, Pennsylvania; suburban Eugene, Oregon; and rural Charlottesville, Virginia. The sample also broadened our representation of cultural diversity, including African American (27.9%), Hispanic American (13.4), biracial (8.9%), and other races (8.9%, including American Indian and Native Hawaiian families).We also expanded the potential targets of change, including multiple aspects of child behavior, parenting, and parental depression, as well as examining potential mediating mechanisms underlying change. Finally, the Multisite Study gave us the opportunity to see if the effects of the intervention could be amplified by repeated dosage administered at child age of 2 and 3.

With the exception of moving the age of child eligibility criterion from 1.75 to 2.0 years, the screening and assessment protocol remained largely intact from the Early Steps Pilot Study, with translation of all materials generated in Spanish for recently immigrated Latino families. Videoconferencing, used extensively for contact between Dr. Dishion and the Pittsburgh site in the pilot study for supervision of intervention cases, was expanded to include all three sites to facilitate intervention fidelity among parent consultants across sites. Both assessment examiners and parent consultants were certified and recertified every few months to ensure reliability in both the administration of assessments and delivery of intervention services.

To address continuing concerns about cultural differences about parenting, focus groups were also conducted with African American families at the Pittsburgh and Virginia sites and Latino families at the Oregon site to find out more about how parents viewed caregiving practices in general and issues that might prevent them from engaging with parent consultants in our intervention specifically. For African American families, there was a focus on commanding respect and compliance to authority in terms of parenting and a concern that parent consultants would not condone their use of corporal punishment to maintain this respect from children. For Latino families, many of whom were recent immigrants, there was a greater emphasis on warmth and family unity with respect to parenting and concerns about their ability to provide proper care for their children without a better understanding of the English language.

Results from the Early Steps Multisite Study. The Early Steps Multisite Study is currently ongoing with funding provided from the National Institute on Drug Abuse to continue the intervention and follow-up of child outcomes through middle childhood; however, data on its efficacy are now available up to age 4. There were a few important differences in the findings from the Early Steps Pilot and Multisite studies. On the one hand, in the ES-M we had more power to detect group differences compared to the Early Steps Pilot Study because of the much larger sample size. On the other hand, there is often a *dilution* effect when intervention programs are expanded in size and/or delivered across new populations and types of communities (e.g., work of Olds, Webster-Stratton). In the current case, this meant testing the intervention's efficacy for the first time with female toddlers, children living in suburban and rural communities, and Latino families, as well as coordinating the complexities of reliably delivering the intervention across three sites.

All of the findings reported in the following were again analyzed using an intention-to-treat design, knowing that a significant minority of families in the intervention group never had contact with parent consultants (77% and 70% rates of engagement at ages 2 and 3, respectively). Note that an important initial finding consistent with a dilution effect is that our rate of engagement was still relatively high, but it was lower than that found in the pilot study (i.e., 92% in the pilot study).

Our first goal was to attempt to replicate and expand the findings from the Early Steps Pilot Study as to whether the intervention was effective in reducing child conduct problems from ages 2 to 4. Using latent growth modeling, we found a consistent pattern of intervention effects for our primary target of change: child conduct problems. In addition, we examined the extent to which intervention effects on conduct problems were mediated by changes in two factors consistently associated with conduct problems and more serious forms of antisocial behavior in our basic work: parenting and maternal depression. In the domain of parenting, we included aspects of positive parenting (e.g., responsivity, involvement, low frequencies of rejecting behavior) found to be important in the author's earlier work, but we also incorporated more proactive dimensions of parenting, including anticipating and structuring potentially problematic situations (e.g., providing structure for the child while preparing a meal, making sure the child understands the goals of a clean-up task at the task's outset). As can be seen in Figure 8.4, not only was the intervention condition associated with reduced growth in child

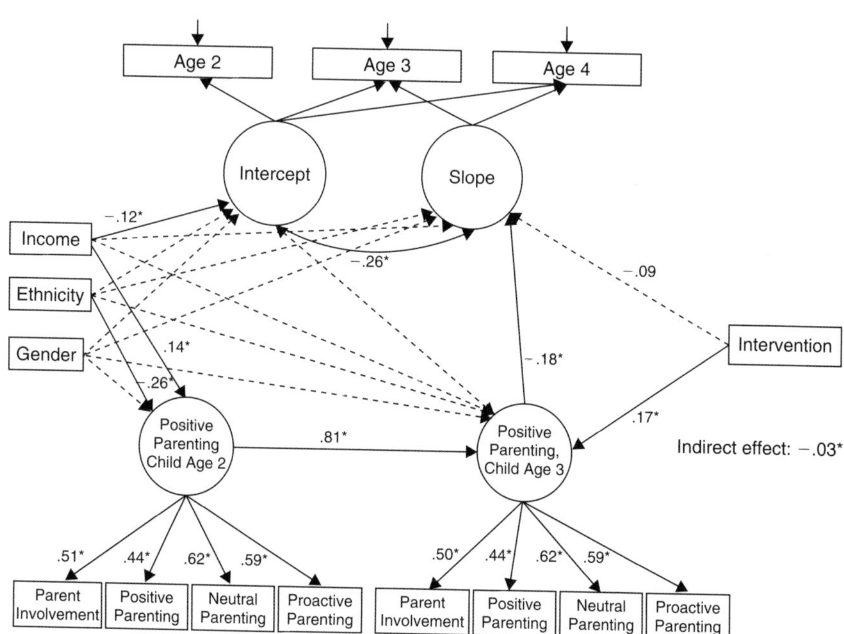

Figure 8.4 Mediation model: CBCL Externalizing.

conduct problems from ages 2 to 4 and found to improve parenting from ages 2 to 3, but slope in child conduct problems was found to be reduced as a function of increases in positive parenting (Dishion, Shaw, Connell, Wilson, Gardner, & Weaver, 2008).

We also examined whether the FCU was associated with reductions in maternal depressive symptoms, and if found, whether reductions in maternal depression mediated reductions in both child internalizing and externalizing symptoms from ages 2 to 4 (Shaw, Dishion, Connell, Wilson, & Gardner, in press). Similar to the intervention effects found for child conduct problems, the FCU was associated with reduced growth in child internalizing problems. Additionally, reductions in maternal depression were found from ages 2 to 3, and reductions in both child conduct problems and internalizing problems were mediated by decreases in maternal depression.

We recently explored the extent to which the intervention is effective in reducing distinct constellations of children's behavior problems, including co-occurring versus conduct-only versus internalizing-only problems at age 4 (Connell et al., in press). Latent transition analysis was used for this analysis, in which broad-band CBCL Externalizing and Internalizing factors were aggregated and then dichotomized into nonclinical and clinical groups, then modeled to create 4 latent groups: Internalizers, Externalizers, Comorbid, and Normal. Intervention effects were subsequently found for both the Comorbid and Internalizing groups, indicating reductions in problem behavior for children in these groups compared to those in the Externalizing and Normal groups. These results may have particular implications for the FCU to prevent pathways leading to early onset drug use because of the high risk of drug use among comorbid children.

Extending the scope of child outcomes to areas that would be particularly relevant to school readiness, we also examined whether the intervention was associated with improvements in language development and inhibitory control, and whether changes in positive parenting would mediate these changes (Lunkenheimer et al., in press). Again, intervention effects were found for language skills and inhibitory control, and these changes were mediated by improvement in parenting.

Finally, we examined moderators of intervention effects among initial sample characteristics, exploring whether families at relatively higher or lower risk are more likely to benefit from the intervention in relation to improvements in child conduct problems at age 4 (Gardner et al., in press). As direct contact with the intervention remained brief in the multisite study, albeit slightly higher than in the pilot study (i.e., M = 3.7 sessions annually versus 3.3 in the pilot study), there is some worry that the intervention might be more effective for families who are less distressed or relatively more economically advantaged. In fact, results suggest that the intervention was comparably effective for parents who varied in sociodemographic and family risk factors (e.g., maternal depression, low income, history of parental drug use), with two exceptions: lower educational attainment predicted greater improvement in conduct problems following intervention, and single-parent status predicted lesser improvement in conduct problems following intervention. Overall, findings suggest that a brief family-centered intervention can be equally effective for reaching the most distressed and disadvantaged families, as well as those who are relatively more advantaged, within a high-risk, low-income sample. The findings present a relatively optimistic picture of outcomes for the most hard-to-reach families, compared to some of the extant literature on parenting interventions. The results also have implications for the FCU's application with other comparable high-risk samples.

PART FOUR: SUMMARY AND FUTURE DIRECTIONS

Informed by a program of basic research on the developmental precursors of conduct problems, the Early Steps Projects represent an effort to target reliable predictors of child conduct problems using motivational interviewing to promote change among families with toddlers at risk for early conduct problems that do not typically use mental health services. In addition to extending the range of child and parent outcomes shown to improve as a result of the intervention and demonstrating that changes in both positive parenting and maternal depression mediate these intervention effects, the multisite study found intervention effects to be similar across child gender, culture, and community type.

In terms of the mechanisms of change, empirical support was found to explain that improvements in child behavior were accounted for by changes in positive parenting and maternal depression (Shaw & Gross, 2008). The mediation of changes in child problem behavior by positive parenting was posited a priori and corroborates findings from other family-based interventions conducted during early and middle childhood (Baydar et al., 2003; Forgatch et al., 2005). Although in the author's basic research, dimensions of rejecting and positive caregiving have been related to later child conduct problems, in the two trials of the Early Steps intervention, greater support has been found for the causal role of positive parenting, as it has been shown to mediate intervention effects on conduct problems, inhibitory control, and language development. A couple of plausible explanations may explain this difference in emphasis in the intervention work. First, it could be that in high-risk samples such as the Early Steps' cohorts, there are *ceiling effects* for rejecting parenting because a disproportionately high percentage of parents show high rates compared to nongated samples of low-income families. Second, as a result of increasing parent ability to anticipate and attend to children in potentially aversive situations (e.g., long car rides, providing the child with an activity when the parent is busy with chores), parents in the intervention group might be reducing rates of harsh and punitive discipline. This is an issue that we are currently exploring in the Early Steps–Multisite data set.

The mediational contribution of maternal depression was less expected but consistent with a large body of research suggesting a consistent association between maternal depression and child conduct and internalizing problems (Farmer, McGuffin, & Williams, 2002). Although maternal depression was explicitly treated in less than 20% of cases, improvements in depressive symptoms were likely related to generic aspects of the establishment of the parent-parent consultant relationship, including such factors as trust, having a confidant to talk to (even if this contact does not occur often), and access to an expert to discuss the challenges of raising a toddler (Shaw et al., in press). Cumulatively, these factors may have resulted in improving maternal depressed mood. In addition, parent consultants were available to provide assistance to mothers who suffered short-term crises (e.g., lack of food, no money to pay for electricity) or long-term challenges in living (e.g., recent immigrants' lack of familiarity with the English language and American culture, moving out of project neighborhoods, social isolation). As families were screened on the basis of multiple risk domains and during a development period known to be challenging even for parents with greater economic and family resources, it is likely that having repeated contact with someone to help navigate these challenges may have reduced initial levels of depression.

Despite our optimism regarding the intervention's effectiveness across 2-year follow-ups in two studies, we realize there are many issues that lie ahead for further consideration. First, although we presented evidence to suggest that the FCU is associated with improvements in child problem behaviors and maternal depressive symptoms, effect sizes, albeit meaningful from a public health perspective, were relatively modest (*d*s ranged from .18 to .23), particularly in relation to the pilot study, in which *d*s ranged from .45 to .65. Consistent with the dilution effect, further work is needed to recapture effect sizes found in the pilot study. However, unique to the multisite project, gains were seen in many more domains of child and parent functioning, as well as support for the mediational contributions of positive parenting and maternal depression.

Second, it will also be important to continue to follow the course of intervention effects through middle childhood to truly test whether the FCU is effective in preventing the onset and early starting pathways of antisocial behavior. It is not necessarily the case that interventions conducted in the context of the home will translate to reductions in child problem behaviors in such settings as schools, after-school care, or in the neighborhood. Whereas some of our intervention effects were corroborated by standardized tests (i.e., language development), most were based on maternal reports of child problem behavior; thus, it will be important to see whether improvements in child adjustment are maintained across time and context from the viewpoints of teachers and after-school care providers. In this regard, while retaining an emphasis on parent–child functioning in the home, we are expanding the scope of assessments to include children's behaviors with peers and adults at school, in after-school care, and in the neighborhood, providing feedback to parents with the help of teachers and after-school care providers to motivate parents to increase their involvement in their children's lives as they spend proportionately more time outside of the home. We also hope to increase parental involvement in these settings to monitor child problem behaviors before they become functionally impaired.

The current findings corroborate previous evidence that changes in child disruptive behaviors can be achieved with a brief intervention and that such change appeared to be mediated by improving parenting practices (Shaw et al., in press). This was achieved using a nationally available service-delivery setting with low-income children at risk for early starting conduct problems whose families do not typically use mental health services (Haines et al., 2002).

The goal of the chapter was to present *a* model for how basic research on developmental processes could be translated into an intervention; however, it should be noted that there are many models for achieving this aim. Consistent with the principle of equifinality, there are many examples of interventions developed using different frameworks and starting points (e.g., works of Olds, Webster-Stratton) than the current perspective. The current approach is specifically directed at researchers studying basic processes who might be a bit hesitant about moving into intervention work. Although intervention research does present a number of idiosyncratic challenges (e.g., training and supervision of therapists, refinement of intervention across child gender and culture), it represents the logical extension of many researchers' current work on basic developmental processes and provides the opportunity to test hypotheses using a truly experimental design. Thus, this author found it to be an exceptionally rewarding experience that also provides a feedback loop to inform his basic program of research.

REFERENCES

Achenbach, T. M. (1991). *Manual for the Teacher's Report Form and 1991 profile*. Burlington: University of Vermont, Department of Psychiatry.

Ackerman, B. P., Kogos, J., Youngstrom, E., Schoff, K., & Izard, C. (1999). Family instability and the problem behaviors of children from economically disadvantaged families. *Developmental Psychology*, 35, 258–268.

Aguilar, B., Sroufe, L. A., Egeland, B., & Carlson, E. (2000). Distinguishing the early onset/persistent and adolescence-onset antisocial behavior types: From birth to 16 years. *Development and Psychopathology, 12*, 109–132.

Bates, J. E., Maslin, C. A., & Frankel, K. A. (1985). Attachment security, mother-child interaction, and temperament as predictors of behavior-problem ratings at age three years. In I. Bretherton & E. Waters (Eds.), *Monographs of the Society for Research in Child Development*, 50(1–2), 167–193.

Baydar, N., Reid, M. J., & Webster-Stratton, C. (2003). The role of mental health factors and program engagement in the effectiveness of a preventive parenting program for Head Start mothers. *Child Development, 74*, 1433–1453.

Beardslee, W. R., Versage, E. M., & Gladstone, T. G. (1998). Children of affectively ill parents: A review of the past 10 years. *Journal of the American Academy of Child & Adolescent Psychiatry, 37*, 1134–1141.

Beck, A. T., Steer, R. A., & Garbin, M. G. (1988). Psychometric properties of the Beck Depression Inventory. Twenty-five years of evaluation. *Clinical Psychology Review*, 8, 77–100.

Bell, R. Q. (1968). A reinterpretation of the direction of effects in studies of socialization. *Psychological Review, 75*, 81–95.

Belsky, J. (1984). The determinants of parenting: A process model. *Child Development*, 55, 83–96.

Bullock, B. M., & Forgatch, M. S. (2005). Mothers in transition: Model-based strategies for effective parenting. In W. M. Pinsof & J. L. Lebow (Eds.), *Family psychology: The art of science* (pp. 349–371). New York: Oxford University Press.

Campbell, S. B. (1990). *Behavior problems in preschool children: Clinical and developmental issues*. New York: Guilford.

Campbell, S. B., Pierce, E. W., Moore, G., Marakovitz, S., & Newby, K. (1996). Boys' externalizing problems at elementary school: Pathways from early behavior problems, maternal control, and family stress. *Development and Psychopathology*, 8, 701–720.

Campbell, S. B., Shaw, D. S., & Gilliom, M. (2000). Early externalizing behavior problems: Toddlers and preschoolers at risk for later maladjustment. *Development and Psychopathology, 12*, 467–488.

Caspi, A., McClay, J., Moffitt, T. E., Mill, J., Martin, J., Craig, I. W., et al. (2002). Role of genotype in the cycle of violence in maltreated children. *Science, 297*, 851–853.

Chambless, D. L., & Ollendick, T. H. (2001). Empirically supported psychological interventions: Controversies and evidence. *Annual Review of Psychology*, 52, 685–716.

Cicchetti, D., & Rogosch, F. A. (1996). Equifinality and multifinality in developmental psychopathology. *Development and Psychopathology, 8*, 597–600.

Conduct Problems Prevention Research Group. (1999). Initial impact of the Fast Track prevention trial for conduct problems: I. The high-risk sample. *Journal of Consulting and Clinical Psychology, 67*, 631–647.

Conger, R. D., Patterson, G. R., & Ge, X. (1995). It takes two to replicate: A meditational model for the impact of parents' stress on adolescent adjustment. *Child Development, 66*, 80–97.

Connell, A., Bullock, B. M., Dishion, T. J., Shaw, D., Wilson, M., & Gardner, F. (in press). Family intervention effects on co-occurring behavior and emotional problems in early childhood: A latent transition analysis approach. *Journal of Abnormal Child Psychology.*

Connell, A. M., Dishion., T. J., Yasui, M., & Kavanagh, K. (2007). An adaptive approach to family intervention: Linking engagement in family-centered intervention to reductions in adolescent problem behavior. *Journal of Counseling and Clinical Psychology, 75*, 568–579.

Corbie-Smith, G. (1999). The continuing legacy of the Tuskegee Syphilis Study: Considerations for clinical investigation. *American Journal of the Medical Sciences, 317*, 5–8.

Crnic, K. A., & Greenberg, M. T. (1990). Minor parenting stresses with young children. *Child Development, 61*, 1628–1637.

Crnic, K. A., Greenberg, M. T., Ragozin, A. S., Robinson, N. M., & Basham, R. B. (1983). Effects of stress and social support on mothers and premature and full-term infants. *Child Development, 57*, 209–217.

Cunningham, C. E., Bremner, R., & Boyle, M. (1995). Large group community-based parenting programs for families of preschoolers at risk for disruptive behavior disorders: Utilization, cost effectiveness, and outcome. *Journal of Child Psychology and Psychiatry, 36*, 1141–1159.

Dishion, T. J., & Kavanagh, K. (2003). *Intervening in adolescent problem behavior: A family-centered approach.* New York: Guilford.

Dishion, T. J., & Patterson, G. R. (1992). Age effects in parent training outcome. *Behavior Therapist, 23*, 719–729.

Dishion, T. J., Shaw, D. S., Connell, A., Wilson, M. N., Gardner, F., & Weaver, C. (2008). The Family Check Up with high-risk families with toddlers: Outcomes on positive parenting and early problem behavior. *Child Development, 79*, 1395–1414.

Erickson, M. F., Sroufe, L. A., & Egeland, B. (1985). The relationship between quality of attachment and behavior problems in preschool in a high-risk sample. In I. Bretherton & E. Waters (Eds.), *Growing points of attachment theory and research. Monographs of the Society for Research in Child Development*, 50(1–2), 147–167.

Fagot, B. I., & Kavanagh, K. (1993). Parenting during the second year: Effects of children's age, sex, and attachment classification. *Child Development*, *64*, 258–271.

Farmer, A., McGuffin, P., & Williams, J. (2002). *Measuring psychopathology*. Oxford, UK: Oxford University Press.

Forgatch, M. S., Patterson, G. R., & DeGarmo, D. S. (2005). Evaluating fidelity: Predictive validity for a measure of competent adherence to the Oregon Model of Parent Management Training. *Behavior Therapy*, *36*, 3–13.

Gardner, F., Shaw, D. S., Dishion, T. J., Supplee, L. A., & Burton, J. (2007). Family centered approach to prevention of early conduct problems: Positive parenting as a contributor to change in toddler problem behavior. *Journal of Family Psychology*, *21*, 398–406.

Gardner, F., Sonuga-Barke, E., & Sayal, K. (1999). Parents anticipating misbehaviour: An observational study of strategies parents use to prevent conflict with behaviour problem children. *Journal of Child Psychology and Psychiatry*, *40*, 1185–1196.

Gardner, F., Trentacosta, C., Connell, A., Shaw, D. S., Dishion, T. J., & Wilson, M. N. (in press). Moderators of family intervention effects on early conduct problems. *Journal of Consulting and Clinical Psychology*.

Gill, A., Hyde, L. W., Shaw, D. S., Dishion, T. J., & Wilson, M. N. (in press). The Family Check-Up in early childhood: A case study of intervention process and change. *Journal of Clinical Child and Adolescent Psychology*.

Greenberg, M. T., & Speltz, M. L. (1988). Contributions of attachment theory to the understanding of conduct problems during the preschool years. In J. Belsky & T. Negworski (Eds.), *Clinical implications of attachment* (pp. 177–218). Hillsdale, NJ: Erlbaum.

Haines, M. M., McMunn, A., Nazroo, J. Y., & Kelly, Y. J. (2002). Social and demographic predictors of parental consultation for child psychological difficulties. *Journal of Public Health Medicine*, *24*, 276–284.

Henggeler, S. W., & Bourdin, C. M. (1990). *Family therapy and beyond: A multisystemic approach to treating the behavior problems of children and adolescents*. Pacific Grove, CA: Brooks/Cole.

Hirschi, T. (1969). *Causes of delinquency*. Berkeley: University of California.

Jersild, A. T., & Markey, F. V. (1935). Conflicts between preschool children. *Child Development*, *21*, 170–181.

Kazdin, A. E. (1995). *Conduct disorders in childhood and adolescence* (2nd ed.). Newbury Park, CA: Sage.

Lunkenheimer, E. S., Skuban, E. M., Dishion, T. J., Connell, A. Shaw, D. S., Gardner, F., et al. (2008). Early family intervention, positive parenting, and school readiness in young children at risk: The effects of the Family Check-Up. Manuscript under review.

Malcolm, J. (1978, May 15). The one-way mirror. *New Yorker*, *54*, 39.

Marchand, J. F., Hock, E., & Widaman, K. (2002). Mutual relations between mothers' depressive symptoms and hostile-controlling behavior and young children's externalizing and internalizing behavior problems. *Parenting: Science and Practice*, *2*, 335–353.

Martin, J. (1981). A longitudinal study of the consequences of early mother-infant interaction: A microanalytic approach. *Monographs of the Society for Research in Child Development*, *46*(3, Serial No. 190).

Miller, W. R., & Rollnick, S. (2002). *Motivational interviewing: Preparing people for change* (2nd ed.). New York: Guilford.

Moffitt, T. E., & Caspi, A. (2001). Childhood predictors differentiate life-course persistent and adolescence-limited antisocial pathways among males and females. *Development and Psychopathology*, *13*, 355–375.

Moffitt, T. E., Caspi, A., Dickson, N., Silva, P., & Stanton, W. (1996). Childhood-onset versus adolescent-onset antisocial conduct problems in males: Natural history from ages 3 to 18 years. *Development and Psychopathology*, *8*, 399–424.

Nagin, D. S. (2005). *Group-based modeling of development.* Cambridge, MA: Harvard University Press.

Nagin, D. S., & Tremblay, R. E. (1999). Trajectories of boys' physical aggression, opposition, and hyperactivity on the path to physically violent and nonviolent juvenile delinquency. *Child Development*, *70*, 1181–1196.

Olds, D. (2002). Prenatal and infancy home visiting by nurses: From randomized trials to community replication. *Prevention Science*, *3*, 153–172.

Offord, D. R., Boyle, M. H., & Racine, Y. A. (1991). The epidemiology of antisocial behavior in childhood and adolescence. In D. J. Pepler & K. H. Rubin (Eds.), *The development and treatment of childhood aggression* (pp. 31–54). Hillsdale, NJ: Erlbaum.

Patterson, G. R. (1982). A *social learning approach: 3. Coercive family process.* Eugene, OR: Castalia.

Patterson, G. R., Capaldi, D., & Bank, L. (1991). An early starter model for predicting delinquency. In D. Pepler & R. K. Rubin (Eds.), *The development and treatment of childhood aggression* (pp. 139-168). Hillsdale, NJ: Erlbaum.

Patterson, G. R., & Chamberlain, P. (1994). A functional analysis of resistance during parent training therapy. *Clinical Psychology: Science and Practice, 1,* 53–70.

Patterson, G. R., Reid, J. B., & Dishion, T. J. (1992). *Antisocial boys.* Eugene, OR: Castalia.

Puig-Antich, J., Orvaschel, H., Tabrizi, M.A., & Chambers, W. (1980). *The schedule for affective disorders and schizophrenia for school-age children–epidemiologic version* (3rd edition). New York: New York State Psychiatric Institute and Yale University School of Medicine.

Renken, B., Egeland, B., Marvinney, D., Mangelsdorf, S., & Sroufe, L. A. (1989). Early childhood antecedents of aggression and passive-withdrawal in early elementary school. *Journal of Personality, 57,* 257–281.

Richman, M., Stevenson, J., & Graham, P. J. (1982). *Preschool to school: A behavioral study.* London: Academic Press.

Rutter, M., Yule, B., Quinton, D., Rowlands, O., Yule, W., & Berger, W. (1975), Attainment and adjustment in two geographical areas: 3. Some factors accounting for area differences. *British Journal of Psychiatry, 126,* 520–533.

Sameroff, A. J., & Chandler, M. J. (1975). Reproductive risk and the continuum of caretaking casualty. In F. D. Horowitz (Ed.), *Review of child development research* (Vol. 4, pp. 187–241). Chicago: University of Chicago Press.

Sameroff, A. J., Seifer, R., & Bartko, T. (1997). Environmental perspective on adaptation during childhood and adolescence. In S. S. Luthar, J. A. Burack, D. Cicchetti, & J. R. Weisz (Eds.), *Developmental psychopathology* (pp. 507–526). Cambridge, UK: Cambridge University Press.

Shaw, D. S., & Bell, R. Q. (1993). Developmental theories of parental contributors to antisocial behavior. *Journal of Abnormal Child Psychology, 21,* 493–518.

Shaw, D. S., Bell, R. Q., & Gilliom, M. (2000). A truly early starter model of antisocial behavior revisited. *Clinical Child and Family Psychology Review, 3,* 155–172.

Shaw, D. S., Dishion, T. J., Connell, A., Wilson, M. N., & Gardner, F. (in press). Maternal depression as a mediator of intervention in reducing early child problem behavior. *Development and Psychopathology.*

Shaw, D. S., Dishion, T. J., Supplee, L., Gardner, F., & Arnds, K. (2006). A family centered approach to the prevention of early-onset antisocial behavior: Two-year effects of the Family Check-Up in early childhood. *Journal of Consulting and Clinical Psychology, 74,* 1–9.

Shaw, D. S., Gilliom, M., & Giovannelli, J. (2000). Aggressive behavior disorders. In C. H. Zeanah (Ed.), *Handbook of infant mental health* (2nd ed., pp. 397–411). New York: Guilford.

Shaw, D. S., Gilliom, M., Ingoldsby, E. M., & Nagin, D. (2003). Trajectories leading to school-age conduct problems. *Developmental Psychology, 39,* 189–200.

Shaw, D. S., & Gross, H. (2008). Early childhood and the development of delinquency: What we have learned from recent longitudinal research. In A. Lieberman (Ed.), *The long view of crime: A synthesis of longitudinal research* (pp. 79-127). New York: Springer.

Shaw, D. S., Vondra, J. I., Dowdell Hommerding, K., Keenan, K., & Dunn, M. (1994). Chronic family adversity and early child behavior problems: A longitudinal study of low income families. *Journal of Child Psychology and Psychiatry, 35,* 1109–1122.

Shaw, D. S., Winslow, E. B., Owens, E. B., Vondra, J. I., Cohn, J. F., & Bell, R. Q. (1998). The development of early externalizing problems among children from low-income families: A transformational perspective. *Journal of Abnormal Child Psychology, 26,* 95–107.

Sroufe, L. A. (1983). Infant-caregiver attachment and patterns of adaptation in preschool: The roots of maladaptation and competence. In M. Perlmutter (Ed.), *Minnesota symposium on child psychology* (Vol. 16, pp. 41–81). Hillsdale, NJ: Erlbaum.

Sroufe, L. A., & Fleeson, J. (1986). Attachment and the construction of relationships. In W. Hartup & Z. Rubin (Eds.), *Relationships and development.* Hillsdale, NJ: Erlbaum.

Tremblay, R. E., Japel, C., Perusse, D., McDuff, P., Boivin, M., Zoccolillo, M., et al. (1999). The search for the age of onset of physical aggression: Rousseau and Bandura revisited. *Criminal Behavior and Mental Health,* 9, 8–23.

Wakschlag., L., & Hans, S. (1999). Relation of maternal responsiveness during infancy and the development of behavior problems in high-risk youths. *Developmental Psychology, 35,* 569–579.

Webster-Stratton, C. (1985). Predictors of treatment outcome in parent training for conduct disordered children. *Behavior Therapy, 16,* 223–243.

Author Index

Subject Index